Enuma Elish

(2 volumes in one)

The Seven Tablets of Creation; The Babylonian and Assyrian Legends Concerning the Creation of the World and of Mankind

LEONARD W. KING

COSIMO CLASSICS

NEW YORK

Enuma Elish (2 volumes in one): The Seven Tablets of Creation; The Babylonian and Assyrian Legends Concerning the Creation of the World and of Mankind

First published in 1902.
Current edition published by Cosimo Classics in 2010.

Cover design by www.popshopstudio.com
Cover image, "Quaerens Quem Devoret" by Jean -Léon Gérôme, 1888.

ISBN: 978-1-61640-510-6

Cosimo, Inc.
P.O. Box 416, Old Chelsea Station
New York, NY 10011

info@cosimobooks.com

or visit us at:
www.cosimobooks.com

She gave him the Tablets of Destiny, on [his] breast she laid them, (saying):
"Thy command shall not be without avail, and [the word of thy mouth shall be established]."
Now Kingu, (thus) exalted, having received [the power of Anu],
[Decreed] the fate among the gods his sons, (saying):
"Let the opening of your mouth [quench] the Fire-god;
"Whoso is exalted in the battle, let him [display (his) might]!"
—from Enuma Elish

Volume I

Introduction

& Transliterations and Translations

Preface.

Perhaps no section of Babylonian literature has been more generally studied than the legends which record the Creation of the world. On the publication of the late Mr. George Smith's work, "The Chaldean Account of Genesis," which appeared some twenty-seven years ago, it was recognized that there was in the Babylonian account of the Creation, as it existed in the seventh century before Christ, much which invited comparison with the corresponding narrative in the Book of Genesis. It is true that the Babylonian legends which had been recovered and were first published by him were very fragmentary, and that the exact number and order of the Tablets, or sections, of which they were composed were quite uncertain; and that, although they recorded the creation of the heavens and of the heavenly bodies, they contained no direct account of the creation of man. In spite of this, however, their resemblance to the Hebrew narrative was unmistakable, and in consequence they at once appealed to a far larger circle of students than would otherwise have been the case.

After the appearance of Mr. Smith's work, other scholars produced translations of the fragments which he had published, and the names of Oppert, Schrader, and Sayce will always be associated with those who were the first to devote themselves to the interpretation of the Creation Legends. Moreover, new fragments of the legends have from time to time been acquired by the Trustees of the British Museum, and of these the most important is the fine text of the Fourth Tablet of the Creation Series, containing the account of the fight between the god Marduk and the dragon Tiamat, which was published in 1887 by Dr. Wallis Budge, and translated by Professor Sayce in the same year. Professor Sayce's translation of the Creation Legends marked a distinct advance upon those of his predecessors, and it was the most complete, inasmuch as he was enabled to make use of the new tablet which restored so much of the central portion of the story. In the year 1890, in his important work *Die Kosmologie der Babylonier*, Professor Jensen of Marburg gave a translation of the legends together with a transliteration and commentary; in 1895 Professor Zimmern of Leipzig translated all the fragments then known, and a year later Professor Delitzsch of Berlin also published a rendering. Finally, two years ago, Professor Jensen issued a new and revised translation of the Creation Legends in the opening pages of the first part of his work *Mythen und Epen*, the second part of which, containing his notes and commentary, appeared some months ago.

In the course of the year 1900, the writer was entrusted with the task of copying the texts of a number of Babylonian and Assyrian legends for publication in the series of *Cuneiform Texts from Babylonian Tablets, etc., in the British Museum*, and, among the documents selected for issue, were those relating to the Creation of the world. Several of the texts of the Creation Legends, which had been used by previous translators, had never been published, and one tablet, which Mr. George Smith had consulted in 1876, had not been identified by subsequent workers. During my work I was so fortunate as to recognize this tablet, and was enabled to make copies of all the texts, not only of those which were previously known, but also of a number of new duplicates and fragments which I had meanwhile identified. These copies appeared in *Cuneiform Texts*, Part XIII (1901), Plates 1–41. The most interesting of the new fragments there published was a tablet which restored a missing portion of the text of the Second Tablet of the Creation Series, and of this, on account of its interest, I gave a translation in a note to the plate on which the text appeared. It was not my intention at that time to publish anything further upon the subject of the Creation Legends.

While I was engaged, however, in searching for fragments of other Babylonian legends for publication officially, it was my good fortune to come across a fine duplicate of the Second Tablet of the Creation

Series. A further prolonged search was rewarded by the finding of other fragments of the poem, and a study of these showed me that the earlier portions of the text of the Creation Story, as already known, could be considerably augmented. Among them, moreover, was a fragment of the poem which refers to the Creation of Man; this fragment is extremely important, for in addition to its valuable contents it also settles the disputed question as to the number of Tablets, or sections, of which the Creation Series was composed. In view of the additional information as to the form and contents of the poem which this new material afforded, it was clearly necessary that a new translation of the Creation Legends should be made, and this I undertook forthwith.

The new fragments of the poem which I had identified up to the summer of last year are inscribed upon tablets of the Neo-Babylonian period. At the conclusion of the examination of tablets of this class, I lithographed the newly identified texts in a series of plates which are published in the second volume of the present work. These plates were already printed off, when, at the beginning of the present year, after my return from Assyria, I identified a fresh group of fragments of the poem inscribed, not upon Neo-Babylonian, but upon Assyrian tablets. At that time I was engaged on making a detailed catalogue, or hand-list, of the smaller fragments in the various collections of Assyrian tablets from

Kuyunjik, and, as a result of previous study of the legends themselves and of the Assyrian commentaries to the Seventh Tablet of the series, I was enabled to identify ten new fragments of the poem which are inscribed upon tablets from the library of Ashur-bani-pal at Nineveh. In order to avoid upsetting the arrangement of the plates in Vol. II, the texts of the new Assyrian fragments are published by means of outline blocks in Appendices I and II to the present volume.

Those who have studied the published texts of the Creation Series will remember that the material used by previous translators of the legends has consisted of some twenty-one tablets and fragments inscribed with portions of the poem. The number of new tablets and fragments belonging to the Creation Series which are here used and translated for the first time reaches the total of thirty-four, but, as I have joined up six of these to other similar fragments, this total has been reduced to twenty-eight. Thus, in place of the twenty-one tablets previously known, forty-nine separate tablets and fragments have now been identified as containing portions of the text of the Creation Series.

The new information, furnished by the recently discovered material regarding the Story of Creation, may here be briefly summarized. Hitherto our knowledge of the contents of Tablets I and II of the series has been very fragmentary. After the narrative of the creation of the great gods in the opening lines of the poem, and a fragmentary reference to the first symptoms of revolt exhibited by the primeval monsters, Apsū and Tiamat, and Mummu, the minister of Apsū, there occurred a great gap in the text, and the story began again with the account of how Tiamat prepared to wage war against the gods. Apsū and Mummu have at this point entirely disappeared from the narrative, and the ally of Tiamat is the god Kingu, whom she appoints to command her forces. What followed the creation of the great gods, what was the cause of the revolt, what was the fate of Apsū and Mummu, and what were the events which led up to Tiamat's preparations for battle, are questions that have hitherto remained unanswered. We now know that the account of the creation of the gods was no fuller than that which has come down to us from Damascius. After the birth of Lakhmu and Lakhamu, Anshar and Kishar, Anu, Bēl (i.e., Enlil, or Illil), and Ea (Nudimmud), the text does not proceed to narrate in detail the coming forth of the lesser deities, but plunges at once into the story of the revolt of the primeval forces of chaos. We now know also that it was Apsū, and not Tiamat, who began the revolt against the gods; and that, according to the poem, his enmity was aroused, not by the creation of light as has been previously suggested, but by the disturbance of his rest in consequence of the new "way" of the gods, which tended to produce order in place of chaos.

One of the most striking facts which the new fragments furnish with regard to the contents of the legends is the prominent part played by the god Ea in the earlier episodes of the story. After Apsū and Mummu had repaired to Tiamat and had hatched with her their plot against the gods, it was the god Ea, who, abounding in all wisdom, detected their plan and frustrated it. The details of Ea's action are still a matter of uncertainty, but, as I have shown in the Introduction, it is clear that Apsū and Mummu were overthrown, and that their conqueror was Ea. Moreover, it was only after their downfall, and in order to avenge them, that Tiamat began her preparations for battle. She was encouraged in her determination by the god Kingu, and it was in consequence of the assistance he then gave her that she afterwards appointed him leader of her host.

Another point which is explained by the new fragments concerns the repetitions in Tablets I, II, and III of the lines containing the account of Tiamat's preparations for battle. The lines describing this episode are given no less than four times: in Tablet I, in Tablet II, and twice in Tablet III. We now know that the first description of Tiamat's preparations occurs after the account of her determination to avenge her former allies; and in the Second Tablet the lines are put into the mouth of Ea, who continues to play a prominent part in the narrative, and carries the tidings to Anshar. How Anshar repeated the lines to Gaga, his messenger, and how Gaga delivered the message to Lakhmu and Lakhamu, is already well known.

Perhaps the most striking of all the new fragments of the poem here published is that which contains the opening and closing lines of the Sixth Tablet, and, at last, furnishes us with a portion of the text describing the Creation of Man. We now know that, as in the Hebrew narrative, the culminating act of Creation was the making of man. Marduk is here represented as declaring to Ea that he will create man from his own blood, and from bone which he will form; it is important to note that the Assyrian word here used for "bone," *iṣṣimtu*, which has not hitherto been known, corresponds to the Hebrew word *'eṣem*, "bone," which occurs in Gen. ii, 23, in connection with the account of the creation of woman. The text thus furnishes another point of resemblance between the Babylonian and the Hebrew stories of Creation. The new fragment also corroborates in a remarkable degree the account given by Berossus of the Babylonian version of the creation of man. According to the writer's rendering of the passage, Marduk declares that he will use his own blood in creating mankind, and this agrees with the statement of Berossus, that Bēl directed one of the gods to cut off his (i.e. Bēl's) head, and to form mankind from his blood mixed with earth. This subject is discussed at length and in detail in the Introduction, as well as a number of new points of resemblance between the Babylonian and the Hebrew accounts of the Creation which are furnished by other recently identified fragments of the poem.

With regard to the extent and contents of the Creation Series, we now know that the Tablets of which the series was composed are seven in number; and we also possess the missing context or framework of the Seventh Tablet, which contains addresses to Marduk under his fifty titles of honour. From this we learn that, when the work of Creation was ended, the gods gathered together once more in Upshukkinakku, their council-chamber; here they seated themselves in solemn assembly and proceeded to do honour to Marduk, the Creator, by reciting before him the remarkable series of addresses which form the contents of the last Tablet of the poem. Many of the missing portions of the Seventh Tablet, including the opening lines, it has been found possible to restore from the new fragments and duplicates here published.

In the following pages a transliteration of the text of the Creation Series is given, which has been constructed from all the tablets and fragments now known to be inscribed with portions of the poem, together with a translation and notes. For comparison with the legends contained in the Creation Series, translations have been added of the other Babylonian accounts of the history of Creation, and of some texts closely connected therewith. Among these mention may be made of the extracts from a Sumerian text, and from a somewhat similar one in Babylonian, referring to the Creation of the Moon and the Sun; these are here published from a so-called "practice-tablet," or student's exercise. A remarkable address to a mythical river, to which the creation of the world is ascribed, is also given.

In the first Appendix the Assyrian commentaries to the Seventh Tablet are examined in detail, and some fragments of texts are described which bear a striking resemblance to the Seventh Tablet, and are of considerable interest for the light they throw on the literary history of the poem. Among the texts dealt with in the second Appendix one of the most interesting is a Babylonian duplicate of the tablet which has been supposed to contain the instructions given by Marduk to man after his creation, but is now shown by the duplicate to be part of a long didactic composition containing moral precepts, and to have nothing to do with the Creation Series. Similarly, in the fourth Appendix I have printed a copy of the text which has been commonly, but erroneously, supposed to refer to the Tower of Babel. The third Appendix includes some hitherto unpublished astrological texts of the period of the Arsacidae, which contain astrological interpretations and explanations of episodes of the Creation story; they indicate that Tiamat, in her astrological character, was regarded as a star or constellation in the neighbourhood of the ecliptic, and they moreover furnish an additional proof of the identification of her monster brood with at any rate some of the Zodiacal constellations.

During the preparation of this work I have, of course, consulted the translations and renderings of the Creation Legends which have been made by other workers on the subject, and especially those of Professors Jensen, Zimmern, and Delitzsch. I have much pleasure in expressing here my indebtedness to their published works for suggestions which I have adopted from them.

To Mr. R. Campbell Thompson I am indebted for the ready assistance he has afforded me during my search for new fragments and duplicates of the legends.

In conclusion, my thanks are due to Dr. Wallis Budge for his friendly suggestions which I have adopted throughout the progress of the work.

L. W. KING.

LONDON, July 31st, 1902.

Contents.

Introduction.

THE great Assyrian poem, or series of legends, which narrates the story of the Creation of the world and of man, was termed by the Assyrians and Babylonians *Enuma eliš*, "When in the height," from the two opening words of the text. The poem consisted of some nine hundred and ninety-four lines, and was divided into seven sections, each of which was inscribed upon a separate Tablet. The Tablets were numbered by the Assyrian scribes, and the separate sections of the poem written upon them do not vary very much in length. The shortest Tablet contains one hundred and thirty-eight lines, and the longest one hundred and forty-six, the average length of a Tablet being about one hundred and forty-two lines. The poem embodies the beliefs of the Babylonians and Assyrians concerning the origin of the universe; it describes the coming forth of the gods from chaos, and tells the story of how the forces of disorder, represented by the primeval water-gods Apsū and Tiamat, were overthrown by Ea and Marduk respectively, and how Marduk, after completing the triumph of the gods over chaos, proceeded to create the world and man. The poem is known to us from portions of several Assyrian and late-Babylonian copies of the work, and from

The Creation Series, "Enuma elish."

The Creation Series, "Enuma elish."

extracts from it written out upon the so-called "practice-tablets," or students' exercises, by pupils of the Babylonian scribes. The Assyrian copies of the work are from the great library which was founded at Nineveh by Ashur-bani-pal, king of Assyria from B.C. 668 to about B.C. 626; the Babylonian copies and extracts were inscribed during the period of the kings of the Neo-Babylonian and Persian periods; and one copy of the Seventh Tablet may probably be assigned to as late a date as the period of the Arsacidae. All the tablets and fragments, which have hitherto been identified as inscribed with portions of the text of the poem, are preserved in the British Museum.

First publication of fragments of the legends by George Smith in 1875.

From the time of the first discovery of fragments of the poem considerable attention has been directed towards them, for not only are the legends themselves the principal source of our knowledge of the Babylonian cosmogony, but passages in them bear a striking resemblance to the cognate narratives in the Book of Genesis concerning the creation of the world. The late Mr. George Smith, who was the first to publish an account of the poem, recognized this resemblance and emphasized it in his papers on the subject in 1875.[1] In the following year in

[1] Mr. Smith described the legends in a letter to the *Daily Telegraph*, published on March 4th, 1875, No. 6,158, p. 5, col. 4. He there gave a summary of the contents of the fragments, and on November 2nd in the same year he read a paper on them before the

his work "The Chaldean Account of Genesis"[1] he gave translations of the fragments of the poem which had been identified, and the copies which he had made of the principal fragments were published.[2] After Smith's death the interest in the texts which he had published did not cease, and scholars continued to produce renderings and studies of the legends.[3]

Smith's publication of the legends.

Society of Biblical Archæology. In noting the resemblance between the Babylonian and the Hebrew legends it was not unnatural that he should have seen a closer resemblance between them than was really the case. For instance, he traced allusions to "the Fall of Man" in what is the Seventh Tablet of the Creation Series; one tablet he interpreted as containing the instructions given by "the Deity" to man after his creation, and another he believed to represent a version of the story of the Tower of Babel. Although these identifications were not justified, the outline which he gave of the contents of the legends was remarkably accurate. It is declared by some scholars that the general character of the larger of the Creation fragments was correctly identified by Sir H. C. Rawlinson several years before.

[1] *The Chaldean Account of Genesis*, London, 1876; German edition, edited by Delitzsch, Leipzig, 1876. New English edition, edited by Sayce, London, 1880.

[2] By November, 1875, Smith had prepared a series of six plates containing copies of portions of the First and Fifth Tablets, and also of the Fourth Tablet which he entitled "War between the Gods and Chaos," and of the Seventh Tablet which he styled "Tablet describing the Fall." These plates were published in the *Transactions of the Society of Biblical Archæology*, vol. iv (1876), and appeared after his death.

[3] See the papers by H. Fox Talbot in *T.S.B.A.*, vol. iv, pp. 349 ff., and vol. v, pp. 1 ff., 426 ff., and *Records of the Past*, vol. ix (1877), pp. 115 ff., 135 ff.; and the translations made by Oppert in an appendix to Ledrain's *Histoire d'Israel, première partie* (1879), pp. 411 ff., and by Lenormant in *Les origines de*

In 1883 Dr. Wallis Budge gave an account of a fine Babylonian duplicate of what proved to be the Fourth Tablet of the Creation Series; this document restored considerable portions of the narrative of the fight between Marduk and the dragon Tiamat, and added considerably to our knowledge of the story of Creation and of the order in which the events related in the story took place.[1] In the Hibbert Lectures for 1887 Professor Sayce translated the new fragment of the text,[2] and in the following year published a complete translation[3] of all fragments of the Creation Legends which had up to that time been identified. In 1890 Professor Jensen, in his studies on the Babylonian cosmogony, included a translation of the legends together with a transliteration and a number of valuable philological notes and discussions.[4] In 1895

Recent translations of the legends.

l'histoire (1880), app. i, pp. 494 ff. The best discussion of the relations of the legends to the early chapters of Genesis was given by Schrader in the second edition (1883) of his *Keilinschriften und das Alte Testament*, English translation, 1885–1888; I hear from Professor Zimmern that the new edition of this work, a portion of which he is editing, will shortly make its appearance.

[1] The tablet was numbered 82-9-18, 3,737; see below, p. cvi, No. 29. Budge gave a description of the tablet in the *Proceedings of the Society of Biblical Archæology* for Nov. 6th, 1883, and published the text in *P.S.B.A.*, vol. x (1887), p. 86, pls. 1–6.

[2] See *Lectures on the Origin and Growth of Religion as illustrated by the Religion of the Ancient Babylonians* (Hibbert Lectures for 1887), pp. 379 ff.

[3] In *Records of the Past*, new series, vol. i (1888), pp. 122 ff.

[4] See *Die Kosmologie der Babylonier* (Strassburg, 1890), pp. 263 ff.

Professor Zimmern published a translation of the legends, similar in plan to Sayce's earlier edition; in it he took advantage of some recently identified fragments and duplicates, and put forward a number of new renderings of difficult passages.[1] In 1896 a third German translation of the legends made its appearance; it was published by Professor Delitzsch and included transliterations and descriptions of the various tablets and fragments inscribed with portions of the text.[2] Finally, in 1900 Professor Jensen published a second edition of his rendering of the legends in his *Mythen und Epen*;[3] this work was the best which could be prepared with the material then available.[4]

Recent translations of the legends.

[1] Zimmern published his translation as an appendix to Gunkel's *Schöpfung und Chaos in Urzeit und Endzeit* (Göttingen, 1895), pp. 401 ff.

[2] *Das Babylonische Weltschöpfungsepos*, published in the *Abhandlungen der philologisch-historischen Classe der Königl. Sächsischen Gesellschaft der Wissenschaften*, xvii, No. ii.

[3] *Assyrisch-Babylonische Mythen und Epen*, published as the sixth volume of Schrader's *Keilinschriftliche Bibliothek*; part 1, containing transliterations and translations (1900); part 2, containing commentary (1901).

[4] In addition to the translations of the legends mentioned in the text, a number of papers and works containing descriptions and discussions of the Creation legends have from time to time been published. Among those which have appeared during the last few years may be mentioned the translations of portions of the legends by Winckler in his *Keilinschriftliches Textbuch zum Alten Testament*, ii (1892), pp. 88 ff.; Barton's article on *Tiamat*, published in the *Journal of the American Oriental Society*, vol. xv (1893), pp. 1 ff.; and the translations and discussions of the

Identification of new texts.

In the most recent translations of the Creation Series, those of Delitzsch and Jensen, use was made in all of twenty-one separate tablets and fragments which had been identified as inscribed with portions of the text of the poem.[1] In the present work thirty-four

legends given in Jastrow's *Religion of Babylonia and Assyria* (1898), pp. 407 ff., in my own *Babylonian Religion and Mythology* (1899), pp. 53 ff., by Muss-Arnolt in *Assyrian and Babylonian Literature*, edited by R. F. Harper (1901), pp. 282 ff., and by Loisy, *Les mythes babyloniens et les premiers chapitres de la Genèse* (1901). Discussions of the Babylonian Creation legends and their connection with the similar narratives in Genesis have been given by Lukas in *Die Grundbegriffe in den Kosmogonien der alten Völker* (1893), pp. 1–46, by Gunkel in *Schöpfung und Chaos in Urzeit und Endzeit* (1895), pp. 16 ff., by Driver in *Authority and Archæology*, edited by Hogarth (1899), pp. 9 ff., and by Zimmern in *Biblische und babylonische Urgeschichte* (*Der alte Orient*, 1901); an exhaustive article on "Creation" has also been contributed by Zimmern and Cheyne to the *Encyclopædia Biblica*, vol. i (1899), cols. 938 ff.

[1] Delitzsch's list of fragments, enumerated on pp. 7 ff. of his work, gave the total number as twenty-two. As No. 21 he included the tablet K. 3,364, but in Appendix II (pp. 201 ff.) I have proved, by means of the Neo-Babylonian duplicate No. 33,851, that this tablet is part of a long composition containing moral precepts, and has no connection with the Creation Series. He also included K. 3,445 + R. 396 (as No. 20), but there are strong reasons for believing that this tablet does not belong to the series *Enuma eliš*, but is part of a variant account of the story of Creation; see further, Appendix II, pp. 197 ff. On the other hand he necessarily omitted from his list an unnumbered fragment of the Seventh Tablet, which had been used by George Smith, but had been lost sight of after his death; this fragment I identified two years ago as K. 9,267. It may be added that the total number of fragments correctly identified up to that time was twenty-five, but, as four of these had been joined to others, the number of separate tablets and fragments was reduced to twenty-one.

Identification of new texts.

additional tablets and fragments, inscribed with portions of the text of the Creation Series, have been employed; but, as six of these join other similar fragments, the number of separate tablets and fragments here used for the first time is reduced to twenty-eight. The total number of separate fragments of the text of the Creation Series is thus brought up to forty-nine.[1] The new material is distributed among the Seven Tablets of the Creation Series as follows:— To the four known fragments of the First Tablet may now be added eight others,[2] consisting of two fragments of an Assyrian tablet and four Babylonian fragments and two extracts inscribed upon Babylonian "practice-tablets." To the three known fragments of the Second Tablet may be added four others,[3] consisting of parts of one Assyrian and of three Babylonian tablets. To the four known fragments of the Third Tablet may be added five others,[4]

[1] On pp. xcvii ff. brief descriptions are given of these forty-nine separate fragments of the Creation Series, together with references to previous publications in which the text of any of them have appeared. The whole of the old material, together with part of the new, was published in *Cuneiform Texts from Babylonian Tablets, etc., in the British Museum*, part xiii. The texts of the new tablets and fragments which I have since identified are published in the lithographed plates of Vol. II, and by means of outline blocks in Appendices I and II (see pp. 159 ff.). For the circumstances under which the new fragments were identified, see the Preface to this volume.

[2] See below, p. xcviii f., Nos. 3, 4, 5, 8, 9, 10, 11, and 12.

[3] See below, p. ci, Nos. 13, 14, 15, and 18.

[4] See below, p. ciii f., Nos. 22, 24, 25, 26, and 27.

Identification of new texts.

consisting of fragments of one Assyrian and one Babylonian tablet and extracts inscribed upon three Babylonian "practice-tablets." To the five known fragments of the Fourth Tablet only one new duplicate can be added,[1] which is inscribed upon a Babylonian "practice-tablet." To the three known fragments of the Fifth Tablet may be added two others,[2] consisting of parts of two Assyrian tablets. Of the Sixth Tablet no fragment has previously been known, and its existence was only inferred from a fragment of the catch-line preserved on copies of the Fifth Tablet; fragments of the text of the Sixth Tablet are published for the first time in the present work from part of a Babylonian tablet.[3] Finally, to the two known fragments of the Seventh Tablet may now be added seven others,[4] inscribed upon five Assyrian fragments and portions of two Babylonian tablets.

The birth of the gods.

The new fragments of the text of the First and Second Tablets of the Creation Series throw light on the earlier episodes in the story of Creation, and enable us to fill up some of the gaps in the narrative. By the identification of the Tablet K. 5,419*c*,[5] George Smith recovered the opening lines of the First Tablet, which describes the condition of things before Creation

[1] See below, p. cvi, No. 32.
[2] See below, p. cviii, Nos. 37 and 38.
[3] See below, p. cix, No. 40.
[4] See below, p. cix f., Nos. 41, 42, 44, 46, 47, 48, and 49.
[5] See below, p. xcvii f., No. 1.

The birth of the gods.

when the primeval water-gods, Apsū and Tiamat, personifying chaos, mingled their waters in confusion. The text then briefly relates how to Apsū and Tiamat were born the oldest of the gods, the first pair, Laḫmu and Laḫamu, being followed after a long interval by Anshar and Kishar, and after a second interval by other deities, of whose names the text of K. 5,419*c* only preserves that of Anu. George Smith perceived that this theogony had been reproduced by Damascius in his summary of the beliefs of the Babylonians concerning the creation of the world.[1] Now, since Damascius mentions Ἴλλινος and Ἀός along with Ἀνός, it was clear that the text of the poem included a description of the birth of the elder Bēl (i.e. Enlil or Illil) and of Ea in the passage in which Anu's name occurs. But as the text inscribed upon the obverse of K. 5,419*c*,

[1] The following is the text of the passage in which Damascius summarizes the Babylonian beliefs:—*Τῶν δὲ Βαρβάρων ἐοίκασι Βαβυλώνιοι μὲν τὴν μίαν τῶν ὅλων ἀρχὴν σιγῇ παριέναι, δύο δὲ ποιεῖν Ταυθὲ καὶ Ἀπασὼν, τὸν μὲν Ἀπασὼν ἄνδρα τῆς Ταυθὲ ποιοῦντες, ταύτην δὲ μητέρα θεῶν ὀνομάζοντες, ἐξ ὧν μονογενῆ παῖδα γεννηθῆναι τὸν Μωϋμῖν, αὐτὸν οἶμαι τὸν νοητὸν κόσμον ἐκ τῶν δυοῖν ἀρχῶν παραγόμενον. Ἐκ δὲ τῶν αὐτῶν ἄλλην γενεὰν προελθεῖν, Δαχὴν καὶ Δαχόν. Εἶτα αὖ τρίτην ἐκ τῶν αὐτῶν, Κισσαρὴ καὶ Ἀσσωρὸν, ἐξ ὧν γενέσθαι τρεῖς, Ἀνὸν καὶ Ἴλλινον καὶ Ἀόν· τοῦ δὲ Ἀοῦ καὶ Δαύκης υἱὸν γενέσθαι τὸν Βῆλον, ὃν δημιουργὸν εἶναί φασιν.*—*Quaestiones de primis principiis*, cap. 125 (ed. Kopp, p. 384). The Δαχην and Δαχον of the text should be emended to Λαχην and Λαχον, which correspond to Laḫamu and Laḫmu. Of the other deities, Ταυθέ corresponds to Tiamat, Ἀπασών to Apsū, Κισσαρή to Kishar, Ἀσσωρός to Anshar, and Ἀνός to Anu; Μωϋμῖς corresponds to Mummu (see below, p. xxxviii, note 1).

The birth of the gods.

and of its Neo-Babylonian duplicate 82-7-14, 402,[1] breaks off at l. 15, the course of the story after this point has hitherto been purely a matter for conjecture. It appeared probable that the lines which followed contained a full account of the origin of the younger gods, and from the fact that Damascius states that Βῆλος, the Creator of the world, was the son of Ἀός (i.e. Ea) and Δαύκη (i.e. Damkina), it has been concluded that at any rate special prominence was given to the birth of Bēl, i.e. Marduk, who figures so prominently in the story from the close of the Second Tablet onwards.

Damascius and the birth of Marduk

The new fragments of the First Tablet show that the account of the birth of the gods in the Creation Series is even shorter than that given by Damascius, for the poem contains no mention of the birth and parentage of Marduk. After mentioning the birth of Nudimmud (i.e. Ea),[2] the text proceeds to describe his marvellous wisdom and strength, and states that he had no rival among the gods; the birth of no other god is recorded after that of Ea, and, when Marduk is introduced later on, his existence, like that of Mummu and of Gaga, appears to be tacitly assumed. It would seem, therefore, that the reference made by

[1] See below, p. xcviii, No. 2.

[2] It is interesting to note that Ea is referred to under his own name and not by his title Nudimmud upon new fragments of the poem in Tabl. I, l. 60 (p. 12 f.), Tabl. II, l. 5 (p. 22 f.), and Tabl. VI, l. 3 (p. 86 f.) and l. 11 (p. 88 f.).

PLATE II.

Part of the First Tablet of the Creation Series (Brit. Mus., No. 45,528+46,614).

Damascius to Marduk's parentage was not derived from the text of the Creation Series, but was added by him to complete his summary of the Babylonian beliefs concerning the origin of the gods.

Ea the hero of the earlier part of the Creation story.

This omission of Marduk's name from the earlier lines of the First Tablet and the prominence given to that of Ea may at first sight seem strange, but it is in accordance with the other newly recovered portions of the text of the First and Second Tablets, which indirectly throw an interesting light on the composite character and literary history of the great poem.[1] It will be seen that of the deities mentioned in these earlier lines Nudimmud (Ea) is the only god whose characteristics are described in detail; his birth, moreover, forms the climax to which the previous lines lead up, and, after the description of his character, the story proceeds at once to relate the rebellion of the primeval gods and the part which Ea played in detecting and frustrating their plans. In fact, Ea and not Marduk is the hero of the earlier episodes of the Creation story.

The cause of Apsū's rebellion.

The new fragments of the text show, moreover, that it was Apsū and not Tiamat who began the rebellion against the gods. While the newly created gods represented the birth of order and system in the universe, Apsū and Tiamat still remained in confusion and undiminished in might. Apsū, however, finding

[1] See further, pp. lxvi ff.

The cause of Apsû's rebellion.

that his slothful rest was disturbed by the new order of beings whom he had begotten, summoned Mummu,[1] his minister, and the two went together to Tiamat, and lying down before her, took counsel with her

[1] The Μωϋμῖς of Damascius; see above, p. xxxiii, n. 1. The title Mummu was not only borne by Apsû's minister, who, according to Damascius, was the son of Apsû and Tiamat, but in Tabl. I, l. 4, it is employed as a prefix to the name of Tiamat herself. In this passage I have conjecturally rendered it as "chaos" (see p. 2 f.), since the explanatory text S. 747, Rev., l. 10 (see below, pp. 162, 170), gives the equation *Mu-um-mu* = *rig-mu*. There is, however, much to be said for Jensen's suggestion of the existence of a word *mummu* meaning "form," or "mould," or "pattern" (cf. *Mythen und Epen*, p. 302 f.). Jensen points out that Ea is termed *mu-um-mu ba-an ka-la*, "the *mummu* (possibly, pattern) who created all" (cf. *Beiträge zur Assyriologie*, ii, p. 261), and he adds that the title might have been applied in this sense to Tiamat, since in Tabl. I, l. 113, and the parallel passages, she is described as *pa-ti-ḳa-at ka-la-ma*, and from her body heaven and earth were created; the explanation, given by Damascius, of Mummu, the son of Apsû and Tiamat, as νοητὸς κόσμος is also in favour of this suggestion. Moreover, from one of the new fragments of the Seventh Tablet, K. 13,761 (see p. 102 f.), we now know that one of Marduk's fifty titles was *Mummu*, which is there explained as *ba-a*[*n* . . . .], i.e., probably, *ba-a*[*n ka-la*], "Creator [of all]" (cf. Ea's title, cited above). In view of the equation *Mu-um-mu* = *rig-mu* (Jensen's suggested alternatives *šim-mu* and *bi-iš-mu* are not probable), we may perhaps conclude that, in addition to the word *mummu*, "form, pattern," there existed a word *mummu*, "chaos, confusion," and that consequently the title *Mummu* was capable of two separate interpretations. If such be the case, it is possible that the application of the title to Tiamat and her son was suggested by its ambiguity of meaning; while Marduk (and also Ea) might have borne the name as the "form" or "idea" of order and system, Tiamat and her son might have been conceived as representing the opposing "form" or "idea" of chaos and confusion.

regarding the means to be adopted to restore the old order of things. It may be noted that the text contains no direct statement that it was the creation of light which caused the rebellion of the primeval gods.[1] Apsū merely states his hatred of the *alkatu* or "way" of the gods, in consequence of which he can get no rest by day or night; and, from the fact that he makes use of the expressions "by day" and "by night," it may be inferred that day and night were vaguely conceived as already in existence. It was therefore the substitution of order in place of chaos which, according to the text of the poem, roused Apsū's resentment and led to his rebellion and downfall.[2]

His hatred of "order," not "light."

[1] Jensen's translation of what is l. 50 of the First Tablet represents Mummu as urging Apsū to make the way of the gods "like night," and implies that it was the creation of light which caused the rebellion. L. 50, however, is parallel to l. 38, and it is certain that the adv. *mu-šiš* is to be rendered "by night," and not "like night." In l. 38 Apsū complains that "by day" he cannot rest, and "by night" he cannot lie down in peace; Mummu then counsels him to destroy the way of the gods, adding in l. 50, "Then by day shalt thou have rest, by night shalt thou lie down (in peace)"; see pp. 8 ff. Jensen's suggested rendering of *im-ma aṣ-ru-nim-ma*, in place of *im-ma-aṣ-ru-nim-ma*, in Tabl. I, l. 109 and the parallel passages, is therefore also improbable.

[2] This fact does not preclude the interpretation of the fight between Marduk and Tiamat as based upon a nature-myth, representing the disappearance of mist and darkness before the rays of the sun. For Marduk was originally a solar deity, and Berossus himself mentions this interpretation of the legend (see further, p. lxxxii, and the quotation on p. liv f., notes 2 and 1).

The overthrow of Apsū and the capture of Mummu by Ea.

Our knowledge of the part played by Ea in the overthrow of Apsū and Mummu is still fragmentary, but we know from l. 60 of the First Tablet that it was he who detected the plot against the gods; it is also certain that the following twenty lines recorded the fate of Apsū and his minister, and there are clear indications that it was Ea to whom their overthrow was due. In Tablet II, ll. 53 ff., Anshar, on learning from Ea the news of Tiamat's preparations for battle, contrasts the conquest of Mummu and Apsū with the task of opposing Tiamat, and the former achievement he implies has been accomplished by Ea. It is clear, therefore, that Ea caused the overthrow of Apsū[1] and the capture of Mummu,[2] but in what way he brought it about, whether by actual fighting or by "his pure incantation,"[3] is still a matter for conjecture. In view of the fact that Anshar at first tried peaceful means for overcoming Tiamat[4] before exhorting Marduk to wage battle against her, the latter supposition is the more probable of the two. The subjugation of Apsū by Ea explains his subsequent disappearance from the Creation story. When Apsū is next mentioned, it is as "the Deep,"[5] and not as an active and malevolent deity.

Tiamat's determination to avenge Apsū and Mummu, due to Kingu's prompting.

After the overthrow of Apṣū, Tiamat remained unconquered, and she continued to represent in her

[1] Cf. Tabl. I, l. 97.
[2] Cf. Tabl. I, l. 98.
[3] Cf. Tabl. I, l. 62.
[4] Cf. Tabl. II, ll. 75 ff.
[5] Cf. Tabl. IV, l. 142.

own person the unsubdued forces of chaos.[1] But, as at first she had not herself begun the rebellion, so now her continuation of the war against the gods was due to the prompting of another deity. The speech in which this deity urges Tiamat to avenge Apsū and Mummu occurs in Tablet I, ll. 93–104, and, inasmuch as she subsequently promoted Kingu to be the leader of her forces "because he had given her support," it may be concluded that it was Kingu who now prompted her to avenge her former spouse.[2] Ea, however, did not cease his active opposition to the forces of disorder, but continued to play the chief rôle on the side of the gods. He heard of Tiamat's preparations for battle, he carried the news to Anshar, his father, and he was sent by him against the monster. It was only after both he and Anu had failed in their attempts to approach and appease Tiamat[3] that Anshar appealed to Marduk to become the champion of the gods.

Ea's continued opposition to the forces of disorder.

The repetitions in the First, Second, and Third Tablets.

Another point completely explained by the new fragments of the text is the reason for the repetitions which occur in the first three tablets of the series. It will be seen that Tablet I, ll. 109–142, are repeated in Tablet II, ll. 15–48; that Tablet II, ll. 11–48, are

[1] It is possible that the fragments of l. 88 f. of Tabl. I are not to be taken as part of a speech, but as a description of Tiamat's state of confusion and restlessness after learning of Apsū's fate.

[2] See also p. 14, n. 1.

[3] On the probable order of the attempts made by Ea and Anu respectively to oppose Tiamat, see Appendix II, p. 188, n. 1.

The repetitions in the First, Second, and Third Tablets.

repeated in Tablet III, ll. 15-52; and that Tablet III, ll. 15-66, are repeated in the same Tablet, ll. 73-124. The lines which are repeated have reference to Tiamat's preparations for battle against the gods, and to Anshar's summons of the gods in order that they may confer power on Marduk as their champion. From the new fragments of the text we now know that the lines relating to Tiamat's preparations occur on the First Tablet in the form of narrative, immediately after she had adopted Kingu's suggestion that she should avenge the overthrow of Apsū and Mummu; and that in the Second Tablet they are repeated by Ea in his speech to Anshar, to whom he carried the news. The context of the repetitions in the Third Tablet is already known; Anshar first repeats the lines to his minister Gaga, when telling him to go and summon the gods to an assembly, and later on in the Tablet Gaga repeats the message word for word to Laḫmu and Laḫamu.

Berossus and the monster-brood of Tiamat.

The constant repetition of these lines was doubtless intended to emphasize the terrible nature of the opposition which Marduk successfully overcame; and the fact that Berossus omits all mention of the part played by Ea in the earlier portions of the story is also due to the tendency of the Babylonian priests to exalt their local god at the expense of other deities. The account which we have received from Berossus of the Babylonian beliefs concerning the origin of the universe is largely taken up with a description of

PLATE III.

Part of the Second Tablet of the Creation Series (No. 40,559).

Berossus and the monster-brood of Tiamat.

the mythical monsters which dwelt in the deep at a time when the world had not come into being and when darkness and water alone existed.[1] Over these monsters, according to Berossus, reigned a woman named Ὀμόρκα, who is to be identified with Tiamat,[2]

[1] The account of the Creation given by Berossus in his history of Babylonia was summarized by Alexander Polyhistor, from whom Eusebius quotes in the first book of his *Chronicon*; the following is his description of the mythical monsters which existed before the creation of the world:—*Γενέσθαι φησὶ χρόνον ἐν ᾧ τὸ πᾶν σκότος καὶ ὕδωρ εἶναι, καὶ ἐν τούτοις ζῶα τερατώδη, καὶ ἰδιοφυεῖς τὰς ἰδέας ἔχοντα ζωογονεῖσθαι· ἀνθρώπους γὰρ διπτέρους γεννηθῆναι, ἐνίους δὲ καὶ τετραπτέρους καὶ διπροσώπους· καὶ σῶμα μὲν ἔχοντας ἓν, κεφαλὰς δὲ δύο, ἀνδρείαν τε καὶ γυναικείαν, καὶ αἰδοῖα δὲ δισσὰ, ἄῤῥεν καὶ θῆλυ· καὶ ἑτέρους ἀνθρώπους τοὺς μὲν αἰγῶν σκέλη καὶ κέρατα ἔχοντας, τοὺς δὲ ἵππου πόδας, τοὺς δὲ τὰ ὀπίσω μὲν μέρη ἵππων, τὰ δὲ ἔμπροσθεν ἀνθρώπων, οὓς ἱπποκενταύρους τὴν ἰδέαν εἶναι. Ζωογονηθῆναι δὲ καὶ ταύρους ἀνθρώπων κεφαλὰς ἔχοντας καὶ κύνας τετρασωμάτους, οὐρὰς ἰχθύος ἐκ τῶν ὄπισθεν μερῶν ἔχοντας, καὶ ἵππους κυνοκεφάλους καὶ ἀνθρώπους, καὶ ἕτερα ζῶα κεφαλὰς μὲν καὶ σώματα ἵππων ἔχοντα, οὐρὰς δὲ ἰχθύων· καὶ ἄλλα δὲ ζῶα παντοδαπῶν θηρίων μορφὰς ἔχοντα. Πρὸς δὲ τούτοις ἰχθύας καὶ ἑρπετὰ καὶ ὄφεις καὶ ἄλλα ζῶα πλείονα θαυμαστὰ καὶ παρηλλαγμένας τὰς ὄψεις ἀλλήλων ἔχοντα· ὧν καὶ τὰς εἰκόνας ἐν τῷ τοῦ Βήλου ναῷ ἀνακεῖσθαι, ἄρχειν δὲ τούτων πάντων γυναῖκα ᾗ ὄνομα Ὀμόρκα εἶναι· τοῦτο δὲ Χαλδαϊστὶ μὲν Θαλὰτθ, Ἑλληνιστὶ δὲ μεθερμηνεύεται θάλασσα [κατὰ δὲ ἰσόψηφον σελήνη].*—*Eusebi chronicorum liber prior*, ed. Schoene, col. 14 f.

[2] The reading Ὀμόρκα is an emendation for *ομορωκα*, cf. op. cit., col. 16, n. 6; while for Θαλατθ we should probably read Θαμτέ, i.e., the Babylonian *Tâmtu*, "sea, ocean" = Tiamat, cf. Robertson-Smith, *Zeits. für Assyr.*, vi, p. 339. The name Ὀμόρκα may probably be identified with Ummu-Ḫubur, "the Mother-Ḫubur," a title of Tiamat which occurs in Tabl. I, l. 113 and the parallel passages. The first part of the name gives the equation Ομ = *Ummu*, but how Ḫubur has given rise to the transcription *ορκα* is not clear. Jensen has attempted to explain the difficulty

Omorka and Bēl.

while the creatures themselves represent the monster-brood which Tiamat formed to aid her in her fight against the gods.[1] Compared with the description of the monsters, the summary from Berossus of the incidents related on the Fourth Tablet is not very full; the text states that Βῆλος (i.e. Bēl) slew 'Ομόρκα,

by suggesting that 'Ομόρκα = *Ummu-urki*, and *urki* he takes as an Assyrian translation of Ḫubur. For *Ḫubur* he suggests the meaning "that which is above, the North" (mainly from the occurrence of *Ḫu-bu-ur*^{KI} = *Su-bar-tum*, the Upper or Northern part of Mesopotamia, in II R, pl. 50, l. 51, cf. also V R, pl. 16, l. 19); and, since what is in the North would have been regarded by the Babylonians as "behind," the title *Ḫubur* might have been rendered in Babylonian as *urku*. This explanation is ingenious, but that the title Ḫubur, as applied to Tiamat, had the meaning "that which is above, the North," cannot be regarded as proved (cf. also *Mythen*, p. 564). Gunkel and Zimmern, on the other hand, see in 'Ομόρκα the equivalent of the Aramaic words *'Om 'orqa*, "Mother of the Deep," the existence of which they trace to the prevalence of the Aramaic dialect in Babylonia at the time of Berossus (see *Schöpfung und Chaos*, p. 18 f., n. 1); according to this explanation the title 'Ομόρκα would be the Aramaic equivalent of Ummu-Ḫubur, for *Ḫubur* may well have had the meaning "deep, depth." Thus, on the fragment S. 2,013 (see below, p. 196 f.) the meaning "depth," rather than "the North," is suggested by the word; in l. 9 of this fragment the phrase *Ḫu-bur pal-ka-ti*, "the broad Ḫubur," is employed in antithesis to *šamē(e) ru-ḳu-u-ti*, "the distant heavens," precisely as in the following couplet *Ti-amat šap-li-ti*, "the Lower Ocean (Tiamat)," is opposed to *Ti-amat e-li-ti*, "the Upper Ocean (Tiamat)." For a possible connection between the lower waters of Tiamat and Ḫubur, the River of the Underworld, see below, p. lxxxiii, n. 2, and p. xciv f., n. 3.

[1] According to the poem, Tiamat is definitely stated to have created eleven kinds of monsters. The summary from Berossus bears only a general resemblance to the description of the monsters in the poem.

PLATE IV.

Part of the Fourth Tablet of the Creation Series (Brit. Mus., No. 93,016).

and having cleft her in twain, from one half of her he made the earth, and from the other the heavens, while he overcame the creatures that were within her, i.e. the monsters of the deep.[1]

The creation of heaven and the heavenly bodies.

The actual account of the creation of the world by Marduk, as related in the Creation Series, begins towards the end of the Fourth Tablet,[2] where the narrative closely agrees with the summary from Berossus. Marduk is there related to have split Tiamat into halves, and to have used one half of her as a covering for heaven. The text then goes on to state that he founded heaven, which is termed E-shara, a mansion like unto the Deep in structure, and that he caused Anu, Bēl, and Ea to inhabit their respective districts therein. The Fifth Tablet does not begin with the account of the creation of the earth, but records the fixing of the constellations of the Zodiac, the founding of the year, and Marduk's charge to the Moon-god and the Sun-god, to the former of whom he entrusted the night, his instructions relating to the phases of the Moon, and the relative positions of the Moon and the Sun during the month. The new fragments of the Fifth Tablet contain some interesting variants to this portion of the text,[3] but,

[1] See below, p. liv f., note 1. [2] Cf. ll. 135 ff.

[3] For instance, the fragment K. 13,774 (see below, pp. 190 ff.) in l. 8, in place of "He set the stations of Bēl and Ea along with him," reads "He set the stations of Bēl and Anu along with him." According to the text Marduk appoints Nibir (Jupiter), Bēl (the

with the exception of the last few lines of the text, they throw no light on what the missing portions of the Tablet contained. In view, however, of the statement of Berossus that from one half of Tiamat Bēl formed the earth, we may conjecture that an account of the creation of the earth occurred upon some part of the Fifth Tablet. It is also probable that the Fifth Tablet recorded the creation of vegetation. That this formed the subject of some portion of the poem is certain from the opening lines of the Seventh Tablet, where Marduk is hailed as "Asari, 'Bestower of planting,' '[Founder of sowing],' 'Creator of grain and plants,' 'who caused [the green herb to spring up]!'"; and the creation of plants and herbs would naturally follow that of the earth.

The creation of the earth and of vegetation.

The creation of man.

From the new fragment of the Sixth Tablet, No. 92,629, we know that this portion of the poem related the story of the creation of man. As at the

north pole of the equator), and Ea (probably a star in the extreme south of the heavens) as guides to the stars, proving that they were already thus employed in astronomical calculations. In place of Ea, K. 13,774 substitutes Anu, who, as the pole star of the ecliptic, would be of equal, if not greater, importance in an astronomical sense. Another variant reading on K. 13,774 is the substitution of *kakkaba-šu*, "his star," in place of *ilu Nannar-ru*, the Moon-god, in l. 12; the context is broken, but we cannot doubt that *šuk-nat mu-ši*, "a being of the night," in l. 13 refers to the Moon-god, and that Marduk entrusted the night to the Moon-god according to this version also. Further variants occur in l. 17 f. in the days enumerated in the course of Marduk's address to the Moon-god; see below, p. 191 f.

PLATE V.

Part of the Fifth Tablet of the Creation Series (K. 3,567 + K. 8,588).

beginning of his work of creation Marduk is said to have "devised a cunning plan"[1] while gazing upon the dead body of Tiamat, so now, before proceeding to man's creation, it is said that "his heart prompted him and he devised [a cunning plan]."[2] In the repetition of this phrase we may see an indication of the importance which was ascribed to this portion of the story, and it is probable that the creation of man was regarded as the culmination of Marduk's creative work. It is interesting to note, however, that the creation of man is not related as a natural sequel to the formation of the rest of the universe, but forms the solution of a difficulty with which Marduk has been met in the course of his work as Creator. To overcome this difficulty Marduk devised the "cunning plan" already referred to; the context of this passage is not very clear, but the reason for man's creation may be gathered from certain indications in the text. The creation of man.

We learn from the beginning of the Sixth Tablet that Marduk devised his cunning plan after he had "heard the word of the gods," and from this it is clear that the Fifth Tablet ends with a speech of the gods. Now in Tablet VI, l. 8, Marduk states that he will create man "that the service of the gods may be established"; in l. 9 f., however, he adds that The reason of man's creation.

[1] See Tabl. IV, l. 136.

[2] See Tabl. VI, l. 2.

The reason of man's creation.

he will change the ways of the gods, and he appears to threaten them with punishment. It may be conjectured, therefore, that after Marduk had completed the creation of the world, the gods came to him and complained that there were no shrines built in their honour, nor was there anyone to worship them. To supply this need Marduk formed the device of creating man, but at the same time he appears to have decided to vent his wrath upon the gods because of their discontent. It is possible, however, that Ea dissuaded Marduk from punishing the gods, though he no doubt assisted him in carrying out the first part of his proposal.[1]

The account by Berossus of man's creation.

In ll. 5 ff. of the Sixth Tablet Marduk indicates the means he will employ for forming man, and this portion of the text corroborates in a remarkable manner the account given by Berossus of the method employed by Bēl for man's creation. The text of the summary from Berossus, in the form in which it has come down to us,[2] is not quite satisfactory, as the

---

[1] See below, p. lviii.

[2] After the description of the monsters of the deep referred to above (see p. xlv), the summary from Berossus records the creation by Bēl of the earth, and the heavens, and mankind, and animals, as follows:—*Οὕτως δὲ τῶν ὅλων συνεστηκότων, ἐπανελθόντα Βῆλον σχίσαι τὴν γυναῖκα μέσην, καὶ τὸ μὲν ἥμισυ αὐτῆς ποιῆσαι γῆν, τὸ δὲ ἄλλο ἥμισυ οὐρανὸν, καὶ τὰ ἐν αὐτῇ ζῶα ἀφανίσαι, ἀλληγορικῶς δέ φησι τοῦτο πεφυσιολογῆσθαι· ὑγροῦ γὰρ ὄντος τοῦ παντὸς καὶ ζώων ἐν αὐτῷ γεγεννημένων, τοῦτον τὸν θεὸν ἀφελεῖν τὴν ἑαυτοῦ κεφαλὴν, καὶ τὸ ῥυὲν αἷμα τοὺς ἄλλους θεοὺς φυρᾶσαι τῇ γῇ, καὶ διαπλάσαι τοὺς ἀνθρώπους· διὸ νοερούς τε εἶναι καὶ φρονήσεως θείας μετέχειν. Τὸν δὲ Βῆλον, ὃν*

course of the narrative is confused. The confusion is apparent in the repetition of the description of man's creation and in the interruption of the naturalistic explanation of the slaying of Omorka. An ingenious but simple emendation of the text, however, was suggested by von Gutschmidt which removes both these difficulties. The passage which interrupts the naturalistic explanation, and apparently describes a first creation of man, he regarded as having been transposed; but if it is placed at the end of the extract it falls naturally into place as a summary by Eusebius of the preceding account of man's creation which is said by Alexander Polyhistor to have been given by Berossus in the First Book of his History.[1] By adopting this emendation we obtain

Confusion in the text.

Δία μεθερμηνεύουσι, μέσον τεμόντα τὸ σκότος χωρίσαι γῆν καὶ οὐρανὸν ἀπ' ἀλλήλων, καὶ διατάξαι τὸν κόσμον. Τὰ δὲ ζῶα οὐκ ἐνεγκόντα τὴν τοῦ φωτὸς δύναμιν φθαρῆναι, ἰδόντα δὲ τὸν Βῆλον χώραν ἔρημον καὶ καρποφόρον κελεῦσαι ἑνὶ τῶν θεῶν τὴν κεφαλὴν ἀφελόντι ἑαυτοῦ τῷ ἀποῤῥυέντι αἵματι φυρᾶσαι τὴν γῆν καὶ διαπλάσαι ἀνθρώπους καὶ θηρία τὰ δυνάμενα τὸν ἀέρα φέρειν. Ἀποτελέσαι δὲ τὸν Βῆλον καὶ ἄστρα καὶ ἥλιον καὶ σελήνην καὶ τοὺς πέντε πλανήτας. Ταῦτά φησιν ὁ πολυΐστωρ Ἀλέξανδρος τὸν Βηρωσσὸν ἐν τῇ πρώτῃ φάσκειν.—Euseb. chron. lib. pri., ed. Schoene, col. 16 f. For the probable transposition of the passage which occurs in the text after *γεγεννημένων*, see the following note.

[1] The transposition of the passage suggested by von Gutschmidt necessitates only one emendation of the text, viz. the reading of *τοιῶνδε* in place of *τον δε* before *Βῆλον*. The context of this passage would then read *ὑγροῦ γὰρ ὄντος τοῦ παντὸς καὶ ζώων ἐν αὐτῷ γεγεννημένων τοιῶνδε, Βῆλον, ὃν Δία μεθερμηνεύουσι, μέσον τεμόντα τὸ σκότος χωρίσαι γῆν καὶ οὐρανὸν ἀπ' ἀλλήλων, καὶ διατάξαι τὸν*

a clear and consecutive account of how Bēl, after the creation of heaven and earth, perceived that the land was desolate ; and how he ordered one of the gods to cut off his (i.e. Bēl's) head, and, by mixing the blood which flowed forth with earth, to create men and animals.

The employment of Marduk's blood for man's creation.

This passage from Berossus has given rise to considerable discussion, and more than one scholar has attempted to explain away the beheading of Bēl, the Creator, that man might be formed from his blood. Gunkel has suggested that in the original legend the blood of Tiamat was used for this purpose ;[1] Stucken,[2] followed by Cheyne,[3] has emended the text so that it may suggest that the head of Tiamat, and not that of Bēl, was cut off ; while Zimmern would take the original meaning of the passage to be that the god

---

κόσμον; and the summary by Eusebius, at the end of the extract, would read **Ταῦτά** *φησιν ὁ πολυΐστωρ* **Ἀλέξανδρος** *τὸν* **Βηρωσσὸν** *ἐν τῇ πρώτῃ φάσκειν· τοῦτον τὸν θεὸν ἀφελεῖν τὴν ἑαυτοῦ κεφαλὴν, καὶ τὸ ῥυὲν αἷμα τοὺς ἄλλους θεοὺς φυρᾶσαι τῇ γῇ, καὶ διαπλάσαι τοὺς ἀνθρώπους· διὸ νοερούς τε εἶναι καὶ φρονήσεως θείας μετέχειν* ; cf. Schoene, *op. cit.*, col. 16 f., note 9. The emendation has been accepted by Budde, *Die Biblische Urgeschichte*, p. 477 f., by Jensen, *Kosmologie*, p. 292, and by Gunkel and Zimmern, *Schöpfung und Chaos*, p. 19 f.

[1] Cf. *Schöpfung und Chaos*, p. 20 f.

[2] For *ἑαυτοῦ* in both passages Stucken would read *αὐτῆς* ; cf. *Astralmythen der Hebraeer, Babylonier und Aegypter*, i, p. 55.

[3] Cheyne, who adopts Stucken's suggestion, remarks : "It "stands to reason that the severed head spoken of in connection "with the creation of man must be Tiāmat's, not that of the "Creator" ; cf. *Encyclopædia Biblica*, i, col. 947, note.

beheaded was not Bēl, but the other deity whom he addressed.[1] In l. 5 of the Sixth Tablet, however, Marduk states that he will use his own blood for creating man;[2] the text of this passage from Berossus is thus shown to be correct, and it follows that the account which he gave of the Babylonian beliefs concerning man's creation does not require to be emended or explained away.

The employment of Marduk's blood for man's creation.

[1] In the *Zeits. für Assyr.*, xiv, p. 282, Zimmern remarks: "Somit "darf man wol doch nicht . . . . annehmen, dass ursprünglich "das Blut der Tiāmat gemeint sei, allerdings auch nicht das Blut "des Schöpfergottes selbst, sondern das irgend eines Gottes . . ., "der zu diesem Zwecke geschlachtet wird." In making this suggestion Zimmern was influenced by the episode related in col. iii of the fragmentary and badly preserved legend Bu. 91–5–9, 269 (cf. *Cuneiform Texts*, pt. vi, and *Mythen*, p. 275, note), which he pointed out contained a speech by a deity in which he gives orders for another god to be slain that apparently a man may be formed from his blood mixed with clay (cf. *Z.A.*, xiv, p. 281). The episode, however, has no connection with the first creation of man, but probably relates to the creation of a man or hero to perform some special exploit, in the same way as Uddushu-namir was created by Ea for the rescue of Ishtar from the Underworld, and as Ea-bani was created by the goddess Aruru in the First Tablet of the Gilgamesh-epic (cf. also Jensen's remarks in his *Mythen und Epen*, p. 275 f.). I learn from Professor Zimmern and Professor Bezold that it was the tablet Bu. 91–5–9, 269, and not an actual fragment of the Creation Series, to which Professor Zimmern refers on p. 14 of his *Biblische und babylonische Urgeschichte*. Although, as already stated, this fragment is not, strictly speaking, part of a creation-legend, it illustrates the fact that the use of the blood of a god for the creation of man was fully in accordance with Babylonian beliefs.

[2] See below, p. 86 f., n. 7.

Ea's share in man's creation.

Jensen has already suggested[1] that the god whom Bēl addressed was Ea, and the new fragment of the Sixth Tablet proves that this suggestion is correct. In the Sixth Tablet Marduk recounts to Ea his intention of forming man, and tells him the means he will employ. We may therefore conclude that it was Ea who beheaded Marduk at his request, and, according to his instructions, formed mankind from his blood. Ea may thus have performed the actual work of making man, but he acted under Marduk's directions, and it is clear from Tablet VII, ll. 29 and 32, that Marduk, and not Ea, was regarded as man's Creator.

The method of man's creation.

According to Berossus, man was formed from the blood of Bēl mixed with earth. The new fragment of the Sixth Tablet does not mention the mixing of the blood with earth, but it is quite possible that this detail was recounted in the subsequent narrative. On the other hand, in the Babylonian poem Marduk declares that, in addition to using his own blood, he will create bone for forming man. Berossus makes no mention of bone, but it is interesting to note that *iṣṣimtu*, the Assyrian word here used for "bone,"[2] is doubtless the equivalent of the Hebrew word *'eṣem*,

[1] See *Kosmologie*, p. 293.

[2] The word is here met with for the first time, the reading of GIR-PAD-DU(var. DA), the ideogram for "bone," not having been known previously.

"bone," which occurs at the end of the narrative of the creation of woman in Gen. ii, 23.

The creation of animals.

The blood of Bēl, according to Berossus, was employed not only in man's creation but in that of animals also, and it is possible that this represents the form of the legend as it was preserved upon the Sixth Tablet. Though, in that case, the creation of animals would follow that of man, the opening lines of the Sixth Tablet prove that man's creation was regarded as the culmination of Marduk's creative work. The "cunning plan," which Marduk devised in order to furnish worshippers for the gods, concerned the creation of man, and if that of animals followed it must have been recorded as a subsidiary and less important act.[1] In this connection it may be noted that the expression *τὰ δυνάμενα τὸν ἀέρα φέρειν*, which Berossus applies to the men and animals created from the blood of Bēl, was probably not based on any description or episode in the Creation story as

[1] On p. 200 it is remarked that, until more of the text of the Fifth and Sixth Tablets is recovered, it would be rash to assert that the fragment K. 3,445 + R. 396 (cf. *Cun. Texts*, pt. xiii, pl. 24 f.) cannot belong to the Creation Series. The phrase *iš-kun ḳaḳḳada* (Obv., l. 35) might perhaps refer to the head of Tiamat (cf. *ru-pu-uš-tu ša Ti-a*[*mat*], in l. 29), which would not be inconsistent with the fragment forming part of the Fifth Tablet as suggested on p. 198. If the fragment were part of the Sixth Tablet, the *ḳaḳḳadu* in l. 35 might possibly be Marduk's head (compare also *ik-ṣur-ma* in l. 31 with *lu-uk-ṣur* in Tabl. VI, l. 5). In view, however, of the inconsistencies noted on p. 199 f., it is preferable to exclude the fragment at present from the Creation Series.

recorded on the Seven Tablets, but was suggested by the naturalistic interpretation of the legend furnished by Berossus himself.

The supposed instructions to man after his creation.

With reference to the creation of man, it was suggested by George Smith that the tablet K. 3,364 was a fragment of the Creation Series, and contained the instructions given to man after his creation by Marduk. This view has been provisionally adopted by other translators of the poem, but in Appendix II[1] I have shown by means of a duplicate, No. 33,851, that the suggestion must be given up. Apart from other reasons there enumerated, it may be stated that there would be no room upon the Sixth Tablet of the Creation Series for such a long series of moral precepts as is inscribed upon the tablets K. 3,364 and No. 33,851. It may be that Marduk, after creating man, gave him some instructions with regard to the worship of the gods and the building of shrines in their honour, but the greater part of the text must have been taken up with other matter.

The final scene in the Creation story.

The concluding lines of the Sixth Tablet are partly preserved, and they afford us a glimpse of the final scene in the Creation story. As the gods had previously been summoned to a solemn assembly that they might confer power upon Marduk before he set out to do battle on their behalf, so now, when he had vanquished Tiamat and had finished his work of

[1] See pp. 201 ff.

PLATE VI.

Part of the Seventh Tablet of the Creation Series (Brit. Mus., No. 91,139+93,073).

creation, they again gathered together in Upshukkinaku, their council-chamber, and proceeded to magnify him by every title of honour. We thus obtain the context or setting of the Seventh, and last, Tablet of the Creation Series, the greater part of which consists of the hymn of praise addressed by the gods to Marduk as the conqueror of Tiamat and the Creator of the world.

The final scene in the Creation story.

The hymn of the gods takes up lines 1-124 of the Seventh Tablet, and consists of a series of addresses in which Marduk is hailed by them under fifty titles of honour. The titles are Sumerian, not Semitic, and each is followed by one or more Assyrian phrases descriptive of Marduk, which either explain the title or are suggested by it. Of the fifty titles which the hymn contained, the following list of eleven occur in the first forty-seven lines of the text :—

The Seventh Tablet of the Creation Series.

The Fifty Titles of Marduk.

Asari : [ilu]*Asar-ri*, Tabl. VII, l. 1 ; p. 92 f.
Asaru-alim : [ilu]*Asaru-alim*, Tabl. VII, l. 3 ; p. 92 f.
Asaru-alim-nuna : [ilu]*Asaru-alim-nun-na*, Tabl. VII, l. 5 ; p. 92 f.
Tutu : [ilu]*Tu-tu*, Tabl. VII, l. 9 ; p. 92 f.
Zi-ukkina : [ilu]*Zi-ukkin-na*, var. [ilu]*Zi-ukkin*, Tabl. VII, l. 15 ; p. 94 f.
Zi-azag : [ilu]*Zi-azag*, Tabl. VII, l. 19 ; p. 96 f. ; var. [ilu]*Na-zi-azag-g*[*a*], p. 161.
Aga-azag : [ilu]*Aga-azag*, Tabl. VII, l. 25 ; p. 96 f.
Mu-azag : [ilu]*Mu*(i.e. KA + LI)-*azag*, Tabl. VII, l. 33 ; var. [ilu]*Mu*(i.e. ŠAR)-*azag*, p. 173.

The Fifty Titles of Marduk.

Shag-zu : ^{ilu}*Šag-zu*, Tabl. VII, l. 35 ; p. 98 f.

Zi-si : ^{ilu}*Zi-si*, Tabl. VII, l. 41 ; p. 100 f.

Suḫ-kur : ^{ilu}*Suḫ-kur*, Tabl. VII, l. 43 ; p. 100 f.

In the gap in the text of the Seventh Tablet, between ll. 47 and 105, occur the following ten titles of Marduk, which are taken from the fragments K. 13,761 and K. 8,519 (and its duplicate K. 13,337), and from the commentary K. 4,406 :—

Agi[l . . . .] : ^{ilu}*A-gi*[*l*- . . . .], Tabl. VII (K. 13,761); p. 102 f. ; var. ^{ilu}*Gil*[ ], p. 163.

Zulummu : ^{ilu}*Zu-lum-mu*, Tabl. VII (K. 13,761) ; p. 102 f.

Mummu : ^{ilu}*Mu-um-mu*, Tabl. VII (K. 13,761) ; p. 102 f.

Mulil : ^{ilu}*Mu-lil*, Tabl. VII (K. 13,761); p. 102 f.

Gishkul : ^{ilu}*Giš-kul*, Tabl. VII (K. 13,761) ; p. 102 f.

Lugal-ab[. . . .] : ^{ilu}*Lugal-ab*-[. . . .], Tabl. VII (K. 13,761) ; p. 102 f.

Pap-[. . . .] : ^{ilu}*Pap*-[. . . .], Tabl. VII (K. 13,761); p. 102 f.

Lugal - durmaḫ : ^{ilu}*Lugal - dur - maḫ*, Tabl. VII (K. 8,519), and K. 4,406, Rev., col. ii, l. 8 ; pp. 104 f., 165.

Adu-nuna : ^{ilu}*A-du-nun-na*, Tabl. VII (K. 8,519) and K. 4,406, Rev., col. ii, l. 23 ; pp. 104 f., 166.

Lugal-dul(*or* du)-azaga : ^{ilu}*Lugal-dul-azag-ga*, Tabl. VII (K. 8,519) ; p. 106 f.

The Fifty Titles of Marduk.

Four other titles, occurring in the concluding portion of the text of the Seventh Tablet, are :—

Nibiru : *^{ilu}Ni-bi-ru*, var. [^{ilu}]*Ne-bi-ri*, Tabl. VII, l. 109 ; p. 108 f.

Bēl-mātāti : *be-el mātāti*, var. *^{ilu}Bēl mātāti*, Tabl. VII, l. 116, p. 110 f. ; cf. also EN KUR-KUR (i.e. *bēl mātāti*), p. 168.

Ea : *^{ilu}E-a*, Tabl. VII, l. 120 ; p. 110 f.

Ḫansha : *Ḫanšā$^{A-AN}$*, var. *Ḫa-an-ša-a*, Tabl. VII, l. 123, p. 110 f. ; cf. also *^{ilu}Ḫanšā*, p. 178.

From the above lists it will be seen that the recovered portions of the text of the Seventh Tablet furnish twenty-five out of the fifty names of Marduk. From the list of the titles of Marduk preserved on K. 2,107 + K. 6,086,[1] and from No. 54,228, a parallel text to the Seventh Tablet,[2] seven other names may be obtained, which were probably among those occurring in the missing portion of the text ; these are :—

Lugal-en-ankia : *^{ilu}Lugal-en-an-ki-a*, K. 2,107, col. ii, l. 19 ; p. 173.

Gugu : *^{ilu}Gu-gu*, K. 2,107, col. ii, l. 22 ; p. 173.

Mumu : *^{ilu}Mu-mu*, K. 2,107, col. ii, l. 23 ; p. 173.

Duṭu : *^{ilu}Du-ṭu*, K. 2,107, col. ii, l. 24 ; p. 173.

[1] See pp. 171 ff.

[2] See pp. 175 ff.

The Fifty Titles of Marduk.

Dudu : *ilu Du-du*, K. 2,107, col. ii, l. 25 ; p. 173.
Shag-gar (?): *Šag-gar*, No. 54,228, Obv., l. 13; p. 177.
En-bilulu : *ilu En-bi-lu-lu*, No. 54,228, Obv., l. 14 ; p. 178.[1]

By these titles of honour the gods are represented as conferring supreme power upon Marduk, and the climax is reached in ll. 116 ff. of the Seventh Tablet, when the elder Bēl and Ea, Marduk's father, confer their own names and power upon him. Marduk's name of Ḫanshā, "Fifty," by which he is finally addressed, in itself sums up and symbolizes his fifty titles. At the conclusion of these addresses there follows an epilogue[2] of eighteen lines, in which the study of the poem is commended to mankind, and prosperity is promised to those that rejoice in Marduk and keep his works in remembrance.

The epilogue to the Creation Series.

The composite nature of the Creation Series.

The story of the Creation, in the form in which it has come down to us upon tablets of the seventh and later centuries before Christ, is of a distinctly

[1] In view of the fact that the Semitic name *Bēl-mātāti* occurs as one of Marduk's titles, it is not impossible that the title *Bēl-ilāni*, which is applied to him in the Epilogue to the Seventh Tablet (l. 129, see p. 112), also occurred as one of his fifty titles in the body of the text. It is unlikely that the name Marduk itself was included as one of the fifty titles, and in support of this view it may be noted that the colophon to the commentary R. 366, etc. (see p. 169), makes mention of "fifty-one names" of Marduk, which may be most easily explained by supposing that the scribe reckoned in the name Marduk as an additional title.

[2] See below, p. 169.

composite character, and bears traces of a long process of editing and modification at the hands of the Babylonian priests. Five principal strands may be traced which have been combined to form the poem; these may be described as (1) The Birth of the gods; (2) The Legend of Ea and Apsū; (3) The Dragon-Myth; (4) The actual account of Creation; and (5) The Hymn to Marduk under his fifty titles. Since the poem in its present form is a glorification of Marduk as the champion of the gods and the Creator of the world, it is natural that more prominence should be given to episodes in which Marduk is the hero than is assigned to other portions of the narrative in which he plays no part. Thus the description of Tiamat and her monster-brood, whom Marduk conquered, is repeated no less than four times,[1] and the preparations of Marduk for battle and his actual fight with the dragon take up the greater part of the Fourth Tablet. On the other hand, the birth of the older gods, among whom Marduk does not figure, is confined to the first twenty-one lines of the First Tablet; and not more than twenty lines are given to the account of the subjugation of Apsū by Ea. That these elements should have been incorporated at all in the Babylonian version of the Creation story may be explained by the fact that they serve to enhance the position of prominence subsequently attained by

Component parts of the Creation Series.

Elements in the poem unconnected with Marduk.

[1] See above, p. xli f.

Marduk. Thus the description of the birth of the older gods and of the opposition they excited among the forces of disorder, was necessarily included in order to make it clear how Marduk was appointed their champion; and the account of Ea's success against Apsū served to accentuate the terrible nature of Tiamat, whom he was unable to withstand. From the latter half of the Second Tablet onwards, Marduk alone is the hero of the poem.

The Dragon-Myth.

The central episode of the poem is the fight between Marduk and Tiamat, and there is evidence to prove that this legend existed in other forms than that under which it occurs in the Creation Series. The conquest of the dragon was ascribed by the Babylonian priests to their local god, and in the poem the death of Tiamat is made a necessary preliminary to the creation of the world. On a fragment of a tablet from Ashur-bani-pal's library we possess, however, part of a copy of a legend[1] which describes the conquest of a dragon by some deity other than Marduk.[2] Moreover, the fight is there described as taking place, not before creation, but at a time when men existed and cities had been built. In this version

[1] See below, pp. 116 ff.

[2] Jensen makes Bēl the slayer of the dragon in this legend (cf. *Mythen und Epen*, p. 46), from which it might be argued that Marduk is the hero in both versions of the story. But Jensen's identification of the deity as Bēl was due to a mistake of Delitzsch, who published an inaccurate copy of the traces of the deity's name upon the tablet; see below, p. 120, n. 1.

men and gods are described as equally terrified at the dragon's appearance, and it was to deliver the land from the monster that one of the gods went out and slew him. This fragmentary tablet serves to prove that the Dragon-Myth existed in more than one form in Babylonian mythology, and it is not improbable that many of the great cities of Babylonia possessed local versions of the legend in each of which the city-god figured as the hero.[1]

Variant accounts of the Creation.

In the Creation Series the creation of the world is narrated as the result of Marduk's conquest of the dragon, and there is no doubt that this version of the story represents the belief most generally held during the reigns of the later Assyrian and Babylonian kings. We possess, however, fragments of other legends in which the creation of the world is not connected with the death of a dragon. In one of these, which is written both in Sumerian and Babylonian,[2] the great Babylonian cities and temples are described as coming into existence in consequence of a movement in the waters which alone existed before the creation of the world. Marduk in this

[1] The so-called "Cuthaean Legend of the Creation" (cf. pp. 140 ff.) was at one time believed to represent another local version of the Creation story, in which Nergal, the god of Cuthah, was supposed to take the place of Marduk. But it has been pointed out by Zimmern that the legend concerns the deeds of an Old-Babylonian king of Cuthah, and is not a Creation legend; see below, p. 140 f., note 1.

[2] See below, pp. 130 ff.

Variant accounts of the Creation.

version also figures as the Creator, for, together with the goddess Aruru,[1] he created man by laying a reed upon the face of the waters and forming dust which he poured out beside it; according to this version also he is described as creating animals and vegetation. In other legends which have come down to us, not only is the story of Creation unconnected with the Dragon-Myth, but Marduk does not figure as the Creator. In one of these "the gods" generally are referred to as having created the heavens and the earth and the cattle and beasts of the field;[2] while in another the creation of the Moon and the Sun is ascribed to Anu, Bel, and Ea.[3]

From the variant accounts of the story of Creation and of the Dragon-Myth, which are referred to in the preceding paragraphs, it will be clear that the priests of Babylon made use of independent legends in the composition of their great poem of Creation[4]; by

[1] Elsewhere this goddess figures in the rôle of creatress, for from the First Tablet of the Gilgamesh-epic, col. ii, ll. 30 ff., we learn that she was credited with the creation of both Gilgamesh and Ea-bani. Her method of creating Ea-bani bears some resemblance to that employed in the creation of man according to the Sumerian and Babylonian version above referred to; she first washed her hands, and then, breaking off a piece of clay, she cast it upon the ground and thus created Ea-bani (cf. Jensen, *Mythen und Epen*, p. 120 f.).

[2] See below, p. 122 f.

[3] See below, pp. 124 ff.

[4] In addition to the five principal strands which have been described above as forming the framework of the Creation Series,

assigning to Marduk the conquest of the Dragon[1] and the creation of the world they justified his claim to the chief place among the gods. As a fit ending to the great poem they incorporated the hymn to Marduk, consisting of addresses to him under his fifty titles. This portion of the poem[2] is proved by the Assyrian commentary, R. 366, etc.,[3] as well as by fragments of parallel, but not duplicate, texts[4] to have been an independent composition which had at one time no connection with the series *Enuma eliš*. In the poem the hymn is placed in the mouth of the gods, who at the end of the Creation have assembled together in Upshukkinaku; and to it is added the epilogue of eighteen lines, which completes the Seventh Tablet of the series.

The hymn to Marduk under his fifty titles.

it is possible to find traces of other less important traditions which have been woven into the structure of the poem. Thus the association of the god Kingu with Tiamat is probably due to the incorporation of a separate legend with the Dragon-Myth.

[1] It may be here noted that the poem contains no direct description of Tiamat, and it has been suggested that in it she was conceived, not as a dragon, but as a woman. The evidence from sculpture and from cylinder-seals, however, may be cited against this suggestion, as well as several phrases in the poem itself (cf. e.g., Tabl. IV, ll. 97 ff.). It is true that in one of the new fragments of the poem Tiamat is referred to as *sinnišatu*, i.e. "woman" or "female" (cf. Tabl. II, l. 122), but the context of this passage proves that the phrase is employed with reference to her sex and not to her form.

[2] Tabl. VII, ll. 1–124.

[3] See below, p. 169.

[4] See below, pp. 175 ff.

The date of the Creation legends.

In discussing the question as to the date of the Creation legends, it is necessary to distinguish clearly between the date at which the legends assumed the form in which they have come down to us upon the Seven Tablets of the series *Enuma eliš*, and the date which may be assigned to the legends themselves before they were incorporated in the poem. Of the actual tablets inscribed with portions of the text of the Creation Series we possess none which dates from an earlier period than the seventh century B.C. The tablets of this date were made for the library of Ashur-bani-pal at Nineveh, but it is obvious that the poem was not composed in Assyria at this time. The legends in the form in which we possess them are not intended to glorify Ashur, the national god of Assyria, but Marduk, the god of Babylon, and it is clear that the scribes of Ashur-bani-pal merely made copies for their master of older tablets of Babylonian origin. To what earlier date we may assign the actual composition of the poem and its arrangement upon the Seven Tablets, is still a matter for conjecture; but it is possible to offer a conjecture, with some degree of probability, after an examination of the various indirect sources of evidence we possess with regard to the age of Babylonian legends in general, and of the Creation legends in particular.

Internal evidence of date.

With regard to the internal evidence of date furnished by the Creation legends themselves, we may note that the variant forms of the Dragon-Myth and of the account of the Creation, to which reference has already been made, presuppose many centuries of tradition during which the legends, though derived probably from common originals, were handed down independently of one another. During this period we may suppose that the same story was related in different cities in different ways, and that in course of time variations crept in, with the result that two or more forms of the same story were developed along different lines. The process must have been gradual, and the considerable differences which can be traced in the resultant forms of the same legend may be cited as evidence in favour of assigning an early date to the original tradition from which they were derived.

Evidence from sculpture and from cylinder-seals.

Evidence as to the existence of the Creation legends at least as early as the ninth century B.C. may be deduced from the representations of the fight between Marduk and the dragon Tiamat, which was found sculptured upon two limestone slabs in the temple of Ninib at Nimrūd.[1] The temple was built by Ashur-naṣir-pal, who reigned from B.C. 884 to B.C. 860, and across the actual sculpture was inscribed the text of a dedication to Ninib by this king. The slab therefore furnishes direct proof of the existence of the legend more than two hundred years before the

[1] The slabs are preserved in the British Museum, Nimroud Gallery, Nos. 28 and 29.

formation of Ashur-bani-pal's library. Moreover, the fight between Marduk and Tiamat is frequently found engraved upon cylinder-seals, and, although the majority of such seals probably date from the later Assyrian and Persian periods, the varied treatment of the scene which they present points to the existence of variant forms of the legend, and so indirectly furnishes evidence of the early origin of the legend itself.

Evidence from historical inscriptions.

From an examination of the Babylonian historical inscriptions which record the setting up of statues and the making of temple furniture, we are enabled to trace back the existence of the Creation legends to still earlier periods. For instance, in a text of Agum,[1] a Babylonian king who reigned not later than the seventeenth century B.C., we find descriptions of the figures of a dragon[2] and of other monsters[3] which he set up in the temple E-sagil at Babylon; and in this passage we may trace an unmistakable reference to the legend of Tiamat and her monster-brood. Agum also set up in the temple beside the dragon a great basin, or laver, termed in the inscription a *tāmtu*, or "sea."[4] From the name of the laver, and from its position beside the figure of the dragon,

[1] An Assyrian copy of this inscription, which was made for the library of Ashur-bani-pal, is preserved in the British Museum, and is numbered K. 4,149; the text is published in V R, pl. 33.

[2] Cf. col. iii, l. 13.

[3] Cf. col. iv, ll. 50 ff.

[4] Cf. col. iii, l. 33.

we may conclude that it was symbolical of the abyss of water personified in the Creation legends by Tiamat and Apsū. Moreover, in historical inscriptions of still earlier periods we find allusions to similar vessels termed *apsē*, i.e. "deeps" or "oceans,"[1] the presence of which in the temples is probably to be traced to the existence of the same traditions.

Evidence from historical inscriptions.

The three classes of evidence briefly summarized above tend to show that the most important elements in the Creation legends were not of late origin, but must be traced back in some form or other to remote periods, and may well date from the first half of the third millennium B.C., or even earlier. It remains to consider to what date we may assign the actual weaving together of these legends into the poem termed by the Babylonians and Assyrians *Enuma eliš*. Although, as has already been remarked, we do not possess any early copies of the text of the Creation Series, this is not the case with other Babylonian legends. Among the tablets found at Tell el-Amarna, which date from the fifteenth century B.C., were fragments of copies of two Babylonian legends, the one containing the story of Nergal and Ereshkigal,[2] and

Evidence from early copies of other legends :—

(1) Copies of legends about B.C. 1500.

[1] Such "deeps" were set up by Bur-Sin, King of Ur about B.C. 2500 (cf. I R, pl. 3, No. xii, 1), and by Ur-Ninā, a still earlier king of Shirpurla (cf. De Sarzec, *Découvertes en Chaldée*, pl. ii, No. 1, col. iii, l. 5 f.).

[2] Two separate fragments of this legend were found, of which one is in the British Museum and the other, made up of four

the other inscribed with a part of the legend of Adapa and the South Wind.[1] Both these compositions, in style and general arrangement, closely resemble the legends known from late Assyrian copies, while of the legend of Adapa an actual fragment, though not a duplicate, exists in the library of Ashur-bani-pal.[2] Fragments of legends have also been recently found in Babylonia which date from the end of the period of the First Dynasty of Babylon, about B.C. 2100, and the resemblance which these documents bear to certain legends previously known from Assyrian copies only is not only of a general nature, but extends even to identity of language. Thus one of the recovered fragments is in part a duplicate of the so-called "Cuthaean Legend of Creation";[3] two others contain phrases found upon the legend of Ea and Atar-ḫasis, while upon one of them are traces of a new version

(2) Copies of legends about B.C. 2100.

smaller fragments, is in Berlin. Their texts are published by Budge and Bezold, *The Tell el-Amarna Tablets*, p. 140 f. and pl. 17 (Bu. 88–10–13, 69), and by Winckler and Abel, *Der Thontafelfund von El-Amarna*, p. 164 f. (Nos. 234, 236, 237, and 239); cf. also Knudtzon, *Beiträge zur Assyr.*, iv, pp. 130 ff. For a translation of the fragments, see Jensen, *Mythen und Epen*, pp. 74 ff.

[1] For the text, see Winckler and Abel, *op. cit.*, p. 166 *a* and *b*, and cf. Knudtzon, *B.A.*, iv, pp. 128 ff. For translations, see E. T. Harper, *B.A.*, ii, pp. 420 ff., Zimmern in Gunkel's *Schöpfung und Chaos*, pp. 420 ff., and Jensen, *Mythen und Epen*, pp. 94 ff.

[2] K. 8,214, published by Strong, *P.S.B.A.*, xvi, p. 274 f.; see Jensen, *Mythen und Epen*, pp. 98 ff.

[3] See below, p. 146 f., n. 4.

of the Deluge-story.[1] Still more recently the Trustees of the British Museum have acquired three fragments of Babylonian legends inscribed upon tablets which date from a still earlier period, i.e. from the period of the kings of the Second Dynasty of Ur, before B.C. 2200;[2] (3) Copies of legends before B.C. 2200.

[1] The old Babylonian fragment Bu. 91–5–9, 269 (cf. *Cun. Texts*, vi, and see above, p. lvii, n. 1), and the Deluge-fragment of the reign of Ammizaduga (published by Scheil, *Receueil de travaux*, xx, pp. 55 ff.) both contain phrases found upon the legend of Atar-ḫasis, K. 3,399; cf. Zimmern, *Zeits. für Assyr.*, xiv, p. 278 f. The text of K. 3,399, which has not hitherto been published, is included as plate 49 in part xv of *Cuneiform Texts*; for translations, see Zimmern, *op. cit.*, pp. 287 ff., and Jensen, *Mythen*, pp. 274 ff.

[2] The tablets are numbered 87,535, 93,828, and 87,521, and they are published in *Cuneiform Texts*, pt. xv (1902), plates 1–6. The opening addresses, especially that upon No. 87,535, are of considerable interest; in this tablet the poet states that he will sing the song of Mama, the Lady of the gods, which he declares to be better than honey and wine, etc. (col. i, (1) [*z*]*a-ma-ar* *ilu* *Bi-li-it-ili a-za-ma-ar* (2) *ib-ru uṣ-ṣi-ra ku-ra-du ši-me-a* (3) *ilu* *Ma-ma za-ma-ra-ša-ma e-li di-iš-pi-i-im u ka-ra-nim ṭa-bu* (4) *ṭa bu-u e-li di-iš-pi u ka-ra-ni-i-im*, etc.). The goddess Mama is clearly to be identified with Mami, who also bore the title *Bêlit-ili* (cf. Jensen, *Mythen*, p. 286 f., n. 11); and with the description of her offspring in col. i, ll. 8 ff. (*ilu* *Ma-ma iš-ti-na-am u-li-id-ma* . . . . *ilu* *Ma-ma ši-e-na u-li-id-ma* . . . . *ilu* *Ma-ma ša-la-ti u-l*[*i*]-*i*[*d-ma*]) we may compare Mami's creation of seven men and seven women in the legend of Atar-ḫasis (cf. Jensen, *op. cit.*, p. 286 f.). The legend No. 93,828 also concerns a goddess referred to as *Bêlit-ili*, whom Bêl summons into his presence (cf. col. i, ll. 10 ff.). The texts are written syllabically almost throughout, and simple syllables preponderate; and it is interesting to note that the ending *iš* with the force of a preposition, which occurs in the Creation legends, is here also employed, cf. No. 87,521, col. iii, l. 4, *mu-uṭ-ṭi-iš um-mi-šu*, and possibly col. vi, l. 3, *gi-ir-bi-iš*. The texts are

Copies of legends before B.C. 2200.

and to the same period is to be assigned the fragment of a legend which was published a few weeks ago by Dr. Meissner,[1] and probably also the new fragment of the Etana-myth, published last year by Father Scheil.[2] These five fragments are of peculiar interest, for they show that early Semitic, as opposed to Sumerian, legends were in existence, and were carefully preserved and studied in other cities of Mesopotamia

carefully written (it may be noted that a *na* has been omitted by the scribe in No. 93,828, col. i, l. 7), the lines vary considerably in length, and the metre is not indicated by the arrangement of the text. Though fragmentary the episodes described or referred to in the texts are of considerable interest, perhaps the most striking being the reference to the birth of Ishum in col. viii of No. 87,521, and the damming of the Tigris with which the text of No. 87,535 concludes. I intend elsewhere to publish translations of the fragments.

[1] *Ein altbabylonisches Fragment des Gilgamosepos*, in the *Mitteilungen der Vorderasiatischen Gesellschaft*, 1902, 1. The fragment here published refers to episodes in the Gilgamesh-epic, the name of Gilgamesh being written *ilu* GIŠ, i.e. *ilu* GIŠ-ṬU-BAR. From the photographic reproductions published by Dr. Meissner, it is clear that the Gilgamesh fragment, in the nature of the clay employed, and in the archaic forms of the characters, resembles the three fragments in the British Museum. Unlike them, however, the lines of its text do not appear to be separated by horizontal lines ruled upon the clay.

[2] Father Scheil has published the text in late Assyrian characters in the *Recueil de travaux*, xxiii, pp. 18 ff., and he does not give a photograph of the tablet. From his description ("C'était une "belle grande tablette de terre cuite, avec, par face, trois ou quatre "colonnes . . . L'écriture en est archaïque et, sans aucun doute "possible, antérieure à Ḥammurabi"), we may conclude that it dates from the same period as the three tablets in the British Museum described above.

than Babylon, and at a period before the rise of that city to a position of importance under the kings of the First Dynasty.

Sumerian origin of much of the Creation legends.

The evidence furnished by these recently discovered tablets with regard to the date of Babylonian legends in general may be applied to the date of the Creation legends. While the origin of much of the Creation legends may be traced to Sumerian sources,[1] it is clear that the Semitic inhabitants of Mesopotamia at a very early period produced their own versions of the compositions which they borrowed, modifying and augmenting them to suit their own legends and beliefs. The connection of Marduk with the Dragon-Myth, and with the stories of the creation of the world and

[1] See above, p. lxxv. Cf. also the Sumerian influence exhibited by the names of the older pairs of deities Laḫmu and Laḫamu, Anshar and Kishar, as well as in the names of Kingu, Gaga, etc.; while the ending *iš*, employed as it constantly is in the Creation Series with the force of a preposition, may probably be traced to the Sumerian *ku*, later *šu*, *ši* (cf. Jensen, *Kosmologie*, p. 266). The Assyrian commentaries to the Seventh Tablet, moreover, prove the existence of a Sumerian version of this composition, and as the hymn refers to incidents in the Creation legends, the Sumerian origin of these, too, is implied. The Sumerian version of the story of the Creation by Marduk and Aruru (see below, pp. 130 ff.) cannot with certainty be cited as evidence of its Sumerian origin, as from internal evidence it may well be a later and artificial composition on Sumerian lines. That we may expect, however, one day to find the original Sumerian versions of the Creation legends is not unreasonable; with respect to the recovery of the ancient religious literature of the Sumerians, the remarkable series of early Sumerian religious texts published in *Cun. Texts*, pt. xv, plates 7–30, may be regarded as an earnest of what we may look for in the future.

man, may with considerable probability be assigned to the subsequent period during which Babylon gradually attained to the position of the principal city in Mesopotamia. On tablets inscribed during the reigns of kings of the First Dynasty we may therefore expect to find copies of the Creation legends corresponding closely with the text of the series *Enuma eliš*. It is possible that the division of the poem into seven sections, inscribed upon separate tablets, took place at a later period; but, be this as it may, we may conclude with a considerable degree of confidence that the bulk of the poem, as we know it from late Assyrian and Neo-Babylonian copies, was composed at a period not later than B.C. 2000.

Probable date of the association of Marduk with the Creation legends.

Probable date of the composition of the poem *Enuma eliš*.

The political influence which the Babylonians exerted over neighbouring nations during long periods of their history was considerable, and it is not surprising that their beliefs concerning the origin of the universe should have been partially adopted by the races with whom they came in contact. That Babylonian elements may be traced in the Phoenician cosmogony has long been admitted, but the imperfect, and probably distorted, form in which the latter has come down to us renders uncertain any comparison of details.[1] Some of the beliefs concerning the

Influence of the Babylonian Creation legends.

[1] For the account of the Phoenician cosmogony according to Sanchuniathon, see Eusebius, *Praep. ev.*, i, 9 f., who quotes from the Greek translation of Philo Byblius; the accounts of Eudemus and Mochus are described by Damascius, cap. 125 (ed. Kopp,

creation of the world which were current among the Egyptians bear a more striking resemblance to the corresponding legends of Babylonia. Whether this resemblance was due to the proto-Semitic strain which probably existed in the ancient Egyptian race,[1] or is to be explained as the result of later Babylonian influence from without, is yet uncertain. But, whatever explanation be adopted, it is clear that the conception of chaos as a watery mass out of which came forth successive generations of primeval gods is common to both races.[2] It is in Hebrew literature, however, that the most striking examples of the influence of the Babylonian Creation legends are to be found.

Points of resemblance between the Creation legends and Gen. i, 1–ii, 4*a*:—

The close relation existing between the Babylonian account of the Creation and the narrative in Genesis i, 1 – ii, 4*a* has been recognized from the time of the

p. 385). For summaries and comparisons of these cosmogonies, see Lukas, *Die Grundbegriffe in den Kosmogonien der alten Völker*, pp. 139 ff.

[1] Cf. Budge, *History of Egypt*, vol. i, pp. 39 ff.

[2] Other Egyptian beliefs, according to which the god Shû separated heaven and earth and upheld the one above the other, may be compared to the Babylonian conception of the making of heaven and earth by the separation of the two halves of Tiamat's body. For detailed descriptions of the Egyptian cosmogonies, see Brugsch, *Religion und Mythologie der alten Aegypter*, pp. 100 ff.; and for a convenient summary of the principal systems, see Lukas, *op. cit.*, pp. 47 ff. Though the Babylonian and Egyptian cosmogonies, in some of their general features, resemble one another, the detailed comparisons of the names of deities, etc., which Hommel attempts in his *Babylonische Ursprung der ägyptischen Kultur*, are rather fanciful.

first discovery of the former,[1] and the old and new points of resemblance between them may here be briefly discussed. According to each account the existence of a watery chaos preceded the creation of the universe; and the Hebrew word *tehōm*, translated "the deep" in Gen. i, 2, is the equivalent of the Babylonian *Tiamat*, the monster of the deep personifying chaos and confusion. In the details of the Creation there is also a close resemblance between the two accounts. In the Hebrew narrative the first act of creation is that of light (Gen. i, 3–5), and it has been suggested that a parallel possibly existed in the Babylonian account, in that the creation of light may have been the cause of the revolt of Tiamat. From the new fragments of the poem we now know that the rebellion of the forces of disorder, which was incited by Apsū and not Tiamat, was due, not to the creation of light, but to his hatred of the way of the gods which produced order in place of chaos.[2] A parallelism may still be found, however, in the original form of the Babylonian myth, according to which the conqueror of the dragon was undoubtedly a solar deity.[3] Moreover, as has been pointed out above,[4] day and night are vaguely conceived in the poem as already in existence at the

(1) The description of chaos.

(2) The creation of light.

[1] See above, p. xxvi f.
[2] See above, p. xxxix, and below, p. 10, n. 1.
[3] See above, p. xxxix, n. 2.
[4] See above, p. xxxix.

time of Apsû's revolt, so that the belief in the existence of light before the creation of the heavenly bodies is a common feature of the Hebrew and the Babylonian account.

The second act of creation in the Hebrew narrative is that of a firmament which divided the waters that were under the firmament from the waters that were above the firmament (Gen. i, 6-8). In the Babylonian poem the body of Tiamat is divided by Marduk, and from one-half of her he formed a covering or dome for heaven, i.e. a firmament, which kept her upper waters in place. Moreover, on the fragment S. 2,013 [1] we find mention of a *Ti-amat e-li-ti* and a *Ti-amat šap-li-ti*, that is, an Upper Tiamat (or Ocean) and a Lower Tiamat (or Ocean), which are the exact equivalents of the waters above and under the firmament.[2] (3) The creation of a firmament.

[1] See below, p. 196 f.

[2] According to Babylonian belief the upper waters of Tiamat formed the heavenly ocean above the covering of heaven; but it is not clear what became of her lower waters. It is possible that they were vaguely identified with those of Apsû, and were believed to mingle with his around and beneath the earth. It may be suggested, however, that perhaps all or part of them were identified with Ḫubur, the River of the Underworld which was believed to exist in the depths of the earth (cf. Jensen, *Mythen*, p. 307). The fact that Tiamat bore the title Ummu-Ḫubur, "the Mother Ḫubur," may be cited in support of this suggestion, as well as the occurrence upon S. 2,013 (cf. p. 197) of the phrases *šamē(e) ru-ḳu-u-ti* and *Ḫu-bur pal-ka-ti*, corresponding to *Ti-amat e-li-ti* and *Ti-amat šap-li-ti* respectively; see also p. xlvi, note.

(4) The creation of the earth and of vegetation.

The third and fourth acts of creation, as narrated in Gen. i, 9-13, are those of the earth and of vegetation. Although no portion of the Babylonian poem has yet been recovered which contains the corresponding account, it is probable that these acts of creation were related on the Fifth Tablet of the series.[1] Berossus expressly states that Bēl formed the earth out of one half of Omorka's body, and as his summary of the Babylonian Creation story is proved to be correct wherever it can be controlled, it is legitimate to assume that he is correct in this detail also. Moreover, in three passages in the Seventh Tablet the creation of the earth by Marduk is referred to: l. 115 reads, "Since he created the heaven and fashioned the firm earth";[2] the new fragment K. 12,830 (restored from the commentary K. 8,299) states, "He named the four quarters (of the world)";[3] and another new fragment, K. 13,761 (restored from the commentary K. 4,406), definitely ascribes to Marduk the title "Creator of the earth."[4] That the creation of vegetation by Marduk was also recorded in the poem may be concluded from the opening lines of the Seventh Tablet, which are inscribed on the new fragment K. 2,854, and (with restorations from the commentary S. 11, etc.) ascribe to him the titles "Bestower of

[1] See above, p. l.
[2] See below, p. 109.
[3] See below, p. 101.
[4] See below, p. 103.

planting," "Founder of sowing," "Creator of grain and plants," and add that he "caused the green herb to spring up."[1]

(5) The creation of the heavenly bodies.

To the fifth act of creation, that of the heavenly bodies (Gen. i, 14-19), we find an exceedingly close parallel in the opening lines of the Fifth Tablet of the series.[2] In the Hebrew account, lights were created in the firmament of heaven to divide the day from the night, and to be for signs, and for seasons, and for days, and years. In the Babylonian poem also the stars were created and the year was ordained at the same time; the twelve months were to be regulated by the stars; and the Moon-god was appointed "to determine the days." As according to the Hebrew account two great lights were created in the firmament of heaven, the greater light to rule the day and the lesser to rule the night, so according to the Babylonian poem the night was entrusted to the Moon-god, and the Moon-god's relations to the Sun-god are described in detail. On the Seventh Tablet, also, the creation of heaven and the heavenly bodies is referred to; in l. 16 Marduk is stated "to have established for the gods the bright heavens,"[3] and l. 111 f. read, "For the stars of heaven he upheld the paths, he shepherded all the gods like sheep!"[4]

[1] See above, p. l, and below, p. 93.
[2] See below, pp. 78 ff.
[3] See below, p. 95.
[4] See below, p. 109.

(6) The creation of animals.

To the sixth and seventh acts of creation, i.e., the creation of creatures of the sea and winged fowl, and of beasts and cattle and creeping things (Gen. i, 20-25), the Babylonian poem as yet offers no parallel, for the portion of the text which refers to the creation of animals is still wanting. But since Berossus states that animals were created at the same time as man, it is probable that their creation was recorded in a missing portion either of the Fifth or of the Sixth Tablet. If the account was on the lines suggested by Berossus, and animals shared in the blood of Bēl, it is clear that their creation was narrated, as a subsidiary and less important episode, after that of man.[1] But, although this episode is still wanting in the poem, we find references on other Assyrian Creation fragments to the creation of beasts. Thus, for the creation of the creatures of the sea in Genesis, we may compare the fragmentary text K. 3445 + R. 396, which records the creation of *naḫirē*, "dolphins (?)."[2] And for the creation of beasts of the earth and cattle, we may compare the tablet D.T. 41,[3] which, after referring generally to the creation of "living creatures" by "the gods," proceeds to classify them as the cattle and beasts of the field, and the creatures of the city, the two

[1] See above, p. lix.
[2] See above, p. lix, n. 1, and below, p. 198.
[3] See below, p. 122 f.

classes referring respectively to wild and domesticated animals.[1]

(7) The creation of man.

The account of the creation of man, which is recorded as the eighth and last act of creation in the Hebrew account (Gen. i, 26-31), at length finds its parallel in the Babylonian poem upon the new fragment of the Sixth Tablet, No. 92,629.[2] It has already been pointed out that the Babylonian account closely follows the version of the story handed down to us from Berossus,[3] and it may here be added that the employment by Marduk, the Creator, of his own blood in the creation of man may perhaps be compared to the Hebrew account of the creation of man in the image and after the likeness of Elohim.[4] Moreover, the use of the plural in the phrase "Let us make man" in Gen. i, 26, may be compared with the Babylonian narrative which relates that Marduk imparted his purpose of forming man to his father Ea,

[1] The portion of the text on which this reference to the creation of beasts is inscribed forms an introduction to what is probably an incantation, and may be compared to the Creation legend of Marduk and Aruru which is employed as an introduction to an incantation to be recited in honour of the temple E-zida (see below, p. 130 f., n. 1). The account given of the creation of the beasts is merely incidental, and is introduced to indicate the period of the creation by Nin-igi-azag of two small creatures, one white and one black, which were probably again referred to in the following section of the text.

[2] See below, pp. 86 ff.

[3] See above, pp. liv ff.

[4] See also below, p. xciii. It may be also noted that, according to Babylonian belief, the great gods (cf. the plural of Elohim) were always pictured in human form.

whom he probably afterwards instructed to carry out the actual work of man's creation.[1]

(8) The instructions to man after his creation.

A parallel to the charge which, according to the Hebrew account, Elohim gave to man and woman after their creation, has hitherto been believed to exist on the tablet K. 3,364, which was supposed to contain a list of the duties of man as delivered to him after his creation by Marduk. The new Babylonian duplicate of this text, No. 33,851, proves that K. 3,364 is not part of the Creation Series, but is merely a tablet of moral precepts, so that its suggested resemblance to the Hebrew narrative must be given up. It is not improbable, however, that a missing portion of the Sixth Tablet did contain a short series of instructions by Marduk to man, since man was created with the special object of supplying the gods with worshippers and building shrines in their honour. That to these instructions to worship the gods was added the gift of dominion over beasts, birds, and vegetation is possible, but it must be pointed out that the Babylonian version of man's creation is related from the point of view of the gods, not from that of man. Although his creation forms the culmination of Marduk's work, it was conceived, not as an end and aim in itself, but merely as an expedient to satisfy the discontented gods.[2] This expedient is referred to in the Seventh

[1] See above, p. lviii.

[2] See above, p. liii f., and below, p. 85, note 3, and p. 88 f., notes 1 and 3.

Tablet, l. 29, in the phrase "For their forgiveness (i.e., the forgiveness of the gods) did he create mankind," and other passages in the Seventh Tablet tend to show that Marduk's mercy and goodness are extolled in his relations, not to mankind, but to the gods.[1] In one passage man's creation is referred to, but it is in connection with the charge that he forget not the deeds of his Creator.[2]

(9) The dominion of man over creation.

The above considerations render it unlikely that the Babylonian poem contained an exact parallel to the exalted charge of Elohim in which He placed the rest of creation under man's dominion. It is possible, however, that upon the new fragment of the Seventh Tablet, K. 12,830 (restored from the commentary K. 8,299),[3] we have a reference to the superiority of man over animals, in the phrase "mankind [he created], [and upon] him understanding [he bestowed (?) . . .]"; and if this be so, we may compare it to Gen. i, 28*b*. Moreover, if my suggested restoration of the last word in l. 7 of the Sixth Tablet be correct, so that it may read "I will create man who shall inhabit [the earth],[4]" we may

---

[1] See especially, ll. 7 f., 9 ff., 15 ff., 23, and 27 f.

[2] L. 31 f., which read, "May his (i.e. Marduk's) deeds endure, may they never be forgotten in the mouth of mankind whom his hands have made!"

[3] See below, p. 100 f.

[4] See below, p. 87; the account of Berossus is in favour of this restoration.

compare it to Gen. i, 28*a*, in which man is commanded to be fruitful, and multiply, and replenish the earth.[1]

(10) The word of the Creator.

A suggestion has been made that the prominence given to the word of the Creator in the Hebrew account may have found its parallel in the creation by a word in the Babylonian poem. It is true that the word of Marduk had magical power and could destroy and create alike; but Marduk did not employ his word in any of his acts of creation which are at present known to us. He first conceived a cunning device, and then proceeded to carry it out by hand. The only occasion on which he did employ his word to destroy and to create is in the Fourth Tablet, ll. 19-26,[2] when, at the invitation of the gods, he tested his power by making a garment disappear and then appear again at the word of his mouth. The parallelism between the two accounts under this heading is not very close.

(11) The order of Creation.

The order of the separate acts of creation is also not quite the same in the two accounts, for, while in the Babylonian poem the heavenly bodies are created immediately after the formation of the firmament, in the Hebrew account their creation is postponed until after the earth and vegetation have been made. It is possible that the creation of the earth and plants has been displaced by the writer to whom the present form of the Hebrew account is due, and that the

[1] The new parallel to Gen. ii, 23, furnished by l. 5 of the Sixth Tablet, is referred to below, p. xciv.

[2] See below, p. 60 f.

order of creation was precisely the same in the original forms of the two narratives. But even according to the present arrangement of the Hebrew account, there are several striking points of resemblance to the Babylonian poem. These may be seen in the existence of light before the creation of the heavenly bodies; in the dividing of the waters of the primeval flood by means of a firmament also before the creation of the heavenly bodies; and in the culminating act of creation being that of man.

(12) The Seven Days and the Seven Tablets of Creation.

It would be tempting to trace the framework of the Seven Days of Creation, upon which the narrative in Genesis is stretched, to the influence of the Seven Tablets of Creation, of which we now know that the great Creation Series was composed. The reasons for the employment of the Seven Days in the Hebrew account are, however, not the same which led to the arrangement of the Babylonian poem upon Seven Tablets. In the one the writer's intention is to give the original authority for the observance of the Sabbath; in the other there appears to have been no special reason for this arrangement of the poem beyond the mystical nature of the number "seven." Moreover, acts of creation are recorded on all of the first six Days in the Hebrew narrative, while in the Babylonian poem the creation only begins at the end of the Fourth Tablet.[1] The resemblance, therefore, is somewhat superficial, but

[1] There is, however, a parallel between the Seventh Day on

The Seven Days and the Seven Tablets of Creation.

it is possible that the employment of the number "seven" in the two accounts was not fortuitous. Whether the Sabbath was of Babylonian origin (as seems probable) or not, it is clear that the writer of the narrative in Genesis was keenly interested in its propagation and its due observance. Now in Exilic and post-Exilic times the account of the Creation most prevalent in Babylonia was that in the poem *Enuma eliš*, the text of which was at this time absolutely fixed and its arrangement upon Seven Tablets invariable. That the late revival of mythology among the Jews was partly due to their actual study of the Babylonian legends at this period is sufficiently proved by the minute points of resemblance between the accounts of the Deluge in Genesis and in the poem of Gilgamesh.[1] It is probable, therefore, that the writer who was responsible for the final form of Gen. i - ii, 4*a*, was familiar with the Babylonian legend of Creation in the form in which it has come down to us. The supposition, then, is perhaps not too

which Elohim rested from all His work, and the Seventh Tablet which records the hymns of praise sung by the gods to Marduk after his work of creation was ended.

[1] See my *Babylonian Religion and Mythology*, pp. 138 ff. The fact that the Jews of the Exile were probably familiar with the later forms of Babylonian legends explains some of the close resemblances in detail between the Babylonian and Hebrew versions of the same story. But this is in perfect accordance with the borrowing of that very story by the Hebrews many centuries before; indeed, to the previous existence of ancient Hebrew versions of Babylonian legends may be traced much of the impetus given to the revival of mythology among the exiled Jews.

fanciful, that the connection of the Sabbath with the story of Creation was suggested by the mystical number of the Tablets upon which the Babylonian poem was inscribed.

Points of resemblance between Babylonian legends and the second Hebrew account of the Creation.

Further resemblances to the Babylonian Creation legends may be traced in the second Hebrew account of the Creation which follows the first in Gen. ii, 4*b*–7. According to this version man was formed from the dust of the ground, which may be compared to the mixing of Bēl's blood with earth according to the account of Berossus, the use of the Creator's blood in the one account being paralleled by the employment of His breath in the other for the purpose of giving life to the dust or earth. Earth is not mentioned in the recovered portion of the Sixth Tablet, but its use in the creation of men is fully in accordance with Babylonian beliefs. Thus, according to the second Babylonian account of the Creation,[1] Marduk formed man by pouring out dust beside a reed which he had set upon the face of the waters. Clay is also related to have been employed in the creation of special men and heroes; thus it was used in Ea-bani's creation by Aruru,[2] and it is related to have been mixed with divine blood for a similar purpose in the fragmentary legend Bu. 91-5-9, 269.[3] To the account of the creation of woman in Gen. ii, 18 ff. we find a new parallel in l. 5 of the

[1] See below, pp. 130 ff.
[2] See above, p. lxx, n. 1.
[3] See above, p. lvii, n. 1.

Sixth Tablet of the Creation Series, in the use of the word *iṣṣimtu*, "bone," corresponding to the Hebrew *'eṣem* which occurs in the phrase "bone of my bones" in Gen. ii, 23.

Paradise and the River of Creation.

In addition to the Babylonian colouring of much of the story of Paradise we may now add a new parallel from the Babylonian address to a mythical River of Creation, inscribed on S. 1704 and the Neo-Babylonian Tablet 82-9-18, 5311.[1] This short composition is addressed to a River to whom the creation of all things is ascribed,[2] and with this river we may compare the mythical river of Paradise which watered the garden, and on leaving it was divided into four branches. That the Hebrew River of Paradise is Babylonian in character is clear; and the origin of the Babylonian River of Creation is also to be found in the Euphrates, from whose waters southern Babylonia derived its great fertility.[3] The

[1] See below, p. 128 f.

[2] With the Babylonian River of Creation, suggested by the Euphrates, we may compare the Egyptian beliefs concerning Ḥāp or Ḥāpi, the god of the Nile, who became identified with most of the great primeval Creation gods and was declared to be the Creator of all things. Considering the importance of the Nile for Egypt, it is easy to understand how he came to attain this position. Brugsch sums up his account of this deity in the words: "So ist der Nilgott im letzten Grunde der geheimnissvolle Urheber "aller Wohlthaten, welche die von ihm befruchtete ägyptische Erde "den Göttern und Menschen zu bieten vermag, er ist 'der starke "Schöpfer von allem'"; see *Religion und Mythologie der alten Aegypter*, p. 641.

[3] It is possible that this River, though suggested by the

life-giving stream of Paradise is met with elsewhere in the Old Testament, as, for instance, in Ezekiel xlvii, and it is probable that we may trace its influence in the Apocalypse.[1]

Probable dates of Babylonian influence on Hebrew mythology.

It is unnecessary here to discuss in detail the evidence to prove that the Hebrew narratives of the Creation were ultimately derived from Babylonia, and were not inherited independently by the Babylonians and Hebrews from a common Semitic ancestor.[2] For the local Babylonian colouring of the stories, and the great age to which their existence can be traced, extending back to the time of the Sumerian inhabitants of Mesopotamia,[3] are conclusive evidence against the second alternative. On the other hand, it is equally unnecessary to cite the well-known arguments to prove

Euphrates, is to be identified with *Ḫubur*, the River of the Underworld, to whom an incantation in the terms of the one under discussion might well have been addressed. A connection between Tiamat and the river Ḫubur has been suggested above (cf. p. lxxxiii, n. 2), and, should this prove to be correct, we might see in the phrase *banat(at) ka-la-ma*, applied to the River, a parallel to *pa-ti-ka-at ka-la-ma*, the description of Ummu-Ḫubur (Tiamat) in Tablet I, l. 113 and the parallel passages.

[1] The connection which Gunkel and Zimmern would trace between the River of Paradise and the River of Water of Life in the Apocalypse on the one side and the "water of life," mentioned in the legend of Adapa, on the other, cannot be regarded as proved. The resemblance in the expressions may well be fortuitous, since there are few other points of resemblance between the narratives in which the expressions occur.

[2] On these subjects, see my *Bab. Rel. and Myth.*, pp. 108 ff.

[3] See above, pp. lxxv and lxxix.

Probable dates of Babylonian influence on Hebrew mythology.

the existence among the Hebrews of Creation legends similar to those of Babylonia for centuries before the Exile. The allusions to variant Hebrew forms of the Babylonian Dragon-Myth in Amos ix, 3, Isaiah li, 9, Psalm lxxiv, 13 f., and lxxxix, 9 f., and Job xxvi, 12 f., and ix, 13, may be cited as sufficient proof of the early period at which the borrowing from Babylonian sources must have taken place ; and the striking differences between the Biblical and the known Babylonian versions of the legends prove that the Exilic and post-Exilic Jews must have found ready to their hand ancient Hebrew versions of the stories, and that the changes they introduced must in the main have been confined to details of arrangement and to omissions necessitated by their own more spiritual conceptions and beliefs. The discovery of the Tell el-Amarna tablets proved conclusively that Babylonian influence extended throughout Egypt and Western Asia in the fifteenth century B.C., and the existence of legends among the letters demonstrated the fact that Babylonian mythology exerted an influence coextensive with the range of her political ties and interests. We may therefore conjecture that Babylonian myths had become naturalized in Palestine before the conquest of that country by the Israelites. Many such Palestinian versions of Babylonian myths the Israelites no doubt absorbed ; while during the subsequent period of the Hebrew kings Assyria and Babylonia exerted a direct influence upon them. It is clear, therefore, that at the time of their exile the captive Jews did not find in Babylonian mythology an entirely new and unfamiliar subject, but recognized in it a series of kindred beliefs, differing much from their own in spiritual conceptions, but presenting a startling resemblance on many material points.

The forty-nine tablets and fragments inscribed with the text of the Creation Series.

Now that the principal problems with regard to the contents, date, and influence of the Creation Series, *Enuma eliš*, have been dealt with, it remains to describe in some detail the forty-nine fragments and tablets from which the text, transliterated and translated in the following pages, has been made up. After each registration-number is given a reference to the published copy of the text in *Cuneiform Texts from Babylonian Tablets, etc., in the British Museum*, pt. xiii, or in Vol. II of this work, or in Appendices I and II of this volume; a brief description of each tablet is added, together with references to any previous publication of the text. After the enumeration of the known copies of each tablet, a list is given of the authorities for the separate lines of the tablet, in order to enable the reader to verify any passage in the text with as little delay as possible.

Copies of the First Tablet of the Creation Series.

The following twelve tablets and fragments are inscribed with portions of the text of the First Tablet of the series :—

1. K. 5,419*c* : *Cuneiform Texts*, pt. xiii (1901), pl. 1. Obverse : ll. 1 - 16 ; Reverse : catch-line and colophon.

Copies of the First Tablet of the Creation Series.

Upper part of an Assyrian tablet, 3¼ in. by 1⅞ in. For earlier publications of the text, see George Smith, *T.S.B.A.*, vol. iv, p. 363 f., pl. i; Fox Talbot, *T.S.B.A.*, vol. v, pp. 428 ff.; Menant, *Manuel de la langue Assyrienne*, p. 378 f.; Delitzsch, *Assyrische Lesestücke*, 1st ed., p. 40, 2nd ed., p. 78, 3rd ed., p. 93; Lyon, *Assyrian Manual*, p. 62; and my *First Steps in Assyrian*, p. 122 f.

2. No. 93,015 (82-7-14, 402): *Cun. Texts*, pt. xiii, pls. 1 and 3. Obverse: ll. 1-16; Reverse: ll. 124-142 and colophon.

Uppet part of a Neo-Babylonian tablet, 2⅛ in. by 2¼ in. For an earlier publication of the text, see Pinches, *Bab. Or. Rec.*, vol. iv, p. 26 f. The fragment is probably part of the same tablet as that to which No. 10 belonged.

3. No. 45,528 + 46,614: Vol. II, pls. i-vi. Obverse: ll. 1-48; Reverse: ll. 111-142, catch-line, and colophon.

Part of a Neo-Babylonian tablet, formed from two fragments, which I have joined; 2¼ in. by 5½ in. This text has not been previously published.

4. No. 35,134: Vol. II, pl. vii. Obverse: ll. 11-21; no reverse.

Part of a Neo-Babylonian tablet, 1⅜ in. by 2 in. This text has not been previously published.

5. No. 36,726: Vol. II, pl. viii. Obverse: ll. 28-33.

Neo-Babylonian "practice-tablet"; the text, which forms an extract, measures 2⅞ in. by 1¼ in. This text has not been previously published.

6. 81-7-27, 80: *Cun. Texts*, pt. xiii, pl. 2. Obverse: ll. 31-56; Reverse: ll. 118-142.

Part of an Assyrian tablet, 2⅝ in. by 3 in. This text, which was referred to by Pinches in the *Bab. Or. Rec.*, vol. iv, p. 33, was used by Zimmern for his translation in Gunkel's *Schöpfung und Chaos*, p. 402 f.; it was given in transliteration by Delitzsch, *Weltschöpfungsepos*, p. 25 f., and by Jensen, *Mythen und Epen*, pp. 2 ff.

Copies of the First Tablet of the Creation Series.

7. K. 3,938: *Cun. Texts*, pt. xiii, pl. 3. Obverse: ll. 33-42; Reverse: ll. 128-142.

Part of an Assyrian tablet, 1 in. by 1⅝ in. This fragment was used by George Smith, *Chaldean Account of Genesis*, p. 93 f., and by subsequent translators; the text was given in transliteration by Delitzsch, *Weltschöpfungsepos*, p. 27.

8. K. 7,871: Vol. I, Appendix II, pp. 183 ff. Obverse: ll. 33-47; no reverse.

Part of an Assyrian tablet, 1⅛ in. by 1¾ in. The fragment may belong to the same tablet as No. 11. This text has not been previously published.

9. No. 36,688: Vol. II, pl. vii. Obverse: ll. 38-44.

Part of a Neo-Babylonian "practice-tablet"; the text, which forms an abstract, measures 1½ in. by 1⅛ in. This text has not been previously published.

10. No. 46,803: Vol. II, pls. ix-xi. Obverse: ll. 46-67; Reverse: ll. 83-103.

Part of a Neo-Babylonian tablet, 2 in. by 2 in. The fragment is probably part of the same tablet as that to which No. 2 belonged. This text has not been previously published.

11. K. 4,488: Vol. I, Appendix II, pp. 185 ff. Obverse: ll. 50-63; no reverse.

Part of an Assyrian tablet, 1¾ in. by 1½ in.; see above, No. 8. This text has not been previously published.

12. 82-9-18, 6,879: Vol. II, pls. xii and xiii. No obverse; Reverse: ll. 93-118.

Part of a Neo-Babylonian tablet, 1⅞ in. by 2⅝ in. This text has not been previously published.

Authorities for the lines of the First Tablet.

The authorities for the lines of the First Tablet are as follows :—

TABLET I.

ll. 1-10	: Nos. 1, 2, and 3.
ll. 11-16	: Nos. 1, 2, 3, and 4.
ll. 17-21	: Nos. 3 and 4.
ll. 22-27	: No. 3.
ll. 28-30	: Nos. 3 and 5.
ll. 31-32	: Nos. 3, 5, and 6.
l. 33	: Nos. 3, 5, 6, 7, and 8.
ll. 34-37	: Nos. 3, 6, 7, and 8.
ll. 38-42	: Nos. 3, 6, 7, 8, and 9.
l. 43	: Nos. 3, 6, and 8.
l. 44	: Nos. 3, 6, 8, and 9.
l. 45	: Nos. 3, 6, and 8.
ll. 46-47	: Nos. 3, 6, 8, and 10.
l. 48	: Nos. 3, 6, and 10.
l. 49	: Nos. 6 and 10.
ll. 50-56	: Nos. 6, 10, and 11.
ll. 57-63	: Nos. 10 and 11.
ll. 64-67	: No. 10.
ll. 68-82	: Wanting.
ll. 83-92	: No. 10.
ll. 93-103	: Nos. 10 and 12.
ll. 104-110	: No. 12.
ll. 111-117	: Nos. 3 and 12.
l. 118	: Nos. 3, 6, and 12.
ll. 119-123	: Nos. 3 and 6.
ll. 124-127	: Nos. 2, 3, and 6.
ll. 128-142	: Nos. 2, 3, 6, and 7.

The following seven tablets and fragments are inscribed with portions of the text of the Second Tablet of the series :— *Copies of the Second Tablet of the Creation Series.*

13. No. 40,559 : Vol. II, pls. xiv - xxi. Obverse : ll. 1-40 ; Reverse : ll. (111)-(140), catch-line, and colophon.

Upper part of a Neo-Babylonian tablet, 2⅝ in. by 4⅛ in. This text has not been previously published.

14. No. 38,396 : *Cun. Texts*, pt. xiii, pl. 4. Obverse : ll. 11-29 ; Reverse : ll. (105)-(132).

Part of a Neo-Babylonian tablet, 3¼ in. by 2 in. This text has not been previously published.

15. No. 92,632 + 93,048 : Vol. II, pls. xxii - xxiv. Obverse : ll. 14-29 ; Reverse : ll. (114)-(131).

Part of a Neo-Babylonian tablet, formed from two fragments which I have joined ; 1⅞ in. by 1⅝ in. This text has not been previously published.

16. K. 4,832 : *Cun. Texts*, pt. xiii, pl. 5. Obverse : ll. 32-58 ; Reverse : ll. (104)-(138).

Part of an Assyrian tablet, 1½ in. by 3¼ in. This tablet was known to George Smith, see *Chald. Acc. of Gen.*, p. 92 ; its text was published by S. A. Smith, *Miscellaneous Texts*, pl. 8 f.

17. 79-7-8, 178 : *Cun. Texts*, pt. xiii, pl. 6. Obverse : ll. (69)-(75) ; Reverse : ll. (76)-(85).

Part of an Assyrian tablet, 3⅛ in. by 1¾ in. This text, which was identified by Pinches, was given in transliteration by Delitzsch, *Weltschöpfungsepos*, p. 30, and by Jensen, *Mythen und Epen*, p. 10 f.

18. K. 10,008 : Vol. I, App. II, pp. 187 ff. No obverse ; Reverse : probably between ll. 85 and 104.

Part of an Assyrian tablet, 1⅝ in. by 2¼ in. This text has not been previously published.

19. K. 292: *Cun. Texts*, pt. xiii, pl. 6. No obverse; Reverse: ll. (131)-(140).

Lower part of an Assyrian tablet, 2½ in. by 2¼ in. The text of this tablet, which was known to George Smith, was given in transliteration by Delitzsch, *Weltschöpfungsepos*, p. 31, and by Jensen, *Mythen und Epen*, p. 10.

Authorities for the lines of the Second Tablet.

The authorities for the lines of the Second Tablet are as follows:—

TABLET II.

ll. 1-10	: No. 13.
ll. 11-13	: Nos. 13 and 14.
ll. 14-29	: Nos. 13, 14, and 15.
ll. 30-31	: No. 13.
ll. 32-40	: Nos. 13 and 16.
ll. 41-58	: No. 16.
ll. 59-(68)	: Wanting.
ll. (69)-(85)	: No. 17.
between ll. (86) and (103)	: No. 18.
l. (104)	: No. 16.
ll. (105)-(110)	: Nos. 14 and 16.
ll. (111)-(113)	: Nos. 13, 14, and 16.
ll. (114)-(126)	: Nos. 13, 14, 15, and 16.
l. (127)	: Nos. 13, 15, and 16.
ll. (128)-(129)	: Nos. 13, 14, 15, and 16.
l. (130)	: Nos. 13, 15, and 16.
l. (131)	: Nos. 13, 15, 16, and 19.
l. (132)	: Nos. 13, 14, 16, and 19.
ll. (133)-(138)	: Nos. 13, 16, and 19.
ll. (139)-(140)	: Nos. 13 and 19.

The following nine tablets and fragments are inscribed with portions of the text of the Third Tablet :—

Copies of the Third Tablet of the Creation Series.

20. K. 3,473 + 79-7-8, 296 + R. 615 : *Cun. Texts*, pt. xiii, pls. 7-9. Obverse : ll. 1-85 ; Reverse : ll. 86-138.

Parts of an Assyrian tablet, $2\frac{1}{2}$ in. by $8\frac{3}{8}$ in. The three fragments of this tablet, which have been recovered, join, but, as they are much warped by fire, they have not been stuck together. For earlier publications of the text, see S. A. Smith, *Miscellaneous Texts*, pls. 1–5, and my *First Steps in Assyrian*, pp. 124 ff. The text of K. 3,473 had been already recognized by George Smith, see *Chald. Acc. Gen.*, p. 92 f.

21. No. 93,017 [88-4-19, 13] : *Cun. Texts*, pt. xiii, pls. 10 and 11. Obverse : ll. 47-77 ; Reverse : ll. 78-105.

Part of a Neo-Babylonian tablet, $2\frac{1}{2}$ in. by $3\frac{4}{8}$ in. This text, which was identified by Pinches, was given in transliteration by Delitzsch, *Weltschöpfungsepos*, p. 36 f., and by Jensen, *Mythen und Epen*, pp. 14 ff.

22. 82-9-18, 1,403 + 6,316 [No. 61,429] : Vol. II, pls. xxv-xxviii. Obverse : ll. 5-15, 52-61 ; Reverse : ll. 62-76, 124-128.

Part of a Neo-Babylonian "practice-tablet," inscribed with a series of five-line extracts from the text ; 2 in. by 3 in. A copy of the text of 82–9–18, 1,403, is given in *Cun. Texts*, pt. xiii, pl. 13 ; since then I have joined to it the fragment 82–9–18, 6,316, and the text is therefore repeated in Vol. II. This text has not been previously published.

23. K. 8,524 : *Cun. Texts*, pt. xiii, pl. 12. Fragment from the end of Obv. or beginning of Rev. : ll. 75-86.

Part of an Assyrian tablet, $1\frac{7}{8}$ in. by $1\frac{3}{8}$ in. The text was

Copies of the Third Tablet of the Creation Series.

referred to by Pinches in the *Bab. Or. Rec.*, vol. iv, p. 30, and was given in transliteration by Delitzsch, *Weltschöpfungsepos*, p. 31.

24. 82-9-18, 6,950 + 83-1-18, 1,868 : Vol. II, pl. xxix. Duplicate of ll. 19-26 and 77-84 ; variants are noted in the text under ll. 19-26.

Neo-Babylonian "practice-tablet"; the text forms an extract measuring $2\frac{5}{8}$ in. by $1\frac{1}{4}$ in. A copy of the text of 83-1-18, 1,868, is given in *Cun. Texts*, pt. xiii, pl. 12; since then I have joined to it the fragment 82-9-18, 6,950, and the text is therefore repeated in Vol. II. This text has not been previously published.

25. K. 6,650 : *Cun. Texts*, pt. xiii, pl. 9. Duplicate of ll. 38-55 and 96-113 ; variants are noted in the text under ll. 38-55.

Part of an Assyrian tablet, 3 in. by $3\frac{3}{8}$ in. This text has not been previously published.

26. No. 42,285 : Vol. II, pls. xxx-xxxiii. Obverse : ll. 46-68 ; Reverse : ll. 69-87.

Part of a Neo-Babylonian tablet, $2\frac{1}{2}$ in. by $2\frac{5}{8}$ in. This text has not been previously published.

27. 82-9-18, 5,448 + 83-1-18, 2,116 : Vol. II, pl. xxxiv. Obverse : ll. 64-72.

Part of a Neo-Babylonian "practice-tablet"; the text, which forms an extract, measures $2\frac{3}{4}$ in. by $1\frac{1}{2}$ in. A copy of the text of 83-1-18, 2,116, is given in *Cun. Texts*, pt. xiii, pl. 12 ; since then I have joined to it the fragment 82-9-18, 5,448, and the text is therefore repeated in Vol. II. This text has not been previously published.

28. K. 8,575 : *Cun. Texts*, pt. xiii, pl. 12. Obverse : ll. 69-76 ; Reverse : ll. 77-85.

Part of an Assyrian tablet, $2\frac{3}{8}$ in. by $2\frac{1}{8}$ in. This text, which was identified by Bezold, *Catalogue*, p. 941, was given in transliteration by Delitzsch, *Weltschöpfungsepos*, p. 38.

The authorities for the lines of the Third Tablet are as follows :—

Authorities for the lines of the Third Tablet.

Tablet III.

ll. 1-4	: No. 20.
ll. 5-15	: Nos. 20 and 22.
ll. 16-18	: No. 20.
ll. 29-26	: Nos. 20 and 24.
ll. 27-37	: No. 20.
ll. 38-45	: Nos. 20 and 25.
l. 46	: Nos. 20, 25, and 26.
ll. 47-51	: Nos. 20, 21, 25, and 26.
ll. 52-55	: Nos. 20, 21, 22, 25, and 26.
ll. 56-63	: Nos. 20, 21, 22, and 26.
ll. 64-68	: Nos. 20, 21, 22, 26, and 27.
ll. 69-72	: Nos. 20, 21, 22, 26, 27, and 28.
ll. 73-74	: Nos. 20, 21, 22, 26, and 28.
ll. 75-76	: Nos. 20, 21, 22, 23, 26, and 28.
ll. 77-84	: Nos. 20, 21, 23, 24, 26, and 28.
l. 85	: Nos. 20, 21, 23, 26, and 28.
l. 86	: Nos. 20, 21, 23, and 26.
l. 87	: Nos. 20, 21, and 26.
ll. 88-95	: Nos. 20 and 21.
ll. 96-105	: Nos. 20, 21, and 25.
ll. 106-113	: Nos. 20 and 25.
ll. 114-123	: No. 20.
ll. 124-128	: Nos. 20 and 22.
ll. 129-138	: No. 20.

Copies of the Fourth Tablet of the Creation Series.

The following six tablets and fragments are inscribed with portions of the text of the Fourth Tablet :—

29. No. 93,016 [82-9-18, 3,737] : *Cun. Texts*, pt. xiii, pls. 14-15. Obverse: ll. 1-44; Reverse: ll. 116-146.

Upper part of a Neo-Babylonian tablet, 3⅜ in. by 4⅞ in. For an earlier publication of the text, see Budge, *P.S.B.A.*, vol. x, p. 86, pls. 1–6.

30. K. 3,437 + R. 641 : *Cun. Texts*, pt. xiii, pls. 16-19. Obverse : ll. 36-83 ; Reverse : ll. 84-119.

Part of an Assyrian tablet, 3 in. by 5½ in. For an earlier publication of the text of K. 3,437, see George Smith, *T.S.B.A.*, vol. iv, p. 363 f., pls. 5 and 6 ; and of K. 3,437+ R. 641, see Delitzsch, *Assyrische Lesestücke*, pp. 97 ff., and my *First Steps in Assyrian*, pp. 137 ff.

31. 79-7-8, 251 : *Cun. Texts*, pt. xiii, pl. 20. Obverse : ll. 35-49 ; Reverse : ll. 103-107.

Part of an Assyrian tablet, 1 in. by 2⅛ in. The text, which was identified by Pinches, was used in transliteration by Delitzsch, *Weltschöpfungsepos*, pp. 41 ff., and by Jensen, *Mythen und Epen*, pp. 22 ff. This fragment probably belongs to the same tablet as No. 34.

32. No. 93,051 : *Cun. Texts*, pt. xiii, pl. 20. Obverse : ll. 42-54 ; Reverse : ll. 85-94.

Part of a Neo-Babylonian "practice-tablet," inscribed with the text divided into sections of five lines ; 2¼ in. by 1¾ in. This text has not been previously published.

33. K. 5,420*c* : *Cun. Texts*, pt. xiii, pl. 21. Obverse : ll. 74-92 ; Reverse : ll. 93-119.

Part of an Assyrian tablet, 3⅜ in. by 3⅛ in. Restorations and variants were taken from this tablet by George Smith for his edition of K. 3,437 ; see above, No. 30.

34. R. 2, 83 : *Cun. Texts*, pt. xiii, pl. 19. No obverse ; Reverse : ll. 117-129.

Part of an Assyrian tablet, 2¼ in. by 1⅝ in. The text, which was identified by Pinches, was given in transliteration by Delitzsch, *Weltschöpfungsepos*, p. 45. This fragment probably belongs to the same tablet as No. 31.

The authorities for the lines of the Fourth Tablet are as follows:— Authorities for the lines of the Fourth Tablet.

TABLET IV.

ll. 1-34	: No. 29.
l. 35	: Nos. 29 and 31.
ll. 36-41	: Nos. 29, 30, and 31.
ll. 42-44	: Nos. 29, 30, 31, and 32.
ll. 45-49	: Nos. 30, 31, and 32.
ll. 50-54	: Nos. 30 and 32.
ll. 55-73	: No. 30.
ll. 74-84	: Nos. 30 and 33.
ll. 85-94	: Nos. 30, 32, and 33.
ll. 95-102	: Nos. 30 and 33.
ll. 103-107	: Nos. 30, 31, and 33.
ll. 108-115	: Nos. 30 and 33.
l. 116	: Nos. 29, 30, and 33.
ll. 117-119	: Nos. 29, 30, 33, and 34.
ll. 120-129	: Nos. 29 and 34.
ll. 130-146	: No. 29.

The following five tablets and fragments are inscribed with portions of the text of the Fifth Tablet:— Copies of the Fifth Tablet of the Creation Series.

35. K. 3,567 + K. 8,588 : *Cun. Texts*, pt. xiii, pl. 22.
Obverse : ll. 1-26 ; Reverse : catch-line.

Upper part of an Assyrian tablet, 3⅛ in. by 2⅞ in. For earlier publications of the text, see George Smith, *T.S.B.A.*, vol. iv, p. 363 f., pl. 2 ; Delitzsch, *Assyrische Lesestücke*, 3rd ed., p. 94 ; and my *First Steps in Assyrian*, pp. 158 ff.

Copies of the Fifth Tablet of the Creation Series.

36. K. 8,526 : *Cun. Texts*, pt. xiii, pl. 23. Obverse : ll. 1-18 ; Reverse : ll. (138)-(140).

Upper part of an Assyrian tablet, 1½ in. by 2¼ in. The text was used by George Smith for his edition of No. 35, and in the other copies of that tablet mentioned above ; it was given in transliteration by Delitzsch, *Weltschöpfungsepos*, p. 48 f.

37. K. 13,774 : Vol. I, Appendix II, pp. 190 ff. Obverse : ll. 6-19 ; no reverse.

Part of an Assyrian tablet, 1¼ in. by 1½ in. This text has not been previously published.

38. K. 11,641 : Vol. I, Appendix II, pp. 192 ff. Obverse : ll. 14-22 ; Reverse : ll. (128)-(140), catch-line, and colophon.

Part of an Assyrian tablet, 2⅝ in. by 3⅜ in. This text has not been previously published.

39. K. 3,449*a* : *Cun. Texts*, pt. xiii, pl. 23. Obverse : ll. (66)-(74) ; Reverse : ll. (75)-(87).

Part of an Assyrian tablet, 2½ in. by 1½ in. This text, which was first identified and translated by George Smith, *Chald. Acc. of Gen.*, p. 94 f., was given in transliteration by Delitzsch, *Weltschöpfungsepos*, p. 50, and the reverse by Jensen, *Mythen und Epen*, p. 32.

Authorities for the lines of the Fifth Tablet.

The authorities for the lines of the Fifth Tablet are as follows :—

TABLET V.

ll. 1-5	: Nos. 35 and 36.
ll. 6-13	: Nos. 35, 36, and 37.
ll. 14-18	: Nos. 35, 36, 37, and 38.
l. 19	: Nos. 35, 37, and 38.
ll. 20-22	: Nos. 35 and 38.
ll. 23-26	: No. 35.

ll. 27-(65) : Wanting.
ll. (66)-(87) : No. 39.
ll. (88)-(127) : Wanting.
ll. (128)-(137) : No. 38.
ll. (138)-(140) : Nos. 36 and 38.

The following fragment is inscribed with a portion of the text of the Sixth Tablet :—

Copy of the Sixth Tablet of the Creation Series.

40. No. 92,629 : Vol. II, pls. xxxv and xxxvi. Obverse : ll. 1-21 ; Reverse : ll. 138-146, catch-line, and colophon.

Part of a Neo-Babylonian tablet, 2⅛ in. by 2¼ in. This text has not been previously published.

The following nine tablets and fragments are inscribed with portions of the text of the Seventh Tablet :—

Copies of the Seventh Tablet of the Creation Series.

41. K. 2,854 : Vol. I, Appendix I, p. 159. Obverse : ll. 1-18 ; Reverse uninscribed.

Upper part of an Assyrian tablet, 2⅛ in. by 1¾ in. This text has not been previously published.

42. No. 91,139 + 93,073 : Vol. II. pls. xxxviii - xlv. Obverse : ll. 3-40 ; Reverse : ll. 106-141.

Part of a Neo-Babylonian tablet, 2¾ in. by 4⅞ in. This text is made up of two fragments which I have joined ; it has not previously been published.

43. K. 8,522 : *Cun. Texts*, pt. xiii, pls. 26 and 27. Obverse : ll. 15-45 ; Reverse : ll. 105-137.

Part of an Assyrian tablet, 2½ in. by 3¼ in. For earlier publications of the text, see George Smith, *T.S.B.A.*, vol. iv, p. 363 f., pls. 3 and 4, and Delitzsch, *Assyrische Lesestücke*, 3rd ed., p. 95 f.

Copies of the Seventh Tablet of the Creation Series.

44. No. 35,506: Vol. II, pls. xlvi-xlviii. Obverse: ll. 14-36; Reverse: ll. 105-142.

Part of a Neo-Babylonian tablet, 2¼ in. by 4¼ in. This text, which probably dates from the period of the Arsacidae, has not been previously published.

45. K. 9,267: *Cun. Texts*, pt. xiii, pl. 28. Obverse: ll. 40-47; Reverse: ll. 109-138.

Part of an Assyrian tablet, 3⅜ in. by 2 in. Restorations and variants were taken from this tablet by George Smith for his edition of K. 8,522; see above, No. 43.

46. K. 12,830: Vol. I, Appendix I, p. 163. Obverse or Reverse: between ll. 47 and 105.

Part of an Assyrian tablet, ⅞ in. by ⅞ in. This text has not been previously published.

47. K. 13,761: Vol. I, Appendix I, p. 164. End of Obverse and beginning of Reverse: between ll. 47 and 105.

Part of an Assyrian tablet, 1⅛ in. by 1⅝ in. This text has not been previously published.

48. K. 8,519: Vol. I, Appendix I, p. 165. End of Obverse and beginning of Reverse: between ll. 47 and 105.

Part of an Assyrian tablet, 1¾ in. by 1⅜ in. This text has not been previously published.[1]

49. K. 13,337: Vol. I, Appendix I, p. 166. Duplicate of No. 48; between ll. 47 and 105.

Part of an Assyrian tablet, ⅞ in. by 1 in. This text, which is a duplicate of K. 8,519, has not been previously published.

[1] I learn from Professor Zimmern that he also has identified this fragment as part of the Seventh Tablet by its correspondence with the commentary K. 4,406, published in II R, pl. 31 (see below, p. cxviii).

The authorities for the lines of the Seventh Tablet are as follows :—

Authorities for the lines of the Seventh Tablet.

TABLET VII.

ll. 1-2	: No. 41.
ll. 3-13	: Nos. 41 and 42.
l. 14	: Nos. 41, 42, and 44.
ll. 15-18	: Nos. 41, 42, 43, and 44.
ll. 19-36	: Nos. 42, 43, and 44.
ll. 37-39	: Nos. 42 and 43.
l. 40	: Nos. 42, 43, and 45.
ll. 41-45	: Nos. 43 and 45.
ll. 46-47	: No. 45.
between ll. 47 and 105	: Nos. 46, 47, 48, and 49.
l. 105	: Nos. 43 and 44.
ll. 106-108	: Nos. 42, 43, and 44.
ll. 109-137	: Nos. 42, 43, 44, and 45.
l. 138	: Nos. 42, 44, and 45.
ll. 139-141	: Nos. 42 and 44.
l. 142	: No. 44.

The above forty-nine tablets and fragments, inscribed with portions of the text of the Creation Series, belong to two distinct periods. The older class of tablets were made for the library of Ashur-bani-pal at Nineveh, and they are beautifully written in the Assyrian character upon tablets of fine clay.[1] The

Description of the tablets.

[1] That the copies were not always made from Babylonian tablets is proved by the colophon of K. 292 (cf. *Cun. Texts*, pt. xiii, pl. 6), which states that this copy of the Second Tablet was made from

Description of the tablets.

Neo-Babylonian tablets, on the other hand, are, as a rule, less carefully written; they vary considerably in size and shape, and were made at different periods for private individuals, either for their own use,[1] or that they might be deposited in the temples as votive offerings.[2] Some of these Babylonian copies

---

an Assyrian archetype (*gab-ri* ${}^{m\bar{a}tu}$*Aššur*^{KI}). Upon some tablets Ashur-bani-pal's label was scratched after the tablet had been baked, e.g., K. 3,567 + K. 8,588 (*Cun. Texts*, pt. xiii, pl. 22). Other Assyrian copies, though giving the catch-line to the next tablet, are without colophons, e.g., K. 3,473, etc. (cf. *Cun. Texts*, pt. xiii, pl. 9), and K. 8,526 (cf. *Cun. Texts*, pt. xiii, pl. 23); the copy of the last tablet, K. 2,854 (see below, p. 159), the reverse of which is blank, was probably also without a colophon.

[1] Cf. No. 40,559 (vol. ii, pl. xxi), a copy of the Second Tablet which was made for a certain Nabū-aḫē-iddina; and No. 45,528 + 46,614 (vol. ii, pl. vi), a copy of the First Tablet, which is described as the property of Nabū-meshētiḳ-urri, a worshipper of Marduk and Ṣarpanitu, and is said to have been copied from an original at Babylon on the ninth day of Iyyar, in the twenty-seventh year of Darius. A certain Nabū-balāṭsu-iḳbi, the son of Na'id-Marduk, appears to have owned a complete set of the Seven Creation Tablets, for we possess fragments of the First and of the Sixth Tablet in the series which belonged to him (cf. No. 93,015, *Cun. Texts*, pl. 3, where the first word of the second line of the colophon, which puzzled Delitzsch, is clearly *bušū*; No. 46,803, vol. ii, pls. ix ff.; and No. 92,629, vol. ii, pl. xxxvii).

[2] Thus the fine copy of the Fourth Tablet, No. 93,016, which was written by the scribe Nabū-bēlishu, was, according to its colophon (cf. *Cun. Texts*, pt. xiii, pl. 15), deposited by the smith Na'id-Marduk as a votive offering in the temple E-zida. In his transliteration of this colophon Delitzsch has made an odd blunder; he has not recognized the common phrase *ana balāṭ napšāti*^{pl}*-šu*, "for the preservation of his life," which occurs at the end of line 3 of the colophon, and has taken it as a proper name

are fine specimens of their class, e.g. Nos. 3, 13, 21, 29, and 42,[1] and the characters and words upon them are carefully written and spaced; others, however, consist of small, carelessly made tablets, on to which the poem is crowded.[2] On all the tablets, whether Assyrian or Babylonian, which possess colophons, the number of the Tablet in the Series is carefully given.[3] The extracts from the text, which were written out by students upon "practice-tablets," no doubt in order to give them practice in writing and at the same time to enable them to learn the text by heart, are naturally rather rough productions.[4] One characteristic which applies to all the tablets,

Description of the tablets.

^{m}TIN-ZI^{pl}-*šu* (see *Weltschöpfungsepos*, p. 41), a transliteration which turns the sentence into nonsense.

[1] See pls. ii, iii, iv, and vi, and the frontispiece to Vol. II. Photographic reproductions of the reverse of No. 21 and the obverse of No. 29 are given in the *Guide to the Babylonian and Assyrian Antiquities* in the British Museum, pls. vi and vii.

[2] Cf. e.g., Nos. 93,015 (No. 2), 46,803 (No. 10), and 92,629 (No. 40), all of which were probably written by the same scribe.

[3] Cf. the notes *duppu I*^{KAN} *E-nu-ma e-liš* on No. 45,528, etc. (vol. ii, pl. vi); *duppu E-nu-ma e-liš ri-eš* on No. 93,015 (*Cun. Texts*, pt. xiii, pl. 3); [*dupp*]*u II*^{KAM} *E-nu-ma e-liš* on K. 292 (*Cun. Texts*, pt. xiii, pl. 6); *duppu IV*$^{KAN\text{-}MA}$ *E-nu-ma e-liš*, which follows a note as to the number of lines in the text upon No. 93,016 (*Cun. Texts*, pt. xiii, pl. 15); and *dup-pi V*$^{KAM\text{-}ME}$ *E-nu-ma e-liš* on K. 3,567 (*Cun. Texts*, pt. xiii, pl. 22).

[4] The "practice-tablets" fall into two classes. In one class the tablets are wholly taken up with portions of the text of the Creation Series, which is written out upon them in sections of five verses separated by horizontal lines; cf. Nos. 82-9-18,

whether Assyrian or Neo-Babylonian, is that the text is never written in columns, but each line of the poem is written across the tablet from edge to edge.[1] As a result, the tablets are long and narrow in shape, and are handled far more conveniently than broader tablets inscribed with two or more columns of writing on each side.

The Assyrian and Neo-Babylonian forms of the text.

The forms of the text of the poem, which were in use in the Assyrian and Neo-Babylonian periods, are identical, and it is incorrect to speak of an Assyrian and a Babylonian "recension." At the time of Ashur-bani-pal the text had already been definitely fixed, and, with the exception of one or two phrases, the words of each line remained unchanged from that time forward. It is true that on the Babylonian tablets the words are, as a rule, written more syllabically, but this is a general characteristic of Babylonian copies of historical and literary texts. Moreover, upon several of the more carefully written tablets, the metre is indicated by the division of the

1,403 + 6,361 (No. 22) and 93,051 (No. 32). In the other class short extracts from the text are inscribed upon tablets containing other matter, all of which the pupil has written out for practice; cf. Nos. 36,726 (No. 5), 36,688 (No. 9), 82–9–18, 6,950 + 83–1–18, 1,868 (No. 24), and 82–9–18, 5,448 + 83–1–18, 2,116 (No. 27). The second class are the more carelessly written of the two.

[1] The only apparent exceptions to this rule occur on some of the Neo-Babylonian tablets, in which two lines of the text are occasionally written on one line of the tablet when they are separated from each other by a division-mark. This is simply due to want of space, which necessitated the crowding of the text.

halves of each verse,[1] an arrangement which is not met with on any of the Assyrian tablets. But both the Assyrian and Neo-Babylonian copies represent the same "recension" of the text, and, as has already been indicated,[2] are probably the descendants of a common Babylonian original. The following table will serve to show the number of Assyrian and Neo-Babylonian copies of each of the Seven Tablets under which the forty-nine separate fragments of the text may be arranged :—

Table showing the number of Assyrian and Neo-Babylonian copies of the Seven Tablets.

TABLET.	ASSYRIAN TEXT.	NEO-BAB. TEXT.	NEO-BAB. EXTRACTS.
I	Four copies (Nos. 1, 6, 7, 8, 11). Nos. 8 and 11 are probably parts of the same tablet.	Four copies (Nos. 2, 3, 4, 10, 12). Nos. 2 and 10 are probably parts of the same tablet.	Two "practice-tablets" (Nos. 5, 9).
II	Four copies (Nos. 16, 17, 18, 19). Nos. 18 and 19 are probably not parts of the same tablet.	Three copies (Nos. 13, 14, 15).	
III	Four copies (Nos. 20, 23, 25, 28). Nos. 23 and 25 are probably not parts of the same tablet ; it is possible, however, that No. 23 is part of a copy of Tabl. II, its text corresponding to ll. 13–24.	Two copies (Nos. 21, 26).	Three "practice-tablets" (Nos. 22, 24, 27).

[1] See below, p. cxxii.

[2] See above, pp. lxxii ff.

Table showing the number of Assyrian and Neo-Babylonian copies of the Seven Tablets.

Tablet.	Assyrian Text.	Neo-Bab. Text.	Neo-Bab. Extracts.
IV	Three copies (Nos. 30, 31, 33, 34). Nos. 31 and 34 are probably parts of the same tablet.	One copy (No. 29).	One "practice-tablet" (No. 32).
V	Four, or five, copies (Nos. 35, 36, 37, 38, 39). Nos. 35 and 39 are possibly parts of the same tablet.		
VI		One copy (No. 40).	
VII	Four, or five, copies (Nos. 41, 43, 45, 46, 47, 48, 49). Nos. 41 and 46 are probably parts of the same tablet, and Nos. 47 and 49 are probably parts of another tablet; it is possible that No. 45 is a part of the same tablet as Nos. 41 and 46.	Two copies (Nos. 42, 44).	

Assyrian Commentaries to the Seventh Tablet.

In the arrangement and interpretation of the text of the Seventh Tablet we receive considerable assistance from some fragments of Assyrian commentaries which have come down to us. These were compiled by the Assyrian scribes in order to explain that composition, and they are of the greatest value for the study of the text. The contents of these documents, and their relation to the text of the Seventh

Tablet, are described in detail in Appendix I,[1] but the following facts with regard to the size of the tablets inscribed with the commentaries, and to previous publications of portions of them, may here be conveniently given.

Commentary of the first class.

The most important class of commentary takes the form of a bilingual list, and, as has been pointed out elsewhere,[2] presupposes the existence of a Sumerian version of part of the text of the Seventh Tablet of the Creation Series. The text of the commentary is inscribed in a series of double columns; in the left half of each column it gives a list of the Sumerian words, or ideograms, and, in the right half, opposite each word is added its Assyrian equivalent. It is noteworthy that the list is generally arranged in the order in which the words occur in the Assyrian text of the Seventh Tablet. The columns of the commentary are divided into a number of compartments, or sections, by horizontal lines impressed upon the clay, and the words within each compartment refer either to separate couplets, or to separate lines, of the Seventh Tablet. Of this class of commentary we possess six fragments of two large tablets which were inscribed with five or six double columns of writing on each side; the two tablets are duplicates of one another, having been inscribed with the same

[1] See below, pp. 157 ff.
[2] See above, p. lxxix, n. 1, and below, p. 158.

version of the commentary. The following is a description of the six separate fragments, the two large tablets, to which they belong, being headed respectively A and B :—

Fragments of the first class of Commentary.

A. (1) S. 11 + S. 980 + S. 1,416. For the text, see Vol. II, pls. li-liii and lv; cf. also App. I, pp. 158 ff., 167 f.

The fragment is the top left hand portion of the tablet; it measures 4 in. by 7 in. The text of S. 11 + S. 980 was published in V R., pl. 21, No. 4. The fragment S. 1,416, which I have joined to the other two, has not been previously published.

(2) K. 4,406. For the text, see Vol. II, pls. liv-lv; cf. also App. I, pp. 163 ff.

The fragment is the top right hand portion of the tablet; it measures 4¼ in. by 4⅞ in. The text has been previously published in II R., pl. 31, No. 2.

(3) 82-3-23, 151. For the text, see Vol. II, pl. liv; cf. also App. I, p. 162.

The fragment measures 1⅞ in. by 2⅛ in.; it has not been previously published.

B. (1) R. 366 + 80-7-19, 288 + 293. For the text, see Vol. II, pls. lvi-lviii; cf. also App. I, pp. 160, 168 f.

The fragment is from the left side of the tablet; it measures 2⅞ in. by 5⅛ in. The fragment R. 366 was published in V R., pl. 21, No. 3; 80-7-19, 293, was joined to it by Bezold, *Catalogue*, p. 1,608. The third fragment, 80-7-19, 288, was identified by Zimmern and published in the *Zeits. für Assyr.*, xii, p. 401 f.

(2) K. 2,053. For the text, see Vol. II, pls. lix-lx; cf. also App. I, pp. 161, 167 f.

This fragment measures 2⅝ in. by 2½ in.; it has long been known to be a duplicate of S. 11 + S. 980 (see Bezold, *Catalogue*, p. 396), but its text has not been previously published.

(3) K. 8,299. For the text, see Vol. II, pl. lx; cf. also App. I, p. 162 f.

This fragment measures 3 in. by 1½ in.; it has not been previously published.

The second and third classes of Commentary.

In addition to the above commentary in the form of a bilingual list, we possess single specimens of a second and a third class of explanatory text. The second class contains a running commentary to passages selected from other Tablets of the Creation Series in addition to the Seventh, and is represented by the tablet S. 747.[1] The third class, represented by the obverse of the tablet K. 2,107 + K. 6,086,[2] gives explanations of a number of titles of Marduk, several of which occur in the recovered portions of the text of the Seventh Tablet. Each of these two commentaries furnishes information on various points with regard to

[1] The tablet S. 747, which measures 4⅛ in. by 3⅛ in., is published in *Cun. Texts*, pt. xiii, pl. 32, and its connection with the text of the Creation Series is described in Appendix I, p. 170 f. The text was given in transliteration by Delitzsch, *Weltschöpfungsepos*, p. 58 f.

[2] The tablet K. 2,107+K. 6,086, which measures 4 in. by 5⅛ in., is published in Vol. II, plate lxi f., and a transliteration and a translation of the text are given in Appendix I, pp. 171 ff. Col. ii of the single fragment K. 2,107 was given in transliteration by Delitzsch, *Weltschöpfungsepos*, p. 155.

the interpretation of the Seventh Tablet, but, as may be supposed, they do not approach in interest the six fragments of the commentary of the first class.

The reconstruction of the text of the Creation Series.

The transliteration of the text of the Creation Series, which is given in the following pages, has been made up from the tablets, fragments, and extracts enumerated on pp. xcvii ff.; while several passages in the Seventh Tablet have been conjecturally restored from the Assyrian Commentaries just described. In the reconstruction of the text preference has usually been given to the readings found upon the Assyrian tablets, and the variant readings of all duplicates, both Assyrian and Neo-Babylonian, are given in the notes at the foot of the page. The lines upon each tablet of the Series have been numbered, and, where the numbering of a line is conjectural, it is placed within parentheses. Great assistance in the numbering of the lines of detached fragments of the text has been afforded by the fact that upon many of the Neo-Babylonian copies every tenth line is marked with a figure "10" in the left-hand margin; in but few instances can the position of a detached fragment be accurately ascertained by its shape. The lines upon the Second and Fifth Tablets have been conjecturally numbered up to one hundred and forty. Upon the Sixth Tablet the total number of lines was one hundred and thirty-six or one hundred and forty-six; and, in view of the fact that the scribe of No. 92,629 has continued the text to the bottom of

Numbering of the lines.

The number of lines upon the Tablets.

the reverse of the tablet, the larger number is the more probable of the two. The following is a list of the total number of lines inscribed upon each of the Seven Tablets of the Series :—

Tablet	I,	142	lines.
,,	II,	(140)	,,
,,	III,	138	,,
,,	IV,	146	,,
,,	V,	(140)	,,
,,	VI,	146	,,
,,	VII,	142	,,

Gaps in the text.

Although it is now possible to accurately estimate the number of lines contained by the Creation Series, there are still considerable gaps in the text of several of the Tablets. The only Tablets in which the whole or portions of every line are preserved are the Third and Fourth of the Series. Gaps, where the text is completely wanting, occur in Tablet I, ll. 68-82, and in Tablet II, ll. 59-(68).[1] The greater part of the text of Tablet V is wanting, but by roughly estimating the position of the fragment K. 3,449*a*, which occurs about in the centre of the text, we obtain two gaps, between ll. 26 and (66) and between ll. (87) and (128). Of Tablet VI we possess only the opening and closing lines, the rest of the text, from l. 22 to l. 137, being wanting. Finally, the gap in the text of

[1] In the gap in Tablet II, ll. 86–103, may probably be inserted the new fragment K. 10,008 ; see Appendix II, pp. 187 ff.

Tablet VII, between ll. 47 and 105, is partly filled up by the fragments KK. 12,830, 13,761, 8,519, 13,337, which together give portions of thirty-nine lines.

The metre of the poem.

Upon some of the Babylonian copies the metre is indicated in writing by the division of the halves of each verse,[1] and, wherever this occurs upon any tablet or duplicate, the division has, as far as possible, been retained in the transliteration of the text. In accordance with the rules of Babylonian poetry, the text generally falls into couplets, the second verse frequently echoing or supplementing the first; each of the two verses of a couplet is divided into halves, and each half-verse may be further subdivided by an accented syllable.[2] This four-fold division of each

[1] On Nos. 45,528 + 46,614 (No. 3), 82-9-18, 6,879 (No. 12), 38,396 (No. 14), 42,285 (No. 26), and 93,016 (No. 29); cf. also the "practice-tablets," Nos. 82-9-18, 1,403 + 6,316 (No. 22) and 82-9-18, 5,448 + 83-1-18, 2,116 (No. 27).

[2] For the first description of the metre of the poem, see Budge, *P.S.B.A.*, vol. vi, p. 7; and for later discussions of the metre of Babylonian poetry in general, see Zimmern's papers in the *Zeits. für Assyr.*, viii, pp. 121 ff., x, pp. 1 ff., xi, pp. 86 ff., and xii, pp. 382 ff.; cf. also D. M. Mueller, *Die Propheten in ihrer ursprünglichen Form*, i, pp. 5 ff. It may be noted that in addition to the division of the text into couplets, the poem often falls naturally into stanzas of four lines each. That the metre was not very carefully studied by the Neo-Babylonian scribes is proved by the somewhat faulty division of the verses upon some of the tablets on which the metre is indicated, and also by the fact that the pupils of the scribes were allowed, and perhaps told, to write out portions of the poem in sections, not of four, but of five lines each (see above, p. cxiii f., n. 4).

verse will be apparent from the following connected transliteration of the first half-dozen lines of the poem, in which the subdivisions of the verses are marked in accordance with the system of the Babylonian scribes as found upon the tablet Sp. ii, 265*a*[1] :—

The metre of the poem.

1 f.	*enuma* |	*eliš* ‖	*lā nabū* |	*šamamu*
	šapliš |	*ammatum* ‖	*šuma* |	*lā zakrat*
3 f.	*Apsūma* |	*rištū* ‖	*zaru* -	*šun*
	mummu |	*Tiamat* ‖	*muallidat* |	*gimrišun*
5 f.	*mē* -	*šunu* ‖	*ištenis* |	*iḫīḳūma*
	gipāra |	*lā kiṣṣura* ‖	*ṣuṣā* |	*lā še'i*

It will be seen that the second verse of each couplet balances the first, and the caesura, or division, in the centre of each verse is well marked. The second half of verse 3 and the first half of verse 5, each of which contains only one word, may appear rather short for scansion, but the rhythm is retained by dwelling on the first part of the word and treating the suffix almost as an independent word. It is unnecessary to transliterate more of the text of the poem in this manner, as the simple metre, or rather rhythm, can be detected without difficulty from the syllabic transliteration which is given in the following pages.

[1] Published by Zimmern, *Z.A.*, x, p. 17 f.

Transliterations

and

Translations.

I.

The Seven Tablets of the History of Creation.

The First Tablet.

1. *e - nu - ma e - liš*[1] *la na - bu - u ša - ma - mu*
2. *šap - liš*[2] *am - ma - tum šu - ma*[3] *la zak - rat*
3. *Apsū - ma*[4] *riš - tu - u za - ru - šu - un*
4. *mu - um - mu Ti - amat mu-al-li-da-at*[5] *gim-ri-šu-un*
5. *mē*^{pl} *- šu - nu*[6] *iš - te - niš i - ḫi - ḳu - u - ma*
6. *gi-pa-ra la ki-iṣ-ṣu-ra*[7] *ṣu - ṣa - a*[8] *la še - '*
7. *e - nu - ma ilāni*^{pl}[9] *la šu - pu - u ma - na - ma*
8. *šu - ma la zuk - ku - ru*[10] *ši - ma - tu la [ši - ma]*[11]
9. *ib-ba-nu-u-ma*[12] *ilāni ki - ri[b]*[13] *š[a - ma - mi]*[14]

---

[1] No. 45,528 + 46,614, *e-li-iš*. For the principles on which the text has been made up, see the Introduction.

[2] No. 45,528, etc., *šap-li-iš*. [3] No. 93,015, *šu-mu*.

[4] No. 45,528, etc., omits *ma*; No. 93,015 reads *Apsū(u)*.

[5] No. 93,015, *mu-um-ma-al-li-da-at* (see the Glossary).

[6] No. 93,015, *mē*^{pl}*-šu-un*; No. 45,528, etc., *mu-u-šu-nu*.

[7] No. 93,015, *gi-par-ra la ku-zu-ru*.

[8] No. 93,015, *ṣu-ṣa-'*. [9] No. 45,528, etc., *ilāni*.

[10] No. 93,015, *šu-um la zu-uk-ku-ru*.

[11] Conjectural restoration; it is probable that not more than two signs are wanting on K. 5,419*c*.

I.

The Seven Tablets of the History of Creation.

The First Tablet.

1. When in the height heaven was not named,
2. And the earth beneath did not yet bear a name,
3. And the primeval Apsū, who begat them,
4. And chaos, Tiamat, the mother of them both,—
5. Their waters were mingled together,
6. And no field was formed, no marsh was to be seen ;
7. When of the gods none had been called into being,
8. And none bore a name, and no destinies [were ordained][11] ;
9. Then were created the gods in the midst[13] of [heaven],[14]

---

[12] *ma* is omitted by Nos. 93,015 and 45,528, etc.

[13] The traces of the character upon No. 45,528, etc., suggest *rib.*

[14] The first sign of the word in No. 45,528, etc., is probably *ša* ; the restoration of the second half of the line as *ki-ri*[*b*] *š*[*a-ma-mi*], "in the midst of heaven," is therefore possible. The existence of *šamāmu*, or "heaven," so early in the Creation-story is not inconsistent with Marduk's subsequent acts of creation. After slaying Tiamat his first act was to use half of her body as a covering for the *šamāmu* (cf. Tabl. IV, l. 138, *ša-ma-ma u-ṣa-al-lil*) ; it is therefore clear that the *šamāmu* was vaguely conceived as already in existence.

10. *ilu Laḫ-mu*[1] *ilu La-ḫa-mu uš-ta-pu-u* [. . .][2]
11. *a - di*[3] *ir - bu - u* *i -* [. . . . .]
12. *An-šar*[4] *ilu Ki-šar ib-ba-nu-u*[5] *e - l*[*i*] *- šu -* [*nu*[6] . . .]

13. *ur - ri - ku*[7] *ūmē pl* *uṣ - ṣi*[8] [. . . . . . .]
14. *ilu A - nu*[9] *a - pil*[10] *- šu - nu* [. . .] *nu*[11] [. . . .]
15. *An - šar* *ilu A - num* [. . . . .]
16. *u* *ilu A - num*[12] *ut -* [. . . . .]
17. *ilu Nu-dim-mud ša abē pl -šu* *a - lid*[13] - [. . . . .]
18. *pal - ka*[14] *uz - nu ḫa - sis* *e* (?) - [. . . . . .][15]
19. *gu - uš - šur ma - a - di - iš* [. . . . .]
20. *la i-ši š*[*a*]*-n*[*i*]*-na*[16] [. . . . .]
21. *in-nin-du-ma*[17] [. . .]*-u*[18] [. . . . .]

---

[1] Nos. 45,528, etc., and 93,015 insert the copula *u*.

[2] The end of the line should possibly be restored as [*mit-ḫa-riš*], "together," or "at one time."

[3] No. 93,015 reads *a-di-i*. It is preferable to take the word as the plur. of the subs. *adū*, rather than as the prep. *adi*, which is not written with the long final vowel.

[4] Nos. 45,528, etc., and 35,134 insert the copula *u*.

[5] No. 45,528, etc., *ib-ba-nu-ma*.

[6] If the reading *e-l*[*i*]*-šu-*[*nu* . . .] be correct, the second half of the line possibly refers to the precedence in rank taken by Anšar and Kišar over Laḫmu and Laḫamu. This suggestion is based on the fact that it is Anšar, and not Laḫmu, to whom Ea appeals on hearing of the revolt of Tiamat, and that it is Anšar who subsequently directs the movements of the gods.

[7] No. 45,528, etc., *u-ur-ri-ku*; No. 35,134, *u-úr-ri-ku*; No. 93,015, *u-ri-ki*.

[8] K. 5,419*c* reads *u*[*ṣ*- . . .]; No. 45,528, etc., *u-uṣ-ṣi*; in the translation I have taken the word as the Pret. Ḳal. from *aṣū*, but it is possible that the word is not complete.

10. Laḫmu and Laḫamu were called into being [. .].[2]
11. Ages[3] increased, [. . . . .],
12. Then Anšar and Kišar were created, and over them [. . . . .].[6]
13. Long were the days, then there came forth[8] [. .]
14. Anu, their son, [. . . . .]
15. Anšar and Anu [. . . . .]
16. And the god Anu [. . . . .]
17. Nudimmud, whom his fathers [his] begetters[13] [. .]
18. Abounding in all wisdom, [. . . . . . .][15]
19. He was exceeding strong [. . . . .]
20. He had no rival [. . . . .]
21. (Thus) were established and [were . . . . . .[18] the great gods (?)].

---

[9] Nos. 45,528, etc., 93,015, and 35,134 read ^{ilu}*A-num*.

[10] Nos. 45,528, etc., and 35,134 prove that the traces of this sign on K. 5,419*c* and No. 93,015 are those of *pil*, not *bi*.

[11] The traces upon No. 45,528, etc., suggest the reading [*da-ni*]-*nu*.

[12] No. 35,134, ^{ilu}*A-nu-um*. The traces which follow upon No. 45,528, etc., are not clear.

[13] The word may possibly be restored *a-lid*-[*di-šu*], as suggested in the translation.

[14] No. 35,134, *pal-ku*. *ḫa-sis* is probably a participle.

[15] L. 18 evidently contains a description of Nudimmud (Ea), and, in view of the important part he plays in the First and Second Tablets, it is not improbable that ll. 19 and 20 also refer to him.

[16] This restoration is in accordance with the traces upon Nos. 35,134 and 45,528, etc.

[17] No. 35,134, [*in-nin-d*]*u-u*[. . .].

[18] *u* is evidently the final syllable of a second verb. The subject of both verbs (possibly some such phrase as *ilâni rabûti*, "the great gods," cf. l. 29) was contained in the second half of the line.

22. *e-šu-u T*[*i-amat u Apsū*[1] . . . .]

23. *da - al - ḫu - nim - ma* [. . . . .]
24. *i-na šu-'-a-ru*[2] *šu*-[[3] . . . .]
25. *la na - ši - ir Apsū* [. . . . .]
26. *u Ti-amat* [*šu*]-*ḳa-am-mu-m*[*a*]-*a*[*t*][4] [. . . . . .]
27. *im-ḫaṣ-ṣa-am-m*[*a i*]*p*[5]-*še-ta*[6]-*šu-un* [. . . . . . .]
28. *la ṭa-bat al - kat - su - nu šu-nu*(-)[*t*]*i*[7] *i - ga - me*[8] *- la*
29. *i - nu - šu Apsū za - ri ilāni ra-bi-u-tim*
30. *is - si - ma Mu - um - mu*[9] *suk-kal-la-šu i-zak-kar-šu*

31. *Mu-um-mu*[9] *suk-kal-li*[10] *mu - ṭib - ba ka - bit - ti - ia*
32. *al-kam-ma ṣi-ri-iš*[11] *Ti-amat*[12] *i ni -* [*il - li - ik*][13]
33. *il - li - ku - ma ḳu-ud-mi- iš*[14] *Ti -* [*amat*][15] *sak - pu*
34. *a-ma-ti im-tal-li-ku aš-šum ilāni* [*ma - ri - e - šu - un*][16]

35. *Ap*[*sū pa*] *- a - šu i - pu -* [*šam - ma i - ḳab - bi*]

---

[1] This restoration is not certain, but it is consistent with the traces upon No. 45,528, etc., and it gives good sense. L. 21 thus concludes the account of the creation of the gods, and in l. 22 the narrative returns to Apsû and Tiamat.

[2] The signs should possibly be divided as *i-na šu-'-a*.

[3] The traces of the character after *šu* suggest *du*.

[4] This restoration is not quite certain. One sign is wanting at the beginning of the word; the traces of the two signs with which it concludes suggest the reading *-ma-at*. For the meaning of *šuḳammumu*, cf. II R, pl. 21, col. iv, l. 18, *šu-ḳam-mu-mu* (not *šu-gam-mu-mu* as H-W-B., p. 640) *ša u-me* (i.e. "storms"). The word is peculiarly applicable to Tiamat.

[5] The traces seem to me to be those of *ip*, but *kal* is possible.

[6] I think the signs are clearly *še-ta*, and not *li*; if the reading were *li*, the restoration [*suk*]-*kal-li-šu-un* would be possible.

22. But T[iamat and Apsū][1] were (still) in confusion [. . . .],
23. They were troubled and [. . . . .]
24. In disorder(?) . . [. . . . .]
25. Apsū was not diminished in might [. . . . .]
26. And Tiamat roared[4] [. . . . .]
27. She smote, and their deeds [. . . . . . .]
28. Their way was evil . . [.] . . . . .
29. Then Apsū, the begetter of the great gods,
30. Cried unto Mummu, his minister, and said unto him:
31. " O Mummu, thou minister that rejoicest my spirit,
32. " Come, unto Tiamat let us [go][13]!"
33. So they went and before Tiamat they lay down,
34. They consulted on a plan with regard to the gods [their sons].[16]
35. Apsū opened his mouth [and spake],

---

[7] The sign upon No. 36,726 may be a carelessly written *ti*; we can hardly read TIL-TIL (cf. Brünnow, No. 1,512). The text is taken from a practice-tablet, and several of the characters upon it are roughly made.

[8] The reading of *ta aš* for *ga me* is also possible.

[9] No. 36,726, [ilu]*Mu-um-mu*.

[10] No. 36,726, *suk-kal-lu*; 81–7–27, 80, *sukkallu*.

[11] 81–7–27, 80, *riš*.

[12] No. 36,726, *Ta-a-ma-ti*; 81–7–27, 80, [ilu][. . . .].

[13] Conjectural restoration. The end of the line should perhaps be restored as *i ni-*[*il-lik ni-i-ni*]; in any case the line must have run over upon the edge of the tablet No. 36,726.

[14] 81–7–27, 80, *ḳud-meš*. [15] No. 36,726, *Ta-a-ma-ti*.

[16] The restoration of this and the following line is conjectural.

36. *a-na* [*T*]*i-am*[*at*] *el-li-tu-ma* *i-za*[*k-kar* *a-ma-tum*][1]

37. *im*-[. . . . .] *al-kat-su-n*[*u* . . . . .]
38. *ur*-[*r*]*a la šu-up-šu-ḫa-ak*[2] *mu-ši* [*la* *ṣal-la-ak*][3]

39. *lu-uš-ḫal-liḳ-ma al-kat-su-nu lu*[4] - [. . . . . . .]
40. *ḳu-u-lu*[5] *liš-ša-kin-ma* *i*[6] *ni-iṣ-lal* [*ni-i-ni*][7]

41. *Ti-amat* *an-ni-ta* *i-na* [*še-mi-ša*][8]
42. *i-zu-uz-ma*[9] *il-ta-si* *e-li*-[*ta*[10] . . . .]
43. [. .] *mar-ṣi-iš* *ug*-[. .] *e*-[. . . . .]
44. *li-mut-ta*[11] *it-ta-di* *a-na* [*Apsū* *i-zak-kar*][12]
45. [*mi*]-*na-a* *ni-i-nu* *ša ni-i*[*p-pu-uš*][13]
46. [*a*]*l-kat-su-nu lu šum-ru-ṣa-at-ma* *i ni*-[*iṣ-lal* *ni-i-ni*][14]

47. [*i*]-*pu-ul-ma* *ilu* *Mu-um-mu* *Apsū*[15] *i-ma-al*-[*li-ku*]
48. [. . .] *u*[16] *la ma-gi-ru*[17] *mi-lik* *Mu*-[*um-mu* (?)][18]

[1] This line is conjecturally restored.

[2] 81–7–27, 80, [*šu-up*]-*šu-ḫa-ku*.

[3] The end of the line obviously contained some parallel phrase to *la šu-up-šu-ḫa-ak*; this has been restored from l. 50.

[4] On No. 45,528, etc., there are traces of the character which follows *lu*; it does not seem to be *uš*.

[5] K. 3,938 and 81–7–27, 80, *ḳu-lu*.

[6] *i* is omitted by 81–7–27, 80.

[7] For this restoration, see ll. 96, 100, and 102.

[8] Cf. Tablet IV, l. 87.

[9] K. 3,938 reads [*e*]-*ziz-m*[*a*].

[10] For this restoration, cf. Tablet IV, l. 89, and Tablet III, l. 125.

[11] No. 36,688, *ti*.

36. And unto Tiamat, the glistening one, he addressed [the word][1]:
37. "[. . . .] their way [. . . . .],
38. " By day I cannot rest, by night [I cannot lie down (in peace)].[3]
39. " But I will destroy their way, I will [. . .],
40. " Let there be lamentation, and let us lie down (again in peace)."
41. When Tiamat [heard][8] these words,
42. She raged and cried aloud [. . . . .].
43. [She . . .] grievously [. . . . .],
44. She uttered a curse, and unto [Apsū she spake][12]:
45. " What then shall we [do][13]?
46. " Let their way be made difficult, and let us [lie down (again) in peace].[14]"
47. Mummu answered, and gave counsel unto Apsū,
48. [. . .] and[16] hostile (to the gods) was the counsel Mu[mmu gave][18]:

---

[12] Conjecturally restored; another possible restoration is *a-na* [*ilāni mārēša*], i.e., "She uttered a curse against [the gods, her sons]."

[13] The line is conjecturally restored.

[14] For the restoration, cf. l. 40, and p. 8, note 7.

[15] No. 45,528, etc., *Ap*-[. . .].

[16] The traces upon 81-7-27, 80 suggest the copula *u* before *la*; the first word of the line was probably another adj. descriptive of Mummu's counsel.

[17] No. 46,803, *ra*.

[18] The restoration *Mu*-[*um-mu*] is not certain, as in l. 47 on 81-7-27, 80 the name is written with the determinative.

49. *[a]-lik li-'*[1]*-at al-ka-s[u]-u[n]*[2] *e-ši-[. . .]*

50. *[ur-r]iš lu š[u]p-šu-ḫa-at mu-šiš lu ṣal-la-[at]*

51. *[iš-me]*[3]*-šum-ma Apsū im-me*[4]*-ru pa-nu-uš-[š]u*

52. *[ša lim]*[3]*-ni-e-ti ik-pu-du a-na ilāni*[5] *m[a]*[6]*-ri-e-šu*

53. [. . . . .] . *i-te-dir ki-[. . . . .]*
54. [. . . *-u]š*[7]*-[. . .] bir-ka-a-šu [i]-na-ša-ḳu*[8] *ša-a-šu*

55. *[eli lim-ni-e-ti]*[3] *ik-pu-du bu-[u]k-ri-šu-un*

56. [. . . . . . .]*-ri-šu-nu uš-tan-nu-ni*
57. [. . . . .]*-lu*
58. *ḳu-l[u* . . . . . *ša-ḳu-um]*[9]*-mi-iš uš-bu*
59. [. . . . .][10]

[1] This passage is very broken, but the sign is possibly '; it is probably not *ma*, as Jensen suggests. In the following line the reading of *š[u]p-šu-ḫa-at* upon 81-7-27, 80 is certain; and the precatives are to be taken as in the 2 m. s., not the 3 f. s. The parallelism of this passage with l. 38, moreover, proves that *mu-šiš* is to be rendered "by night," not "like the night"; and the expression cannot therefore be cited as proving that it was the creation of light which caused the revolt of Apsū. For a further discussion of this point and of the suggested reading of *im ma aṣ-ru-nim-ma* in l. 109, see the Introduction.

[2] The last sign of the line preserved by 81-7-27, 80 is either *e* or *un*. If *e*, it is to be identified with the *e* of No. 46,803, and the preceding word must be read as *al-ka-s[u]*; to read *al-ka-t[a]* is consistent with the traces upon the tablet, but is hardly probable.

49. "Come, their way is strong, but thou shalt destroy [it];
50. "Then by day shalt thou have rest, by night shalt thou lie down (in peace)."
51. Apsū [hearkened unto][3] him and his countenance grew bright,
52. [Since] he (i.e. Mummu) planned evil against the gods his sons.
53. [. . . . .] he was afraid [. . . . .],
54. His knees [became weak (?)], they gave way[8] beneath him,
55. [Because of the evil][3] which their first-born had planned.
56. [. . . . .] their [. . .] they altered (?).
57. [. . . . .] they [. . . . .],
58. Lamentation [. . . . .] they sat in [sorrow][9]
59. [. . . . .][10]

---

[3] Conjectural restoration. [4] No. 46,803, *mi*.

[5] The traces on No. 46,803 suggest the reading [*ilāni*]*pl*.

[6] This seems to be the reading of No. 46,803.

[7] No. 46,803, Obv., l. 8, contains ll. 53 and 54 of the text, and the division-mark is not preserved; the sign [*u*]*š* may therefore belong to the second half of l. 53.

[8] 81–7–27, 80 reads *u*(?)-*na-aš-ša*[*ḳ* . . .]. In K. 2,056, col. i *b* (last three lines), a verb *na-ša-ku* forms a group with *nadū* and *maḳūtu*; cf. also H-W-B., p. 486, col. *a*.

[9] Cf. Tablet II, l. 6.

[10] L. 59 formed the first half of l. 11 of the Obverse of No. 46,803, but none of it has been preserved. The scribe of Nos. 46,803 and 93,015 has written several couplets of the text in single lines on his tablet.

60. [*e-l*]*i-e* *ilu* *E-a* *ḫa-sis mi im* [*b*]*a*-[*š*]*u*[1] *i-še-'-a me-ki-šu-un*[2]

61. [. . . . .][3]
62. [. . . . *k*]*i* *il-ku* *šu* (?)-*tu-ru*[4] *ta-a-šu* *el-lum*
63. [. . . .]-*te-eš* *ša* *kit-tu* *kit*-[. . . .][4]
64. [. . . . .][5]
65. [. . . . . . .] *ku-tal-la*[4] [. . . . .] *ku-u-ru*
66. [. . . . .] 67. [. . . . . - *na*]*m*[6]

[Lines 68-82 are wanting.]

83. [. . . . . . . - *r*]*a* 84. [. . . . . - *a*]*m* - *ra*
85. [. . . . .] *ilu* *A* - *num*
86. [. . . . . *mu* - *tir* *gi*][7] - *mil* - *li*
87. [. . . . .][8]
88. [. . . . . .]-*ga-am-ma*[9] *i-dal-laḫ*[10] *ilu* *Ti-amat*
89. [. . . . .] *i* - *du* - *ul* - [*li*][11]
90. [. . . . .] *da* - *a* - *ri* - *šam*
91. [. . . . .] *li* - *mut* - *tum*

[1] The reading [*b*]*a*-[*š*]*u* is not quite certain; there are traces of only two signs.

[2] The word *meku* occurs again in Tablet II, l. 81 (*me-ku-uš Ti-a-ma-ti*), and Tablet IV, l. 66 (*ša* *ilu* *Kin-gu* . . . . *me-ki-šu*), and from the context of these passages it is clear that the word describes an act or state capable of inspiring terror. II R, pl. 36, No. 3, Obv., l. 49 f., explains the group [KA]-SAL as *me-ku-u ša* KA (i.e. *pū* or *šinnu*), and a following group as "ditto" (i.e. *me-ku-u*) *ša amēli*. If we may connect this *me-ku-u* with the *meku* in the passages quoted above, we may perhaps assign to it some such meaning as "muttering, growling, snarling." It is probable that Apsū, Mummu, and Kingu, as well as Tiamat, were conceived as monsters and not endowed with human forms.

60. Then Ea, who knoweth all that [is],[1] went up and he beheld their muttering.[2]

61. [. . . . .][3]

62. [. . . . .] . . . . his pure incantation

63. [. . . . .] . . . . [. . .]

64. [. . . . .][5]

65. [. . . . . .] . . . [. . . .] misery

66. [. . . . . . .] 67. [. . . . . . .][6]

[Lines 68–82 are wanting.]

83. [. . . . . . .] 84. [. . . . .] . .

85. [. . . . .] the god Anu,

86. [. . . . . an aven]ger.[7]

87. [. . . . .][8]

88. [. . . . .] and[9] he shall confound Tiamat.[10]

89. [. . . . .] he . . . . . . ,[11]

90. [. . . . .] for ever.

91. [. . . . .] the evil,

---

[3] No. 46,803, Obv., l. 12, contained ll. 61 and 62 of the text.

[4] Ll. 62 ff. are so broken that the reading of the signs which are preserved is not certain.

[5] No. 46,803, Obv., l. 14, contained ll. 64 and 65 of the text.

[6] It is probable that No. 46,803, Obv., l. 15, contained ll. 66 and 67 of the text.

[7] Conjectural restoration; the reading of *gi* is not certain.

[8] No. 46,803, Rev., l. 5, contained ll. 87 and 88 of the text.

[9] Perhaps read *a-ga-am-ma*, "swamp"; but the *a* is not certain.

[10] Tiamat is possibly the subject of the verb.

[11] It is possible that the verb in Tablet IV, ll. 63 and 64, should be transliterated *i-dul-lu-šu*, and connected with the verb in the present passage and with *ta-du-ul-l*[*i*] in l. 99.

92. [. . . . .] *tur-ṣa iz-zak-kar*[1]
93. [. . . . .] [. .]-*ba-ki i-na-ru-ma*
94. [. . . . .]-*ki-ma ḳa-li-iš uš-bu*[2]
95. [. . . . .] *ša*[3] *pu-luḫ-tum*
96. [. . . . .] *ul ni-ṣa-al-lal ni-i-ni*
97. [. . . . .] *Ap-su-u ḫar-ba*-[. .][4]
98. [. . .]-*šu*[5] *u* ^{ilu}*Mu-um-mu ša ik-ka-mu-u ina su*-[. .][6]

99. [. . . . .]-*hi-iš ta-du-ul-l*[*i*][7]
100. [. . . . .] *i ni-iṣ-lal ni-i*-[*ni*][8]
101. [. . . . . . .] [*ḫ*]*u*-[*u*]*m-mu-ra*[9] *e-na-tu-u*-[. .][10]
102. [. . . . .] *i ni-iṣ-lal ni-i*-[*ni*]
103. [. . . . .] *gi-mil-la-šu-nu tir-ri*-[. .][11]
104. [. . . . .] *a-na za-ki-ḳu šu-uk*-[. . .]
105. [. . . . .][12] *a*-[*m*]*a-tum i-lu el*-[*lu*]

---

[1] The speech that follows is evidently addressed to Tiamat. The speaker refers to the evil fate which has overtaken Apsû and Mummu in their revolt against the gods (cf. ll. 97 and 98); he encourages Tiamat to take vengeance for them (l. 103), and, by continuing the struggle, to obtain with him the slothful peace which she desires (ll. 100 ff.). From the fact that Tiamat subsequently promoted Kingu to lead her forces "because he had given her support" (cf. l. 127), and addressed him as her "chosen spouse," it may be inferred that the speaker of ll. 93 ff. was Kingu.

[2] 82–9–18, 6,879, *tu-uš*-[. . .].

[3] No. 46,803 also reads *ša*, preceded by traces of another sign.

[4] One sign is wanting at the end of the line, perhaps *ma*.

[5] No. 46,803, Rev., l. 14, contains ll. 97 and 98 of the text. It is possible that l. 98 begins with the words *u* ^{ilu}*Mu-um-mu*, in which case *šu* (or *ku*) would form the last sign of line 97. Elsewhere on the tablet, however, the scribe has not omitted the division-signs when writing two lines of the text together; cf. No. 46,803, Obv., ll. 9 and 10. It is safer to assume that no part of l. 98 has been preserved by No. 46,803.

92\. [. . . . . . .] . . . he spake :[1]
93\. "[. . .] thy [. .] he hath conquered and
94\. "[. . .] he [weepeth] and sitteth in tribulation(?).
95\. "[. . . . .] of fear,
96\. "[. . . .] we shall not lie down (in peace).
97\. "[. . . . . . .] Apsū is laid waste (?),[4]
98\. "[. . .] and Mummu, who were taken captive, in [. . .].
99\. "[. . . . .] . . thou didst . . . ;[7]
100\. "[. . . . . .] let us lie down (in peace).
101\. "[. . . . .] . . . they will smite (?) [. . .].
102\. "[. . . . . .] let us lie down (in peace).
103\. "[. . .] thou shalt take vengeance for them,
104\. "[. . .] unto the tempest shalt thou [. . .]!"
105\. [And Tiamat hearkened unto][12] the word of the bright god, (and said):

---

[6] 82-9-18, 6,879 gives a variant reading for the second half of the line: *la e-diš ina ma-a-*[. . .].

[7] Cf. l. 89, and p. 13, note 11.

[8] 82-9-18, 6,879 gives a variant reading for the second half of the line: *ul(-)ta-ra-mi(-)na*[. . .].

[9] The first two signs of the word are not quite certain.

[10] 82-9-18, 6,879, *i-na-tu-u-*[. . .].

[11] The word should probably be restored as *tir-ri-*[*i*], or *tir-ri-*[*ma*].

[12] The first half of the line may possibly be restored as [*iš-me-ma Ti-amat*], as suggested in the translation; or [*iḫ-du-ma Ti-amat a-na*], cf. Tablet II, l. (113). According to this interpretation the speech of the god (Kingu) ends with l. 104, Tiamat replies in l. 106, and with l. 107 the narrative begins the description of Tiamat's preparations for battle. It is possible that the speech does not end with l. 104, but continues to l. 106; in that case l. 106 may be restored in some such way as "[The leadership of the gods unto me] shalt thou entrust," and for *a-*[*m*]*a-tum* in l. 105 we should perhaps read *a-*[*b*]*a-tum*. The former interpretation seems to me preferable, as it assigns a line to Tiamat in which she assents to Kingu's proposals.

106. [. . . . .] *lu ta-ad-di-nu i ni-pu-uš* [. .][1]
107. [. . . . .] *ilāni ki-rib* [. . .]
108. [. . . . .] *an ilāni ba-ni-*[. . .][2]
109. [*im-ma-aṣ-ru-nim-ma*] *i-du-uš Ti-amat ti-bi-*[*u-ni*][3]

110. [*iz-zu kap-du la sa-ki-pu*] *mu-ša u* [*im-ma*]

111. [*na-šu-u tam-ḫa-r*]*a na-zar-bu-bu la-*[*ab-bu*]
112. [*unken-na šit-ku-nu*]*-ma i-ban-nu-u ṣu-l*[*a-a-ti*]
113. [*Um-mu-Hu-bu*]*r*[4] *pa-ti-ḳa-at ka-l*[*a-ma*]
114. [*uš-rad-di ka*]*k-ku la maḫ-ru it-t*[*a-l*]*ad ṣirmaḫē*[^{pl}]

115. [*zaḳ-tu-ma ši*]*n-ni la pa-d*[*u-u*] *at-ta-*[*'-i*]
116. [*im-tu ki-ma*] *da-mu zu-mur-*[*šu-nu*] *uš-ma-al-*[*li*]

117. [*ušumgallē*^{pl}] *na-ad-ru-tum pu-ul-ḫa-*[*a*]*-ti u-šal-*[*biš-ma*]
118. [*me-lam-m*]*e uš-daš-ša-a i-li-iš*[5] [*um-taš-šil*]

119. [*a-mi*]*r-šu-nu šar-ba-ba* [*l*]*iš-ḫ*[*ar-mi-im*][6]
120. [*zu*]*-mur-šu-nu liš-taḫ-ḫi-dam-ma la i-ni-'-u* [*i-rat-su-un*]

---

[1] We may perhaps restore the end of the line as *i ni-pu-uš* [*ša-aš-ma*]; cf. Tablet IV, l. 86.

[2] The word may possibly be restored as *ba-ni-*[*at*].

[3] Lines 109–142 have been restored from Tablet III, ll. 19–52.

[4] A title of Tiamat.

[5] In the parallel passages the majority of the duplicates read *eliš*, not *iliš*, which precludes the translation "she made them even as

106. "[. . .] shalt thou entrust! let us wage [war]!"[1]
107. [. . . .] the gods in the midst of [. . .]
108. [. . . . .] for the gods did she create.[2]
109. [They banded themselves together and] at the side of Tiamat [they] advanced;[3]
110. [They were furious, they devised mischief without resting] night and [day].
111. [They prepared for battle], fuming and raging;
112. [They joined their forces] and made war.
113. [Ummu-Ḫubu]r,[4] who formed all things,
114. [Made in addition] weapons invincible, she spawned monster-serpents,
115. [Sharp of] tooth, and merciless of fang;
116. [With poison instead of] blood she filled [their] bodies.
117. Fierce [monster-vipers] she clothed with terror,
118. [With splendour] she decked them, [she made them] of lofty stature.[5]
119. [Whoever beheld] them, terror overcame him,[6]
120. Their bodies reared up and none could withstand [their attack].

---

gods." The same variety of reading occurs in a parallel expression in IV R, pl. 60* [67], B, Obv., l. 31, and C, Obv., l. 11, *ta-na-da a-ti šarri e-liš* (so B; C, *i-liš*) *u-maš-šil*, "I have made the honour of the king to be exalted."

[6] No. 45,528, etc., *šar-ba-bi-iš li-iḫ-ḫ[ar-mi-im]*, "he was overcome by terror," or possibly, "his terror overcame him"; of the two I think it preferable to assign a passive meaning to *li-iḫ-ḫar-mi-im* and to take *šar-ba-bi-iš* as an adverb.

121. [*uš-zi*]*z*[1] *ba-aš-mu*[2] *ṣir-ruš u* ^{ilu}[*La-ḫa-mi*]

122. [*ugall*]*ē*^{pl} UR-BE^{pl}[3] [4]*aḳrab-am*[*ēlu*]

123. [*u-m*]*e da-ab-ru-te*[5] *nūn-amēlu u ku-*[*sa-riḳ-ḳu*][6]

124. [*na-š*]*i kak-ku la pa-du-u la a-di-ru* [*ta-ḫa-zi*]

125. [*gab-ša*] *te-ri-tu-ša la maḫ-ra ši-*[*na-a-ma*]

126. [*a*]*p-pu-na-ma*[7] *iš-ten eš-rit*[8] *kīma*[9] *šu-a-ti u*[*š-tab-ši*]

127. *i-na ilāni*[11] *bu-uk-ri-ša*[12] *šu-ut iš-ku-nu-*[*ši pu-uḫ-ri*]

128. *u-ša-aš-ki*[13] ^{ilu}*Kin-gu ina bi-ri-šu-nu ša-a-š*[*u uš-rab-bi-iš*]

129. *a-li-kut*[14] *maḫ-ri*[15] *pa-an*[16] *um-ma-ni mu-'-ir-ru-*[*ut puḫri*][17]

130. [*na*]*-aš*[18] *kakku ti-iṣ-bu-tu*[19] *te-bu-*[*u*][20] *a-na-*[*an-tu*]

---

[1] No. 45,528, etc., [*uš-ziz-m*]*a*, or [*uš-zi-i*]*z*.

[2] In the list of monsters created by Tiamat, both here and in the parallel passages, it is probable that the words which occur in the singular are used collectively.

[3] In II R, pl. 6, col. i, l. 26, [UR]-BE is explained as *kal-bu še-gu-u*, "raging hound"; the reading of the ideogram is not certain.

[4] No. 45,528, etc., inserts *u*.

[5] No. 45,528, etc., *tum*.

[6] Restored from Tablet II, l. 29; No. 45,528, etc., BI (or GUD, but not *ḳu*)[. . .].

[7] No. 93,015, [*a*]*p-pu-na-a-ta*.

[8] No. 93,015, *eš-ri-e-ti*.

[9] No. 45,528, etc., *ki-ma*.

[10] That is, eleven kinds of monsters; since the plural is used in

121. [She set] up vipers,[2] and dragons, and the (monster) [Laḫamu],
122. [And hurricanes], and raging hounds,[3] and scorpion-men,
123. And mighty [tempests], and fish-men, and [rams];
124. [They bore] cruel weapons, without fear of [the fight].
125. Her commands [were mighty], [none] could resist them ;
126. After this fashion, huge of stature, [she made] eleven (monsters).[10]
127. Among the gods who were her[12] sons, inasmuch as he had given [her support],
128. She exalted Kingu ; in their midst [she raised] him [to power].
129. To march before the forces, to lead [the host],
130. To give the battle-signal, to advance to the attack,

---

the case of many of the classes, it is clear that Tiamat created more than one of each.

[11] No. 45,528, etc., [*ilâni*]^{pl}.

[12] No. 93,015, *bu-uk-ri-šu-nu*, i.e. the sons of Apsû and Tiamat.

[13] Nos. 45,528, etc., and 93,015, *ḳa*.

[14] No. 93,015, *-ku-tu* ; No. 45,528, etc., [. . . *-k*]*u*-[. . .].

[15] No. 45,528, etc., [*m*]*a-aḫ-ra* ; No. 93,015, *maḫri*.

[16] Nos. 45,528, etc., and 93,015, *pa-ni*.

[17] No. 93,015, *um-ma-nu mu-'-ir-ru-tu pu-u*[*ḫ-ri*].

[18] K. 3,938, *na-še-e* ; No. 45,528, etc., *na-še*.

[19] No. 45,528, etc., *te-iṣ-bu-tum*.

[20] 81-7-27, 80 reads *di-ku-u*, "to summon to the attack."

131. *šu - ud tam - ḫa - ru*[1] *ra - ab šik - ka - tu - tu*[2]
132. *ip - ḳid - ma ḳa - tuš - šu*[3] *u-še-ši-ba-aš-šu ina [kar-ri]*

133. *ad-di*[4] *ta-a-ka ina puḫur*[5] *ilāni*^{pl}[6] *u - šar - bi - ka*

134. *ma-li-kut*[7] *ilāni*^{pl}[8] *gim-ra-at-su-nu ḳa tuš-[šu uš-mal-li]*

135. *lu*[9] *šur-ba-ta-ma ḫa-'-i-ri*[10] *e - du - u at - ta*
136. *li-ir-tab-bu u zik-ru-ka eli kalī-[šu-nu . . ilu A-nun-na-ki]*[11]

137. *id-din-šu-ma*[12] *dupšīmāti*^{pl} *i-ra-[tu-uš]*[13] *u-šat-mi-iḫ*

138. *ka-ta*[14] *ḳibīt-ka la in-nin-na-a l[i-kun ṣi-it pi-i-ka]*

139. *e-nin-na*[15] *ilu Kin-gu*[16] *šu*[17]*-uš-ḳu-u li-ḳu-u [ilu A-nu-ti]*

140. *ina ilāni [ma-r]i-e-šu*[18] *ši - ma - [ta iš - ti - mu]*

141. *ip-ša pi-ku-nu*[19] *ilu Gibil*[20] *l[i - ni - iḫ - ḫa]*

142. *nā'id ina*[21] *kit-mu-ru ma-ag-ša-ru*[22] *liš - [rab - bi - ib]*

---

[1] No. 45,528, etc., *ta-am-ḫa-ru* ; No. 93,015, *ta-am-ḫa-a-ta.*
[2] No. 93,015, *rab šik-kat-tu-tu.* [3] No. 45,528, etc., *ḳa-tu-[u]š-šu.*
[4] K. 3,938, *a-di*; No. 93,015 reads KU, i.e. *addi.*
[5] No. 45,528, etc., *i-[na] pu-ḫur.*
[6] No. 93,015. *ilāni.* [7] No. 45,528, etc., *ku-ut.*
[8] K. 3,938, *ilā[ni].* [9] No. 45,528, etc., *lu-u.*
[10] No. 93,015, *lu šu-ur-ba-ta-a ḫa-'-a-ri.*
[11] Restored from Tablet III, l. 104. The Anunnaki are possibly the subject of the sentence.
[12] No. 45,528, etc., *id-din-[š]um-ma* ; No. 93,015, *id-din-ma.*

131. To direct the battle, to control the fight,
132. Unto him she entrusted ; in [costly raiment] she made him sit, (saying) :
133. " I have uttered thy spell, in the assembly of the gods I have raised thee to power.
134. " The dominion over all the gods [have I entrusted unto him].
135. " Be thou exalted, thou my chosen spouse,
136. " May they magnify thy name over all [of them . . . the Anunnaki]." [1]
137. She gave him the Tablets of Destiny, on [his] breast she laid them, (saying) :
138. " Thy command shall not be without avail, and [the word of thy mouth shall be established]."
139. Now Kingu, (thus) exalted, having received [the power of Anu],
140. [Decreed] the fate among the gods his sons, (saying) :
141. " Let the opening of your mouth [quench] the Fire-god ;
142. " Whoso is exalted in the battle, let him [display (his) might] ! "

---

[13] No. 93,015, *i-rat-šu*. [14] No. 93,015, *ka-at*[. . .].

[15] No. 45,528, etc., *in-na-an-*[*n*]*a* ; No. 93,015, *in-na-nu*.

[16] 81–7–27, 80, [*ilu Ki*]*-in-gu*.

[17] The scribe of No. 93,015 has written *ma* for *šu* by mistake.

[18] No. 45,528, etc., *a-na ilāni pl mārē pl-ṣu*, " for the gods his sons."

[19] Nos. 45,528, etc., and 93,015, *pi-i-ku-nu*.

[20] No. 93,015, *ilu* BIL-GI ; 81–7–27, 80 and No. 45,528, *ilu* GIŠ-BAR.

[21] *ina* is omitted by Nos. 45,528, etc., and 93,015.

[22] 81–7–27, 80, *r*[*a*].

The Second Tablet.

1. *u - kab - bi*[*t*] *- ma*[1] *Ti - a - ma - tum pi - ti - iḳ - šu*
2. [*lim - ni - e - ti iḳ*][2]*- ta - ṣar a-na ilāni ni - ip - ri - šu*
3. [*ana tu-ur gi-mil*][3]*-li Apsū u-lam-mi-in Ti-amat*
4. [. . . . *-u*]*š*[4] *ki-i iṣ-mi-da a-na* ^{ilu}*E-a ip-ta-šar*[5]

5. [*iš - me - ma*][6] ^{ilu}*E - a a - ma - tum šu - a - tim*
6 [*mar-ṣi*]*-iš uš - ḫa - ri - ir - ma ša-ḳu-um-mi-iš uš - bu*
7. [*ūmē*^{pl} *u*] *- ri - ku - ma uz - za - šu i - nu - ḫu*
8. [*ur-ḫa-šu aš - ri*] *- iš An-šar a - bi - šu šu - u uš - tar - di*

9. [*il - lik*] *- ma maḫ - ru*[7] *a - bi a - li - di - šu An - šar*

10. [*mim-mu*]*-u Ti-amat ik-pu-du u-ša-an-na-a a-na ša-a-šu*
11. [*um-ma Ti*][8]*-amat a-lit-ti-a-ni i - zi - ir - ra - an - na - a - ti*

12. [*pu*]*-uḫ-ru šit*[9]*-ku-na-at-ma ag - gi - iš la - ab - bat*
13. [*is*]*-ḫu - ru - šim - ma ilāni gi - mi - ir - šu - un*
14. [*a-di*] *ša at-tu-nu tab-na-a i - da - a - ša al - ka*[10]

---

[1] The beginning of l. 1 has been restored from the catch-line on Tablet I, preserved by No. 45,528 + 46,614.

[2] Conjectural restoration.

[3] For this restoration cf. Tablet I, l. 103.

[4] The sign is possibly *ta*.

[5] The rendering of this line is a little uncertain. The beginning may perhaps be restored as [*pu-uḫ-ru-u*]*š*; in that case a passive meaning must be assigned to *ip-ta-šar*, and the line translated, "How she had collected her [forces] unto Ea was divulged."

The Second Tablet.

1. Tiamat made weighty[1] her handiwork,
2. [Evil][2] she wrought against the gods her children.
3. [To avenge][3] Apsū, Tiamat planned evil,
4. But how she had collected her [forces, the god . . . .] unto Ea divulged.[5]
5. Ea [hearkened to][6] this thing, and
6. He was [grievous]ly afflicted and he sat in sorrow.
7. [The days] went by, and his anger was appeased,
8. And to [the place of] Anšar his father he took [his way].
9. [He went] and standing before[7] Anšar, the father who begat him,
10. [All that] Tiamat had plotted he repeated unto him,
11. [Saying, "Ti]amat our mother hath conceived a hatred for us,
12. "With all her force she rageth, full of wrath.
13. "All the gods have turned to her,
14. "[With] those, whom ye created, they go at her side.

For *ip-ta-šar* we may also read *ip-ta-ḫir*, and for the object of *iṣ-mi-da* we may perhaps restore [*narkabtu*]*š*; the line may then be translated, "But when [. . . .] had yoked his [chariot], unto Ea he repaired." It may be noted that not very much is missing from the beginning of the line.

[6] Lines 5–10 have been conjecturally restored.

[7] Or, possibly, "addressing Anšar."

[8] Lines 11–19 have been restored from Tablet III, ll. 73–81.

[9] No. 38,396, *ši-it.*

[10] No. 38,396, *al-ku.*

15. [*im*]-*ma-aṣ-ru-nim-ma i-du-uš Ti-amat te-bu-u-ni*[1]

16. [*iz*]-*zu kap-du la sa-ki-pu mu-ša u im-ma*[2]

17. [*na*]-*šu-u tam-ḫa-ra*[3] *na-zar-bu-bu la-ab-bu*[4]
18. *unken-na šit-ku-nu-ma i*[5]-*ban-nu-u ṣu-la-a-tum*[6]
19. [*U*]*m-ma-Ḫu-bu-ur*[7] *pa-ti-iḳ-ḳa-at*[8] *ka-la-mu*
20. *uš-rad*[9]-*di kak-ku la maḫ-ru*[10] *it-ta-lad ṣir-ma-ḫu*[11]

21. *zaḳ-tu-ma šin-nu la pa-du-u at-ta-'-um*[12]
22. *im-tu ki-ma da-am*[13] *zu-mur-šu-nu uš-ma-al-lu*[14]

23. *ušumgallē*^{pl} *na-ad-ru-ti pu-ul ḫa-a-ti*[15] *u-šal-biš-'ma*

24. *me-lam-mu uš-daš-ša-a i-li-iš um-taš-ši-il*[16]

25. *a-mi-ir-šu-nu šar-ba-bi-iš li-iḫ-ḫar-mi-im*[17]
26. *zu-mur-šu-nu liš-taḫ-ḫi-da-am*[18]-*ma la i-ni-'-e*[19] *i-rat*[20]-*su-un*

27. *uš-zi-iz-ma ba-aš-mu* ^{ilu}*ṣirruššu*[21] *u* ^{ilu}*La-ḫa-mu*

---

[1] No. 38,396, *te-bi-u-nu*.
[2] No. 92,632 + 93,048, *mu*.
[3] No. 38,396, *ri*.
[4] No. 92,632, etc., *bi*.
[5] No. 38,396, *a*.
[6] No. 92,632, etc., *ti*.
[7] No. 38,396, [*U*]*m-mu-Ḫu-bur*.
[8] Nos. 38,396 and 92,632, etc., *pa-ti-ḳa at*.
[9] No. 38,396, *ra-ad*.
[10] No. 38,396, *ma-ḫar*.
[11] No. 92,632, etc., *ṣir-maḫ*; No. 38,396, *ṣirmaḫē*^{pl}.
[12] No. 38,396, *at-ta-'-u-um*; No. 92,632, etc., *at-ta-'-am*.
[13] No. 38,396, *da-mu*; No. 92,632, etc., *da-mi*.

15. " They are banded together and at the side of Tiamat they advance ;
16. " They are furious, they devise mischief without resting night and day.
17. " They prepare for battle, fuming and raging ;
18. " They have joined their forces and are making war.
19. " Ummu-Ḫubur, who formed all things,
20. " Hath made in addition weapons invincible, she hath spawned monster-serpents,
21. " Sharp of tooth, and merciless of fang.
22. " With poison instead of blood she hath filled their bodies.
23. " Fierce monster-vipers she hath clothed with terror,
24. " With splendour she hath decked them, she hath made them of lofty stature.[16]
25. " Whoever beholdeth them is overcome by terror,[17]
26. " Their bodies rear up and none can withstand their attack.
27. " She hath set up vipers, and dragons, and the (monster) Laḫamu,

---

[14] Nos. 38,396 and 92,632, etc., *la*.

[15] No. 38,396, [GA]L-BUR *na-ad-ru-tum pu-ul-ḫa-a-tum*.

[16] So No. 38,396; No. 92,632, etc., reads *um-ta-aš ši-il*, and No. 45,528 + 46,614, *um-taš-ši-ir* (= *umtaššil*). For the phrase *i-li-iš um-taš-ši-il*, see above, p. 16 f., note 5.

[17] See above, p. 17.

[18] Nos. 38,396 and 92,632, etc., *dam*.

[19] No. 38,396, *i-ni-'-im*; No. 92,632, *i-ni-'-u*.

[20] No. 92,632, *ra-at*.

[21] No. 92,632, *ṣirruššê^{pl}*.

28. *u - gal - la* UR - BE^{pl} [1] *u aḳrab* [2] *- amēlu*

29. *u - me da - ab - ru -ti nūn - amēlu u ku - sa - riḳ - ḳu*
30. *na - ši kak - ku la pa - du - u la a - di - ru ta - ḫa - zi*

31. *gab - ša te - ri - tu - ša la ma - ḫar - ra ši - na - ma*
32. *ap-pu-na-ma iš - ten eš - rit ki-ma šu-a-ti uš - tab - ši*

33. *i-na ilāni*^{pl} *bu-uk-ri-ša šu-ut iš-ku-nu-ši pu-uḫ-ru*

34. *u-ša-aš-ḳa* ^{ilu}*Kin-gu ina bi-ri-šu-nu ša-a-šu uš-rab-bi-iš* [3]

35. *a-li-ku-ut maḫ-ru pa-ni um-ma-nu mu-ir-ru-tum* [4] *pu-uḫ-ru* [5]
36. *na-še-e kak-ku ti-iṣ-bu-tum te-bu-u a-na-an-tum* [6]

37. *[šu - u]d* [7] *ta - am - ḫa - ra ra - ab šik - kat - u - tum* [8]
38. *[ip-ḳid-m]a ḳa-tu-uš-šu u-še-ši-ba-aš-ši i-na* [9] *kar-ri*

39. *[ad-di ta-a]-ka i-na pu-ḫur ilāni*^{pl} *u-šar-bi-ka*

40. *[ma-li-kut] ilāni [gim-rat-su-nu ḳa-tuk-ka] uš-mal-li*

41. *[lu - u šur - ba - ta - ma ḫa - i - ri e - du - u a]t - ta*

---

[1] For this ideogram see above, p. 18, note 3.
[2] No. 38,396 prefixes the determinative ^{ilu}.
[3] K. 4,832, *[uš]-rab-bi.*
[4] K. 4,832, *tu.*
[5] K. 4,832, *puḫri.*
[6] K. 4,832, *ti.*

28. "And hurricanes and raging hounds, and scorpion-men,
29. "And mighty tempests, and fish-men and rams;
30. "They bear cruel weapons, without fear of the fight.
31. "Her commands are mighty, none can resist them;
32. "After this fashion, huge of stature, hath she made eleven (monsters).
33. "Among the gods who are her sons, inasmuch as he hath given her support,
34. "She hath exalted Kingu; in their midst she hath raised him to power.
35. "To march before the forces, to lead the host,
36. "To give the battle-signal, to advance to the attack,
37. "[To direct][7] the battle, to control the fight,
38. "Unto him [hath she entrusted]; in costly raiment she hath made him sit, (saying):
39. "'[I have uttered] thy [spell], in the assembly of the gods I have raised thee to power,
40. "'[The dominion over all] the gods have I entrusted [unto thee].
41. "'[Be thou exalted], thou [my chosen spouse],

[7] Lines 37–48 have been restored from Tablet III, ll. 41–52 and 99–110.

[8] K. 4,832, [. . .]-*tu u-ti.* [9] K. 4,832, *ina.*

42. *[li-ir-tab-bu-u zik-ru-ka eli kalī-šu-nu . . . .]-uk-ki*[1]

43. *[id-din šum-ma dupšīmāti*^{pl} *i-ra-tu-uš] u-[šat-m]e-iḫ*

44. *[ka-ta ḳibīt-ka la in-nin-na-a] li-kun ṣ[i-i]t pi i-ka*

45. *[in-na-nu* ^{ilu}*Kin-gu šu-uš-ḳu]-u li-ḳu-u* ^{ilu}*A-nu-ti*

46. *[an ilāni mārē*^{pl} *- ša] ši - ma - ta iš - ti - mu*

47. *[ip - šu pi - ku - nu]* ^{ilu}*Gibil li - ni - iḫ - ḫa*

48. *[nā'id ina kit - mu - ri] ma - ag - ša - ra liš - rab - bi - ib*

49. *[iš - me - ma* ^{ilu}*Anšar ša Ti-a-ma]*[2]*-tu rabiš dal-ḫat*

50. [. . . . .[3] *ša] - pat - su it - taš - ka*
51. [. . . . .] *la na - ḫat*[4] *ka - ras - su*
52. [. . . . . .]*-šu ša - gi - ma - šu uš - taḫ - ḫa - aḫ*
53. [. . . . .] *- u tu - ḳu - un - tu*
54. [. . . . .] *- pu - šu i(-)taš - ši at - ta*
55. [^{ilu}*Mu - um - mu u]*[2] *Apsū ta - na - ra*[5]

---

[1] In the parallel passage, Tablet III, l. 104, No. 93,017 reads at the end of the line ^{ilu}*A-nun-na-ki*. This is in favour of Jensen's suggestion that the present passage should be restored as ^{ilu}*E-nu]-uk-ki*; cf. the list of gods, K. 2,100 (published by Bezold, P.S.B.A., vol. xi, March, 1889), col. iv, l. 8, which explains ^{ilu}*E-nu-uk-ki* as ^{ilu}*A-nun-na-[ki]*.

[2] Conjectural restoration.

[3] For the first half of the line Delitzsch suggests the restoration *šunšu imḫaṣma*, "he smote his loins."

42. " '[May they magnify thy name over all of them . . .] . . .'[1]
43. " [She hath given him the Tablets of Destiny, on his breast she] laid them, (saying):
44. " '[Thy command shall not be without avail], and the [word] of thy mouth shall be established.'
45. " [Now Kingu, (thus) exalted], having received the power of Anu,
46. " Decreed the fate [for the gods, her sons], (saying):
47. " 'Let [the opening of your mouth] quench the Fire-god;
48. " '[Whoso is exalted in the battle], let him display (his) might!' "
49. [When Anšar heard how Tiamat][2] was mightily in revolt,
50. [. . . . .],[3] he bit his lips,
51. [. . . . . . .], his mind was not at peace,
52. His [. . .], he made a bitter lamentation:
53. "[. . . . .] battle,
54. "[. . . . .] thou . . . .
55. " [Mummu and][2] Apsū thou hast smitten,[5]

[4] The reading *ḫat* is certain.

[5] *ta-na-ra* I take as the Pret., not the Pres. From ll. 93 ff. of the First Tablet it may be inferred that Apsū was conquered before Tiamat made her preparations for battle. It is clear, therefore, that in the present passage *ta-na-ra* is to be taken as the Pret. and not as the Pres.; and, as Anšar is addressing Ea, it may be concluded that Ea was the conqueror of Apsū. In accordance with this conclusion is the fact that it was the god Ea who first discovered the conspiracy of Apsū and Tiamat (see Tablet I, l. 60).

56. [*Ti-amat u-ša-aš-ki* ^{ilu}*Kin*]*-gu a-li*[1] *ma-ḫar-ša*

57. [. . . . .]*-e ta-šim-ti*
58. [. . . . .] *il*[*āni*] ^{ilu}*N*[*u*]*-di*[*m-mud*][2]

[A gap of about ten lines occurs here.]

(69)[3] [. . . . .]*-ta*
(70) [. . . . .]*-ni*
(71) [. . . . . . .]*zi iš*[. . . . .]*-si*
(72) [^{ilu}*An-šar ana*] *ma-ri-šu* [*a-ma-tu i*]*-zak-kar*
(73) [. . . . *a*]*n-nu-u ka-šu-*[*šu*] *ḳar-ra-di*
(74) [*ša ša-ḳa-a e-mu*]*-ḳa-a-šu la ma-ḫar te-bu-šu*

(75) [*al-kam*]*-ma mut-tiš Ti-amat i-ziz-za at-ta*
(76) [. . . .][4] *kab-ta-taš lib-bu-uš lip-pu-uš*

(77) [*šum-ma-ma*] *la še-ma-ta a-mat-ka*
(78) [*a-ma-t*]*u-ni at-me-šim-ma ši-i lip-pa-aš-ḫa*[5]

(79) [*iš-me-e*]*-ma zik-ri abi-šu An-šar*
(80) [*uš-te-šir ḫar*]*-ra-an-ša-ma u-ru-uḫ-ša uš-tar-di*

(81) [*iṭ-ḫi-ma*][6] ^{ilu}*A-num me-ku-uš*[7] *Ti-a-ma-ti i-še-'-am-ma*

---

[1] I think there is no doubt *a-li* should be taken as the adv. "where?" The beginning of the line is conjecturally restored.

[2] The reading of Nudimmud at the end of the line is certain. Before the determinative the sign AN is visible.

[3] The numbers of the lines, when conjectural, are enclosed within parentheses.

56. "[But Tiamat hath exalted Kin]gu, and where[1] is one who can oppose her?"
57. [. . . . .] deliberation
58. [. . . . the . . of] the gods, N[u]di[mmud][2]

[A gap of about ten lines occurs here.]

(69)[3] [. . . . .]
(70) [. . . . .]
(71) [. . . . . .] . . . [. . . . . .]
(72) [Anšar unto] his son addressed [the word]:
(73) "[. . . . .] . . . my mighty hero,
(74) "[Whose] strength [is great] and whose onslaught cannot be withstood,
(75) "[Go] and stand before Tiamat,
(76) "[That] her spirit [may be appeased],[4] that her heart may be merciful.
(77) "[But if] she will not hearken unto thy word,
(78) "Our [word] shalt thou speak unto her, that she may be pacified."[5]
(79) [He heard the] word of his father Anšar
(80) And [he directed] his path to her, towards her he took the way.
(81) Anu [drew nigh],[6] he beheld the muttering[7] of Tiamat,

[4] The first part of the line probably contained some such phrase as *lip-pa-aš-šir*, as suggested in the translation.

[5] The sense of the couplet seems to be that, should Tiamat not listen to Anu, she might perhaps respect the authority of Anšar.

[6] For this restoration, cf. Tablet IV, l. 65.

[7] See above, p. 12, note 2.

(82) [*ul i-li-'-a ma-ḫar-ša*][1] *i-tu-ra ar-kiš*

(83) [. . . . .]-*šu An-šar*
(84) [. . . . . *i*]-*zak-kar-šu*
(85) [. . . . . *e*]*li-ia*

[A gap of about twenty lines occurs here.]

(104) [. . . . .]
(105) [. . . . . *mu-tir*] *gi-mil-lu a*-[. .][2]
(106) [. . . . .] *ḳar*-[*du*][3]
(107) [. . . . .] *a-šar pi-ris-ti-š*[*u*]
(108) [. . . . .] *i-ta-mi*[4]-*šu*
(109) [. . . . .] *abi-ka*
(110) *at-ta-ma ma-ri mu-nap-pi-šu*[5] *lib-bi-šu*

(111) [. . . . . . . *ḳi*]*t-ru-bi-iš*[6] *ṭi-ḫi-e-ma*[7]
(112) [. . . . . .] *e-ma-ru-uk-ka*[8] *ni-i-ḫu*[9]

(113) *iḫ-du-ma be-lum a-na a-ma-tum a-bi-šu*
(114) *iṭ-ḫi-e-ma it-ta-zi-iz ma-ḫa-ri-iš*[10] *An-šar*
(115) *i-mur-šu-ma An-šar lib-ba-šu tu-ub-ba-a-ti im-la*[11]

---

[1] This line has been restored from Tablet III, l. 53.

[2] The last word of the line may possibly be restored as *a*-[*na-ku*], in which case the line would form part of a speech of Marduk to Anšar.

[3] This restoration is not certain. [4] K. 4,832, *me*.

[5] Literally, "who maketh broad his heart"; cf. l. 71, *lib-bu-uš lip-pu-uš*, "that her heart may be merciful." The phrase, as applied to Marduk, implies that he shows mercy on the gods by

(82) [But he could not withstand her], and he turned back.
(83) [. . . . .] Anšar
(84) [. . . . .] he spake unto him :
(85) "[. . . . .] upon me

[A gap of about twenty lines occurs here.]

(104) [. . . . .]
(105) [. . . . . . .] an avenger [. . .][2]
(106) [. . . . .] va[liant][3]
(107) [. . . . . .] in the place of his decision
(108) [. . . . .] he spake unto him :
(109) "[. . . . .] thy father
(110) "Thou art my son, who maketh merciful[5] his heart.
(111) "[. . .] to the battle shalt thou draw nigh,
(112) "[. . .] he that shall behold thee shall have peace."
(113) And the lord rejoiced at the word of his father,
(114) And he drew nigh and stood before Anšar.
(115) Anšar beheld him and his heart was filled with joy,

---

consenting to become their avenger. This seems to me preferable to my previous translation, "who maketh valiant his heart" (cf. *Cun. Texts*, part xiii, pl. 4, note).

[6] K. 4,832, *biš*. [7] No. 40,559, *ṭi-ḫi-ma*.

[8] K. 4,832, [. . .]-*uk*.

[9] No. 40,559, *ni-i-ḫi*; K. 4,832, *ni-iḫ-ḫa*.

[10] K. 4,832, and Nos. 40,559 and 92,632, etc., *riš*.

[11] Nos. 40,559 and 92,632, etc., *tu-ub-ba-ta im-li*.

(116) [*i*]*š-ši-iḳ šap*[1]*-ti-šu a-di-ra-šu ut-te-is-si*[2]

(117) [*a-bi*][3] *la šuk-tu-mat pi-ti*[4] *ša-ap-tu-uk*[5]

(118) *lu-ul-lik-ma lu-ša-am-ṣa-a ma-la lib-bi-ka*

(119) [*An-šar*][6] *la šuḳ-tu-mat pi-ti*[4] *ša-ap-tu-uk*[5]

(120) [*lu-ul-li*]*k-ma lu-ša-am-ṣa-a ma-la lib-bi-ka*[7]

(121) *ai-u zik-ri ta-ḫa-za-šu u-še-ṣi-ka*[8]

(122) [. .] *Ti-amat ša si-in-ni-ša-tum*[9] *ia-ar-ka*[10] *i-na kak-ku*[11]

(123) [. . .][12]*-nu-u ḫi-di u šu-li-il*[13]
(124) *ki-ša-ad Ti-amat ur-ru-ḫi-iš ta-kab-ba-as at-ta*

(125) [. . . .][12]*-nu-u ḫi-di u šu-li-il*[13]
(126) [*ki-ša-ad*] *Ti-amat ur-ru-ḫi-iš ta-kab-ba-as at-ta*

---

[1] Nos. 40,559 and 92,632, etc., *ša-ap*.
[2] No. 40,559, *su*.
[3] Conjectural restoration; the traces of the second sign in the line on No. 38,396 may be those of *bi* or *šar*.
[4] No. 40,559, *pi-ta*.
[5] Nos. 40,559 and 92,632, *šap-tu-uk*; K. 4,832, *šap-tuk*.
[6] Conjectural restoration; for a somewhat similar change of one word when a couplet is repeated, see Tablet IV, ll. 3–6.
[7] It is clear that at this point Marduk ceases to speak, and that Anšar's answer begins with the following line.
[8] Literally, "Of what man has his battle caused thee to go

(116) He kissed him on the lips and his fear departed from him.
(117) "[O my father],[3] let not the word of thy lips be overcome,
(118) "Let me go, that I may accomplish all that is in thy heart.
(119) "[O Anšar],[6] let not the word of thy lips be overcome,
(120) "[Let me] go, that I may accomplish all that is in thy heart."[7]
(121) "What man is it, who hath brought thee forth to battle?[8]
(122) "[. . .] Tiamat, who is a woman, is armed and attacketh thee.[10]
(123) "[. . .] . . rejoice and be glad;[12]
(124) "The neck of Tiamat shalt thou swiftly trample under foot.
(125) "[. . .] . . rejoice and be glad;[12]
(126) "[The neck] of Tiamat shalt thou swiftly trample under foot.

forth." No. 40,559 reads *u-še-ṣi-ma*; according to this reading it is possible to take *zik-ri* as the subject, and *ta-ḫa-za-šu* as the object, of the verb.

[9] No. 40,559, *ša si-in-ni-ša-at.*

[10] *ia-ar-ka* I take as the Pres. Ḳal. from *āru*, followed by the direct accusative.

[11] K. 4,832, *ina kakki.*

[12] It is possible that the first word of the line should be restored [*li-ib-ba*]-*nu-u*, in which case *ḫi-di* and *šu-li-il* must be taken as substantives, "let there be joy and gladness."

[13] K. 4,832, *lil.*

(127) [*ma*] - *ri* *mu* - *du* - *u* *gim* - *ri*[1] *uz* - *nu*
(128) [*Ti* - *ama*]*t* *šu* - *up* - *ši* - *iḫ* *i* - *na* *te* - *e* - *ka*[2] *el* - *lu*[3]
(129) [*ur* - *ḫa* - *ka*] *ur* - *ru* - *ḫi* - *iš* *šu* - *tar* - *di* - *ma*
(130) [. . . .] *la* *ut-tak-ka*[4] *šu-te-e-ri*[5] *ar-ka-niš*

(131) [*iḫ* - *d*]*u* - *m*[*a* *b*]*e* - *lum* *a* - *na*[6] *a* - *mat* *a* - *bi* - *šu*
(132) [*e*]-*li-iṣ* *lib-ba-šu-ma* *a-na* *a-bi-šu*[7] *i-zak-kar*
(133) *be* - *lum* *ilāni*[8] *ši* - *mat*[9] *ilāni*[10] *rabūti*^{pl}
(134) *šum* - *ma* - *ma* *ana* - *ku* *mu* - *tir* *gi* - *mil* - *li* - *ku* - *un*
(135) *a-kam-me* *Ti-amat-ma*[11] *u* - *bal* - *laṭ* *ka* - *a* - *šu* - *un*
(136) *šuk-na-ma* *pu-uḫ-ra* *šu-te-ra* *i-ba-a* *šim-ti*[12]

(137) *ina* *Up-šu-ukkin-na-ki* *mit-ḫa-riš* *ḫa-diš* *tiš-ba-ma*[13]

(138) *ip-šu* *pi-ia* *ki-ma* *ka-tu-nu-ma*[14] *ši-ma-ta*[15] *lu-ši-im*

(139) *la* *ut-tak-kar* *mim*[16]-*mu-u* *a-ban-nu-u* *a-na-ku*
(140) *ai* *i-tur* *ai* *i-in-nin-na-a*[17] *se-ḳar* *ša-ap*[18]-*ti-ia*

---

[1] K. 4,832, [*gi-m*]*ir*. [2] No. 38,396, *ina te-e-ki*.

[3] K. 4,832, *el-li*.

[4] *ut-tak-ka* is possibly Pres. Iftaal from *naḳū*, or Pres. Piel from *etēḳu*, with (or without) the 2 m. s. pron. suffix; if the former, the beginning of the line may perhaps be restored as [*da-mi-ka*], as suggested in the translation.

[5] K. 4,832, [. . . -*i*]*r*; No. 92,632, *š*[*a-* . . .].

[6] K. 4,832 seems to have read [*in*]*a*.

[7] K. 4,832, *abi-šu*. [8] No. 40,559, [*ilāni*]^{pl}.

(127) "O my [son], who knoweth all wisdom,
(128) "Pacify [Tiama]t with thy pure incantation.
(129) "Speedily set out upon thy way,
(130) "For [thy blood (?)] shall not be poured out,[4] thou shalt return again."
(131) The lord rejoiced at the word of his father,
(132) His heart exulted, and unto his father he spake:
(133) "O Lord of the gods, Destiny of the great gods,
(134) "If I, your avenger,
(135) "Conquer Tiamat and give you life,
(136) "Appoint an assembly, make my fate pre-eminent and proclaim it.[12]
(137) "In Upšukkinaku seat yourselves joyfully together,
(138) "With my word in place of you will I decree fate.
(139) "May whatsoever I do remain unaltered,
(140) "May the word of my lips never be changed nor made of no avail."

---

[9] No. 40,559, *šīmāt*^{pl}. [10] K. 4,832 and No. 40,559, *ilāni*^{pl}.

[11] No. 40,559, [*T*]*i-amat-am-ma*.

[12] In No. 40,559, l. 136 reads: [. . .]-*uḫ-ru šu-te-ir-ba-' šim-tum*, "[Appoint an as]sembly, make my fate pre-eminent."

[13] In No. 40,559, l. 137 reads: [. . . -š]*u-ukkin-na-kam mit-ḫa-ri-iš ha-di-iš ti-iš-b*[*a*]*-ma*.

[14] No. 40,559, *ka-a-tu-nu-ma*. [15] No. 40,559, *tum*.

[16] No. 40,559, *mi-im*. [17] No. 40,559, *in-ni-na-a*.

[18] K. 292, *š*[*ap*].

The Third Tablet.

1. *An - šar pa - a - šu*[1] *i - pu - šam - ma*
2. [*a-na* ^{ilu}*Ga-ga suk-kal-li*][2]*-šu a-ma-tu i-zak-kar*
3. [^{ilu}*Ga - ga suk - kal*][2] *- lum mu - ṭib ka - bit - ti - ia*

4. [*a-na* ^{ilu}*Laḫ-mu u* ^{ilu}*La-ḫ*]*a*[2]*-mu ka-a-ta lu-uš-pur-ka*
5. [. . . . .][3] *ti - iṣ - bu - ru te - li - '*
6. [. . . . .] *šu-bi-ka ana maḫ-ri-ka*[4]

7. [. . . . . *il*]*āni*[5] *na - gab*[6] *- šu - un*
8. [*li - ša - nu liš - ku - n*]*u*[7] *ina ki - ri - e - ti liš - bu*[8]

9. [*aš - na - an li - k*]*u - [l*]*u*[7] *lip - ti - ḳu ku - ru - na*[9]
10. [*a-na* ^{ilu}*Marduk mu*][10]*-tir-ri gi-mil-li-šu-nu*[11] *li-ši-mu šim-ta*[12]

11. [*a - lik*][10] ^{ilu}*Ga - ga ḳud - me - šu - nu i - ziz - ma*[13]
12. [*mim-mu-u*][10] *a-zak-ka-ru-ka šu-un-na-a ana*[14] *ša-a-šu-un*

---

[1] The first two words in the line are restored from the catch-line in Tablet II; see K. 292 and No. 40,559.

[2] Lines 2–4 are conjecturally restored; for the restoration of l. 3, cf. the similar line spoken by Apsû when addressing Mummu in Tablet I, l. 31.

[3] Jensen compares l. 14, and suggests the restoration [*te-rit lib-bi-ia*], i.e. "[The purpose of my heart] thou canst understand."

[4] 82–9–18, 1,403 + 6,316 reads *ma-aḫ-ri-ia*, i.e. "thou shalt bring before *me*"; this reading gives better sense, as it is possible to refer the phrase to an answer to the summons, which Gaga is directed to bring from Laḫmu and Laḫamu. As, however, the duplicate is merely a practice-tablet containing extracts from the text, I have retained the reading of K. 3,473, etc.

The Third Tablet.

1. Anšar opened his mouth,[1] and
2. [Unto Gaga], his [minister],[2] spake the word:
3. "[O Gaga, thou minis]ter[2] that rejoicest my spirit,
4. "[Unto Laḫmu and Laḫ]amu[2] will I send thee.
5. "[. . . . .][3] thou canst attain,
6. "[. . . . .] thou shalt cause to be brought before thee.[4]
7. "[. . . . . let][5] the gods, all of them,
8. "[Make ready for a feast],[7] at a banquet let them sit,
9. "[Let them eat bread],[7] let them mix wine,
10. "[That for Marduk],[10] their avenger, they may decree the fate.
11. "[Go,][10] Gaga, stand before them,
12. "[And all that][10] I tell thee, repeat unto them, (and say):

---

[5] Jensen suggests the restoration [*li-il-li-ku-u-ni il*]*āni*, "let the gods come."

[6] 82–9–18, 1,403 + 6,316, [*g*]*a-ab*.

[7] Lines 8 and 9 are restored from ll. 133 and 134.

[8] 82–9–18, 1,403 + 6,316, *lu-uš-bu*.

[9] 82–9–18, 1,403 + 6,316, *ku-ru-un-nu*.

[10] Conjecturally restored.

[11] K. 3,437, etc., reads ŠU-*šu-nu*, i.e. *gimilli-šu-nu*.

[12] 82–9–18, 1,403 + 6,316, *šim-tum*.

[13] 82–9–18, 1,403 + 6,316, *ku-ud-mi-šu-nu i-zi-iz-ma*.

[14] 82–9–18, 1,403 + 6,316, *a-na*.

13. *[An - šar]*[1] *ma - ru - ku - nu u - ma - ' - i - ra - an - ni*
14. *[te - rit]*[2] *libbi - šu u - ša - aṣ - bi - ra - an - ni ia - a - ti*

15. *[um-ma Ti-a]mat*[3] *a-lit-ta-ni*[4] *i-zir-ra-an-na-ši*[5]

16. *[pu - uḫ - ru šit - k]u*[6] *- na - at - ma ag - giš lab - bat*
17. *is - ḫu - ru - šim - ma ilāni gi - mir - šu - un*
18. *a - di ša aṭ - tu - nu tab - na - a i - da - ša al - ka*

19. *im-ma-aṣ-ru-nim-ma i-du-uš*[7] *Ti-amat te-bu-u-ni*[8]

20. *iz - zu kap - du la sa - ki - pu mu - ša u im - ma*[9]

21. *na - šu - u tam - ḫa - ri*[10] *na - zar - bu - bu lab - bu*[11]
22. *unken-na šit*[12]*-ku-nu-ma i-ban-nu-u ṣu-la-a-[ti]*[13]

23. *Um - mu - Ḫu - bur*[14] *pa - ti - ḳat*[15] *ka - la - [ma]*[16]
24. *uš-rad-di ka-ak-ki la maḫ-ri it-ta-lad ṣirmaḫē[pl]*[17]

25. *zaḳ - tu - ma šin - ni*[18] *la pa - du - u at - ta - ' - [i]*[19]
26. *im-tu ki-ma da-mi*[20] *zu-mur-šu-nu uš-ma-al-l[i]*[21]

---

[1] Restored from l. 71.
[2] Restored from l. 72.
[3] Restored from l. 73.
[4] 82–9–18, 1,403 + 6,316, *nu*.
[5] 82–9–18, 1,403 + 6,316, *i-zi-ir-ra-an-na-a-ti*.
[6] Restored from l. 74.
[7] 82–9–18, 6,950 + 83–1–18, 1,868, *i-du-šu*.
[8] 82–9–18, 6,950, etc., *te-bi-u-ni*.
[9] 82–9–18, 6,950, etc., *im-mu*.
[10] 82–9–18, 6,950, etc., *ru*.
[11] 82–9–18, 6,950, etc., *la-ab-bu*.
[12] 82–9–18, 6,950, etc., *[š]i-it*.

13. " [Anšar],[1] your son, hath sent me,
14. " [The purpose][2] of his heart he hath made known unto me.
15. " [He saith that Tia]mat[3] our mother hath conceived a hatred for us,
16. " [With all][6] her force she rageth, full of wrath.
17. " All the gods have turned to her,
18. " With those, whom ye created, they go at her side.
19. " They are banded together, and at the side of Tiamat they advance;
20. " They are furious, they devise mischief without resting night and day.
21. " They prepare for battle, fuming and raging;
22. " They have joined their forces and are making war.
23. " Ummu-Ḫubur, who formed all things,
24. " Hath made in addition weapons invincible, she hath spawned monster-serpents,
25. " Sharp of tooth and merciless of fang.
26. " With poison instead of blood she hath filled their bodies.

---

[13] Restored from l. 80; 82–9–18, 6,950, etc., reads *tum*.

[14] 82–9–18, 6,950, etc., *bu-ur*. [15] 82–9–18, 6,950, etc., *ḳa-at*.

[16] Restored from l. 81; 82–9–18, 6,950, etc., reads *mu*.

[17] Restored from l. 82. [18] 82–9–18, 6,950, etc., *ši-in-na*.

[19] Restored from l. 83; 82–9–18, 6,950, etc., reads *an-ta-'-a[m]*.

[20] 82–9–18, 6,950, etc., *da-me*.

[21] Lines 26–32 have been restored from ll. 84–90.

27. *ušumgallē*^{pl} *na-ad-ru-u-ti* *pul-ḫa-a-ti* *u-šal-biš-*[*ma*]

28. *me - lam - me* *uš - daš - ša - a* *e - liš* *um - taš -* [*šil*][1]

29. *a - mir - šu - nu* *šar - ba - ba* *liš - ḫar -* [*mi - im*]

30. *zu-mur-šu-nu* *liš-taḫ-ḫi-dam-ma* *la* *i-ni-'-u* *i-rat-su-*[*un*]

31. *uš - ziz* *ba - aš - mu* *ṣir - ruš - šu* *u* ^{ilu}*La - ḫa -* [*mi*]

32. *u - gal - lum* UR - BE[2] *u* *akrab - amēl*[*u*]

33. *u - mi* *da - ab - ru - ti* *nūn - amēlu* *u* *ku - sa - riḳ -* [*ḳu*][3]
34. *na - aš* *kakkē*^{pl} *la* *pa - di - i* *la* *a-di-ru* *ta-ḫ*[*a-zi*][4]

35. *gab - ša* *te - ri - tu - ša* *la* *ma - ḫar* *ši - na - a -* [*ma*]

36. *ap-pu-un-na-ma* *eš-tin* *eš-ri-tum* *kīma* *šu-a-tu* *uš-tab-*[*ši*]

37. *i-na* *ilāni* *bu-uk-ri-ša* *šu-ut* *iš - kun - ši* [*pu-uḫ-ri*]

38. *u-ša-aš-ki* ^{ilu}*Kin-gu* *ina* *bi-ri-šu-*[*nu* *ša-a-šu*] *uš-rab-*[*bi-iš*]

39. [*a*]*-li-kut* *maḫ-ri* *pa-an* *um-ma-ni* [*mu-ir-ru-ut* *puḫri*]
40. [*na-a*]*š* *kakkē*^{pl}[5] *ti-iṣ-bu-tu* *ti-*[*bu-u* *a-na-an-tu*]

41. [*šu - ud*] *tam - ḫa - ri* *ra - ab* *šik -* [*ka - tu - ti*]

---

[1] See above, p. 16 f., note 5. [2] See above, p. 18, note 3.
[3] Restored from Tablet II, l. 29.

27. " Fierce monster-vipers she hath clothed with terror,
28. " With splendour she hath decked them, she hath made them of lofty stature.
29. " Whoever beholdeth them, terror overcometh him,
30. " Their bodies rear up and none can withstand their attack.
31. " She hath set up vipers, and dragons, and the (monster) Laḫamu,
32. " And hurricanes, and raging hounds, and scorpion-men,
33. " And mighty tempests, and fish-men, and rams ;
34. " They bear merciless weapons, without fear of the fight.
35. " Her commands are mighty, none can resist them ;
36. " After this fashion, huge of stature, hath she made eleven (monsters).
37. " Among the gods who are her sons, inasmuch as he hath given her [support],
38. " She hath exalted Kingu ; in their midst she hath raised [him] to power.
39. " To march before the forces, [to lead the host],
40. " [To] give the battle-signal, to advance [to the attack],
41. " [To direct] the battle, to control the [fight],

[4] Lines 34–45 have been restored from ll. 92–103.
[5] K. 6,650, [*na-ša-*]*a*, or [*na-še-*]*e*, *kakku*.

42 [*ip-ḳid*]-*ma ḳa-tuš-šu u-še-ši-ba-aš*-[*šu ina kar-ri*]

43. [*ad-d*]*i ta-a-ka ina puḫur ilāni* [*u-šar-bi-ka*]

44. [*ma*]-*li-ku-ut ilāni gi-mir*-[*šu-nu*[1] *ḳa-tuk-ka*[2] *uš-mal-li*]

45. [*lu-u*] *šur-ba-ta-ma ḫa-'-i-ri*[3] *e-du*-[*u at-ta*]

46. *li-ir-tab-bu-u zik-ru-ka eli kalī-šu-n*[*u* . . ^{ilu}*A-nun-na-ki*][4]

47. *id-din-šum*[5]-*ma dupšīmāti*^{pl} *i-ra-tu-uš*[6] *u-šat-mi-iḫ*

48. *ka-ta ḳibīt-ka la in-nin-na-a li-kun ṣi-it pi-i*-[*ka*][7]

49. *in-na-nu* ^{ilu}*Kin-gu šu-uš-ḳu-u li-ḳu-u* [^{ilu}*A-nu-ti*][8]

50. *an ilāni mārē*^{pl}-*ša*[9] *ši-ma-ta*[10] *iš-t*[*i-mu*][11]

51. *ip-šu*[12] *pi-ku-nu*[13] ^{ilu}*Gibil*[14] *li-ni-iḫ-ḫa*

52. *nā'id ina*[15] *kit-mu-ri*[16] *ma-ag-ša-ri liš-rab-bi-ib*[17]

---

[1] K. 6,650, *gim-rat-su-nu.*

[2] K. 6,650, *ḳa-tuš-š*[*u*]; according to this reading, l. 44 does not form part of Tiamat's speech, or we may suppose that in this line Tiamat addresses her followers and not Kingu (cf. note 7).

[3] K. 6,650, *ḫa-'-ri.*

[4] Restored from l. 104; the Anunnaki are possibly the subject of the sentence (see below, p. 52 f., note 8).

[5] K. 6,650, *šu.*

[6] So No. 42,285; K. 6,650 reads *i-ra-a*[*t-su*].

[7] Restored from Tablet II, l. 44; No. 42,285 reads *pi-i-šu,* "the word of his mouth shall be established," i.e., Tiamat addresses her followers in the second half of the line.

[8] Restored from Tablet II, l. 45; No. 42,285 reads *e-nu-ti,* "lordship, rule."

42. "Unto him [hath she entrusted; in costly raiment] she hath made him sit, (saying):
43. "'[I have] uttered thy spell, in the assembly of the gods [I have raised thee to power],
44. "'[The] dominion over all the gods [have I entrusted unto thee].
45. "'[Be] thou exalted, [thou] my chosen spouse,
46. "'May they magnify thy name over all of [them . . . . the Anunnaki].'
47. "She hath given him the Tablets of Destiny, on his breast she laid them, (saying):
48. "'Thy command shall not be without avail, and the word of [thy][7] mouth shall be established.'
49. "Now Kingu, (thus) exalted, having received [the power of Anu],[8]
50. "Decreed the fate for the gods, her sons, (saying):
51. "'Let the opening of your mouth quench the Fire-god[14];
52. "'Whoso is exalted in the battle, let him display (his) might!'

---

[9] K. 6,650, *mārē-ša*; No. 93,017, *ma-ri-e-ša*.

[10] No. 93,017, *ši-ma-tu*; No. 42,285, *ši-ma-ti*.

[11] Restored from Tablet II, l. 46; No. 42,285 reads *uš-ti-u*, or *uš-ti-šam*.

[12] K. 6,650, [*ip-š*]*a*.

[13] K. 6,650, *pi-i-ku-nu*; No. 93,017, *pi-ku-un*.

[14] K. 6,650 and No. 93,017, *ilu* BIL-GI; K. 3,473, etc., and No. 42,285, *ilu* GIŠ-BAR.

[15] *ina* is omitted by K. 6,650 and No. 93,017.

[16] No. 93,017, *kit-mu-ra*; 82–9–18, 1,403 + 6,316, *kit-mu-ru*. K. 6,650 probably reads *kit* (not *šit*)-*mu-ra*.

[17] 82–9–18, 1,403, etc., *li-ra-ab-bi-ib*.

53. *aš-pur-ma ilu A-nu-um*[1] *ul i-li-'-a*[2] *ma-ḫar*[3]*-ša*
54. *ilu Nu-dim-mud i-dur-ma*[4] *i-tu-ra ar-kiš*[5]
55. *'-ir ilu Marduk ab-kal-lu*[6] *ilāni ma-ru-ku-un*[7]

56. *ma-ḫa-riš*[8] *Ti-amat*[9] *lib*[10]*-ba-šu a-ra ub-la*

57. *ip-šu pi-i-šu i-ta-ma-a a-na ia-a-ti*

58. *šum-ma-ma a-na-ku mu-tir*[11] *gi-mil-li-ku-un*
59. *a-kam-me Ti-amat-ma*[12] *u-bal-laṭ ka-šu-un*[13]
60. *šuk-na-a-ma*[14] *pu-uḫ-ru*[15] *šu-ti*[16]*-ra i-ba-a šim-ti*

61. *i-na Up-šu-ukkin-na-ki*[17] *mit-ḫa-riš*[18] *ḫa-diš*[19] *taš-ba-ma*[20]

62. *ip-šu pi-ia ki-ma ka-tu-nu-ma*[21] *ši-ma-tu lu-šim-ma*[22]
63. *la ut-tak-kar mim*[23]*-mu-u a-ban-nu-u a-na-ku*
64. *ai i-tur*[24] *ai in-nin-na-a se-ḳar šap-ti-ia*[25]

65. *ḫu-um-ṭa-nim-ma ši-mat-ku-nu ar-ḫiš*[26] *ši-ma-šu*

---

[1] K. 6,650, No. 93,017, and 82–9–18, 1,403, etc., *ilu A-num.*
[2] 82–9–18, 1,403, etc., *i-li-'-im*; No. 42,285, *i-li-'-i.*
[3] No. 42,285, *ḫa-ar.*
[4] 82–9–18, 1,403, etc., *i-du-ur-ma.*
[5] No. 42,285, *ki-iš.*
[6] No. 93,017, 82–9–18, 1,403, etc., and No. 42,285, *abkal.*
[7] No. 42,285, *ma-ruk-ku-un.*
[8] 82–9–18, 1,403, etc., *ri-iš.*
[9] No. 93,017, *Ti-a-ma-ti.*
[10] 82–9–18, 1,403, etc., *li-ib.*
[11] 82–9–18, 1,403, etc., *mu-tir-ri.*
[12] No. 93,017, *Tam-tam-ma*; 82–9–18, 1,403, etc., and No. 42,285, *Ti-amat-am-ma.*

53. " I sent Anu, but he could not withstand her;
54. " Nudimmud was afraid and turned back.
55. " But Marduk hath set out, the director of the gods, your son;
56. " To set out against Tiamat his heart hath prompted (him).
57. " He opened his mouth and spake unto me, (saying):
58. " ' If I, your avenger,
59. " ' Conquer Tiamat and give you life,
60. " ' Appoint an assembly, make my fate pre-eminent and proclaim it.
61. " ' In Upšukkinaku seat yourselves joyfully together;
62. " ' With my word in place of you will I decree fate.
63. " ' May whatsoever I do remain unaltered,
64. " ' May the word of my lips never be changed nor made of no avail.'
65. " Hasten, therefore, and swiftly decree for him the fate which you bestow,

---

[13] No. 42,285, *ka-a-šu-un.* [14] No. 93,017, *šuk-na-ma.*
[15] No. 93,017, *ra.* [16] 82-9-18, 1,403, etc., *te.*
[17] No. 93,017, *ku*; 82-9-18, 1,403, etc., *kam.*
[18] 82-9-18, 1,403, etc., *mi-it-ha-ri-*[*iš*].
[19] No. 42,285, *di-iš.* [20] No. 42,285, *ta-aš-ba-ma.*
[21] 82-9-18, 1,403, etc., *ka-a-tu-*[*nu-ma*].
[22] No. 42,285, *ši-ma-tum lu-ši-im.* [23] 82-9-18, 1,403, etc., *mi-im.*
[24] 82-9-18, 1,403, etc., *tu-ur.* [25] No. 42,285, *šap-ti-i.*
[26] 82-9-18, 1,403, etc., No. 42,285 and 82-9-18, 5,448 + 83-1-18, 2,116, *ar-ḫi-iš.*

66. *lil - lik*[1] *lim - ḫu - ra*[2] *na - kar - ku - nu dan - nu*
67. *il - lik* *ilu Ga - ga ur - ḫa - šu u - šar - di - ma*
68. *aš - riš* *ilu Laḫ-mu u* *ilu La-ḫa-me*[3] *ilāni pl*[4] *abē pl-šu*[5]

69. *uš - kin - ma iš - šiḳ*[6] *ḳaḳ - ḳa - ra*[7] *ša - pal - šu - un*[8]

70. *i - šir*[9] *iz - ziz - ma*[10] *i - zak - kar - šu - un*

71. *An - šar*[11] *ma - ru*[12] *- ku - nu u - ma - ' - ir - an - ni*[13]
72. *te - rit lib - bi - šu*[14] *u - ša - aṣ - bi - ra - an - ni*[15] *ia-a-ti*

73. *um - ma Ti - amat a - lit - ta - ni*[16] *i-zir-ra-an-na-ši*[17]

74. *pu-uḫ-ru*[18] *šit*[19] *- ku - na - at - ma ag - giš*[20] *lab*[21] *- bat*
75. *iš - ḫu - ru - šim - ma ilāni gi - mir*[22] *- šu - un*
76. *a - di ša at - tu - nu tab - na - a i - da - ša*[23] *al - ku*[24]
77. *im-ma-aṣ-ru-nim-ma i-du-uš*[25] *Ti-a-ma-ti*[26] *te-bu-ni*[27]

---

1 82–9–18, 1,403, etc., and 82–9–18, 5,448, etc., insert *ma*.
2 No. 42,285, [. . .]-*ḫir*.
3 82–9–18, 1,403, etc., and 82–9–18, 5,448, etc., *ilu La-ḫa-mu*.
4 82–9–18, 1,403, etc., No. 42,285 and 82–9–18, 5,448, etc., *ilāni*.
5 No. 42,285 and 82–9–18, 5,448, etc., *ab-bi-e-šu*.
6 82–9–18, 1,403, etc., *ši-iḳ*.
7 No. 42,285 and 82–9–18, 5,448, etc., *ru*; K. 8,575, *ri*.
8 82–9–18, 1,403, etc., No. 42,285 and 82–9–18, 5,448, etc., read *ma-ḫar-šu-un*, "before them."
9 No. 93,017 reads *ik-mis*, "he bowed himself down."
10 82–9–18, 1,403, etc., *iz-za-az*; No. 42,285 and 82–9–18, 5,448, etc., [. . .]-*az*.
11 No. 93,017 and 82–9–18, 1,403, *An-šar-ma*.
12 No. 93,017, *ri*.

66. "That he may go and fight your strong enemy!"
67. Gaga went, he took his way and
68. Humbly before Laḫmu and Laḫamu, the gods, his fathers,
69. He made obeisance, and he kissed the ground at their feet.[8]
70. He humbled himself;[9] then he stood up and spake unto them, (saying):
71. "Anšar, your son, hath sent me,
72. "The purpose of his heart he hath made known unto me.
73. "He saith that Tiamat our mother hath conceived a hatred for us,
74. "With all her force she rageth, full of wrath.
75. "All the gods have turned to her,
76. "With those, whom ye created, they go at her side.
77. "They are banded together and at the side of Tiamat they advance;

[13] 82–9–18, 1,403, etc., and 82–9–18, 5,448, etc., *u-ma-'-i-ra-an-*[*ni*].

[14] 82–9–18, 1,403, etc., [*te-r*]*i-it libbi-šu*.

[15] No. 93,017, *u-ša-aṣ-bir-an-ni*. [16] 82–9–18, 1,403, *nu*.

[17] 82–9–18, 1,403, *i-zi-ir-ra-an-na-ti*; No. 42,285, *iz-zi-ir-ra-an-na-a-ti*.

[18] No. 93,017, *ra*. [19] 82–9–18, 1,403, etc., *ši-it*.

[20] 82–9–18, 1,403, etc., and No. 42,285, *gi-iš*.

[21] No. 93,017, 82–9–18, 1,403, etc., and No. 42,285, *la-ab*.

[22] 82–9–18, 1,403, etc., and No. 42,285, *mi-ir*.

[23] K. 8,575, *i-da-a-ša*. [24] No. 42,285, *al ka*.

[25] K. 8,575, *i-du-šu*.

[26] K. 8,524 and K. 8,575, *Ta-a-ma-ti*; No. 42,285, *Ti-amat*.

[27] No. 42,285, *te-bi-ni*.

78. *iz - zu kap - du la sa - ki - pu mu - ši*[1] *u im - ma*[2]

79. *na - šu - u tam - ḫa - ri*[3] *na - zar - bu - bu lab - bu*[4]
80. *unken-na*[5] *šit-ku-nu-ma i - ban - nu - u*[6] *ṣu - la - a - ti*[7]

81. *Um - mu - Ḫu - bur pa - ti - ḳat*[8] *ka - la - ma*[9]
82. *uš - rad - di kakkē*[pl] *la maḫ-ri*[10] *it-ta-lad ṣirmaḫē*[pl][11]

83. *zaḳ - tu - ma šin - ni la pa - du - u at - ta - ' - i*[12]
84. *im-ta kīma da-a-mi*[13] *zu-mur-šu-nu*[14] *uš-ma-al-li*[15]

85. *ušumgallē*[pl] *na-ad-ru-ti pul-ḫa-a-ti*[16] *u - šal - biš - ma*

86. *me - lam - me uš - daš - ša - a i - liš*[17] *um - taš - šil*[18]

87. *a - mir - šu - nu šar - ba - ba li - iḫ - ḫar - mi - im*
88. *zu-mir-šu-nu*[19] *liš-taḫ-ḫi-dam-ma la i-ni-'-u irat-su-un*

89. *uš - ziz ba - aš - mu ṣir - ruš - šu*[20] *u* [ilu]*La - ḫa - mi*

90. *u - gal - lum* UR - BE[21] *u aḳrab - amēlu*

---

[1] K. 8,575 and No. 42,285, *mu-ša*.
[2] No. 42,285, *im-mu*.
[3] No. 93,017, *ra*.
[4] No. 42,285 and No. 93,017, *la-ab-bu*.
[5] No. 93,017, *un-ki-en-na*.
[6] No. 42,285, [*i-ba*]*n-nu-ma*.
[7] No. 93,017, *tum*.
[8] No. 42,285, *ḳa-at*.
[9] No. 42,285, *mu*.
[10] No. 93,017, *kakku la ma-ḫar*.
[11] No. 42,285, *ṣir-maḫ*; No. 93,017, *ṣir-maḫ-i*.
[12] No. 42,285 reads *la-at-'-im*, a scribal error for *at-ta-'-im*.

78. "They are furious, they devise mischief without resting night and day.
79. "They prepare for battle, fuming and raging;
80. "They have joined their forces and are making war.
81. "Ummu-Ḫubur, who formed all things,
82. "Hath made in addition weapons invincible, she hath spawned monster-serpents,
83. "Sharp of tooth and merciless of fang.
84. "With poison instead of blood she hath filled their bodies.
85. "Fierce monster-vipers she hath clothed with terror,
86. "With splendour she hath decked them, she hath made them of lofty stature.[17]
87. "Whoever beholdeth them, terror overcometh him,
88. "Their bodies rear up and none can withstand their attack.
89. "She hath set up vipers, and dragons, and the (monster) Laḫamu,
90. "And hurricanes, and raging hounds, and scorpion-men,

[13] No. 93,017, *im-tu ki-ma da-mi.*

[14] No. 42,285 seems to have had a variant reading.

[15] No. 42,285, *la.*

[16] K. 8,524, *pul-ḫa-ta.*

[17] K. 8,524, *e-liš*; see above, p. 16 f., note 5.

[18] No. 42,285, [*u*]*m-taš-ši-il.*

[19] No. 93,017, *zu-mur-šu-nu.*

[20] No. 93,017, [ilu] ṢIR-RUŠ[pl].

[21] No. 93,017, UD-GAL[pl] UR-BE[pl]; for the ideogram UR-BE, see above, p. 18, note 3.

91. *ūmē*^{pl} *da-ab-ru-ti nūn-amēlu u* [*ku-sa-riḳ-ḳu*][1]

92. *na-aš kakkē*^{pl}[2] *la pa-di-i la a-di-ru ta-ḫa-zi*

93. *gab-ša te-ri-tu-ša la ma-ḫar ši-na-ma*
94. *ap-pu-un-na-ma*[3] *iš-tin eš-rit ki-ma šu-a-tu uš-tab-ši*

95. *i-na*[4] *ilāni bu-uk-ri-ša šu-ut iš-ku-nu-ši pu-uḫ-ri*

96. *u-ša-aš-ki* ^{ilu}*Kin-gu ina bi-ri-šu-nu ša-a-šu uš-rab-bi-iš*

97. *a-li-ku-ut maḫ-ri*[5] *pa-an um-ma-ni mu-ir-ru-ut puḫri*
98. *na-aš kakkē*^{pl}[6] *ti-iṣ-bu-tu te-bu-u a-na-an-tu*
99. *šu-ud tam-ḫa-ri*[7] *ra-ab šik-ka-tu-ti*
100. *ip-ḳid-ma ḳa-tuš-šu u-še-ši-ba-aš-šu ina kar-ri*

101. *ad-di ta-a-ka ina puḫur ilāni u-šar-bi-ka*

102. *ma-li-kut ilāni gim-rat-su-nu ḳa-tuk-ka uš-mal-li*

103. *lu-u šur-ba-ta-ma ḫa-i-ri e-du-u at-ta*
104. *li-ir-tab-bu-u zik-ru-ka eli kalī-šu-nu . . .* ^{ilu}*A-nun-na-*[*ki*][8]

105. *id-d*[*in-š*]*um-ma dupšīmāti*^{pl} *i-ra-a*[*t-su u-šat-mi-iḫ*][9]

---

[1] Restored from Tablet II, l. 29; No. 93,017 reads ḪA[erasure]-KI.
[2] No. 93,017, *kak-ku.*
[3] No. 93,017, *ap-pu-na-ma.*
[4] No. 93,017, *ina.*
[5] No. 93,017, *a-li-kut ma-ḫar.*
[6] No. 93,017, *na-še-e kakku.*
[7] No. 93,017, *ra.*
[8] In the parallel passage in l. 46, K. 6,650 reads KAK (i.e. *kalī*)-

91. "And mighty tempests, and fish-men, and [rams];[1]
92. "They bear merciless weapons, without fear of the fight.
93. "Her commands are mighty, none can resist them;
94. "After this fashion, huge of stature, hath she made eleven (monsters).
95. "Among the gods who are her sons, inasmuch as he hath given her support,
96. "She hath exalted Kingu; in their midst she hath raised him to power.
97. "To march before the forces, to lead the host,
98. "To give the battle-signal, to advance to the attack,
99. "To direct the battle, to control the fight,
100. "Unto him hath she entrusted; in costly raiment she hath made him sit, (saying):
101. "'I have uttered thy spell, in the assembly of the gods I have raised thee to power,
102. "'The dominion over all the gods have I entrusted unto thee.
103. "'Be thou exalted, thou my chosen spouse,
104. "'May they magnify thy name over all of them . . . . the Anunna[ki].'
105. "She hath given him the Tablets of Destiny, on [his] breast [she laid them], (saying):

šu-n[u . . .]. In the present line on No. 93,017 there are traces of *kalī-šu-nu* followed by traces of two signs and by the word *ilu A-nun-na-[ki]* which ends the line. The Anunnaki are possibly the subject of the sentence.

[2] Line 105 has been restored from l. 47.

106. *ka-ta ḳibīt-ka la in-nin-*[*na-a li-kun ṣi-it pi-i-ka*][1]

107. *in-na-na* ^{ilu}*Kin-gu šu-uš-ḳu-*[*u li-ḳu-u* ^{ilu}*A-nu-ti*]

108. *an ilāni mārē*^{pl} *- ša ši -* [*ma - ta iš - ti - mu*]

109. *ip - šu pi - i - ku - nu* ^{ilu}*Gibil* [*li - ni - iḫ - ḫa*][2]

110. *nā'id ina kit-mu-ru ma-ag-š*[*a-ri liš - rab - bi - ib*]

111. *aš - pur - ma* ^{ilu}*A-nu-um ul i-*[*li - ' - a ma - ḫar - ša*]
112. ^{ilu}*Nu - dim - mud e - dur - ma i -* [*tu - ra ar - kiš*]
113. *' - ir* ^{ilu}*Marduk ab - kal -* [*lu i*]*lā*[*ni ma - ru - ku - un*]

114. *ma - ḫa - riš Ti - amat li*[*b-ba-šu a - ra ub - la*]

115. *ip - šu pi - i - šu* [*i - ta - ma - a a - na ia - a - ti*]

116. *šum - ma - ma a-na-ku* [*mu - tir gi - mil - li - ku - un*]
117. *a - kam - me Ti - amat - m*[*a u - bal - laṭ ka - šu - un*]
118. *šuk-na-a-ma pu-uḫ-ru š*[*u - ti - ra i - ba - a šim - ti*]

119. *i-na Up-šu-ukkin-na-ki mi*[*t-ḫa-riš ḫa-diš taš-ba-ma*]

120. *ip-šu pi-ia ki-ma k*[*a-tu-nu-ma ši-ma-tu lu-šim-ma*]
121. *la ut-tak-kar mim-m*[*u*]*-u a-ban-nu-u* [*a-na-ku*]
122. [*a*]*i i - tur* [*ai in*] *- nin - na - a se - ḳar* [*šap - ti - ia*]

---

[1] Lines 106–108 have been restored from ll. 48–50 and Tablet II, ll. 44–46.

106. " 'Thy command shall not be without avail, [and the word of thy mouth shall be established].' [1]
107. " Now Kingu, (thus) exalted, [having received the power of Anu],
108. " [Decreed the fate] for the gods, her sons, (saying):
109. " 'Let the opening of your mouth [quench] [2] the Fire-god;
110. " 'Whoso is exalted in the battle, [let him display] (his) might!'
111. " I sent Anu, but he could not [withstand her];
112. " Nudimmud was afraid and [turned back].
113. " But Marduk hath set out, the director of the [gods, your son];
114. " To set out against Tiamat [his heart hath prompted (him)].
115. " He opened his mouth [and spake unto me], (saying):
116. " 'If I, [your avenger],
117. " 'Conquer Tiamat and [give you life],
118. " 'Appoint an assembly, [make my fate pre-eminent and proclaim it].
119. " 'In Upšukkinaku [seat yourselves joyfully together];
120. " 'With my word in place of [you will I decree fate].
121. " 'May whatsoever [I] do remain unaltered,
122. " 'May the word of [my lips] never be changed nor made of no avail.'

[2] Lines 109–124 have been restored from ll. 51–66.

123. *[ḫ]u-um-ṭa-nim-ma ši-mat-ku-nu ar-ḫiš [ši-ma-šu]*

124. *[l]il-lik lim-ḫu-ra na-kar-ku-nu dan-nu*
125. *[i]š-mu-ma* ^ilu^ *Laḫ-ḫa* ^ilu^ *La-ḫa-mu is-su-u e-li-tum*
126. ^ilu^ *Igigi nap-ḫar-šu-nu i-nu-ḳu mar-ṣi-iš*
127. *mi-na-a nak-ra a-di ir-šu-u ṣi-bi-it n[e- . . .]*[1]

128. *la ni-i-di ni-i-ni ša Ti-amat e-p[iš-ti-ša]*[2]
129. *ik-ša-šu-nim-ma il-lak-[ku-ni]*[3]
130. *ilāni rabūti ka-li-šu-nu mu-šim-[mu šim-ti]*[3]
131. *i-ru-bu-ma mut-ti-iš An-šar im-lu-u [. . . .]*
132. *in-niš-ḳu*[4] *a-ḫu-u a-ḫi ina puḫri [. . . .]*
133. *li-ša-nu iš-ku-nu ina ki-ri-e-ti [uš-bu]*[5]

134. *aš-na-an i-ku-lu ip-ti-ḳu [ku-ru-na]*[6]
135. *ši-ri-sa mat-ḳu u-sa-an-ni [. . .]-[r]a-[d]i*[7]*-šu-[un]*
136. *ši-ik-ru ina ša-te-e ḫa-ba-ṣu zu-um-[ri]*[3]

137. *ma-'-diš e-gu-u ka-bit-ta-šu-un*[8] *i-te-el-[li]*[3]
138. *a-na* ^ilu^ *Marduk mu-tir gi-mil-li-šu-nu i-šim-mu šim-[tu]*[3]

---

[1] The characters *ṣi-bi-it* are clearly written on 82–9–18, 1,403, etc., and they are followed by traces of the sign *ne*.

[2] There is room for this restoration.

[3] Conjectural restoration.

[4] *in-niš-ḳu* may be taken as the Nifal of *našāḳu*; cf. Tablet II, l. 116, where Anšar is described as kissing Marduk upon the lips.

123. " Hasten, therefore, and swiftly [decree for him] the fate which you bestow,
124. " That he may go and fight your strong enemy ! "
125. Laḫmu and Laḫamu heard and cried aloud,
126. All of the Igigi wailed bitterly, (saying) :
127. " What has been altered so that they should . . . [. . . .]
128. " We do not understand the d[eed] of Tiamat ! "
129. Then did they collect and go,
130. The great gods, all of them, who decree [fate].
131. They entered in before Anšar, they filled [. . .] ;
132. They kissed one another,[4] in the assembly [. . .].
133. They made ready for the feast, at the banquet [they sat] ;
134. They ate bread, they mixed [sesame-wine].[6]
135. The sweet drink, the mead, confused their [. .],
136. They were drunk with drinking, their bodies were filled.
137. They were wholly at ease, their spirit was exalted ;
138. Then for Marduk, their avenger, did they decree the fate.

---

[5] It is possible that more than two signs are wanting, in which case a longer form of the verb must have been employed.

[6] Restored from l. 9.

[7] The traces are possibly those of *mi*; one sign is wanting at the beginning of the word.

[8] The reading *ka-bit-ta-šu-un* is certain.

The Fourth Tablet.

1. *id - du - šum - ma   pa - rak   ru - bu - tim*[1]
2. *ma-ḫa-ri-iš   ab-bi-e-šu   a-na   ma-li-ku-tum   ir-me*[2]
3. *at - ta - ma   kab - ta - ta   i - na   ilāni   ra - bu - tum*
4. *ši-mat-ka   la   ša-na-an   se - ḳar - ka* ^{ilu}*A - num*
5. ^{ilu}*Marduk   kab - ta - ta   i - na   ilāni   ra - bu - tum*

6. *ši-mat-ka   la   ša-na-an   se - ḳar - ka* ^{ilu}*A - num*
7. *iš - tu   u - mi - im - ma   la   in - nin - na - a   ki - bit - ka*

8. *šu - uš - ḳu - u   u   šu - uš - pu - lu   ši - i   lu - u   ga - at - ka*
9. *lu-u   ki-na-at   ṣi-it   pi-i-ka   la   sa-ra-ar   se-ḳar-ka*

10. *ma-am-ma-an   i-na   ilāni   i - tuk - ka   la   it - ti - iḳ*

11. *za - na - nu - tum   ir - šat   pa - rak   ilāni - ma*
12. *a - šar   sa - gi - šu - nu   lu-u   ku-un   aš - ru - uk - ka*

13. ^{ilu}*Marduk   at - ta - ma   mu - tir - ru   gi - mil - li - ni*
14. *ni-id-din-ka   šar-ru-tum   kiš - šat   kal   gim - ri - e - ti*
15. *ti-šam-ma   i-na   pu-ḫur*[3]   *lu - u   ša - ga - ta   a-mat-ka*

16. *kak-ki-ka   ai   ip-pal-tu-u   li - ra - i - su   na - ki - ri - ka*

---

[1] The catch-line on the Third Tablet, preserved by K. 3,473, etc., reads *ru-bu-u-ti*.

[2] The lines which follow contain the words addressed by the gods to Marduk, after he had taken his seat in their presence.

The Fourth Tablet.

1. They prepared for him a lordly chamber,
2. Before his fathers as prince he took his place.[2]
3. "Thou art chiefest among the great gods,
4. "Thy fate is unequalled, thy word is Anu!
5. "O Marduk, thou art chiefest among the great gods,
6. "Thy fate is unequalled, thy word is Anu!
7. "Henceforth not without avail shall be thy command,
8. "In thy power shall it be to exalt and to abase.
9. "Established shall be the word of thy mouth, irresistible shall be thy command;
10. "None among the gods shall transgress thy boundary.
11. "Abundance, the desire of the shrines of the gods,
12. "Shall be established in thy sanctuary, even though they lack (offerings).
13. "O Marduk, thou art our avenger!
14. "We give thee sovereignty over the whole world.
15. "Sit thou down in might,[3] be exalted in thy command.
16. "Thy weapon shall never lose its power, it shall crush thy foe.

---

[3] This is preferable to the rendering "take thy seat in the assembly (of the gods)"; for the other gods had an equal right to sit in the assembly.

17. *be - lum ša tak - lu - ka na - piš - ta - šu gi - mil - ma*

18. *u ilu ša lim-ni-e-ti i-ḫu-zu tu - bu - uk nap - šat - su*

19. *uš - zi - zu - ma i - na bi-ri-šu-nu lu - ba - šu iš - ten*
20. *a-na* ^{ilu}*Marduk bu-uk-ri-šu-nu šu - nu iz - zak - ru*
21. *ši - mat - ka be - lum lu-u maḫ-ra-at ilāni-ma*

22. *a - ba - tum u ba - nu - u ki - bi li - ik - tu - nu*

23. *ip - ša pi - i - ka li - ' - a - bit lu - ba - šu*
24. *tu - ur ki - bi - šum - ma lu - ba - šu li - iš - lim*

25. *iḳ - bi - ma i-na pi - i - šu ' - a - bit lu - ba - šu*

26. *i - tu - ur iḳ - bi - 'um - ma lu - ba - šu it - tab - ni*

27. *ki - ma ṣi - it pi - i - šu i-mu-ru ilāni ab-bi-e-šu*

28. *iḫ - du - u ik - ru - bu* ^{ilu}*Marduk - ma šar - ru*

29. *u - uṣ - ṣi - pu - šu* ^{iṣu}*ḫaṭṭa* ^{iṣu}*kussā u palā(a)*[1]

30. *id-di-nu-šu kak-ku la ma-aḫ-ra da-'-i-bu za-ai-ri*

31. *a - lik - ma ša Ti - amat nap-ša-tu-uš pu - ru - ' - ma*[2]
32. *ša-a-ru da-mi-ša a-na pu - uz - ra - tum li - bil - lu - ni*

---

[1] The translation of *palū* as "ring" is provisional; the *palū* was certainly a symbol of power.

17. "O lord, spare the life of him that putteth his trust in thee,
18. "But as for the god who began the rebellion, pour out his life."
19. Then set they in their midst a garment,
20. And unto Marduk their first-born they spake:
21. "May thy fate, O lord, be supreme among the gods,
22. "To destroy and to create; speak thou the word, and (thy command) shall be fulfilled.
23. "Command now and let the garment vanish;
24. "And speak the word again and let the garment reappear!"
25. Then he spake with his mouth, and the garment vanished;
26. Again he commanded it, and the garment reappeared.
27. When the gods, his fathers, beheld (the fulfilment of) his word,
28. They rejoiced, and they did homage (unto him, saying), "Marduk is king!"
29. They bestowed upon him the sceptre, and the throne, and the ring,[1]
30. They give him an invincible weapon, which overwhelmeth the foe.
31. "Go, and cut off the life of Tiamat,[2]
32. "And let the wind carry her blood into secret places."

[2] Lines 31 and 32 contain the final address of the gods to Marduk before he armed for the fight.

33. *i-ši-mu-ma ša* ^{ilu}*Bēl ši-ma-tu-uš ilāni ab-bi-e-šu*

34. *u-ru-uḫ šu-ul-mu u taš-me-e uš-ta-aṣ-bi-tu-uš ḫar-ra-nu*

35. *ib - šim - ma* ^{iṣu}*ḳašta kak - ka - šu u - ad - di*
36. *mul-mul-lum*[1] *uš-tar-ki-ba u - kin - šu*[2] *ba*[3] *- at - nu*
37. *iš - ši - ma* ^{iṣu}*miṭṭa*[4] *im - na - šu u - ša - ḫi - iz*
38. ^{iṣu}*ḳašta u* ^{mašku}*iš-pa-tum*[5] *i - du - uš - šu i - lu - ul*[6]
39. *iš - kun bi - ir - ḳu*[7] *i - na pa - ni - šu*
40. *nab-lu*[8] *muš - taḫ - mi*[9]*-ṭu zu - mur - šu um-ta-al-la*[10]
41. *i - pu - uš - ma sa - pa - ra šul-mu-u kir-biš Ti-amat*[11]

42. *ir-bit-ti ša-a-ri*[12] *uš-te-iṣ-bi-ta ana la a-ṣi-e mim-mi-ša*[13]

43. *šūtu iltānu šadū aḫarrū*

44. *i-du-uš sa-pa-ra*[14] *uš-tak-ri-ba*[15] *ki-iš-ti abi-šu*[16] ^{ilu}*A-nim*

45. *ib-ni im-ḫul-la šāra lim-na*[17] *me-ḫa-a*[18] *a-šam-šu-tum*

46. *šār arba'i šār sibi*[19] *šāra ēšā šāra lā šanān*[20]

---

[1] K. 3,437, etc., omits *lum*. [2] K. 3,437, etc., *ši*.

[3] The scribe of No. 93,016 does not make a clear distinction between the signs *ba* and *ma*, and it is possible that the word is *ma-at-nu*; its meaning is not certain.

[4] K. 3,437, etc., *miṭ-ṭa*.

[5] K. 3,437, etc., omits the determinative.

[6] K. 3,437, etc., *i-lul*.

[7] K. 3,437, etc., and 79-7-8, 251, NUM-GIR, i.e. *birḳu*.

[8] K. 3,437, etc., and 79-7-8, 251, *la*.

[9] K. 3,437, etc., *me*. [10] K. 3,437, etc., *um-tal-li*.

[11] No. 93,016, *ki[r]-b[i]-iš Tam-tim*.

[12] No. 93,016, *irbittim(tim) šārē*^{pl}.

33. After the gods his fathers had decreed for the lord his fate,
34. They caused him to set out on a path of prosperity and success.
35. He made ready the bow, he chose his weapon,
36. He slung a spear upon him and fastened it . . . [3]
37. He raised the club, in his right hand he grasped (it),
38. The bow and the quiver he hung at his side.
39. He set the lightning in front of him,
40. With burning flame he filled his body.
41. He made a net to enclose the inward parts of Tiamat,
42. The four winds he stationed so that nothing of her might escape;
43. The South wind and the North wind and the East wind and the West wind
44. He brought near to the net, the gift of his father Anu.
45. He created the evil wind,[17] and the tempest, and the hurricane,
46. And the fourfold wind, and the sevenfold wind, and the whirlwind, and the wind which had no equal;

---

[13] No. 93,016, *mi-im-me-ša*. [14] No. 93,051, *ru*.
[15] After *uš-tak-ri-ba*, No. 93,051 reads *a-na*[. . .].
[16] No. 93,016, [*a-b*]*i-š*[*u*]
[17] No. 93,051, *ša-ar lim-nu*. This phrase must be taken as an explanation of *im-ḫul-la*, i.e. "the evil wind," and not as the name of a separate wind; for the list only comprises seven winds (cf. l. 47).
[18] No. 93,051, *me-ḫu-u*. [19] No. 93,051, VII-*bi-im*.
[20] For IM-NU-DI-A, No. 93,051 reads IM-DI-A-NU-DI-[A].

47. *u-še-ṣa-am-ma* *šārē*^pl[1] *ša* *ib-nu-u* *si-bit-ti-šu-un*

48. *kir-biš*[2] *Ti-amat* *šu-ud-lu-ḫu* *ti*[3]*-bu-u* *arki-šu*[4]

49. *iš-ši-ma* *be-lum* *a-bu-ba*[5] *kakka-šu* *rabā(a)*[6]

50. ^iṣu *narkabta* *u-mu*[7] *la* *maḫ-ri*[8] *ga-lit-ta*[9] *ir-kab*[10]

51. *iṣ-mid-sim*[11]*-ma* *ir-bit* *na-aṣ-ma-di*[12] *i-du-uš-ša* *i-lul*[13]
52. [*ša*] *gi-šu*[14] *la* *pa du-u* *ra-ḫi-ṣu* *mu-up-par-ša*[15]

53. [. . . .][16]*-ti* *šin-na-šu-nu* *na-ša-a* *im-ta*[17]

54. [. . . . .[18] *i*[19]]*-du-u* *sa-pa-na* *lam-du*[20]

55. [. . . . .]*-za* *ra-aš-ba* [*t*]*u-ḳu-un-tum*
56. *šu-me-la* *u* [*im-na* . . .]*-a* *i-pat* *t*[*u* . . . . *e*]*n-d*[*i*][21]
57. *na-aḫ-l*[*ap-ti-šu* . . . .]*-ti* *pul-ḫa-ti* [*ḫa*]*-lip-ma*

---

[1] No. 93,051, *ša-a-ri.* [2] No. 93,051, [*kir-bi-i*]*š.*
[3] No. 93,c51, *te.* [4] No. 93,051, *ar-ki-šu.*
[5] No. 93,051, *bu.* [6] No. 93,051, *kak-ka-šu ra-ba-a-am.*
[7] K. 3,437, etc., reads *u-mu*, "a storm," not *ši-kin*, "a construction"; and this reading is supported by the duplicate No. 93,051. Marduk is represented driving the storm as his chariot, drawn by fiery steeds.
[8] No. 93,051, *ru.* [9] No. 93,051, *tum.*
[10] No. 93,051, *ir-ka-ab.* [11] No. 93,051, *šum.*
[12] No. 93,051, *IV na-aṣ-ma-du.* [13] No. 93,051, *i-du-uš-šu i-lu-ul.*
[14] No. 93,051 reads [. . .]*-gi-šu*; only one sign is wanting from the beginning of the line, and this is conjecturally restored

47. He sent forth the winds which he had created, the seven of them ;
48. To disturb the inward parts of Tiamat, they followed after him.
49. Then the lord raised the thunderbolt, his mighty weapon,
50. He mounted the chariot, the storm [7] unequalled for terror,
51. He harnessed and yoked unto it four horses,
52. Destructive,[14] ferocious, overwhelming, and swift of pace ;
53. [. . . . .][16] were their teeth, they were flecked with foam ;
54. They were skilled in [. . .],[18] they had been trained to trample underfoot.
55. [. . . . .], mighty in battle,
56. Left and [right . . . .].[21]
57. His garment was [. . . .], he was clothed with terror,

---

as *ša* in the transliteration. The new duplicate disproves the restorations which have previously been suggested.

[15] No. 93,051, *šu*.

[16] Delitzsch suggests the restoration, [*malā rū*]*ti*, "full of slaver."

[17] No. 93,051, *tum*.

[18] Delitzsch suggests the restoration *lasāma*, "galloping" ; Jensen, *kamāra*, "casting down."

[19] K. 3,437, etc., gives traces of *i*.

[20] No. 93,051, [*l*]*a-a*[*m*]-*d*[*u*].

[21] Lines 55 and 56 are taken by Delitzsch as referring to Marduk, and by Jensen as referring to the horses ; their suggested restorations differ accordingly.

58. *me-lam-mi-šu saḫ-[pu a]-pi-ir r[a]-šu-uš-šu*

59. *uš-te-šir-ma [ḫar-ra-an-šu*[1] *u]r-ḫa-šu u-šar-di-ma*
60. *aš-riš Ti-amat [ša ag]*[2]*-gat pa-nu-uš-šu iš-kun*
61. *i-na šap-ti[. . . . . . .]*[3] *u-kal-lu*
62. *u-mi-im-ta [. . .]-i*[4] *ta-me-iḫ lak-tuš-šu*
63. *i-na u-mi-šu i-t[ul]-lu-šu*[5] *ilāni i-ṭul-lu-šu*
64. *ilāni abē-šu i-ṭul-lu-šu ilāni i-ṭul-lu-šu*

65. *iṭ-ḫi-ma be-lum ḳab-lu-uš Ti-a-ma-ti i-bar-ri*

66. *ša* ^{ilu}*Kin-gu ḫa-'-ri-ša i-še-'-a me-ki-šu*[6]
67. *i-na-aṭ-ṭal-ma e-ši ma-lak-šu*

68. *sa-pi-iḫ ṭe-ma-šu-ma si-ḫa-ti ip-šit-su*
69. *u ilāni*^{pl} *ri-ṣu-šu a-li-ku i-di-šu*
70. *i-mu-ru[. . -a]m*[7]*-ṭa a-ša-ri-du ni-ṭil-šu-un i-ši*

71. *[i]d-di-[. .]*[8] *Ti-amat ul u-ta-ri ki-šad-sa*
72. *i-na šap-t[i] ša lul-la-a*[9] *u-kal sar-ra-a-ti*[10]

---

[1] There is just room upon the tablet for this restoration.

[2] It is possible that more than two signs are wanting.

[3] In the broken portion of the line there is not room for more than three signs.

[4] Jensen reads *šam-mi-im ta-m[i]-i*, "a plant of magical power." If, however, *ta* and *i* are parts of the same word it is certain that at least two signs are wanting between them.

[5] The verb is possibly not to be taken from *naṭālu*, but should perhaps be transliterated *i-dul-lu-šu*; see above, p. 13, note 11.

58. With overpowering brightness his head was crowned.
59. Then he set out, he took his way,
60. And towards the [rag]ing Tiamat he set his face.
61. On his lips he held [. . .],
62. . . . . . [. .][4] he grasped in his hand.
63. Then they beheld[5] him, the gods beheld him,
64. The gods his fathers beheld him, the gods beheld him.
65. And the lord drew nigh, he gazed upon the inward parts of Tiamat,
66. He perceived the muttering[6] of Kingu, her spouse.
67. As (Marduk) gazed, (Kingu) was troubled in his gait,
68. His will was destroyed and his motions ceased.
69. And the gods, his helpers, who marched by his side,
70. Beheld their leader's [. . .],[7] and their sight was troubled.
71. But Tiamat [. . .], she turned not her neck,
72. With lips that failed not[9] she uttered rebellious words :[10]

---

[6] See above, p. 12, note 2.

[7] The sign is *am* or *ḳar*; not more than one sign is wanting before it.

[8] The first sign in the line seems to be *id*; there is not more than one sign wanting.

[9] Lit., "that were full"; *lul-la-a* is probably Perm. Piel from *lalû* (cf. H-W-B., p. 377).

[10] Lit., "she held fast rebellion."

73. [. .]-*ta*-[. . .][1] *ša be-lum ilāni ti-bu-ka*
74. [*aš*]-*ru-uš-šu-un ip-ḫu-ru šu-nu aš-ruk-ka*[2]

75. [*iš-ši*][3]-*ma be-lum a-bu-ba kakka-šu rabā(a)*

76. [. . . *Ti*][4]-*amat ša ik-mi-lu ki-a-am iš-pur-ši*

77. [. . . . . .][5]-*ba-a-ti e-liš na-ša-ti*-[*ma*]

78. [. . . . . .][6]-*ba-ki-ma di-ki a-na-an*-[*ti*]

79. [. . . . . . .] *abē-šu-nu i-da*-[. . .]
80. [. . . . .]-*šu-nu ta-zi-ri*[7] *ri-e*-[. . .]
81. [. . . ^{ilu}*Kin-g*]*u*[8] *a-na ḫa-'-ru-t*[*i*[9]-*ki*]
82. [. . . . .]-*šu a-na pa-ra-aṣ* ^{ilu}*An-nu-ti*[10]

83. [. . . . . *lim-n*]*i-e-ti te-še-'-e-ma*[11]
84. [. . . *il*]*āni*[12] *abē(e)-a li-mut-ta-ki*[13] *tuk-tin-ni*

85. [*lu ṣ*]*a-an-da-at um-mat-ki lu rit-ku-su šu-nu kakkē*^{pl}-*ki*

86. *en-di-im-ma a-na-ku u ka-a-ši*[14] *i ni-pu-uš ša-aš-ma*

---

[1] One sign is wanting at the beginning of the line, and there are traces of three signs after *ta*.

[2] As the beginning of l. 73 is wanting, the meaning of Tiamat's taunt is not quite clear.

[3] Conjectural restoration ; cf. l. 37.

[4] Possibly restore [*a-na Ti*]-*amat*.

[5] Probably restore [*at-ti-ma ra*]-*ba-a-ti*.

[6] Possibly restore [*u-bi-lu lib*]-*ba-ki-ma*.

73. "[. . . . .] thy coming as lord of the gods,
74. "From their places have they gathered, in thy place are they!"[2]
75. Then the lord [raised][3] the thunderbolt, his mighty weapon,
76. [And against][4] Tiamat, who was raging, thus he sent (the word):
77. "[Thou][5] art become great, thou hast exalted thyself on high,
78. "And thy [heart hath prompted][6] thee to call to battle.
79. "[. . . . . . .] their fathers [. . .],
80. "[. . .] their [. . .] thou hatest [. . .].
81. "[Thou hast exalted King]u[8] to be [thy] spouse,
82. "[Thou hast . . .] him, that, even as Anu, he should issue decrees.
83. "[. . . . .] thou hast followed after evil,
84. "And [against][12] the gods my fathers thou hast contrived thy wicked plan.
85. "Let then thy host be equipped, let thy weapons be girded on!
86. "Stand! I and thou, let us join battle!"

---

[7] K. 5,420*c*, *ta-zir-ri*.

[8] Possibly restore [*tu-ša-aš-ki* ^{ilu}*Kin-g*]*u*; cf. Tablet I, ll. 128 and 135, and the parallel passages in Tablets II and III.

[9] K. 5,420*c* gives traces of *ti*.

[10] K. 5,420*c*, ^{ilu}*A*-[. . .]. [11] K. 5,420*c*, *te-eš*-[. . .].

[12] Probably restore [*a-na il*]*āni*. [13] K. 5,420*c*, *ka*.

[14] No. 93,051, *ka-a-šu*.

87. *Ti - amat an - ni - ta i - na še - mi - ša*[1]
88. *maḫ - ḫu - tiš*[2] *i - te - mi*[3] *u - ša - an - ni*[4] *ṭe - en - ša*
89. *is - si - ma Ti - amat šit - mu - riš*[5] *e - li - ta*
90. *šur - šiš*[6] *ma - al - ma - liš*[7] *it - ru - ra iš - da - a - [ša]*[8]
91. *i - man - ni šip - ta it - ta - nam - di ta - a - [ša]*[9]

92. *u ilāni ša taḫāzi u-ša-'-lu*[10] *šu-nu kakkē*^{pl}*-šu-u[n]*[11]

93. *in - nin - du - ma Ti - amat abkal ilāni*^{pl} ^{ilu}*Marduk*

94. *ša - aš - meš it - tib - bu ḳit - ru - bu ta - ḫa - zi - iš*

95. *uš - pa - ri - ir - ma be-lum sa - pa - ra - šu u-šal-mi*[12]*-ši*
96. *im-ḫul-lu*[13] *ṣa-bit ar-ka-ti pa - nu - uš - šu*[14] *um-daš-šir*

97. *ip - te - ma pi - i - ša Ti - amat a - na la - ' - a - ti - šu*[14]
98. *im-ḫul-la uš - te - ri - ba a-na la ka - tam šap-ti-šu*[14]

99. *iz - zu - ti*[15] *šārē*^{pl} *kar - ša - ša i - ṣa - nu - ma*
100. *in - ni - ḫaz lib - ba - ša - ma pa - a - ša uš - pal - ki*

101. *is - suk mul - mul - la iḫ - te - pi ka - ras - sa*[16]
102. *kir - bi - ša u - bat - ti - ḳa u - šal - liṭ lib - ba*

103. *ik - mi - ši - ma nap - ša - taš u - bal - li*

[1] No. 93,051, *ina še-me-e-šu.*
[2] No. 93,051, *ti-iš.*
[3] No. 93,051, *me.*
[4] No. 93,051, *nu.*
[5] No. 93,051, *ri-iš.*
[6] No. 93,051, *[ši-i]š.*
[7] No. 93,051, *[li-i]š.*
[8] No. 93,051, *it-ru-ru iš-da-a-šu.*
[9] No. 93,051, *ta-a-šu.*

87. When Tiamat heard these words,
88. She was like one possessed, she lost her reason.
89. Tiamat uttered wild, piercing cries,
90. She trembled and shook to her very foundations.
91. She recited an incantation, she pronounced her spell,
92. And the gods of the battle cried out for their weapons.
93. Then advanced Tiamat and Marduk, the counsellor of the gods;
94. To the fight they came on, to the battle they drew nigh.
95. The lord spread out his net and caught her,
96. And the evil wind that was behind (him) he let loose in her face.
97. As Tiamat opened her mouth to its full extent,
98. He drove in the evil wind, while as yet she had not shut her lips.
99. The terrible winds filled her belly,
100. And her courage was taken from her, and her mouth she opened wide.
101. He seized the spear and burst her belly,
102. He severed her inward parts, he pierced (her) heart.
103. He overcame her and cut off her life;

[10] K. 5,420*c*, *u-ša-'-a-lu*; No. 93,051, [. . . -*š*]*a-a-lu*.
[11] No. 93,051, *kak-ki-šu*.
[12] K. 5,420*c*, *me*.
[13] K. 5,420*c*, *la*.
[14] K. 5,420*c*, *ša*.
[15] K. 5,420*c*, *tum*.
[16] K. 5,420*c*, *su*.

104. *ša - lam - ša*[1] *id - da - a* *eli - ša* *i - za - za*[2]
105. *ul - tu* *Ti - amat* *a - lik* *pa - ni* *i - na - ru*
106 *ki - iṣ - ri - ša* *up - tar - ri - ra* *pu - ḫur - ša* *is - sap - ḫa*
107. *u* *ilāni* *ri - ṣu - ša* *a - li - ku* *i - di - ša*

108. *it - tar - ru* *ip - la - ḫu* *u - saḫ - ḫi - ru* *ar - kat - su - un*[3]
109. *u - še - ṣu - ma* *nap - ša - tuš* *e - ṭi - ru*
110. *ni - ta* *la - mu - u* *na - par - šu - diš*[4] *la* *li - ' - e*

111. [*e*] *- sir - šu - nu - ti - ma* *kakkē*^{pl}*- šu - nu* *u - šab - bir*
112. *sa - pa - riš* *na - du - ma* *ka - ma - riš* *uš - bu*

113. [. .][5] *- du* *tub - ḳa - a - ti* *ma - lu - u* *du - ma - mu*

114. *še - rit - su* *na - šu - u* *ka - lu - u* *ki - suk - kiš*

115. *u* *iš - ten* *eš - rit* *nab-ni-ti* *šu-ut* *pul-ḫa-ti* *i-ṣa-nu*[6]

116. [7]*mi - il - la* *gal - li - e* *a - li - ku* *ka -* [. . .[8] *- n*]*i - ša*

117. *it - ta - di*[9] *ṣir - ri - e - ti* *i - di - šu - n*[*u* . . . .]
118. *ga - du* *tuk - ma - ti - šu - nu* *ša - pal - šu* [*ik*]*-b*[*u*]*-us*[10]

---

[1] K. 5,420*c* and 79–7–8, 251, *ša-lam-tuš*. [2] K. 5,420*c*, *iz-zi-za*.
[3] K. 5,420*c*, *u-saḫ-ḫi-ra al-kat-su-un*. [4] K. 5,420*c*, *di-iš*.
[5] The sign begins with a single horizontal wedge; we cannot therefore read [*as*]*-kup*. It is possible that the first word is a verb in the Permansive, parallel to *na-du*, *uš-bu*, and *ma-lu-u*; we may perhaps read [*en*]*-du*, and translate the line, "standing in the *t.* they were filled with lamentation."

104. He cast down her body and stood upon it.
105. When he had slain Tiamat, the leader,
106. Her might was broken, her host was scattered.
107. And the gods her helpers, who marched by her side,
108. Trembled, and were afraid, and turned back.
109. They took to flight to save their lives ;
110. But they were surrounded, so that they could not escape.
111. He took them captive, he broke their weapons ;
112. In the net they were caught and in the snare they sat down.
113. The [. .] . . of the world they filled with cries of grief.
114. They received punishment from him, they were held in bondage.
115. And on the eleven creatures which she had filled with the power of striking terror,
116. Upon the troop of devils, who marched at her [. . . .],
117. He brought affliction, their strength [he . . .];
118. Them and their opposition he trampled under his feet.

---

[6] So K. 5,420*c*; in K. 3,437, etc., the sign which follows *ti* is *ṣ*[*a*], *ḫ*[*a*], or *š*[*a*].

[7] In No. 93,016 the line begins : TE-LAL-MEŠ, i.e. *gallē*^{pl}.

[8] There are traces of at least three signs between *ka* and the last sign but one in the line, which is [*n*]*i*, or [*i*]*r*.

[9] No. 93,016, *it-ta-ad-d*[*i*].

[10] I think there is no doubt that the sign is *us*.

119. *u* ^{ilu}*Kin-gu ša ir-tab-bu-u*[1] *ina* [*e*[2]*-li*]*-šu-un*

120. *ik-mi-šu-ma it-ti* ^{ilu}*Dug-ga(-)e šu*[3]*-a-*[. .]*im-ni-šu*

121. *i-kim-šu-ma dupšīmāti*^{pl} *la si-ma-ti-šu*[4]

122. *i-na ki-šib-bi ik-nu-kam-ma ir-tu-uš*[5] *it-mu-uḫ*

123. *iš-tu lim-ni-šu*[6] *ik-mu-u i-sa-du*

124. *ai-bu*[7] *mut-ta-'-du*[8] *u-ša-pu-u šu-ri-šam*
125. *ir-nit-ti An-šar e-li na-ki-ru*[9] *ka-li-iš uš-zi-zu*

126. *ni-is-mat* ^{ilu}*Nu-dim-mud ik-šu-du* ^{ilu}*Marduk ḳar-du*
127. *e-li ilāni*^{pl} *ka-mu-tum*[10] *ṣi-bit-ta-šu u-dan-nin-ma*

128. *ṣi-ri-iš*[11] *Ti-amat*[12] *ša ik-mu-u i-tu-ra ar-ki-iš*

129. *ik-bu-us-ma be-lum ša Ti-a-ma-tum*[13] *i-šid-sa*
130. *i-na mi-ṭi-šu la pa-di-i u-nat-ti mu-uḫ-ḫa*
131. *u-par-ri-'-ma uš-la-at da-mi-ša*
132. *ša-a-ru il-ta-nu a-na pu-uz-rat uš-ta-bil*

133. *i-mu-ru-ma ab-bu-šu iḫ-du-u i-ri-šu*

---

[1] Rm. 2, 83, *ir-ta-bu-u*.

[2] The beginning of the sign *e* is preserved by K. 5,420*c*.

[3] The sign is clearly written and is *šu*, not *la* as Delitzsch and Jensen transliterate it; the end of the line may perhaps be restored as *šu-a-*[*šu*] *im-ni-šu*.

[4] Rm. 2, 83, *la si-m*[*at-* . . . .].

119. Moreover, Kingu, who had been exalted over them,
120. He conquered, and with the god Dug-ga he counted him.
121. He took from him the Tablets of Destiny that were not rightly his,
122. He sealed them with a seal and in his own breast he laid them.
123. Now after the hero Marduk had conquered and cast down his enemies,
124. And had made the arrogant foe even like . . . ,
125. And had fully established Anšar's triumph over the enemy,
126. And had attained the purpose of Nudimmud,
127. Over the captive gods he strengthened his durance,
128. And unto Tiamat, whom he had conquered, he returned.
129. And the lord stood upon Tiamat's hinder parts,
130. And with his merciless club he smashed her skull.
131. He cut through the channels of her blood,
132. And he made the North wind bear it away into secret places.
133. His fathers beheld, and they rejoiced and were glad;

---

[5] Rm. 2, 83, *ir-tuš.*
[6] Rm. 2, 83, *lim-ni-e-šu.*
[7] Rm. 2, 83, *bi.*
[8] Rm. 2, 83, *mut-ta-du.*
[9] Rm. 2, 83, *eli na-ki-ri.*
[10] Rm. 2, 83, *ilāni ka-mu-u-ti.*
[11] Rm. 2, 83 probably read [*a-d*]*i.*
[12] Rm. 2, 83, *Ti-a-ma-ti.*
[13] Rm. 2, 83, [*T*]*i-a*[*mat*].

134. *ši-di-e šul-ma-nu u-ša-bi-lu šu-nu a-na ša-a-šu*
135. *i-nu-uḫ-ma be-lum ša-lam-tu-uš i-bar-ri*
136. *šir ku-pu*[1] *u-za-a-zu i-ban-na-a nik-la-a-ti*

137. *iḫ-pi-ši-ma ki-ma nu-nu maš-di-e a-na šinā-šu*
138. *mi-iš-lu-uš-ša iš-ku-nam-ma ša-ma-ma u-ṣa-al-lil*[2]

139. *iš-du-ud par-ku ma-aṣ-ṣa-ru u-ša-aṣ-bi-it*
140. *me-e-ša la šu-ṣa-a šu-nu-ti um-ta-'-ir*
141. *šamē(e) i-bi-ir aš-ra-tum i-ḫi-ṭam-ma*

142. *uš-tam-ḫi-ir mi-iḫ-rat apsī šu-bat* ^{ilu}*Nu-dim-mud*

143. *im-šu-uḫ-ma be-lum ša apsī bi-nu-tu-uš-šu*
144. *eš-gal-la tam-ši-la-šu u-ki-in E-šar-ra*
145. *eš-gal-la E-šar-ra ša ib-nu-u ša-ma-mu*
146. ^{ilu}*A-num* ^{ilu}*Bēl u* ^{ilu}*E-a ma-ḫa-zi-šu-un uš-ram-ma*

---

[1] The meaning of *ku-pu* is uncertain; Jensen takes *šir* as a determinative, and assigns to *ku-pu* the meaning "trunk, body."

[2] See above, p. 3, note 14.

134. Presents and gifts they brought unto him.
135. Then the lord rested, gazing upon her dead body,
136. While he divided the flesh of the . . . ,[1] and devised a cunning plan.
137. He split her up like a flat fish into two halves;
138. One half of her he stablished as a covering for heaven.[2]
139. He fixed a bolt, he stationed a watchman,
140. And bade them not to let her waters come forth.
141. He passed through the heavens, he surveyed the regions (thereof),
142. And over against the Deep[3] he set the dwelling of Nudimmud.
143. And the lord measured the structure of the Deep,
144. And he founded E-šara, a mansion like unto it.
145. The mansion E-šara which he created as heaven,
146. He caused Anu, Bēl, and Ea in their districts to inhabit.

---

[3] For the reason of this change in the use of the word *apsū*, in contrast with its personal meaning in the First Tablet, see the Introduction.

The Fifth Tablet.

1. *u - ba - aš - šim man - za - za an ilāni rabūti*^{pl}[1]

2. *kakkabāni*^{pl} *tam - šil - šu - nu lu - ma - ši*[2] *uš - zi - iz*

3. *u - ad - di šatta mi - iṣ - ra - ta u - ma - aṣ - ṣir*
4. *XII arḫē*^{pl} *kakkabāni*^{pl} *III*$^{TA\text{-}A\text{-}AN}$ *uš - zi - iz*
5. *iš - tu u - mi ša šatti uṣ-ṣ[i . . .] u-ṣu-ra-ti*

6. *u-šar-šid man-za-az* ^{ilu}*Ni-bi-ri*[3] *ana ud-du-u rik-si-šu-un*

7. *a - na la e - piš an - ni la e - gu - u ma - na - ma*
8. *man - za - az* ^{ilu}*Bēl u* ^{ilu}*E - a u - [k]in it - ti - šu*
9. *ip - te - ma abullē*^{pl} *ina ṣi - li ki - lal - la - an*
10. *ši - ga - ru ud - dan - ni - na šu - me - la u im - na*

11. *ina ka - bit - ti - ša - ma*[4] *iš - ta - kan e - la - a - ti*
12. ^{ilu}*Nannar - ru uš - te - pa - a mu - ša ik - ti - pa*

13. *u-ad-di-šum-ma šu-uk-nat mu-ši a-na ud-du-u u-me*

14. *ar - ḫu - šam la na - par - ka - a ina a - gi - [e] u - ṣir*

---

[1] The catch-line on the Fourth Tablet, preserved by No. 93,016, reads: *u-ba-aš-šim ma an-za-za an ilāni ra bi-u-tum.*

[2] A list of the seven *lumaši*-stars, or constellations, is given in

The Fifth Tablet.

1. He (i.e. Marduk) made the stations for the great gods;
2. The stars, their images, as the stars of the Zodiac,[2] he fixed.
3. He ordained the year and into sections he divided it;
4. For the twelve months he fixed three stars.
5. After he had [. . .] the days of the year [. . .] images,
6. He founded the station of Nibir[3] to determine their bounds;
7. That none might err or go astray,
8. He set the station of Bēl and Ea along with him.
9. He opened great gates on both sides,
10. He made strong the bolt on the left and on the right.
11. In the midst[4] thereof he fixed the zenith;
12. The Moon-god he caused to shine forth, the night he entrusted to him.
13. He appointed him, a being of the night, to determine the days;
14. Every month without ceasing with the crown he covered (?) him, (saying):

III R, pl. 57, No. 6, ll. 53–56; see further, Jensen, *Kosmologie*, pp. 47 ff.

[3] I.e. Jupiter.

[4] This meaning is conjecturally assigned to *kabittu*.

15. *i - na rēš arḫi - ma na - pa - ḫi [i - na] ma - a - ti*

16. *ḳar - ni na - ba - a - ta*[1] *ana ud - du - u VI u - mi*[2]

17. *i - na ūmi VII*^{KAN} *a - ga - a [šum - šu] - la*
18. *[um]u XIV-tu lu-u šu-tam-ḫu-rat meš - l[i . . .]-u*

19. *[e-n]u-ma* ^{ilu}*Šamaš i-na i-šid šamē(e) [. . . .]-ka*

20. *[. . . .]-ti šu-taḳ-ṣi-ba-am-ma bi-ni ar-[. .]*[3]*-uš*

21. *[. . . .] . .*[4] *a-na ḫar-ra-an* ^{ilu} *Šamaš šu-taḳ-rib-[ma]*

22. *[ina ūmi . . .]*^{KAN} *lu šu-tam-ḫu-rat* ^{ilu}*Šamaš lu ša-na-[. .]*

23. *[. . . . . .] - ši - um*[5] *ba - ' - i u - ru - uḫ - ṣa*
24. *[. . . . . š]u-taḳ-ri-ba-ma di-na di-na*

25. *[. . . . .] ḫa - ba - la*
26. *[. . . . .] ia - a - ti*
[. . . . .]

[1] *na-ba-a-ta* is possibly the Perm. from *nabū*; Jensen takes it as the Infinitive from *nabāṭu* with an Imperative meaning.

[2] The reading of *VI u-mi* is certain. K. 3,567 + K. 8,588 reads *VI [. . .]-mi*, while the duplicate K. 8,526 reads [. . .]*u-mu* (see also *First Steps in Assyrian*, p. 160). George Smith's reading *ša-ma-mu*, "to determine heaven," which has been followed by Zimmern and Delitzsch, gives little sense; Jensen reads *z(ṣ)a(?)-mi*, which he does not translate. The reading *ana ud-du-u VI u-mi*,

15. "At the beginning of the month, when thou shinest upon the land,
16. "Thou commandest[1] the horns to determine six days,[2]
17. "And on the seventh day to [divide] the crown.
18. "On the fourteenth day thou shalt stand opposite, the half [. . .].
19. "When the Sun-god on the foundation of heaven [. . . .] thee,
20. "The [. . .] thou shalt cause to . . . , . and thou shalt make his [. . .].
21. "[. . . .] . . unto the path of the Sun-god shalt thou cause to draw nigh,
22. "[And on the . . . day] thou shalt stand opposite, and the Sun-god shall . . [. . .]
23. "[. . . . .] to traverse her way.
24. "[. . . .] thou shalt cause to draw nigh, and thou shalt judge the right.
25. "[. . . . .] to destroy
26. "[. . . . .] me.
" . . . . "

"to determine six days," agrees well with l. 13, where Marduk is described as appointing the Moon-god *a-na ud-du-u u-me*, "to determine the days"; moreover, the phrase is appropriately followed in l. 17 by the statement of the Moon-god's duty on the seventh day.

[3] One sign is wanting. [4] Perhaps read *arba'i*.

[5] Possibly read *iltu*.

[The following twenty-two lines are taken from K. 3,449*a*, and probably form part of the Fifth Tablet.[1]]

(66) *u* - [. . . . .].
(67) *zar* - *ba* - *bu* [. . . . .]
(68) *iš* - *tu* [. . . . .]
(69) *ina E* - *sag* - *gil* [. . . . .]
(70) *kun* - *na* [. . . . .]
(71) *man* - *za* - *az* ^{ilu}[. . . . .]
(72) *ilāni*^{pl} *rabûti*^{pl} [. . . . .]
(73) *ilāni*^{pl} *ik* - [. . . . .]
(74) *im* - *ḫur* - *ma* [. . . . .]
(75) *sa-pa-ra ša i-te-ip-pu-šu i-mu-ru ilāni*^{pl} [*abē*^{pl}-*šu*]

(76) *i-mu-ru-ma* ^{iṣu}*ḳašta ki-i nu-uk-ku-lat* [*ip*$^{?}$-*šit-sa*]

(77) *ip* - *šit i* - *te* - *ip* - *pu* - *šu i* - *na* - *a* - *d*[*u* . . .]

(78) *iš* - *ši* - *ma* ^{ilu}*A* - *num ina puḫur ilāni*^{pl} [. . .]

(79) ^{iṣu}*ḳašta it* - *ta* - *šik ši* - *i* [. . . . .]
(80) *im* - *bi* - *ma ša* ^{iṣu}*ḳašti ki* - *a* - *am* [*šumē*^{pl} - *ša*]

(81) *iṣ-ṣu a-rik lu iš-te-nu-um-ma ša-nu* [. . .]

(82) *šal-šu šum-ša* ^{kakkabu}*Ḳaštu ina šamē*(*e*) [. . .]

---

[1] If K. 3,449*a* forms part of the Fifth Tablet, the position of the fragment may be roughly ascertained from the fact that the end of the obverse and the beginning of the reverse are preserved. The first line preserved was probably not earlier, though it may have been some lines later, than the 66th line of the text.

[The following twenty-two lines are taken from K. 3,449*a*, and probably form part of the Fifth Tablet.[1]]

(66) . [. . . . .]
(67) . . . [. . . . .]
(68) From [. . . . .]
(69) In E-sagil [. . . . .]
(70) To establish [. . . . .]
(71) The station of [. . . . .]
(72) The great gods [. . . . .]
(73) The gods [. . . . .]
(74) He took and [. . . . .]
(75) The gods [his fathers] beheld the net which he had made,
(76) They beheld the bow and how [its work] was accomplished.
(77) They praised the work which he had done [. . . .].
(78) Then Anu raised [the . . . .] in the assembly of the gods.
(79) He kissed the bow, (saying), "It is [. . . .]!"
(80) And thus he named the names of the bow, (saying),
(81) "'Long-wood' shall be one name, and the second name [shall be . . . .],
(82) "And its third name shall be the Bow-star, in heaven [shall it . . . .]!"

[1] The traces upon the tablet are possibly those of *ip*. For the restoration cf. IV R, pl. 12, Obv., l. 24; Delitzsch suggests the reading *epšissa*.

(83) *u - kin - ma gi - is - gal - la - ša* [. . . . . .]

(84) *ul - tu ši - ma - a - ti ša* [. . . . .]

(85) [*id - d*]*i - ma* *iṣu kussā* [. . . . .]

(86) [. . . .] *ina šamē*[(*e*) . . . .]

(87) [. . . .] - *ru* - [. . . . .]

[The following traces of the last thirteen lines of the Fifth Tablet are taken from the reverse of K. 11,641 and from the reverse of K. 8,526.[1]]

(128) [. . . . .] - *lu - šu* [. . . . .]

(129) [. . . . . . .] - *šu - nu - ti nu* - [. . .]

(130) [. . . . . - *b*]*a - šu e* - [. . . .]

(131) [. . . . .] - *su - nu - ti* [. . . .]

(132) [. . . . . . - *šu - n*]*u lu ḫu* - [. . .]

(133) [. . . . . *i*]*lāni i - ḳab - bu*[- *u*]

(134) [. . . .] *šamē*(*e*)[2] [. . . . .][3]

(135) [. . . .] *ma - a - ru - k*[*u - un* . . . .]

(136) [. . . . . . .] - *ni it* - [. . . . . .]

(137) [. . . . . .] *u - bal - li - i*[*ṭ* . . . . .]

(138) [. . . *me*]-*lam-me mi*-[. . .] *uš*-[. . .]

(139) [. . . .] *la um* - [. . .] *nu* - [. . .]

(140) [. . . . .] *ni - i - nu*

---

[1] The reverse of K. 8,526 gives traces of the last three lines of the text; the greater part of the traces are taken from the reverse of K. 11,641. The obverse of K. 11,641 gives portions of ll. 14–22; for the text, see Appendix II.

[2] The reading *šamē*(*e*) is probable; there is not room on the tablet for the restoration *ilu* [*E*]-*a*.

(83) Then he fixed a station for it [. . . . . .]
(84) Now after the fate of [. . . . .]
(85) [He set] a throne [. . . . .]
(86) [. . . . .] in heaven [. . . . . . .]
(87) [. . . . .] . . [. . . . .]

[The following traces of the last thirteen lines of the Fifth Tablet are taken from the reverse of K. 11,641 and from the reverse of K. 8,526.[1]]

(128) "[. . . . . .] him [. . . . . .]"
(129) "[. . . . . .] them [. . . . . .]"
(130) "[. . . . . .] him [. . . . . .]"
(131) "[. . . . . .] them [. . . . . .]"
(132) "[. . .] their [. . . .] may [. . . .]"
(133) [. . . . .] the gods spake,
(134) [. . . . . .] the heavens [. . .]:[3]
(135) "[. . . . your] son [. . . . . .]"
(136) "[. . . .] our [. . . .] hath he [. . . .]"
(137) "[. . . .] he hath caused to live [. . . .]"
(138) "[. . . . .] splendour [. . . . .]"
(139) "[. . . . . .] not [. . . . . .]"
(140) "[. . . . .] we [. . .]!"

[3] In the speech that follows it may be conjectured that the gods complained that, although Marduk had endowed the heavens with splendour and had caused plants to live upon the earth, yet there were no shrines built in honour of the gods, and there were no worshippers devoted to their service; see below, p. 88, note 1.

The Sixth Tablet.

1. *ilu Marduk zik - ri ilāni ina še - mi - šu* [1]
2. [*ub*] [2] - *bal lib - ba - šu i - ban - na - a* [*nik - la - a - ti*] [3]

3. [*ip*] - *šu pi - i - šu a - na ilu E - a* [*i* [4] - *zak - kar*]
4. [*ša*] [5] *ina lib-bi-šu uš-ta-mu-u i-nam-din* [*ana ša-a-šu*] [6]

5. *da-mi* [7] *lu-uk-ṣur-ma iṣ-ṣi-im-*[*tu*]*m* [8] *lu* - [. . .] [9]
6. *lu-uš-ziz-ma amēla*(*a*) *lu a-me-lu* . . [. . . .]
7. *lu - ub - ni - ma amēla*(*a*) *a - šib* [. . .] [10]

---

[1] The end of the line has been restored from the catch-line of Tablet V, preserved by K. 8,526; the traces upon K. 3,567, etc., suggest the reading *ina še-*[*m*]*i-*[*e-šu*]; K. 11,641 reads [*i*]*na še-me-*[. .].

[2] Conjectural restoration.

[3] For this restoration, cf. Tablet IV, l. 136.

[4] The beginning of the sign *i* is visible.

[5] One sign only is missing at the beginning of the line.

[6] Conjectural restoration.

[7] It is possible that the final vowel of *da-mi* is not the *i* of the 1 sing. pron. suffix; in that case the phrase should be translated "Blood will I take." In view of the fact, however, that, according to Berossus, Bēl first formed mankind from his own blood mixed with earth, it appears to me preferable to take the *i* as the pron. suffix and translate *da-mi* as "my blood." Berossus does not state that Bēl used his own bone for forming man, and this agrees with the

The Sixth Tablet.

1. When Marduk heard the word of the gods,[1]
2. His heart prompted him and he devised [a cunning plan].[2]
3. He opened his mouth and unto Ea [he spake],
4. [That which][5] he had conceived in his heart he imparted [unto him][6]:
5. "My blood[7] will I take and bone[8] will I [fashion],[9]
6. "I will make man, that man may . . [. . .].
7. "I will create man who shall inhabit [the earth],[10]

---

absence of the pronominal suffix from *iṣ-ṣi-im-[tu]m*. According to my rendering of the line, Marduk states his purpose of forming man from his own blood, and from bone which he will create; see further, the Introduction.

[8] The traces of the last sign of the word appear to be those of *tum*. I think there can be no doubt that *iṣ-ṣi-im-[tu]m* corresponds to the Hebrew *'eṣem*, "bone," which is employed in Gen. ii, 23, in the phrase *'eṣem mē'ăṣāmai*, "bone of my bones." In connection with the feminine form of the word *iṣ-ṣi-im-[tu]m*, it may be noted that, in addition to the plur. *'ăṣāmīm*, the fem. form *'ăṣāmōth* is also found.

[9] The verb may perhaps be restored as *lu-[ub-ni]*, as suggested in the translation.

[10] The last word of the line may perhaps be restored as *irṣitim*, as suggested in the translation.

8. *lu-u en-du dul-lu ilāni-ma šu-nu lu-u pa-pa* [[1] . . .]

9. *lu-ša-an-ni-ma al-ka-ka-ti ilāni lu-nak-ki-*[*ir* . . .][2]

10. *iš-te-niš lu kub-bu-tu-ma*[3] *a-na lim-na lu-u* [. . .]

11. *i-pu-ul-lu-šu-ma* ^{ilu}*E-a a-ma-tum i-z*[*ak-kar*]
12. [. .]-*t*[*um š*]*u-ut šal-ḫu*(?)-*tum*[4] *ša ilāni u-ša-an-*[. . .][5]

13. [. . . . . *t*]*a*[6]-*ad-nam-ma iš-ten a-*[. . .]
14. [. . . *li-in-n*]*a*[7]-*ab-bit-ma niše*^{pl} *lul-*[. . .]

15. [. . . . .]-*ma ilāni* [. . . .]
16. [. . . .]-*na-din-ma šu-nu li-*[. . .]
17. [. . . . .]-*ḫi-ir-ma ilāni* [. . . .]
18. [. . . . .]-'-*a-ra i-*[*n*]*am-*[. . .]
19. [. . . . .] *ilāni u-*[. . . . .]
20. [. . . . . . . ^{ilu}*A*]-*nun-na-ki* [. . . .]
21. [. . . . .]-*aḫ-ru* [. . . .]

---

[1] The word is probably *papaḫu*; literally the line reads, "Let the service of the gods be established, and as for them let [their] shrines [be built]." It is interesting to note the reason that is here implied for the creation of mankind, i.e., that the gods may have worshippers. There is clearly a reference to this in l. 29 of the Seventh Tablet, where, after referring to Marduk's mercy upon the gods, his enemies, the text goes on *a-na pa-di-šu-nu ib-nu-u a-me-lu-tu*, "For their forgiveness did he create mankind."

[2] It is probable that the end of the line contained some expression parallel to *al-ka-ka-ti*.

[3] It seems to me preferable to assign to the Piel of [*kabātu*] its usual meaning "to oppress," rather than to render the passage as

8. "That the service of the gods may be established, and that [their] shrines[1] [may be built].
9. "But I will alter the ways of the gods, and I will change [their paths];[2]
10. "Together shall they be oppressed,[3] and unto evil shall [they . . . .]."
11. And Ea answered him and spake the word:
12. "[. . . . .] the [. . . . .] of the gods I have [changed][5]
13. [. . . . .] . . and one . [. . . .]
14. [. . . shall be de]stroyed[7] and men will I [. . . . .]
15. [. . . . . . .] and the gods [. . . . .]
16. [. . . . .] . . and they [. . . . .]
17. [. . . .] . . and the gods [. . . . .]
18. [. . . . . . .] . . . . . [. . . . .]
19. [. . . . .] the gods [. . . . .]
20. [. . . . . . .] the Anunnaki [. . . . .]
21. [. . . . .] . . . [. . . . .]

"Together shall they be honoured." The sense seems to be that Marduk, by the creation of man, will establish the worship of the gods, but at the same time will punish the gods for their complaints. It is possible that in his speech that follows Ea dissuades Marduk from carrying out the second part of his proposal.

[4] The signs at the beginning of the line are not very clear. The signs read as *ut*, *šal*, and *ḫu* are probably not to be taken as the single character *úḫ*.

[5] Possibly, "I have [related]."

[6] Possibly [*n*]*a*.

[7] The word is conjecturally restored.

[The rest of the text is wanting [1] with the exception of the last few lines of the tablet, which read as follows.]

138. [. . . . .] . [. . . . .]

139. [. . . . .] *bi* [. . . . .]

140. *ki - i na* - [. . . . . . .] *nu* [. . . . .]

141. *iḫ - du - u* [. . . .] - *mu - u* [. . . . .]

142. *i - na Up-šu-ukkin-na-ka uš - ta - ad* - [. . . . .]

143. *ša ma-ru ḳar-ra-du mu-tir* [*gi-mil-li-šu-nu* . . .]

144. *ni - i - nu ša za - ni - nu ul - lu* - [. . . . . .]

145. *u-ši-bu-ma ina puḫri-šu-nu i-nam-bu*-[. . .]

146. [. . .]-*su na-gab-šu-nu u-zak-k*[*a-ru-šu* . . .] [2]

---

[1] It is probable that the missing portion of the text corresponded closely with the account of the creation of man and animals given by Berossus; for a further discussion of this subject, see the Introduction. The tablet K. 3,364 (*Cun. Texts*, part xiii, pl. 29 f.) has been thought to belong to the Creation Series, and to contain the instructions given by Marduk to man after his creation. Had this been so, it would have formed part of the Sixth Tablet. On plates lxiv ff. of Vol. II is published the text of a Neo-Babylonian tablet, No. 33,851, which gives a duplicate text to K. 3,364; and in Appendix II I have given reasons for believing that the text inscribed upon K. 3,364 and No. 33,851 has no connection with

[The rest of the text is wanting[1] with the exception of the last few lines of the tablet, which read as follows.]

138. [. . . . .] . [. . . . .]
139. [. . . . .] . [. . . . .]
140. When [. . . . . .] . [. . . . .]
141. They rejoiced [. .] . . [. . . . .]
142. In Upšukkinnaku they set [their dwelling].
143. Of the heroic son, their avenger, [they cried]:
144. "We, whom he succoured, . . [. . .]!"
145. They seated themselves and in the assembly they named [him . . . .],
146. They all [cried aloud (?)], they exalted [him . . .].[2]

---

the Creation Series, but is part of a long composition containing moral precepts. Another fragment which it has been suggested belongs to one of the later tablets of the Creation Series is K. 3,445 + R. 396 (*Cun. Texts*, part xiii, pl. 24 f.; cf. also its duplicate K. 14,949, pl. 24); but there are strong reasons against the identification of the text as a fragment of the series *Enuma eliš*, though it may well be part of a parallel version of the Creation story (see further, Appendix II).

[2] The address of the gods to Marduk forms the subject of the Seventh Tablet of the series.

The Seventh Tablet.

1. ^{ilu}*Asar-ri ša-riḳ mi-riš-t*[*i*[1] *mu-kin iz-ra-ti*][2]

2. *ba-nu-u še-am u ki-e mu-š*[*e-ṣi ur-ki-ti*][3]

3. ^{ilu}*Asaru-alim ša ina bīt mil-ki kab-t*[*u a-tar mil-ki*][4]

4. *ilāni u-taḳ-ḳu-u a-d*[*ir* . . . .][5]

5. ^{ilu}*Asaru-alim-nun-na ka-ru-bu nu-ur* [*a-bi a-li-di-šu*][6]

6. *muš-te-šir te-rit* ^{ilu}*A-nim* ^{ilu}*Bēl* [*u* ^{ilu}*E-a*][7]

7. *šu-u-ma za-nin-šu-nu mu-ud-du-u* [. . . . .]
8. *ša šu-ku-us-su ḫegallu*[8] *uṣ-ṣa*[9] [. . . . .]

9. ^{ilu}*Tu-tu ba-an te-diš-ti-šu-nu* [*šu-u*][10]

---

[1] No. 92,629 (catch-line), *me-ri*[*š*- . .].

[2] The end of the line has been restored from the commentary S. 11 + S. 980, Obv., col. i, ll. 4 and 5; see Appendix I.

[3] Restored from S. 11, etc., Obv., col. i, ll. 9 and 10; see Appendix I.

[4] Restored from S. 11, etc., Obv., col. i, ll. 15 and 16, which gives the words *at-ru* and *mil-ku* as occurring at the end of the line; the restoration *at-ru mil-ki-šu*, "whose counsel is mighty," is also possible.

[5] The end of the line may perhaps be restored from the

The Seventh Tablet.

1. O Asari, "Bestower of planting," "[Founder of sowing]," [2]
2. "Creator of grain and plants," "who caused [the green herb to spring up]!" [3]
3. O Asaru-alim, "who is revered in the house of counsel," "[who aboundeth in counsel]," [4]
4. The gods paid homage, fear [took hold upon them]! [5]
5. O Asaru-alim-nuna, "the mighty one," "the Light of [the father who begat him]," [6]
6. "Who directeth the decrees of Anu, Bel, [and Ea]!" [7]
7. He was their patron, he ordained [their . . . .];
8. He, whose provision is abundance, goeth forth [. . . .]!
9. Tutu [is] [10] "He who created them anew;"

---

commentary S. 11, etc., in some such way as *a-d[ir i-ḫu-us-su-nu-ti]*; see Appendix I.

[6] The restoration is taken from the astrological fragment, No. 32,574, Obv., l. 3; see Appendix III.

[7] Conjectural restoration. [8] No. 91,139 + 93,073, *ḫegalla(la)*.

[9] No. 91,139, etc., *u-uṣ-ṣ[i]*.

[10] Restored from the commentary R. 366+80-7-19, 288+293; Obv., ll. 1-4 (see Appendix I). The title Tutu is there explained as *ba-a-nu*, "creator," while its two component parts (TU + TU) occur in the Sumerian version of the line as the equivalents of *ba-nu-u* and *e-di-šu*.

10. *li-lil sa-gi-šu-nu-ma*[1] *šu-nu lu-u* [*pa-aš-ḫu-ni*][2]

11. *lib - ni - ma*[3] *šipti*[4] *ilāni li* - [*nu - ḫu*][2]

12. *ag - giš*[5] *lu*[6] *te - bu - u li - ni - ' - u* [*i - rat - su - nu*][2]

13. *lu-u šu-uš-ḳu-u-ma ina puḫur*[7] *ilāni* [. . . .][8]

14. *ma-am-man ina ilāni*[pl9] *šu-a-šu*[10] *la um*-[*maš-ša-lu*]
15. [ilu] *Tu-tu* [ilu] *Zi-ukkin-na*[11] *na-piš-ti um-ma-ni* [*ilāni*][12]

16. *ša u - kin - nu an*[13] *ilāni šamē*(*e*) *el - lu* - [*ti*]
17. *al-kat-su-un iṣ-ba-tu-ma*[14] *u-ad-du-u* [. . . .][15]

18. *ai im-ma-ši i-na*[16] *a-pa-ti*[17] *ip-še-ta*-[*šu* . . . .][18]

---

[1] No. 91,139, etc., *sag-gi-šu-nu-ma*.

[2] Lines 10 – 12 have been conjecturally restored from the commentary R. 366, etc., Obv., ll. 5–18 (see Appendix I); the sentences I take as conditionals. For another occurrence of the verb *sagū* (l. 10), see Tablet IV, l. 12.

[3] No. 91,139, etc., [*li-i*]*b*-[*n*]*i-ma*.

[4] No. 91,139, etc., *šip-ti*.

[5] No. 91,139, etc., [*a*]*g-gi-iš*.

[6] No. 91,139, etc., *lu-u*.

[7] No. 91,139, etc., *i-na pu-ḫur*.

[8] It is probable that another precative came at the end of the line, and if this was so the verb was given in l. 24 of the Obv. of the commentary R. 366, etc. In No. 91,139, etc., not very much is wanting at the end of the line.

[9] No. 91,139, etc., *ma-am-ma-an i-na ilāni*.

[10] No. 91,139, etc., *ša-a-šu*.

10. Should their wants be pure, then are they [satisfied];[2]
11. Should he make an incantation, then are the gods [appeased];[2]
12. Should they attack him in anger, he withstandeth [their onslaught]![2]
13. Let him therefore be exalted, and in the assembly of the gods [let him . . . .];[8]
14. None among the gods can [rival him]!
15. Tutu is Zi-ukkina, "the Life of the host [of the gods],"[12]
16. Who established for the gods the bright heavens.
17. He set them on their way, and ordained [their path (?)];[15]
18. Never shall his [. . . .][18] deeds be forgotten among men.

---

[11] No. 35,506, *ilu Zi-ukkin.*

[12] The end of the line is conjecturally restored from K. 2,107+K. 6,086, Obv., col. ii, l. 29 (see pl. lxii), which explains the title *ilu* ZI-UKKIN as *nap-šal nap-ḫar ilāni pl*.

[13] No. 35,506 and K. 8,522, *a-na.*

[14] No. 35,506, *iṣ-ba-tu-u.*

[15] Some such word as *ur-ḫa-šu-nu* should possibly be restored at the end of the line; for a fragment of the commentary to the line, see Appendix I.

[16] K. 8,522, *ina.*

[17] K. 8,522 and No. 35,506, *a-pa-a-ti.*

[18] According to S. 11 + S. 980, Obv., col. ii, l. 7, a word *ku-u[l- . . .]* occurred at the end of the line, but this is not certain, as the commentary evidently gives a variant reading for the beginning of the line (see Appendix I); Jensen's suggested restoration is disproved by No. 35,506 (see pl. xlvi).

19. *ilu Tu-tu ilu Zi-azag šal-šiš im-bu-u mu-kil*[1] *te-lil-ti*

20. *il ša-a-ri ṭa-a-bi be-el taš-me-e u ma-ga-ri*[2]

21. *mu-šab-ši ṣi-im-ri u*[3] *ku-bu-ut-te-e mu-kin ḫegalli*[4]

22. *ša mimma-ni*[5] *i-ṣu*[6] *a-na ma-'-di-e*[7] *u-tir-ru*
23. *i-na pu-uš-ki dan-ni*[8] *ni-ṣi-nu*[9] *šār-šu*[10] *ṭa-a-bu*
24. *liḳ-bu-u lit-ta-'-du*[11] *lid-lu-la*[12] *da-li-li-šu*

25. *ilu Tu-tu*[13] *ilu Aga-azag ina*[14] *ribī(i)*[15] *li-šar-ri-ḫu*[16] *ab-ra-a-te*[17]
26. *be-el*[18] *šip-tu*[19] *ellitim(tim)*[20] *mu-bal-liṭ*[21] *mi-i-ti*

27. *ša an*[22] *ilāni ka-mu-ti*[23] *ir-šu-u ta-ai-ru*[24]
28. *ap-ša-na en-du*[25] *u-ša-as-si-ku*[26] *eli ilāni pl*[27] *na-ki-ri-šu*[28]

---

[1] The text of the commentary read ***mu-kin***, i.e. "the Founder of Purification"; for other variant readings in the line, see Appendix I.

[2] The text of ll. 20 and 21 corresponds to that of the commentary.

[3] *u* is omitted by Nos. 91,139 + 93,073 and 35,506.

[4] No. 91,139, etc., *ḫegalla(la)*.

[5] No. 91,139, etc., [*mi-i*]*m-ma-n*[*i*].

[6] Nos. 35,506 and 91,139, etc., *i-ṣi*.

[7] No. 91,139, etc., *ma-a-di-e*.

[8] No. 91,139, etc., [*p*]*u-uš-ḳu* [*da*]*n-nu*; No. 35,506 reads [*pu-u*]*š-ḳa* and omits the adjective.

[9] No. 35,506, *ni-ṣi-ni*.

[10] Nos. 35,506 and 91,139, etc., *ša-ar-šu*.

[11] No. 35,506, *li-it-ta-'-id*.

[12] No. 91,139, etc., *li-id-lu-lu*; No. 35,506, *li-id-*[. . . .].

[13] K. 8,522, here and in ll. 33, 41, and 43, reads *ilu* MIN (i.e.

19. Tutu as Zi-azag thirdly they named, "the Bringer[1] of Purification,"
20. "The God of the Favouring Breeze," "the Lord of Hearing and Mercy,"
21. "The Creator of Fulness and Abundance," "the Founder of Plenteousness,"
22. "Who increaseth all that is small."
23. "In sore[2] distress we felt his favouring breeze,"
24. Let them say, let them pay reverence, let them bow in humility before him!
25. Tutu as Aga-azag may mankind fourthly magnify!
26. "The Lord of the Pure Incantation," "the Quickener of the Dead,"
27. "Who had mercy upon the captive gods,"
28. "Who removed the yoke from upon the gods his enemies,"

Tutu), which is written in small characters on the edge of the tablet.

[14] No. 35,506, *i-na*.

[15] Nos. 35,506 and 91,139, *ri-bi-i*.

[16] No. 91,139, etc., *ḫa*.

[17] No. 91,139, etc., *ti*.

[18] No. 91,139, etc., *bēl*.

[19] No. 91,139, etc., *šip-ti*; No. 35,506, [*š*]*i-ip-ti*.

[20] Nos. 35,506 and 91,139, etc., *el-li-ti*.

[21] No. 35,506, *l*[*i-iṭ*].

[22] *an* is omitted by No. 91,139, etc.

[23] No. 91,139, etc., *tu*; No. 35,506, *tum*.

[24] No. 91,139, etc., *ri*.

[25] No. 35,506, *di*.

[26] No. 91,139, etc., *ka*.

[27] Nos. 35,506 and 91,139, etc., *e-li ilāni*.

[28] No. 91,139, etc., *ša*.

29. *a - na pa - di - šu - nu*[1] *ib - nu - u a - me - lu - tu*[2]
30. *ri - me*[3] *- nu - u ša bul*[4] *- lu - ṭu ba - šu - u it - ti - šu*

31. *li - ku - na - ma ai im - ma - ša - a a - ma - tu - šu*

32. *ina*[5] *pi-i ṣal-mat ḳaḳḳadu*[6] *ša ib-na-a ḳa-ta-a-šu*

33. ^{ilu}*Tu-tu* ^{ilu}*Mu-azag ina*[8] *ḫanši(ši)*[9] *ta-a šu ellu*[10] *pa-ši-na*[11] *lit*[12]*-tab-bal*
34. *ša ina šipti-šu*[13] *ellitim(tim)*[14] *is-su-ḫu na-gab lim-nu-ti*[15]

35. ^{ilu}*Šag-zu mu-di-e lib-bi ilāni*^{pl} *ša i-bar-ru-u*[16] *kar-šu*

36. *e - piš lim - ni - e - ti la u - še - ṣu - u it - ti - šu*

37. *mu-kin puḫri*[17] *ša ilāni* [. . . . *l*]*ib*[18]*-bi-šu-un*

38. *mu - kan - niš*[19] *la ma - gi - [ri* . . . .]
39. *mu - še - šir kit - ti na -* [. . . . . . .]
40. *ša sa - ar - ti u k[i -* . . . .]

---

[1] See above, p. 88, note 1.
[2] No. 35,506, *a-me-lu-ti*; No. 91,139, etc., *a-me-lu-ut-tum.*
[3] Nos. 35,506 and 91,139, etc., *mi.*
[4] Nos. 35,506 and 91,139, etc., *bu-ul.*
[5] Nos. 35,506 and 91,139, etc., *i-na.*
[6] No. 91,139, etc., *ḳaḳ-ḳa-[d]u.*
[7] Literally, "the black-headed ones."
[8] No. 35,506, *[i]-na.*
[9] No. 35,506, *ḫa-an-šu*; No. 91,139, etc., *ḫa-a[m-* . . .].
[10] No. 35,506, *el-lu.*
[11] No. 91,139, etc., *p[a]-a-ši-na.*

29. "For their forgiveness[1] did he create mankind,"
30. "The Merciful One, with whom it is to bestow life!"
31. May his deeds endure, may they never be forgotten
32. In the mouth of mankind[7] whom his hands have made!
33. Tutu as Mu-azag, fifthly, his "Pure Incantation" may their mouth proclaim,
34. "Who through his Pure Incantation hath destroyed all the evil ones!"
35. Šag-zu, "who knoweth the heart of the gods," "who seeth through the innermost part!"
36. "The evil-doer he hath not caused to go forth with him!"
37. "Founder of the assembly of the gods," "[who . . . .][18] their heart!"
38. "Subduer of the disobedient," "[. . . . .]!"
39. "Director of Righteousness," "[. . . . .],"
40. "Who rebellion and [. . . . .]!"

---

[12] No. 91,139, etc., *li-it.*

[13] No. 91,139, etc., *šip-ti-šu.*

[14] No. 91,139, etc., *el-li-*[. . .]; No. 35,506, [. . .]*-li-ti.*

[15] No. 91,139, etc., *tu.*

[16] No. 35,506, *ib-ru*[. . .].

[17] No. 91,139, etc., *pu-uḫ* [*ru*]; the scribe has omitted the *ru* by mistake.

[18] Jensen suggests the restoration [*mu-ṭi-ib*], i.e., "[who gladdened] their heart."

[19] No. 91,139, etc., *ni-iš.*

41. ^{ilu}[*Tu - tu*] ^{ilu}*Zi - si mu - šat*[1] - [. . . . . . .]
42. *mu - uk - kiš šu - mur - ra - tu* [. . . . . .][2]
43. ^{ilu}[*Tu - tu*] ^{ilu}*Suḫ - kur šal - šiš*[3] *na - si*[*ḫ ai - bi*][4]

44. *mu* - [*sap*] - *pi - iḫ* [*ki*]*p*[5] - *di - šu - nu* [. . . .]
45. *m*[*u - ba*]*l - li* [*nap - ḫ*]*ar rag - g*[*i* . . . . . .]
46. [. . . . .] *liš* - [. . .] - *lu* [. . . . .]
47. [. . . . .] *ḫi r*[*i* . . . .]

[The following lines are taken from the fragment K. 12,830,[6] but their position in the text is uncertain.]

[*ib - bi kib - ra - a - te*] *ṣal-mat* [*ḳaḳḳadi ib-ni-ma*][7]

[*e - li sa*] - *a - šu ṭe* - [*e - mu* . . . .][8]
[. . . . . . .] - *gi mu* - [. . . . . . .]
[. . . . . . .] *Ti - amat* [. . . . . . .]
[. . . . . . .] *uz* - [. . . . . . .]
[. . . . . . .] *ru - u - ḳ*[*u* . . . .]
[. . . . .] *lu* [. . . . . . .]

---

[1] The reading of K. 9,267, I think, is *šat* rather than *še*.

[2] The end of this line may perhaps be restored from K. 2,107, etc., col. ii, l. 30 (see pl. lxii and Appendix I), as ***na-si-iḫ ša-bu-ti***, "who destroyed the mighty."

[3] This does not appear to agree with ll. 25 and 33, but the reading of K. 9,267 is clear.

[4] The sign following *na* is broken, but the reading *siḫ* is possible. On K. 2,107, etc., col. ii, l. 31 the title Suḫ-kur is explained as *mu-bal-lu-u ai-bi*, and, though the following lines give explanations of other titles, they contain the synonymous expressions ***mu-bal-lu-u***

41. Tutu as Zi-si, "the [. . . . .],
42. "Who put an end to anger," "[who . . . .]!"[2]
43. Tutu as Suḫ-kur, thirdly,[3] "the [Destroyer of the foe],"[4]
44. "Who put their plans to confusion," "[. . . .],"
45. "Who destroyed all the wicked," "[. . . . .],"
46. [. . . . . .] let them [. . . . . . .]!
47. [. . . . . . .] . . [. . . . . .]

[The following lines are taken from the fragment K. 12,830,[6] but their position in the text is uncertain.]

[He named the four quarters (of the world)], mankind [he created],[7]
[And upon] him understanding [. . . .][8]
[. . . . .] . . [. . . . . .]
[. . . . .] Tiamat [. . . . . .]
[. . . . . .] . [. . . . . .]
[. . . . .] distant [. . . . . .]
[. . . . .] may [. . . . . .]

nap-ḫar ai-bi na-si-iḫ rag-gi and *na-si-iḫ nap-ḫar rag-gi* (see pl. lxii and Appendix I).

[5] The traces of the sign on K. 9,267 are those of *kip*, not *a*.

[6] That the fragment K. 12,830 belongs to a copy of the Seventh Tablet is proved by the correspondence of its first two lines with the fragment of the commentary K. 8,299, Rev. (see pl. lx). Its exact position in the gap between ll. 47 and 105 is not certain.

[7] The line has been conjecturally restored from the commentary K. 8,299, Rev., ll. 3–6; see Appendix I.

[8] The first part of the line has been restored from the commentary K. 8,299, Rev., ll. 7–9; see Appendix I.

[The following lines are taken from the fragment K. 13,761.[1]]

[. . . .]
[2] ^{ilu}[. . . . .]
rab - bu [. . . . .]
^{ilu}*A - gi*[*l -* . . . .][3]
ba - nu - u [*irṣitim*(*tim*)[4] . . . .]
^{ilu}*Zu - lum - mu ad - di -* [. . . . .]
na - din mil - ki u mim - m[*a* . . . .]

^{ilu}*Mu - um - mu ba - a*[*n* . . . .][5]
^{ilu}*Mu - lil šamē*(*e*) [. . . . .]
ša ana du - un - ni - [. . . . .]
^{ilu}*Giš - kul lit - ba -* [. . . . .]
a - bit ilāni^{pl} [. . . . .]
^{ilu}*Lugal - ab -* [. . . . .]
ša i - na [. . . . .]
^{ilu}*Pap -* [. . . . .]
ša ina [. . . . .]
^{ilu}[. . . . .]

---

[1] That the fragment K. 13,761 belongs to a copy of the Seventh Tablet is proved by the correspondence of its fourth, fifth, sixth, seventh, eighth, and ninth lines with the commentary K. 4,406, Rev., col. i (pls. liv f., and see Appendix I). As the sixth line preserved by the fragment is the first line of the reverse of the tablet, it may be concluded that its place is about in the middle of the text. The arrangement of the text, however, upon different copies of the same tablet varies considerably, a large space being

[The following lines are taken from the fragment K. 13,761.[1]]

[. . . . .]
[2] [. . . . .]
"The mighty one [. . . . .]!"
Agi[l . . . .],[3]
"The Creator of [the earth[4] . . . . .]!"
Zulummu . . [. . . . .],
"The Giver of counsel and of whatsoever [. . . .]!"
Mummu, "the Creator [of . . . .]!"[5]
Mulil, the heavens [. . . . .],
"Who for . . . [. . . . .]!"
Giškul, let [. . . . .],
"Who brought the gods to naught [. . . .]!"
Lugal-ab-[. . . . .],
"Who in [. . . . .]!"
Pap-[. . . . .],
"Who in [. . . . .]!"
[. . . . .]

---

sometimes left blank at the end of the reverse; thus the reverse of the copy of the Seventh Tablet, of which K. 8,519 is a fragment (see p. 104 f.), begins at a different point.

[2] In the margin of the fragment K. 13,761 every tenth line is indicated by the figure "10."

[3] For the commentary to this line, see Appendix I.

[4] Restored from the commentary K. 4,406, Rev., col. i, l. 9.

[5] The commentary K. 4,406 presupposes a variant reading for this line; see Appendix I.

[The following lines are taken from the fragment K. 8,519 and its duplicate K. 13,337;[1] this portion of the text was not separated by much from that preserved by K. 13,761.[2]]

[. . . . .] - *tim*

[. . . . . - *ḳ*]*i - me - ša*

[. . . . . *n*]*ap - ḫar be - lim*[3]

[. . . . . *ša - ḳa*] *- a e - mu - ḳa - šu*[4]

[^{ilu}*Lugal-dur-maḫ šar m*]*ar*[5]-[*k*]*as ilāni*^{pl} *be-el dur-ma-ḫi*[6]

ša ina šu - bat šarru - u - ti šur - bu - u[7]

[*ša*][8] *ina ilāni*^{pl} *ma - ' - diš ṣi - ru*

[^{ilu}*A-du-nun-na*][9] *ma-lik* ^{ilu}*E-a ba-an ilāni*^{pl} *abē*^{pl}*-šu*

ša a - [na] tal - lak - ti ru - bu - ti - šu

---

[1] That the fragments K. 8,519 and K. 13,337 belong to two copies of the Seventh Tablet is proved by their correspondence with the commentary K. 4,406, Rev., col. ii (pl. liv f.).

[2] This is clear from the fact that col. i of the reverse of K. 4,406 gives the commentary to the earlier lines preserved by the preceding fragment, K. 13,761. The three columns of the commentary, parts of which are preserved on one side of K. 4,406, are probably cols. i, ii, and iii of the reverse of the tablet; if this is so, it follows that the lines on K. 8,519 and K. 13,337 follow those on K. 13,761. But, as it is possible that K. 4,406 gives the last three columns of the obverse of the tablet, a conjectural numbering of the lines of the text has not been attempted.

[3] With the phrase [. . . . *n*]*ap-ḫar be-lim*, compare the explanations of a title of Marduk given by K. 2,107 + K. 6,086 (see pl. lxi and Appendix I), Obv., col. ii, l. 5, [. . . . . .] *nap-har be-li a-ša-rid nap-ḫar be-li*, "[The . . .] of all lords, the Chief of all lords."

[4] The commentary K. 4,406 presupposes a variant reading for

[The following lines are taken from the fragment K. 8,519 and its duplicate K. 13,337;[1] this portion of the text was not separated by much from that preserved by K. 13,761.[2]]

[. . . . .].
[. . . . .] . . . .
[. . . . . . . "the Chief (?) of] all lords,"[3]
[. . . . . supreme] is his might![4]
[Lugal-durmaḫ, "the King][5] of the band of the gods," "the Lord of rulers,"[6]
"Who is exalted in a royal habitation,"[7]
"[Who][8] among the gods is gloriously supreme!"
[Adu-nuna],[9] "the Counsellor of Ea," who created the gods his fathers,
Unto the path of whose majesty

this line; cf. Appendix I. With the phrase given in the text, which is repeated ten lines lower down, compare the explanation of a title of Marduk on K. 2,107, etc., l. 16, *be-lum ša e-mu-ḳa-a-šu ša-ḳa-a*, "The Lord whose might is supreme."

[5] For the restoration of the beginning of the line from the commentary K. 4,406, Rev., col. ii, ll. 8 ff., see Appendix I.

[6] The word *durmaḫu* was employed as a Babylonian priestly title. It may here be rendered by some such general phrase as "ruler," unless it is to be taken as a proper name.

[7] This line and the one that follows it are rather shorter than usual, but, according to the commentary K. 4,406 (see Appendix II), nothing appears to be missing at the beginning of either. It may be noted that the arrangement of the four lines that follow differs on the duplicate K. 13,337.

[8] Conjectural restoration.

[9] This line and the two which follow it are restored from the commentary K. 4,406, Rev., col. ii, ll. 23 ff. (see Appendix I); for the title *ilu A-du-nun-na*, cf. also K. 2,107, etc., l. 20.

l[*a - a u*] *- maš - ša - lu ilu ai - um - ma*

[. . . . .] *Dul - azag u - ta - da - šu*

[. . . . . *šu*] *- bat - su el - lit*

[. . . . . .]*-bar la ḫas-su* *ilu* *Lugal-dul-azag-ga*

[. . . . .] *ša - ḳa - a e - mu - ḳa - šu*

[. . . . .]*-šu-nu kir-biš Tam-tim*

[. . . . . -*]*a - bi - ka ta - ḫa - zi*

[The numbering of the following lines is based on the marginal numbers upon No. 91,139 + 93,073.[1]]

105. [. . . . .] *k*[*a* (?) . . . . .] *ša - a - šu*

106. [. . . . *-r*]*u kakkaba š*[*a i-na ša-me-e šu-pu-u*][2]

107. *lu-u ṣa-bit*[3] *rēšu-arkāt*[4] *šu-nu ša-a-šu lu-u pal-su* [. .][6]

108. *ma-a ša kir-biš*[7] *Ti-amat i-tib*[8]*-bi-*[*ru la a-ni-ḫu*][9]

---

[1] See pls. xl, xlii f.

[2] The end of the line has been restored from S. 11, etc., Rev., col. ii, ll. 3–6 (see pl. lii and Appendix I).

[3] No. 91,139, etc., [*bi-i*]*t*.

[4] *rēšu-arkāt* is written KUN-SAG-GI on Nos. 35,506, 91,139, etc., and K. 8,522. The expression *rēšu-arkāt*, literally "the beginning –the future," may be taken as implying Marduk's complete control over the world, both at its creation and during its subsequent existence. It is possible that *šu-nu* is the pronominal suffix and should be attached to the preceding word, i.e. *rēšu-arkātu-šu-nu*, "their beginning and future," that is, "the beginning and future of mankind."

[No] god can ever attain!
[. . . . . . in] Dul-azag he made it known,
[. . . . .] pure is his dwelling!
[. . . . the . . .] of those without understanding is Lugal-dul-azaga!
[. . . . .] supreme is his might!
[. . . . .] their [. . .] in the midst of Tiamat,
[. . . . .] . . . of the battle!

[The numbering of the following lines is based on the marginal numbers upon No. 91,139 + 93,073.[1]]

105. [. . . . . .] . [. . . . . .] him,
106. [. . . . . .] . the star, which [shineth in the heavens].[2]
107. May he hold the Beginning and the Future,[4] may they[5] pay homage[6] unto him,
108. Saying, "He who forced his way through the midst of Tiamat [without resting],[9]

---

[5] I.e., mankind.

[6] Possibly restore *pal-su-*[*u*] or *pal-su-*[*ni*]; it is also possible that nothing is wanting. The meaning assigned to *palāsu* in the translation is conjectural.

[7] No. 91,139, *i-na kir-bi.*

[8] No. 91,139 appears to read *i-ḫ*[*i* (or *ṭi*) . . .].

[9] The end of the line is restored from the commentaries S. 11, etc., Rev., col. ii, ll. 19–21, and K. 2,053, Rev., col. ii, ll. 3–5 (cf. pls. lii and lix, and Appendix I).

109. *šum - šu lu*[1] ^{ilu}*Ni - bi - ru*[2] *a - ḫi - zu*[3] *kir - bi - šu*[4]

110. *ša kakkabāni*^{pl}[5] *ša-ma-me*[6] *al-kat-su-nu li-ki-il-lu*[7]
111. *kīma*[8] *ṣi-e-ni*[9] *li - ir - ta - a*[10] *ilāni gim - ra - šu - un*[11]
112. *lik - me*[12] *Ti - amat ni-ṣir-ta-ša*[13] *li-si-iḳ u lik-ri*

113. *aḫ - ra - taš*[14] *nišē*^{pl} *la - ba - riš*[15] *u - me*[16]
114. *liš - ši - ma*[17] *la uk - ta - li*[18] *li-bi-il*[19] *ana*[20] *ṣa-a-ti*

115. *aš - šu*[21] *aš - ri*[22] *ib-na-a ip - ti - ḳa*[23] *dan - ni - na*[24]

---

[1] No. 91,139, *lu-u.*

[2] Cf. Tablet V, l. 6; No. 35,506, [^{ilu}]*Ne-bi-ri.*

[3] No. 35,506, *a-ḫi-iz.*

[4] It is possible that in No. 35,506, Rev., l. 4 (second half of the line), an additional line of the text was inserted between ll. 109 and 110 of the text; it is also possible that the second half of the line was left blank. From the traces upon the tablet it would seem that at the end of l. 109 the scribe has written his sign of division three times.

[5] No. 91,139, etc., *kakkabu.*

[6] K. 9,267 and Nos. 35,506 and 91,139, etc., *mi.*

[7] For *li-ki-il-lu* the commentaries S. 11, etc., and K. 2,053 (see Appendix I) give the variant reading *likīn*, i.e. "he ordained their paths."

[8] Nos. 35,506 and 91,139, etc., *ki-ma.*

[9] No. 91,139, etc., *nu.*

[10] No. 91,139, etc., *li-ir-'-a.*

[11] The commentaries presuppose a variant text for the end of the line (cf. Appendix I).

[12] No. 91,139, etc., *li-ik-mi*; No. 35,506, [. . . . . *-m*]*i.*

109. "Let his name be Nibiru, 'the Seizer of the Midst'![4]

110. "For the stars of heaven he upheld[7] the paths,

111. "He shepherded all[11] the gods like sheep!

112. "He conquered Tiamat, he troubled and ended her life,"[13]

113. In the future of mankind, when the days grow old,

114. May this be heard without ceasing, may it hold sway[19] for ever!

115. Since he created the realm (of heaven)[22] and fashioned the firm earth,[24]

---

[13] Nos. 35,506 and 91,139, etc., *na-piš-ta-šu*; K. 9,267, *na-*[. . . .], i.e. *na-*[*piš-ta-ša*]; the text of the commentary S. 11, etc., also read *napištu*. *naṣirtu*, lit. "treasure," is evidently to be taken in this passage as synonymous in meaning with *napištu*.

[14] No. 91,139, etc., *ta-aš*.

[15] Nos. 35,506 and 91,139, etc., *ri-iš*.

[16] No. 35,506, *u-mu*.

[17] No. 91,139, etc., *li-is-si-e-ma*; No. 35,506, *li-is-si-e-*[. .].

[18] No. 91,139, etc., *lu*.

[19] No. 91,139, etc., [*li-r*]*i-ik*, "may it endure."

[20] No. 91,139, etc., *a-n*[*a*].

[21] No. 91,139, etc., *aš-šum*.

[22] K. 9,267, *ra*; No. 91,139, etc., *ru*. That *ašru*, lit. "place," in this passage refers to heaven is proved by the commentary R. 366, etc., Rev., col. ii, l. 3 f. (see pl. lvii), which gives the equations AN = *aš-ru*, and *aš-ru* = *ša-mu-u*.

[23] No. 91,139, etc., *ip-ti-ḳu*; No. 35,506, *ip-ti-iḳ*; K. 9,267, [*ip-t*]*iḳ*.

[24] No. 35,506, *ni*; No. 91,139, etc., *nu*. The commentary R. 366, etc. (see above, n. 22), l. 7 f., explains *danninu* as referring to the earth by the equations RU = *dan-ni-ni* and *dan-ni-nu* = *irṣitim*(*tim*).

116. *be - el mātāti*[1] *šum - šu it - ta - bi a - bi*[2] ^{ilu}*Bēl*[3]

117. *zik - ri*[4] ^{ilu}*Igigi im - bu - u na - gab - šu - un*[5]

118. *iš - me - ma*[6] ^{ilu}*E - a ka - bit - ta - šu i - te - en - gu*[7]

119. *ma - a ša abē*^{pl} *- šu*[8] *u - šar - ri - ḫu zik - ru - u - šu*[9]
120. *šu - u ki - ma ia - a - ti - ma* ^{ilu}*E - a lu - u šum - šu*
121. *ri - kis par - ṣi - ia ka - li - šu - nu li - bil - ma*[10]
122. *gim - ri te - ri - ti - ia*[11] *šu - u lit*[12] *- tab - bal*
123. *ina zik - ri Ḫanšā*$^{A\text{-}AN}$[13] *ilāni rabūti*
124. *hanšā*$^{A\text{-}AN}$[14] *šumē*^{pl}*-šu*[15] *im-bu-u u-ša-ti-ru*[16] *al-kat-su*[17]

Epilogue.

125. *li - iṣ - ṣab - tu - ma*[18] *maḫ*[19] *- ru - u li - kal - lim*

---

[1] Nos. 35,506 and 91,139, etc., ^{ilu}*Bēl mātāti.*

[2] No. 91,139, etc., *a-bu.*

[3] The text of ll. 116 and 117 corresponds to that followed by the commentary R. 366, etc. (see Appendix I).

[4] No. 91,139, etc., *ina zik-ri.*

[5] No. 35,506, *nu.* The text of the commentary R. 366, etc., gave a variant and fuller reading for the second half of the line.

[6] Nos. 35,506 and 91,139, etc., *iš-me-e-ma.*

[7] No. 91,139, etc., *it-ta-an-gi.* Lines 118–123 are omitted by K. 9,267, possibly by mistake, in consequence of *zik-ri* occurring at the beginning of l. 117 and also of l. 123.

[8] No. 91,139, etc., *ab-bi-[e]-šu.*

[9] Nos. 35,506 and 91,139, etc., *zi-kir-šu.*

[10] No. 91,139, etc., *li-bi-el-ma.*

116. "The Lord of the World," the father Bēl hath called his name.
117. (This) title, which all the Spirits of Heaven proclaimed,[5]
118. Did Ea hear, and his spirit was rejoiced, (and he said):[7]
119. "He whose name his fathers have made glorious,
120. "Shall be even as I, his name shall be Ea!
121. "The binding of all my decrees shall he control,
122. "All my commands shall he make known!"
123. By the name of "Fifty" did the great gods
124. Proclaim his fifty names, they made his path pre-eminent.[17]

Epilogue.

125. Let them[20] be held in remembrance, and let the first man proclaim them;

---

[11] No. 91,139, etc., *te-ri-e-ti-ia.*

[12] No. 91,139, etc., *li-it.*

[13] Nos. 35,506 and 91,139, etc., *Ḫa-an-ša-a.*

[14] K. 9,267, [. . . . .]-*a*; No. 91,139, etc., [. . .]-*ša-a.*

[15] Nos. 35,506 and 91,139, etc., *šu-mi-e-šu.*

[16] K. 9,267, *u-ša-tir.*

[17] From the commentary R. 366, etc., and the explanatory text S. 747, it may be concluded that the Seventh Tablet, in its original form, ended at l. 124. It is probable that ll. 125–142 were added as an epilogue at the time when the composition was incorporated in the Creation Series (see Appendix I).

[18] No. 91,139, etc., [*li-iṣ*]-*sa-ab-tu.*

[19] No. 91,139, etc., [*ma*]-*aḫ.*

[20] I.e., the names of Marduk.

126. *en - ḳu*[1] *mu - du - u* *mit - ḫa - riš* *lim - tal - ku*[2]

127. *li - ša - an - ni - ma* *a - bu*[3] *ma - ri*[4] *li - ša - ḫi - iz*[5]

128. *ša* *amêlu rē'ī*[6] *u* *na-ki-di*[7] *li-pat-ta-a* *uz-na-šu-un*[8]

129. *li - ig - gi - ma*[9] *a - na* *ilu Bēl* *ilāni* *ilu Marduk*

130. *māt - su* *lid - diš - ša - a*[10] *šu - u* *lu*[11] *šal - ma*[12]

131. *ki - na - at* *a - mat - su* *la* *e - na - at*[13] *ki - bit*[14] *- su*

132. *ṣi - it* *pi - i - šu* *la* *uš - te - pi - il*[15] *ilu* *ai - um - ma*

133. *ik - ki - lim - mu - ma*[16] *ul* *u - tar - ra*[17] *ki - šad - su*[18]

134. *ina sa-ba-si-šu uz-za-šu ul i-maḫ-ḫar-šu ilu ma-am-man*[19]

135. *ru - u - ḳu* *lib - ba - šu*[20] *ra - pa - aš*[21] *ka - ra[s - su]*[22]

---

[1] Nos. 35,506 and 91,139, etc., insert the copula *u*.

[2] No. 91,139, etc., *mi-it-ḫa-ri-iš li-im-tal-ku*.

[3] No. 35,506, *a-ba*; K. 9,267 probably read *abu*.

[4] Nos. 35,506 and 91,139, etc., *ma-ri-iš*; K. 9,267, *māri*.

[5] K. 9,267, *lu-ša-ḫi-*[. . .].

[6] No. 91,139, etc., [. . . . .]*-i*.

[7] K. 9,267, *na-kid*; Nos. 35,506 and 91,139, etc., *na-ki-du*.

[8] K. 9,267, *uznā II -šu-*[. .]; No. 91,139, etc., *uz-ni-šu*.

[9] No. 91,139, etc., [*l*]*a ig-*[. . . . .].

[10] No. 91,139, etc., *li-id-*[*di*]*-eš-ša-a*; K. 9,267 and No. 35,506, *li-*[. . . . . .].

[11] K. 9,267 and No. 91,139, etc., *lu-u*.

[12] No. 91,139, etc., *ša-al-ma*.

126. Let the wise and the understanding consider them together!

127. Let the father repeat them and teach them to his son;

128. Let them be in the ears of the pastor and the shepherd!

129. Let a man rejoice in Marduk, the Lord of the gods,

130. That he may cause his land to be fruitful, and that he himself may have prosperity!

131. His word standeth fast, his command is unaltered;

132. The utterance of his mouth hath no god ever annulled.

133. He gazed in his anger, he turned not his neck;

134. When he is wroth, no god can withstand his indignation.

135. Wide is his heart, broad[21] is his compassion;

---

[13] K. 9,267, [. . . .]-*na-ta*.

[14] No. 35,506, *bi-it*.

[15] No. 91,139, etc., *uš-te-pi-el-l*[*u*].

[16] No. 35,506, [. . . . -*m*]*u-u*.

[17] K. 9,267, [*u*]-*tar*; No. 91,139, etc., *u-ta-ri*.

[18] K. 9,267, *kišād*-[. .].

[19] K. 9,267, *man*-[. .].

[20] No. 91,139, etc., [*li*]-*ib-ba-šu*.

[21] So Nos. 35,506 and 91,139, etc.; K. 9,267, [*r*]*a-pa-aš*. K. 8,522 gives the variant reading *šu-'-id*, "fitmly established (?) is his compassion."

[22] So K. 9,267; K. 8,522 reads *ka*[*r*]- *a*[*s- su*]; No. 35,506, *ka-ra-aš-sa*; No. 91,139, etc., *ka*-[. . . .].

136. *ša an - ni u ḫab - la - ti ma - ḫar - šu ba*[1] - [. . .]

137. *ta*[*k*] - *lim - ti maḫ - ru - u id-bu-bu pa - nu - uš - š*[*u*]
138. [. . .] *tur* [. . .]-*kan a-na te*-[. . . .]
139. [. . . .]-*at* *ilu* *Marduk lu-u ilāni* [. . . .]

140. [. . . . . .]-*mat-tu-u šu-u*[*m*- . . . . . .]
141. [. . . . . . .] *il - ḳu - u - ma* [. . . .]
142. [. . . . .][2]

---

[1] So K. 9,267 and No. 91,139, etc.; K. 8,522, *i*-[. . . .].

[2] This is probably the last line of the tablet. It may here be noted that, for the text of the Seventh Tablet given in the preceding pages, only those fragments have been used which are proved by the commentaries to contain missing portions of the text. Several other fragments, which from their contents and style of writing may possibly belong to copies of the text, have not been

136. The sinner and evil-doer in his presence [. . . .].
137. They received instruction, they spake before him,
138. [. . . . .] unto [. . . .].
139. [. . . . . .] of Marduk may the gods [. . . .];
140. [May] they [. . . . his] name [. . . .]!
141. [. . . .] they took and [. . . .];
142. [. . . . .]![2]

included. The text of one such fragment (S. 2,013) is of peculiar interest and is given in Appendix II; in l. 10 f. it refers to *Ti-amat e-li-ti* and *Ti-amat šap-li-ti*, "The Ocean (Tiamat) which is above" and "The Ocean (Tiamat) which is beneath," a close parallel to "the waters which were above the firmament" and "the waters which were under the firmament" of Gen. i, 7; see the Introduction.

Volume II

Transliterations and Translations, cont.

Appendices, Indices, Glossary, etc.

Contents.

PLATES :—

SUPPLEMENTARY TEXTS.

II.

Other Accounts of the History of Creation.

I. Another Version of the Dragon-Myth.[1]

OBV.

1. The cities sighed, men [. . . . .],
2. Men uttered lamentation, [they . . . . . .],
3. For their lamentation there was none [to help],
4. For their grief there was none to take [them by the hand].
5. Who was the dragon [. . . . .]?
6. Tiamat[2] was the dragon [. . . . .]!
7. Bēl in heaven hath formed [. . . . . . .].
8. Fifty kaspu in his length, one kaspu [his height],[3]

---

second measurement in the line is taken by Zimmern to refer to the dragon's breadth, but, as Jensen points out, this is not consistent with the measurement of the mouth given in the following line. Even Zimmern's readings of 60 GAR in l. 10 and 65 GAR in l. 11 do not explain, but render still more anomalous, the ½ GAR in l. 9. Without going into the question of the probable length of the Babylonian cubit, it is obvious that the dragon's breadth can hardly have been given as so many miles, if its mouth only measures so many feet. This difficulty can be got over by restoring *ṣīrūtišu* in place of the suggested *rupussu* at the end of l. 8. We then have a consistent picture of the dragon as a long thin snake, rearing his head on high.; his coils might well have been believed to extend for three hundred or three hundred and fifty miles, and the raising of his head in the air to a height of six or seven miles would not be inconsistent with the measurement of his mouth as six cubits, i.e., some ten feet or more across.

9 ½ GAR *pi - i - šu I* GAR [. . . . .]
10. *I* GAR *li - ma - a - ti ša u*[*z* - . . . .]
11. *ana*[1] *V* GAR *iṣ - ṣu - ri i* - [. . . . . . .]
12. *i - na mē*^{pl} *IX ammatu i - šad - da* - [*ad* . . .]
13. *u - še - ik - ki zi - im - bat - su i* - [. . . . . .]
14. *ilāni ša šamē*(*e*) *ka - li - šu - nu* [. . . . .]
15. *ina šamē*(*e*) *ilāni*^{pl} *ka-an-šu ana pān* [. . .]

16 *u ša* ^{ilu}*Sin ina ulinni - šu ur - ru* - [. . . .]

17. *man - nu il - lak - ma lab - b*[*i* . . . . . .][2]
18. *ma - a - tum ra - pa - aš - tum u - še - iz* - [. . .]
19. *u šarru - u - ti ip - pu - u*[*š* . . . . . .]
20. *a - lik* ^{ilu}*Tišḫu*[3] *lab - bi d*[*u* - . . . . . .]
21. *ma - a - ta ra - pa - aš - ta šu - zi - b*[*a* . . . .]
22. *u šarru - u - ta e - pu - uš* [. . . . .]
23. *taš-pu-ra-an-ni be-el dal-ḫu-ut*[4] *nāri* [. . . .]

24. *ul i - di - e - ma ša lab - bi* [. . . . . .]

[The rest of the Obverse and the upper part of the Reverse of the tablet is wanting.[5]]

---

[1] See Jensen, *Keilins. Bibl.*, vi, p. 364; Zimmern takes the upright wedge as part of the number, cf. the preceding note.

[2] Lines 17–19 are the appeal of the gods to the Moon-god; ll. 20–22 contain the address of the Moon-god to Tišḫu; and ll. 23 ff. give Tišḫu's answer to the Moon-god.

[3] For this value of the sign SUḪ, cf. Brünnow, No. 3,013, and Jensen, *Keilins. Bibl.*, vi, p. 365.

9. Six cubits is his mouth, twelve cubits [his . . . .],
10. Twelve cubits is the circuit of his [ears . . . .];
11. For the space of[1] sixty cubits he [. . . .] a bird;
12. In water nine cubits deep he draggeth [. . . .].
13. He raiseth his tail on high [. . . . .];
14. All the gods of heaven [. . . . .].
15. In heaven the gods bowed themselves down before [the Moon-god . . . .];
16. The border of the Moon-god's robe they hasti[ly grasped]:
17. "Who will go and [slay] the dragon,[2]
18. "And deliver the broad land [from . . . .].
19. "And become king [over . . . .]?"
20. "Go, Tišḫu,[3] [slay] the dragon,
21. "And deliver the broad land [from . . . .],
22. "And become king [over . . . .]!"
23. "Thou hast sent me, O lord, [to . . . .] the raging (creatures)[4] of the river,
24. "But I know not the [. . . .] of the Dragon!"

[The rest of the Obverse and the upper part of the Reverse of the tablet are wanting.[5]]

---

[4] Jensen, *ri-ḫu-ut*, which he renders as "moisture." The plural, *dalhūti*, may perhaps be explained by supposing that, according to this version also, the dragon had other creatures to help her in the fight.

[5] Of ll. 25 and 26 the following traces are preserved: (25) [. . . . .] *maḫ-r[a- . . . . . .]*, (26) [. . . . . .] *mē*^{pl} [. . . . .].

REV. . . . .

1. [. . .] *pa-a-šu i-pu-uš-ma a-na* ^{ilu}[1][. . .]

2. *šu-uš-ḫi-it ur-pa mi-ḫa-a* [. . . . .]

3. *ku-nu-uk-ku na-piš-ti-ka i-na pa-ni-ka* [. . .]

4. *us-kam-ma lab-ba du*-[. . . . .]

5. *u-ša-aš-ḫi-it ur-pa mi-ḫa-a* [. . . .]

6. *ku-nu-uk-ku na-piš-ti-šu ina pa-ni-šu* [. . . .]

7. *is-su-kam-ma lab-bi* [. . . . .]

8. *III šanāti*^{pl} *III arḫē*^{pl} *ūmu I*^{KAN} *u* [. . . .][2]

9. *ša lab-bi il-la-ku da-mu-šu* [. . . .][3]

---

[1] Jensen suggests the restoration ^{ilu}*B*[*ēl*], which he deduces from the traces upon the tablet as published by Delitzsch; for, as he states, the only other restoration possible would be ^{ilu}*I*[*štar*], and this is rendered unlikely by the masculine form of the imperatives in ll. 2 and 4. This would prove that the slayer of the dragon was Bēl, or Marduk, in both the versions of the story. As a matter of fact, the traces are incorrectly given by Delitzsch; they represent the sign AN and not the conflate sign AN + EN (cf. *Cun. Txts.*, pt. xiii, pl. 34), and it is not possible to conclude from the text who is the hero of this version.

[2] Jensen suggests the restoration *u*[. KAS-PU], i.e., "for three years, three months, a day and [. hours]." The trace of the

REV. . . . .

1. [And . . . .] opened his mouth and [spake] unto the god[1] [. . . . .]:
2. " Stir up cloud, and storm [and tempest]!
3. " The seal of thy life [shalt thou set] before thy face,
4. " Thou shalt grasp it, and thou shalt [slay] the dragon."
5. He stirred up cloud, and storm [and tempest],
6. He [set] the seal of his life before his face,
7. He grasped it, and [he slew] the dragon.
8. For three years and three months, one day and [one night][2]
9. The blood of the dragon flowed [. . . .].[3]

---

next character after *u* is the single diagonal wedge (cf. *Cun. Txts.*, pt. xiii, pl. 34); according to Jensen's restoration this sign can only be the number "10," i.e. X KAS-PU, "twenty hours," a not very probable reading. The diagonal wedge is more probably the beginning of the sign MI, i.e. *mūšu*, and the end of the line may be restored as *umu* I^{KAN} *u* [*mūšu* I^{KAN}]; this may be rendered "one day and one night," or possibly, as Zimmern in his translation suggests, "day and night."

[3] Line 9 is the last line of the text. The lower part of the tablet is taken up with the common colophon found upon tablets from Ašur-bani-pal's palace.

II. A reference to the Creation of the Cattle and the Beasts of the Field.[1]

1. *e-nu-ma ilâni*^pl^ *i-na pu-uḫ-ri-šu-nu ib-nu-u* [. . .][2]

2. *u-ba-aš-šim-mu* [*bu*]-*ru-mi ik-ṣu*-[*ur* . . . . .][3]

3. *u-ša-pu-u* [*šik-na*]-*at na-piš-ti* [. . . . . . .]

4. *bu-ul ṣêri* [*u-ma-a*]*m ṣêri u nam-maš-še-e* [. . . .][4]

5. *u*[*l*]-*tu*[5] [. . . .] *a-na šik-na-at na-piš-ti* [. . . .]

6. [. . . .][6] *ṣêri u nam-maš-še-e ali u-za-'-*[*i-zu* . . .]

7. [. . . *pu-u*]*ḫ-ri nam-maš-ti gi-mir nab-ni-ti* [. . . .]

8. [. . . .] *ša i-na pu-uḫ-ri kim-ti-ia š*[*e-* . . . .]

---

[1] For the text, see *Cuneiform Texts*, part xiii, pl. 34, D.T. 41; for a previous publication, cf. Delitzsch, *Assyrische Lesestücke*, 3rd ed., p. 34 f.; and for previous translations, see George Smith, *The Chaldean Account of Genesis*, p. 76 f., Zimmern in Gunkel's *Schöpfung und Chaos*, and Jensen in Schrader's *Keilins. Bibl.*, vi, p. 42 f. This fragment, which George Smith suggested might be part of the Seventh Tablet of the Creation Series, does not belong to that series; it contains the introduction or opening lines of a text, and describes the creation of two small creatures by Nin-igi-azag,

II. A reference to the Creation of the Cattle and the Beasts of the Field.[1]

1. When the gods in their assembly had made [the world],[2]
2. And had created the heavens, and had formed [the earth],[3]
3. And had brought living creatures into being [. . . .],
4. And [had fashioned][4] the cattle of the field, and the beasts of the field, and the creatures [of the city],—
5. After[5] [they had . . . .] unto the living creatures [. . . .],
6. [And between the beasts][6] of the field and the creatures of the city had divided [. . . .],
7. [And had . . . .] all creatures, the whole of creation [. . . .],
8. [And had . . . .], which in the whole of my family [. . . .],

"The lord of clear vision." The reference to the creation of cattle and beasts of the field is merely incidental; it occurs in the long opening sentence and indicates the period at which the two small creatures were made; see further the Introduction.

[2] Possibly restore *kullatu* at the end of the line.

[3] Possibly restore *irṣiti*; Jensen suggests *dan-ni-nu* (cf. p. 108, l. 115).

[4] Probably restore *ali ibnū* at the end of the line.

[5] The reading *u*[*l*]-*tu* is certain from the traces on the tablet.

[6] Probably restore the beginning of the line as *ana bûl*.

9. [. . . .][1] *-i-ma* [ilu]*Nin-igi-azag šinā ṣu-ḫa-*[*ri* . . . .]

10. [. . . *pu*]*-uḫ-ri nam-maš-ti uš-tar-ri-i*[*ḫ* . . . .][2]

11. [. . . . [ilu]] *Gu-la ḫa-ma-a-ni ir*[. . . . . .]
12. [. . . . . . .] *iš-ḳa pi-ṣi* [*u ṣa-al-mi* . . . .]

13. [. . . . . .] *iš-ḳa pi-ṣi u ṣa-*[*al-mi* . . . . . .]

---

14 [. . . . . . .][3] *- ṣi i - n*[*am* - . . . .]

[The rest of the text is wanting.]

III. A reference to the Creation of the Moon and the Sun.[4]

1. UD[5] AN - NA (DINGIR) EN - LIL - LA (DINGIR) EN - KI DINGIR - [E - NE][6]

---

[1] Possibly restore the verb as [*ib-ni*]*-i-ma*; Jensen suggests the restoration [*i-te-li*]*-i-ma* and adds *ib-na-a* at the end of the line.

[2] Restore *ina* at the beginning of the line; at the end of the line Jensen suggests the reading *nab-nit-su-un*.

[3] The traces of the character before *ṣi* are those of *pa* or *ú*; we cannot, therefore, read [. . . *pi*]*-ṣi i-n*[*am bi*], "[. . . .] he calleth the white one by name [. . . .]." It is probable, however, that the second section of the text also dealt with the two small creatures whose creation is described in the first paragraph.

[4] The text is taken from the obverse of the tablet 82–7–14, 4,005, which is published in vol. ii, pl. xlix. The tablet is one of the so-called "practice-tablets," or students' exercises, and contains on the obverse an extract from a Sumerian composition (ll. 1–7), an extract from a Babylonian composition (ll. 8–14) very similar to the Sumerian extract which precedes it, and on the lower part

9. [Then did] Nin-igi-azag [fashion][1] two small creatures [. . . . .],
10. [Among] all the beasts he made [their form][2] glorious
11. [. . . . .] the goddess Gula . . [. .]
12. [. . . . .] . . one white [and one black . . . . .]
13. [. . . . .] . . one white and one black [. . . . .]

---

14. [. . . . . .][3] . . . . . [. . . . .]

[The rest of the text is wanting.]

III. A reference to the Creation of the Moon and the Sun.[4]

1. When[5] the gods[6] Ana, Enlil, and Enki

---

of the tablet a number of grammatical notes arranged in three columns and referring to the extracts given above. The first word of l. 8 is broken, but the traces suggest the word *š[a]-n[i]-[e]*, which may be rendered "version." Lines 8–14 are not, however, a literal translation of ll. 1–7, though they appear to have been taken from a somewhat similar Babylonian text. It is clear that the extracts formed the opening lines of the compositions to which they belonged, and that the scribe has written them out for comparison, adding notes on some of the expressions which occur.

[5] That both the Sumerian and Babylonian extracts are to be taken as single sentences, and not broken up into separate phrases, is proved by the note in l. 15. Here the scribe equates UD with *e-nu-ma*, and to *e-nu-ma* adds the grammatical note *iš-tu šu-ta-mu-u mal-ma-liš*, "corresponding to *šutamū*."

[6] The end of the line should possibly be restored as DINGIR-[GAL-GAL-LA], "the great gods."

2. (MAL + GAR)¹-NE-NE-GI-NA-TA   ME²-GAL-GAL-LA-[TA]

3. MA-TU³ (DINGIR) EN-ZU-NA MU-·UN-GI-NE-E[Š]
4. U - SIR   SIR - SIR - DA⁴   ITU   U - TU - UD - DA

5. U - ITI⁵   AN - KI - A   MU - UN - GI - NE - EŠ
6. MA - TU⁶ AN - NA   IM - PA - UD - DU   ŠA - A - NE
7. ŠAG   AN - NA   IGI - BAR - RA   TA - UD - DU

8. š[a]-n[i]-[e]⁷ e-nu-ma⁸ ⁱˡᵘA-num ⁱˡᵘBēl ⁱˡᵘE-a
9. ilāniᵖˡ rabūtiᵖˡ ina mil - ki - šu - nu ki - i - nu
10. uṣurātiᵖˡ šamē(e) u irṣitim(tim) iš - ku - nu
11. a - na ḳātē¹¹ ilāniᵖˡ rabūtiᵖˡ u - kin - nu
12. u - mu ba - na - a arḫa ud - du - šu ša inaṭṭalūᵖˡ

13. a-me-lut-tum ⁱˡᵘŠamaš⁹ ina libbi bāb aṣī-šu i-mu-ru

14. ki-rib šamē(e) u irṣitim(tim) ki-niš uš-ta-mu-u¹⁰

---

¹ Cf. Brünnow, No. 5,525.
² Cf. Br., No. 10,374.
³ The group MA-TU occurs in the Cylinder Inscription of Tiglath-pileser I, col. i, l. 6, in the expression ša-ḳu-u MA-TU, applied to Sin; and, from the occurrence of the parallel expression ša-ḳu-u nam-ri-ri on the obelisk of Shalmaneser II, l. 6, MA-TU is rendered namriru, "brightness." In l. 17 of the text the scribe furnishes the new equation MA-TU = ⁱˡᵘŠEŠ-KI-RU, and at the end of the line he adds the explanation RU = e-di-šu. MA-TU, therefore, signifies the brightness of the New Moon, and in the present passage may be translated "renewal."
⁴ The group SIR-SIR = banū (Br., No. 4,304), aṣū (No. 4,302),

2. Through their sure counsel[1] and by their great commands[2]
3. Ordained the renewal[3] of the Moon-god,
4. The reappearance of the moon,[4] and the creation of the month,
5. And ordained the oracle[5] of heaven and earth,
6. The New Moon[6] did Ana cause to appear,
7. In the midst of heaven he beheld it come forth.

8. [Version].[7] When[8] Anu, Bēl and Ea,
9. The great gods, through their sure counsel
10. Fixed the bounds of heaven and earth,
11. (And) to the hands of the great gods entrusted
12. The creation of the day and the renewal of the month which they might behold,
13. (And) mankind beheld the Sun-god[9] in the gate of his going forth,
14. In the midst of heaven and earth they duly created (him).[10]

---

and *napāḫu* (No. 4,327); in l. 18 the scribe equates U-SIR with *ar-ḫa*, but, as ITU occurs in the second half of l. 4, it is preferable to take U-SIR as referring to the moon itself (cf. Br., No. 7,860).

[5] Cf. Br., No. 9,426.

[6] See above, note 3.

[7] See above, p. 125, note 4.

[8] See above, p. 125, note 5.

[9] It is interesting to note that in the Semitic version the creation of the sun is substituted for that of the moon, although in the preceding line the renewal of the month is referred to.

[10] The reverse of the tablet, which is badly preserved (see vol. ii, pl. L), is inscribed with some grammatical and astrological notes.

IV. An Address to the River of Creation.[1]

1. *šiptu at - ti*[2] *nāru banat(at)*[3] *ka - l[a - mu]*
2. *e - nu - ma iḫ - ru - ki ilāni*[pl] *rabūti*[pl]
3. *ina a - ḫi - ki*[4] *[iš - ku - nu] dum - ḳa*[5]
4. *ina libbi-ki* [ilu]*E-a šar ap-si-i ib-na-[a šu-bat-su]*[6]

5. *a - bu - ub la ma - ḫar ka - a - ši iš - ruk - [ku]*[7]
6. *i - ša - tum uz - za na - mur - ra - ti pu - luḫ - t[i]*
7. [ilu]*E - a u* [ilu]*Marduk*[8] *iš - ru - ku - nik - kim - ma*
8. *d[i] - ni te - ni - še - e - ti ta - din - ni at - ti*[9]
9. *nāru rabīti(ti) nāru ṣir - ti nāru eš - ri - e - ti*[10]

---

[1] This mystical river of creation was evidently suggested by the Euphrates, on the waters of which the fertility of Babylonia so largely depended; for a comparison of similar conceptions of a river of creation both in Egyptian and in Hebrew mythology, see the Introduction. The text forms the opening words of an incantation and is taken from the reverse of S. 1,704, with restorations and variant readings from the obverse of 82–9–18, 5,311 (cf. Appendix II). A translation of the former tablet has been given by Sayce, *Hibbert Lectures*, p. 403.

[2] 82–9–18, 5,311, *at-ta.*

[3] 82–9–18, 5,311, *ba-na-a-t[um]*.

[4] 82–9–18, 5,311, *ina a-ḫi-ka.*

[5] 82–9–18, 5,311, *dum-ki*; the division of ll. 2–4 in the text is taken from 82–9–18, 5,311.

[6] 82–9–18, 5,311, *ina kir-bi-ka* [ilu]*Ea* (AN-BAT) *šar apsī ib-na-a šu-bat-su*; it is possible that the line in S. 1,704 read *dum-ḳa ina libbi-ki* [ilu]*E-a šar ap-si-i ib-na-[a]*.

IV. An Address to the River of Creation.[1]

1. O thou River, who didst create all things,
2. When the great gods dug thee out,
3. They set prosperity upon thy banks,[5]
4. Within thee Ea, the King of the Deep, created his dwelling,[6]
5. The deluge they sent not before thou wert![7]
6. Fire, and wrath, and splendour, and terror
7. Have Ea and Marduk[8] presented unto thee!
8. Thou judgest the cause of mankind!
9. O River, thou art mighty! O River, thou art supreme! O River, thou art righteous![10]

---

[7] Upon 82–9–18, 5,311, ll. 5–7 read as follows: (5) *iš-ru-uk-ku im-ma uz-zu na-mur-tum pu-luḫ-tum* (6) *a-bu-bu la maḫ-ri ka-a-šu im-bi-ka* (7) [*p*]*i-ki* ^{ilu}*Ea* (AN.BAT) *u* ^{ilu}*Marduk* (AN.ASAR.LU.ŠAR) *iš-ru-ku im-ma*. It may be noted that the duplicate in l. 5 reads *im-ma*, "daylight," for *i-ša-tum*, "fire," and for l. 7 gives the interesting variant reading "At thy word did Ea and Marduk bestow the daylight."

[8] AN.ASAR.LU.ŠAR.

[9] 82–9–18, 5,311 reads [. .]-*nu te-ni-še-e-tum ta-dan-nu al-ta*.

[10] 82–9–18, 5,311 omits l. 9, and from this point onwards it seems probable that the tablets ceased to be duplicates. The invocation to the river ceases with l. 9, the lines which follow on each tablet containing the personal petitions of the suppliant (cf. Appendix II).

V. Another Version of the Creation of the World by Marduk.[1]

OBV.

1. EN[2] E AZAG-GA E DINGIR-E-NE KI MIN NU MU-UN-RU
bītu el-lim bīt ilāni[pl] *ina aš-ri el-lim ul e-pu-uš*

2. GI NU E GIŠ NU DIM
ḳa-nu-u ul a-ṣi i-ṣi ul ba-ni

3. MUR NU ŠUB GIŠ-U-RU NU DIM
li-bit-ti ul na-da-at na-al-ban-ti ul ba-na-at

4. E NU RU URU NU DIM
bītu ul e-pu-uš alu ul ba-ni

5. URU NU DIM A-DAM NU MU-UN-[GAR]
alu ul e-pu-uš nam-maš-šu-u ul ša-kin

6. EN-LIL(KI) NU RU E-KUR-RA NU DIM
Ni-ip-pu-ru ul e-pu-uš E-kur ul ba-ni

7. UNUG(KI) NU RU E-AN-NA NU DIM
U-ruk ul e-pu-uš E-MIN *ul ba-ni*

8. ABZU NU RU NUN(KI) NU DIM
ap-su-u ul e-pu-[uš] [alu]*Eridu ul ba-ni*

---

[1] For the text, see *Cuneiform Texts*, part xiii, pls. 35 ff. (82-5-22, 1,048); and for previous translations, see Pinches, *J.R.A.S.*, vol. xxiii (new series), pp. 393 ff.; Zimmern in Gunkel's *Schöpfung und Chaos*, p. 419 f.; and Jensen in Schrader's *Keilins. Bibl.*, vi, pp. 38 ff. The variant legend of the creation is contained on the portion of the obverse of the tablet which has been preserved, but it does not form the principal subject of the composition; it

V. Another Version of the Creation of the World by Marduk.

OBV.

1. The holy house, the house of the gods, in the holy place had not yet been made;
2. No reed had sprung up, no tree had been created.
3. No brick had been laid, no building had been set up;
4. No house had been erected, no city had been built;
5. No city had been made, no creature had been created.
6. Nippur had not been made, E-kur had not been built;
7. Erech had not been created, E-ana had not been built;
8. The Deep had not been created, Eridu had not been built;

---

is merely an elaborate introduction to an incantation which was intended to be recited in honour of E-zida, the great temple of Nabû at Borsippa. The reverse of the tablet contains the concluding lines of the incantation. For a further discussion of the legend on the obverse, see the Introduction.

[2] EN, i.e. *šiptu*, "incantation," the word placed at the beginning of most religious and magical compositions intended for recitation.

9. E AZAG DINGIR-RI-E-NE KI-DUR-BI NU DIM
bītu el-lum bīt ilāni[pl] *šu-bat-su ul ip-še-it*

10. [NIGIN] KUR-KUR-RA-GE A-AB-BA-A-BA
nap-ḫar ma-ta-a-tu tam-tum-ma

11. [U] ŠAG A-AB-BA-GE RAD-NA-NAM
i-nu ša ki-rib tam-tim ra-ṭu-um-ma

12. [U-BI-A NUN(KI)] BA-RU E-SAG-IL-LA BA-DIM
ina u-mi-šu [alu]*Eridu e-pu-uš E*-MIN *ba-ni*

13. [E-SAG-IL]A ŠAG ABZU E-E-NE (DINGIR) LUGAL-DUL-AZAG-GA MU-NI-IN-RI-A
E-MIN *ša ina ki-rib ap-si-i* [ilu]*Lugal-dul-azag-ga ir-mu-u*

14. [KA-DINGIR-RA](KI) BA-RU E-SAG-IL-LA ŠU-UL
Bābilu[KI] *e-pu-[uš] E-sag-ila šuk-lul*

15. [(DINGIR) A]-NUN-NA-GE-E-NE URU-BI BA-AN-RU
ilāni[pl] [ilu]*A-nun-na-ki mit-ḫa-riš e-pu-uš*

16. [URU] AZAG-GA KI-DUR ŠAG-DUG-GA GE-E-NE-MU-MAḪ-A MI-NI-IN-SA-A
alu el-lum šu-bat ṭu-ub lib-bi-šu-nu ṣi-riš im-bu-u

17. [(DINGIR)] GI-ŠI-MA GI-DIR I-NE-NA A NAM-MI-NI-IN-KEŠDA
[ilu]*Marduk a-ma-am ina pa-an me-e ir-ku-us*

18. SAḪAR-RA NI-SAR A-KI A-DIR NAM-MI-IN-DUB
e-pi-ri ib-ni-ma it-ti a-mi iš-pu-uk

19. DINGIR-RI-E-NE KI-DUR ŠAG-DUG-GA NE-IN-DUR-RU-NE-EŠ-A-MA
ilāni ina šu-bat ṭu-ub lib-bi ana šu-šu-bi

9. Of the holy house, the house of the gods, the habitation had not been made.

10. All lands were sea.

11. At that time there was a movement in the sea;

12. Then was Eridu made, and E-sagil was built,

13. E-sagil, where in the midst of the Deep the god Lugal-dul-azaga[1] dwelleth;

14. The city of Babylon was built, and E-sagil was finished.

15. The gods, the Anunnaki, he[2] created at one time;

16. The holy city, the dwelling of their hearts' desire, they proclaimed supreme.

17. Marduk laid a reed upon the face of the waters,

18. He formed dust and poured it out beside the reed.

19. That he might cause the gods to dwell in the habitation of their hearts' desire,

---

[1] Or, Lugal-du-azaga. [2] I.e., Marduk.

20. NAM - LU - GIŠGAL - LU BA - RU
a - me - lu - ti ib - ta - ni

21. (DINGIR) A - RU - RU KUL *do.* DINGIR - TA[1] NE - IN - SAR
ilu MIN *zi - ir a - me - lu - ti it - ti - šu ib - la - nu*

22. BIR - ANŠU GAR - ZI - IG EDIN - NA BA - RU
bu-ul ṣēri ši - kin na-piš-ti ina ṣi - e - ri ib - ta - ni

23. (ID) IDIGNA (ID) BURANUNU ME-DIM KI GAR-RA-DIM
MIN *u* MIN *ib - ni - ma ina aš - ri iš - ku - un*

24. MU - NE - NE - A NAM - DUG MI - NI - IN - SA - A
šum - ši - na ṭa - biš im - bi

25. GI-BE GI-ŠE-RU ŠUG GIŠ-GI GIŠ-TER-GID-GE BA-DIM
uš-šu di-it-ta ap-pa-ri ḳa-na-a u ki - šu ib - ta - ni

26. U - RIG EDIN - NA BA - RU
ur - ki - it ṣi - rim ib - ta - ni

27. [KUR - KU]R - RA ŠUG GIŠ - GI - NA - NAM
ma - ta - a - tum ap - pa - ri a - pu - um - ma

28. [. . . .] GUD-LID-BA GE ŠURIM . . . LU AMAŠ-A
lit-tu pu-ur-ša me-ru la-aḫ-ru pu-ḫad-sa im-mir su-pu-ri

29. [. . . .] - TER GIŠ - TER - BI - NA - NAM
ki - ra - tu u ki - ša - tu - ma

30 [. . . . .] MI - NI - IN - LU - UG
a - tu - du šap - pa - ri ız - za - az - ru - šu

31. [. . . . .] ZAG A-AB-BA-GE [. . . .]
be-lum ilu Marduk ina pa-aṭ tam-tim tam-la-a u-mal-li

32. [. . . . .] GIŠ - GI PA - RIM NE - [IN - GAR]
[. . . . - *n*]*a a - pa na - ma - la iš - ku - un*

20. He formed mankind.

21. The goddess Aruru together with him[1] created the seed of mankind.

22. The beasts of the field and living creatures in the field he formed.

23. He created the Tigris and the Euphrates, and he set them in their place;

24. Their names he declared in goodly fashion.

25. The grass, the rush of the marsh, the reed, and the forest he created,

26. The green herb of the field he created,

27. The lands, the marshes, and the swamps;

28. The wild cow and her young, the wild calf; the ewe and her young, the lamb of the fold;

29. Plantations and forests;

30. The he-goat and the mountain-goat . . . . him.

31. The lord Marduk laid in a dam by the side of the sea,

32. [He . . . .] a swamp, he made a marsh,

---

[1] The Sumerian version reads "together with the god."

33. [. . . . . .] MU - UN - TUK
[. . . . . .] *uš - ta - ši*

34. [GI BA - RU] GIŠ BA - DIM
[*ḳa - na - a ib - t*]*a - ni i - ṣa ib - ta - ni*

35. [. . . . .] KI - A BA - DIM
[. . . . .] *ina aš - ri ib - ta - ni*

36. [MUR BA - AN - ŠUB] GIŠ - U - RU BA - AN - RU
[*li - bit - tu id - di na - a*]*l - ban - tu ib - ta - ni*

37. [E BA - RU] URU MU - UN - DIM
[*bītu e - pu - uš alu ib - ta - n*]*i*

38. [URU MU - UN - DIM] A - DAM KI MU-UN-GAR-[RA]
[*alu e - pu - uš nam - maš - šu - u iš - t*]*a - kan*

39 [EN - LIL(KI) BA - RU] E - KUR - RA - GE BA - DIM
[*Ni - ip - pu - ru e - pu - uš E - kur ib - ta - ni*]

40. [UNUG(KI) BA - RU E - AN - N]A BA - D[IM]
[*U - ruk e - pu - uš E* - MIN *ib - ta - ni*]

[The rest of the Obverse and the beginning of the Reverse of the tablet are wanting.]

REV.

1. [. . . . .]
[. . . . . . .] - *mat par - ṣi* [. . . . . .]

2. [. . . . .]
[. . . . . . *i*]*k - ki - lim - mu - u* [. . . . .]

3. [. . . . GAL]-AN-ZU KI-GAL DINGIR-RI-[E-NI-GE]
4. *suk-kal-la-ka ṣi-i-ru ilu Pap-sukal ir-šu ma-lik ilāni pl*

5. (DINGIR) NIN-A-ḪA-KUD-DU DU (DINGIR) EN-KI-GA-GE
ilu MIN *mar - ti ilu E - a*

33. [. . . . . . .] he brought into existence.

34. [Reeds he form]ed, trees he created;

35. [. . . . .] he made in their place.

36. [Bricks he laid], buildings he set up;

37. [Houses he made], cities he built;

38. [Cities he made], creatures he created.

39. [Nippur he made], E-kur he built;

40. [Erech he made, E-an]a he built.

[The rest of the Obverse and the beginning of the Reverse of the tablet are wanting.]

REV.

1. [. . . . . .] the decree [. . . . . .]

2. [. . . . .] . . [. . . . . .]

3 f. Thy exalted minister is Papsukal, the wise counsellor of the gods.

5. May Nin-aḫa-kudu, the daughter of Ea,

6. NIG - NA - [. . . . .] ḪU - MU - RA - AB - EL - LA
ina nik - na - ki el - lu ul - lil - ka

7. GI - BIL - LA EL - [LA] HU - MU - RA - AB - LAḪ - LAḪ - GA
ina MIN *ib - bi ub - bi - ib - ka*

8. DUK-A-GUB-BA [EL-LA ABZU] KI NER-DU-NA-ZU
U-MU-UN-NA-AZAG

9. *ina* MIN-*e el-la ša ap-si-i a-šar tal-lak-ti-ka ul-lu*

10. MU - DUG - GA (DINGIR) ASAR - LU - ŠAR LUGAL
AN - KI - ŠAR - RA - GE
ina MIN-*e* ^{ilu}*Marduk šar kiš-šat šamē(e) u irṣitim(tim)*

11. ḪE-GAL KUR-RA-GE ŠAG-ZU ḪA-BA-RA-AN-TU-TU
nu - ḫuš ma - a - ti ana lib - bi - ka li - ru - ub

12. ME - ZU U - UL - DU - A - ŠU ŠU - ḪA - RA - AN - DU - DU
par - ṣu - ka ana u - mu [ṣa] - a - ti liš - tak - li - lu

13. E - ZI - DA KI - DUR MAḪ AN - NA (DINGIR) NINNI
KI - DUR ME - EN

14. *E* - MIN *šub - tum ṣir - tum na - ram lib - bi* ^{ilu}*A - nu*
u ^{ilu}*Iš - tar at - ta*

15. AN - GIM ḪE - EN - AZAG - GA [KI - GIM ḪE] - EN - EL - LA
ŠAG - AN - GIM ḪE[1]

16. [. . . . .] . . ḪE - IM - TA - GUB[2]

---

[1] The scribe has not written out the rest of the verb; it is probable that he intended it to be read as *ḫe-[en-laḫ-laḫ-ga]*, as indicated in the translation. In Assyrian the line would read *kīma šamē lilil kīma irṣiti libib kīma kirib šamē limmir.*

6. Purify thee with the pure censer,

7. And may she cleanse thee with cleansing fire!

8 f. With a cup of pure water from the Deep shalt thou purify thy way!

10. By the incantation of Marduk, the king of the hosts of heaven and earth,

11. May the abundance of the land enter into thee,

12. And may thy decree be accomplished for ever!

13 f. O E-zida, thou glorious dwelling, thou art dear unto the hearts of Anu and Ishtar!

15. May (Ezida) shine like the heavens, may it be bright like the earth, may it [be glorious][1] like the heart of heaven,

16. [And may . . . . .] be firmly established![2]

[2] In Assyrian *lizziz*. Line 17 gives the title of the prayer as INIM-INIM-MA [. . . .] GA-GA-NE-GE; and l. 18 gives the catch-line to the next tablet, which may perhaps be restored as *šiptu* *kakkabu* [*Mar-gid-da*] *ṣumbu ša-ma-mi*, "O [Margida], thou waggon of the heavens!"

VI. The "Cuthaean Legend of the Creation."[1]

COLUMN I.

[The upper half of the column is wanting.]

1. [*a-* . . . . . .][2] 2. *bēl* ME-GAN [. . . . .]

3. *di - en - šu purussū* [. . . . .]

4. *utukku pirʾu - šu ekimmu pirʾu - š*[*u* . . . . . .]

5. *bēl elāti*[pl] *u šaplāti*[pl] *bēl* [ilu]*A-nun-n*[*a-ki* . . .]

6. *ša mē*[pl] *dal-ḫu-te išatū*(*u*) *mē*[pl] *za-ku-te l*[*ā išatū*(*u*)]

7. *ša ši-ik-la-šu šab - šu ummānu šu - a - tu ik - mu - u ik - šu - du i - na - ru*

8. *ina narī*[3] *ul šaṭir ul ezib-am-ma*[4] *pag-ri u pu-u-ti*[5]

---

[1] The text is taken from the tablet K. 5,418*a* and its duplicate K. 5,460 (see *Cuneiform Texts*, part xiii, pls. 39–41). The legend was for some years known as "the Cuthaean legend of the Creation." It was thought that the text was put in the mouth of the god Nergal, who was supposed to be waging war against the brood of Tiamat; and it was assumed that Nergal took the place of Marduk in accordance with local tradition at Cuthah. It is clear, however, that the speaker is not the god Nergal, but an old Babylonian king, who recounts how the gods delivered him and his land from hordes of monsters. In the description of the monsters in col. i, Tiamat is said to have suckled them, but this reference does not justify their identification with the monster brood of the Creation Series; it is more probable that Tiamat is called their foster-mother in order to indicate their terrible nature. In *The Chaldean Account of Genesis*, pp. 102 ff., George Smith gave

VI. The "Cuthaean Legend of the Creation."[1]

COLUMN I.

[The upper half of the column is wanting.]

1. [. . . . .][2] 2. He was lord of . . [. . . . .];
3. His judgment was the decision [of . . . . .].
4. The fiend was his offspring, the spectre was his offspring [. . . . .];
5. He was lord of the height and of the depths, he was lord of the Anunnaki [. . . . .].
6. A people who drink turbid water, and drink not pure water,
7. Whose sense is perverted, had taken (men) captive, had triumphed over them, and had committed slaughter.
8. On a tablet nought was written, nought was left (to write).[4] In mine own person[5]

---

a translation of the legend, and, though he describes it as a "Legend of Creation," he correctly recognized the general character of its contents. For later translations see Sayce, *Records of the Past*, vol. xi, pp. 109 ff., and vol. i (new series), pp. 149 ff.; Zimmern, *Zeits. für Assyr.*, xii, pp. 319 ff.; and Jensen, *Keilins. Bibl.*, vi, pp. 290 ff. For earlier publications of the text of K. 5,640, see S. A. Smith, *Miscellaneous Texts*, pl. 6 f., and of the text of K. 5,418, see Winckler, *Sammlung von Keilschrifttexten*, ii, pl. 70 f.

[2] The first six lines which are preserved are taken from K. 5,640.

[3] K. 5,640, *abnu narî*.

[4] I.e., the land was in confusion, so that no business was transacted and no records were kept.

[5] Cf. Zimmern, *Z.A.*, xii, p. 323.

9. *ina māti*[1] *ul u - še - ṣi - ma ul aḳ - ta - rab - šu*

10. *ummān*[pl] *pag - ri iṣ - ṣur*[2] *ḫur - ri a - me - lu - ti*[3] *a - ri - bu pa - nu - šu - un*

11. *ib - šu - nu - ti - ma ilāni*[pl] *rabūti*[pl]

12. *ina ḳaḳ - ḳar ib - nu - u ilāni*[pl] *a - lu - šu*

13. *Ti - a - ma - tu u - še - niḳ - šu - nu - ti*

14. *ša - sur - šu - nu* [ilu] *Be - lit - i - li u - ban - ni*

15. *ina ki - rib šadī(i) ir - ti - bu - ma*[5] *i - te - it - lu - ma ir - ta - šu - u mi - na - ti*

16. *VII šarrāni*[pl] *(ni)*[6] *at - ḫu - u šu - pu - u ba - nu - tu*

17. *CCCLX. M*[7 A-AN] *um - ma - na - tu - šu - nu*

18. *An - ba - ni - ni abu - šu - nu šarru ummu - šu - nu [šar] - ra - tu* [f] *Me - li - li*

19. *aḫu-šu-nu rabū(u) a-lik pa-ni-šu-nu* [m] *Me-ma-an-gab šum-šu*

20. *šanū(u) aḫu - [šu - nu]*[8] [m] *Me - du - du šum - šu*

21. *šalšu(šu) aḫu - [šu - nu* [m] . . .] *- lul šum - šu*

---

[1] The reading is not certain; MU is possible, i.e. *šatta*, "for a year." The phrase is omitted by K. 5,640, in which the line begins with *ul*.

[2] K. 5,640, *iṣṣur*.

[3] K. 5,640, *ta*.

[4] Literally, "city."

9. From my land[1] I went not forth, and I did not give them battle.
10. A people who had the bodies of birds of the hollow, men who had the faces of ravens,
11. Had the great gods created,
12. And in the ground the gods created a dwelling-place[4] for them.
13. Tiamat gave them suck,
14. The Lady of gods brought them into the world.
15. In the midst of the mountain (of the world) they became strong, they waxed great, they multiplied exceedingly.
16. Seven kings, brethren, fair and comely,
17. Three hundred and sixty thousand[7] in number were their forces.
18. Anbanini, their father, was king; their mother, Melili, was queen.
19. Their eldest brother, their leader, was named Memangab;
20. [Their][8] second brother was named Medudu;
21. [Their] third brother was named [. . . .]lul;

[5] K. 5,640, *ir-te-[bu]-u-ma*; the scribe has omitted *bu* by mistake.

[6] K. 5,640 omits *ni*.

[7] It is probable that 360,000, and not 6,000, should be read, in view of the large numbers which occur in col. ii, ll. 19 ff.

[8] The restoration of the pronominal suffix in this and the following lines is conjectural.

22. *ribū(u)* *a[ḫu - šu - nu* ^{m} . . . . *- d]a·- da* *šum - šu*
23. *ḫanšu(šu)* *[aḫu - šu - nu* ^{m} . . . . . *] - daḫ* *šum - šu*
24. *se[ššu(šu)* *aḫu - šu - nu* ^{m} . . . . . *- r]u*[1] *šum - šu*
25 *[sibū(u)* *aḫu - šu - nu* ^{m} . . . . . . *]* *šum - šu*[2]

Column II.

[The upper half of the column[3] is wanting.]

1. [. . . .]
2. *[u-tuk(?)]-ki* *[r]a-[b]i-ṣu* *lim-nu-te* [. . . . . .]
3. *ri - du - u* *ṭe - en - šu* *u - t[r -* . . . .]

4. *ina* [. . . .] *- e* *al - p[u -* . . . .]
5. [. . . .]*-si* *arrat* *limutti* *mātāti* ^{pl}[4] *it-ta-[* . . .]

6. *a[l]*[5] *- si* *mārē* ^{pl} ^{amēlu}*barē* ^{pl} *u - ma - ' - [ir]*
7. *[VII a - na* *pa - an]* *VII* ^{immeru}*puḫadu* *al - pu - t[u]*[6]
8. *[u - kin* *guḫḫē]* ^{pl}[7] *ellūti* ^{pl}
9. *a - šal - m[a]* *ilāni* ^{pl} *rabūti* ^{pl}
10. ^{ilu}*Iš-tar* ^{ilu}[. . . . .] ^{ilu}*Za-ma-ma* ^{ilu}*A-nu-ni-tum*

11. ^{ilu}[PA[8] . . . .] ^{ilu}*Šamaš* *ku - ra - du*
12. *iḳ - [* . . . . *]* *ilāni* ^{pl} *ana* *a - la - ki - ia*
[. . . . .] *- e* *ul* *i - di - na - am - ma*

---

[1] Possibly ŠAG.

[2] This is the last line of the column.

[3] The missing portion of the column probably continued the description of the hordes of monsters, who were oppressing the land. The king then enquires of the gods whether he should give the enemy battle (cf. ll. 6 ff.).

[4] This rendering is conjectural.

22. [Their] fourth brother was named [. . . . d]ada;
23. [Their] fifth [brother] was named [. . . .]daḫ;
24. [Their] sixth [brother] was named [. . . . r]u;
25. [Their seventh brother] was named [. . . .].[2]

Column II.

[The upper half of the column[3] is wanting.]

1. [. . . . .]
2. Evil [fiends] and demons that lie in wait [. . .]
3. Pursuing after (a man), turned [him] from his purpose.
4. In [. . . . .] did I [. . . . .]
5. [. . . . .] an evil curse was [cast upon (?)] the lands.[4]
6. [I][5] cried unto the magicians, and I directed them,
7. I set out the lambs for sacrifice [in rows of] seven.
8. [I placed there also] the holy [. . . . .],[7]
9. And I enquired of the great gods,
10. Of Ištar, and [. . . . .], and Zamama, and Anunitum,
11. And [. . . . .], and Šamaš, the warrior.
12. And the gods [commanded me] that I should go, but [. . . . .] they gave not (unto me).

---

[5] The beginnings of ll. 6–8 are restored from col. iii, ll. 18–20.

[6] The sign is TU, not TÚ (= *ut*).

[7] The ideogram is explained as *gu-uḫ-ḫ[u]* in K. 4,174 (see Thompson, *Cun. Texts*, part xi, pl. 47, and Jensen, *K.B.*, vi, p. 294). The traces of the third sign upon the tablet are those of *ḫu*, not *lu*.

[8] Restored from col. iii, l. 23.

13. *ki - a - am ak̦ - bi a - na lib - bi - ia*
um - ma lu - u a - na - ku - ma[1]
14. *ai - u* UR - BAR - [. . . . .] *ib - ri*
15. *ai - u* UR - BAR - [. . . . .] *ša - il - tu*
16. *lul - lik ki - i at*[2] *- kil* [. . .] *- piš lib - bi - ia*

17. *u lu - ud - di*[3] *ša parzilli ia - a - ti lu - uṣ - bat*
18. *šattu maḫ - ri - tu ina ka - ša - di*[4]

---

[1] The exclamatory phrase *lu-u a-na-ku-ma* may perhaps be best rendered in this way.

[2] The sign is AT, not TUR; in other signs the scribe tends to carry through his horizontal wedges.

[3] The word *lu-ud-di* evidently refers to a weapon of some kind.

[4] It was pointed out by Zimmern (*Z.A.*, p. 317 f.) that another version of this portion of the legend is preserved on a fragment of an Old-Babylonian tablet, the text of which is published in Neo-Assyrian characters by Scheil, *Recueil de travaux*, xx, p. 65 f. According to Scheil, the fragment in question forms the third or fourth column of a tablet, and in l. 8 he read the name of the king Tukulti-bēl-niši; but its parallelism with l. 22 f. of col. ii of the "Cuthaean Legend," as Zimmern pointed out, disproved the reading, and in place of Scheil's IZ-KU-*ti* [i.e. *tukulti(ti)*], *a-ka-ṣi* [or *ad*], and *a-na-aṣ* in l. 8 f. we may probably read *is-si-ḫu*, *a-ka-la*, and *a-na-ḫi* (cf. also Jensen's transliteration and translation of the text in *K.B.*, vi, pp. 298 ff.). The column of text preserved by the fragment reads as follows: (1) *im-ta-ḫa-aṣ ta-ap-da-a u-ul i-zi-* [. . . . .] (2) *i-na ša-ni-i II š*[*u*]*-š*[*i*] *li-mu um-ma-ni u-še-ṣi-am-ma* (3) *im-ta-ḫa-aṣ ta-ap-da-a u-ma-al-li ṣi-ra* (4) *i-na ša-al-ši šu-ši li-mi um-ma-na u-še-ṣi-am-ma* (5) *e-li ša pa-na u-wa* (i.e. PI)*-at-te-ir šu-a-ti* (6) *iš-tu VI šu-ši li-mi um-ma-ni i-ni-ru* (7) *im-ta-ḫa-aṣ ta-ap-da-a ra-bi-a* (8) *a-na-ku is-si-ḫu en-ni-ši* (9) *a-ka-la a-na-ḫi a-šu-uš am-ṭi-ma* (10) *um-ma a-na-ku* ŠU(?)-AN *a-na pali-ia mi-nam ub-lam* (11) *a-na-ku šar-rum la mu-ša-lim* [*ma*]*-ti-šu* (12) [*u*] *rē'ū la mu-ša-lim ni-ši-šu* (13) *ia-a-ši palē(e) mi-nam ub-lam* (14) *ki-i lu-uš-ta-ag-*[?]*-ma* (15) *pa-ag-ri u um-ma-ni lu-še-ṣi*

13. Then spake I unto my heart,
Saying: "By my life![1]
14. Who is . . [. . . . .] my friend?
15. Who is . . [. . . . .] a sorcerer?
16. But I will go, since I have put my trust in the [. . . . .] of my heart,
17. And my weapon[3] of iron will I take!"
18. As the first year drew nigh,[4]

(16) *a-na ḫu-ul-lu-uḳ ṣi-ri Ak-ka-di-i* (17) *amîlu nakra da-an-na id-ki-am-ma* (18) [. . . . . .]-*e ta*(?)-*am-ḫa-ri-a ti*-[?]-*gi-a* (19) [. . . . . .] *gu-uk-ka-ni-e* (20) [. . . . . .] *Ak-ka-di-i sa-pa-nu* [. . . . .], "(1) He fought, and conquered (lit. "he fought a defeat"), and left not [one remaining]. (2) The second time, one hundred and twenty thousand warriors I sent forth, and (3) he fought, and conquered, and filled the plain (with their bodies). (4) The third time, sixty thousand warriors I sent forth, and (5) I caused them to be mightier than before. (6) After he had slain the three hundred and sixty thousand warriors, (7) and had fought, and had achieved a mighty victory, (8) I was desperate, powerless, (9) and afflicted, I was cast down and full of woe, and I lamented, (10) saying: 'As for me . . . what have I brought upon my realm? (11) I am a king who hath brought no prosperity unto his country, (12) and a shepherd who hath brought no prosperity unto his people. (13) As for me and my realm, what have I brought upon (upon us) (14) by . . . . and (15) causing myself and my warriors to go forth? (16) To destroy the plain of Akkad (17) he hath summoned a mighty foe, and (18) [. . . .] my battle . . . . (19) [. . . .] . . . . (20) [. . . . .] to overwhelm Akkad [. . . .].'" From the summary in l. 6, the last line of the preceding column may probably be restored, as "The first time, one hundred and eighty thousand warriors I sent forth." Jensen also connects the fragment K. 8,582 (see Haupt, *Nimrodepos*, p. 78) with the "Cuthaean legend," since it describes in the first person the putting to flight and capture of twelve warriors, and contains the formula [*ḳ*]*i-a-am aḳ-bi ana lib-bi-i*[*a*]; cf. *K.B.*, vi, p. 300 f.

19. *II šuši. M ummānu u-še-ṣi-ma ina libbi-šu-nu išten(en) balṭu ul itūra(ra)*

20. *šanītum(tum) šattu ina kašādi(di) XC. M do.*

21. *šalultum(tum) šattu ina kašādi(di) LX. M + VII. C do.*

22. *is-si-ḫu en-ni-šu a-ka-la a-šu-uš uš-ta-ni-iḫ*

23. *ki-a-am ak̦-bi a-na lib-bi-ia um-ma lu-u a-na-ku-ma*

24. *a-na pa-li-e mi-na-a e-ṣip*[1]

25. *a-na-ku šarru la mu-šal-li-mu māti-šu*

COLUMN III.

1. *u ri-e-um la mu-šal-li-mu um-ma-ni-šu*

2. *ki lu-uš-tak-kan-ma pag-ri u pu-ti lu-še-ṣi*

3. *ša-lum-mat ni-ši mu-ši mu-u-tu nam.aru a-ru-ur-tu*

4. *na-mur-ra-tu ḫar-ba-šu ni-pil-su-u ni-ib-ri-tu*

5. *[ḫu-sa-aḫ]-ḫu di-lib-tu ma-la ba-šu-u*

6. *[. . . . .]-šu-nu iṭ-ṭar-da*

7. *[. . . . . li-iš]-ša-kin a-bu-bu*

8. *[. . . . . a]-bu-ba pāni*[2]

[1] Lit., "added to."

19. One hundred and twenty thousand warriors I sent out, but not one returned alive.
20. As the second year drew nigh, ninety thousand warriors I sent out, but not one returned alive.
21. As the third year drew nigh, sixty thousand seven hundred warriors I sent out, but not one returned alive.
22. Despairing, powerless, and afflicted, I was full of woe, and I groaned aloud,
23. And I spake unto my heart, saying: "By my life!
24. "What have I brought upon[1] my realm?
25. "I am a king who hath brought no prosperity unto his country,

COLUMN III.

1. "And a shepherd who hath brought no prosperity unto his people.
2. "But (this thing) will I do. In mine own person will I go forth!
3. "The pride of men, and night, and death, and disease, and trembling,
4. "And fear, and terror, and . . . , and hunger,
5. "And [famine], and misery of every kind
6. "Pursue after their [. . . . .].
7. "[But . . . . let] there be a deluge,
8. "[. . . . . . the] deluge of old time!"

[2] The reading of ŠI as *pāni* is not certain.

9. [1] ^{ilu}[. . . . . *i*] - *ḳab* - *bi* [2]

10. *i* - *zak* - [*ka* - *ru* . . . .] - *e* - *šu*

11. *ilāni* ^{pl} [. . . . .] - *ša*

12. *taḳ* - *ba* - *nim* - *ma* [3] [. . . . .] - *ki*

13. *u* *šub* - *šu* - *u* [. . . . .] - *pa*

ta - *ṣur* - [. . . . .] - *a*

14. *zag* - *muk* *ša* *rıbūti*(*ti*) *ša*[*tti* . . . .] - *pa*

15. *ina* *te* - *me* - *ki* *ša* ^{ilu}*E* - *a* [. . . . .] - *a*

ša *ilāni* ^{pl} [*rabūti*] ^{pl} [4]

16. *niḳē* *zag* - *muk* *ellūti* ^{pl} [. . . . .]

17. *te* - *ri* - *e* - *te* *ellūti* ^{pl} [. . . . .]

18. *al* - *si* *mārē* ^{pl} ^{amēlu}*barē* ^{pl} *u* - [*ma* - ' - *i*]*r*

19. *VII* *a* - *na* *pa* - *an* *VII* ^{immeru}*puḫadu* *al* - *p*[*u* - *t*]*u*

20. *u* - *kin* *guḫhē* ^{pl} [5] *ell*[*ūti*] ^{pl} [4]

21. *a* - *šal* - *ma* *ilāni* ^{pl} *ra*[*būtı*] ^{pl} [4]

22. ^{ilu}*Iš-tar* [^{ilu} . . . . ^{ilu}*Za-ma-ma* ^{ilu}*A*·*nu-ni-t*]*um*

23. ^{ilu}PA[. . . . . ^{ilu}*Šamaš* *ḳu* - *ra* - *d*]*u*

24. *mār* [. . . . .] 25. *i*[*š* - . . . .]

[The lower half of the column is wanting,[6] except for traces of what is probably the last line of the column, preserved by K. 5,640.]

at - [. . . . .]

---

[1] The fragments of the tablet K. 5,418*a* are not quite correctly put together, the beginnings of ll. 9 ff. being one line higher on the tablet than the ends of the lines to which they correspond.

[2] It would seem that one of the gods urged the king to make offerings and supplication at the Feast of the New Year, before undertaking his fourth expedition. From ll. 14 ff. it is clear that the king followed the god's advice; and, from the conclusion of col. iv, it may be inferred that he at last met with success against his enemies.

9. [1] Then the god [. . . . .] spake,[2]
10. And said [. . . . .]:
11. "The gods [. . . . .]
12. "Thou didst speak unto me[3] and [. . . . . .]
13. "And to make [. . . . .]
thou . . . [. . . . .]."
14. The New Year's Feast in the fourth y[ear . . .],
15. With supplication unto Ea, [the . . . . .] of the great gods,
16. Pure offerings for the Feast of the New Year [. . . . .],
17. Pure omens [. . . . . . .].
18. I cried unto the magicians, and I [directed them],
19. I set [out] the lambs for sacrifice in rows of seven.
20. I placed there also the holy . . . ,[5]
21. And I enquired of the great gods,
22. Of Ištar, [and . . . . , and Zamama, and Anunit]um,
23. And [. . . . . , and Šamaš, the warr]ior.
24. The son [. . . . .] 25. [. . . . . . .]

[The lower half of the column is wanting,[6] except for traces of what is probably the last line of the column, preserved by K. 5,640.]

[. . . . .]

[3] Possibly the 2nd pers. plur., "ye commanded and"; but as the god appears to be addressing the king, the rendering in the translation is preferable.

[4] The end of the sign MEŠ is preserved.

[5] See above, p. 145, n. 7.

[6] It is clear that in the missing portion of the column the king describes the defeat of his foes, since in col. iv he refers to the record of his history as an encouragement to future princes who may succeed him on the throne.

COLUMN IV.

1. it - t[i . . . . . .] 2. niše^{pl} la [. . . . .]

3. al nak - [ri . . . . .] 4. alu ša-a-[šu . . .]

5. a - na [. . . . .] i - š[u - u]

6. šarru dan - [nu . . . . .] ul - lu - [. . . . .]
7. ilāni^{pl} [. . . . . - n]e - ti u - [. . . . . .]
8. ḳa - t[i . . . . .] - ki ul [. . . -p]il-šu-nu-ti
9. at - ta šarru iššakku rubū lu mamma ša - na - ma

10. ša ilu i - nam - bu - šu šarru - ta ippuš(uš).
11. duppa - [ši - n]a[1] e - pu - uš - ka narā aš - ṭur - ka

12. i - na Kutū^{KI} ina E - šid - lam
13. i - na pa - paḫ ^{ilu}Nergal e - zi - bak - ka

14. ^{abnu}narā an - na - a a - mur - ma
15. ša pi - i ^{abnu}narā an - na - a ši - me - ma
16. la te - si - iḫ - ḫu[2] la te - en - niš - šu
17. la ta - pal - laḫ[3] la ta - tar - ru - ur
18. iš - da - a[4] - ka lu - u ki - na
19. at-ta ina su-un sinništi-ka ši-pir lu tippuš(uš)
20. dūrāni^{pl} - ka tuk - kil
21. ḫi - ra - ti - ka mē^{pl} mul - li

[1] K. 5,640, šin.
[2] K. 5,640, la te-iš-si-iḫ-ḫu.

COLUMN IV.

1. Together with [. . . . .] 2. The people did not [. . . . .]
3. The city of the [foe . . . . .] 4. That city [. . . . . .]
5. Unto [. . . . .] there was [. . . . .]
6. A mighty king [. . . . .] . . [. . . . .]
7. The gods [. . . . .] . . . [. . . . .]
8. My hand [. . . . .] did not conquer them.
9. Thou, O king, or ruler, or prince, or anyone whatsoever,
10. Whom the god shall call to rule over the kingdom,
11. A tablet concerning these matters have I made for thee, and a record have I written for thee.
12. In the city of Cuthah, in the temple E-shidlam,
13. In the shrine of Nergal, have I deposited it for thee.
14. Behold this memorial tablet,
15. And hearken unto the words thereof,
16. And thou shalt not despair, nor be feeble,
17. And thou shalt not fear, nor be affrighted.
18. Stablish thyself firmly,
19. Sleep in peace beside thy wife,
20. Strengthen thy walls,
21. Fill thy trenches with water,

[3] K. 5,640, *la-aḫ*.
[4] K. 5,640 omits *a*.

22. *pi - sa - an - na - ti - ka* *še - im - ka* *kaspa - ka*
bušā - ka *makkura - ka*
23. [. . .][1] - *k*[*a* *u*] - *nu - ti - ka* *šu - rib*
24. [. . . . *ru - k*]*u - us - ma* *tub - ḳa - a - ti* *e - mid*

25. [*pa - gar - ka*] *u - ṣur* *pu - ut - ka* *šul - lim*
26. [. . . . .] *e* *tu - ṣi - šu*
27. [. . . . .] *- ma* *e* *ta - as - niḳ - šu*
28. [. . . . .] *- ka*[2]

[The lower half of the column is wanting.]

[1] One sign is wanting at the beginning of the line; the traces suggest GUD, i.e. *alpu-ka*, "thy cattle." The reading of the second sign as *ka* is not certain.

[2] In this address to future rulers, the general moral which the king would draw from his own history appears to be, that safety is to be found in following the commands of the gods. Furthermore, he recommends his successors upon the throne, not to take

22. Bring in thy treasure-chests, and thy corn, and thy silver, and thy goods, and thy possessions,
23. And thy [. . .],[1] and thy household stuff.
24. Fix firmly [the . . .], and build surrounding walls.
25. Guard [thy body] and take heed for thy person.
26. [. . . . .], thou shalt not go out unto him,
27. [. . . . .], thou shalt not draw nigh unto him.
28. [. . . . .] thy [. . . . .].[2]

[The lower half of the column is wanting.]

---

the field against an invading foe, but to shelter themselves behind the walls of the city of Cuthah. It will be seen from the above translation that the text does not contain a legend of creation (cf. p. 140 f., note 1). The reference to Tiamat in col. i, however, is of considerable interest from the evidence which it furnishes with regard to the early date of the dragon-myth; see further, the Introduction.

Appendices.

I.

Assyrian Commentaries and Parallel Texts to the Seventh Tablet of the Creation Series.

THE Seventh Tablet of the Creation Series was a composition which received much attention from the Babylonian and Assyrian scribes, and specimens of three classes of commentaries have come down to us, which were compiled to explain the whole, or portions, of its contents. The first and most important class consists of a commentary to each line of the text; and of this class we have a single version inscribed upon fragments of two large tablets, duplicates of one another. A second class seems to have contained a kind of running commentary to passages selected not only from the Seventh Tablet, but also from the other tablets of the Creation Series; the fragment S. 747 belongs to this class of explanatory text. A third class, represented by K. 2,107 + K. 6,086, gives explanations of a number of titles of the god Marduk, several of which occur in those portions of the text of the Seventh Tablet which have been recovered. The greater part of this Appendix deals with these commentaries, and with the information which they supply concerning the contents and interpretation of the Seventh Tablet. At the end of the Appendix some fragments of texts are discussed, which bear a striking resemblance to the Seventh Tablet, and prove that the religious literature of Babylonia included parallel texts composed on very similar lines. The evidence which the commentaries and the fragments of parallel texts furnish, with regard to the form and literary development of the Creation Series, is also of considerable value.

To the commentary of the first class, which refers to every line of the Seventh Tablet, the following fragments belong:

S. 11 + S. 980 + S. 1,416, K. 4,406, 82-3-23, 151, R. 366 + 80-7-19, 288 + 293, K. 2,053, and K. 8,299. These six fragments are separate portions of two large tablets, which were inscribed with duplicate texts. I think there is little doubt that S. 11 + S. 980 + S. 1,416 (vol. ii, pls. li ff. and lv) and K. 4,406 (pl. liv f.) are parts of the same tablet, a large one inscribed with five or six double columns of writing on each side; 82-3-23, 151 (pl. liv) is a smaller fragment of the same tablet. The remaining three fragments R. 366 + 80-7-19, 288 + 293 (pls. lvi ff.), K. 2,053 (pl. lix f.), and K. 8,299 (pl. lx) are parts of a duplicate commentary to the Seventh Tablet. The commentary is in the form of a bilingual list, and presupposes the existence of a Sumerian version of the Seventh Tablet of the Creation Series; it gives a list of the Sumerian words, or ideograms, and opposite each word is added its Assyrian equivalent, generally in the order in which the words occur in the Assyrian text. The compartments, or sections, into which the columns of the commentary are divided, refer to the separate couplets, and frequently to the separate lines of the Seventh Tablet; and it will be seen that it is often possible to restore the text of the Seventh Tablet from the information which they furnish.[1] The following paragraphs deal with the sections of the commentary which have been preserved:—

S. 11 + S. 980, Obv., col. i (pl. li), ll. 1-10, the commentary to ll. 1 and 2 of the text, read: (1) [*ilu*] ASAR-RI *ša-riḳ* (2) RU: *ša-ra-ku* (3) SAR: *mi-riš-tu* (4) A: *iz-ra-tu* (5) SI-DU: *ka-a-nu* (6) RU: *ba-nu-u* (7) SAR: *še-im* (8) SAR: *ḳu-u* (9) MA: *a-ṣu-u* (10) SAR: *ar-ḳu*. From this we may restore ll. 1 and 2 of the Seventh Tablet (see the text of K. 2,854 in the block on p. 159) as *ilu Asar-ri ša-riḳ mi-riš-t[i mu-kin*

[1] For references to previous publications of various portions of the commentary, see the Introduction. The text of five additional fragments of the Seventh Tablet, which I came across after the lithographed texts in vol. ii had been printed off (see Appendix II), are published in this Appendix near the paragraphs dealing with the portions of the commentary which refer to them.

iz-ra-ti], and *ba-nu-u še-am u ki e mu-š*[*e-ṣi ur-ki-ti*]. As the verb *ša-ra-ku* occurs in l. 2 of the commentary, it would be possible to take the signs GAR and RIG in l. 1 as part of the title, and transliterate the line as [*ilu*] ASAR-RI-GAR-RIG; and this would agree with the explanations of the title given in the Seventh Tablet, as GAR = *kānu* (cf. Brünnow, No. 11,962) and RIG = *urḳītu* (cf. Br., No. 5,165). But in l. 1 of the Seventh Tablet the signs GAR-RIG are clearly to be rendered

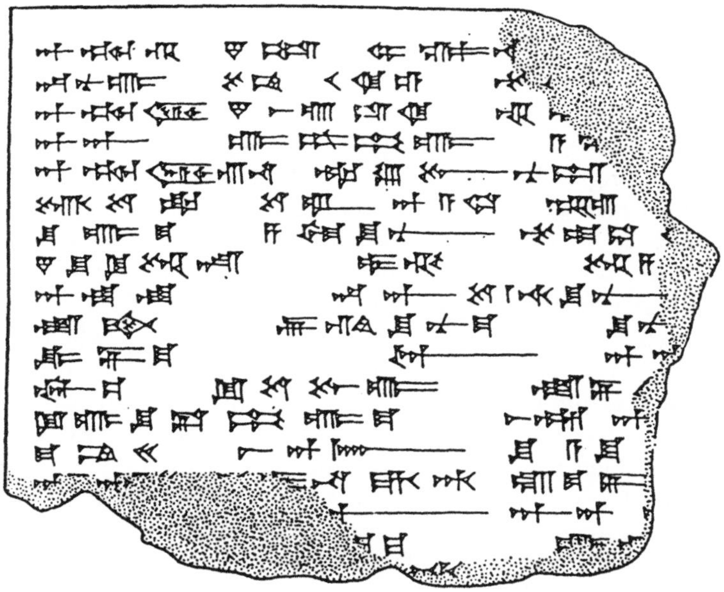

Creation Series, Tablet VII, ll. 1–18 (K. 2,854).

ša-riḳ, and it is preferable to render them in this way also in the commentary. The title *ilu* ASAR-RI is therefore explained as *ša-riḳ* (as in R. 366, etc., Obv., col. i, l. 1, *ilu* TU-TU is explained as *ba-a-nu*); or, which is perhaps preferable, the scribe wrote the two opening words of the Semitic version of the text as a heading to the commentary.

S. 11, etc., Obv., col. i, ll. 11–16, the commentary to l. 3 of the text, read: (11) *ilu* ASARU-ALIM (12) SA: *bi-i-tu* (13) SA: *mil-ku* (14) ALIM: *kab-tu* (15) SA: *at-ru* (16) SA: *mil-ku*.

The text reads ^{ilu}*Asaru-alim ša ina bīt mil-ki kab-t*[*u* . . . .]; the end of the line may therefore be restored as *a-tar mil-ki*, or possibly as *at-ru mil-ki-šu*. Lines 17–20, the commentary to l. 4 of the text, read (17) DINGIR : *i-lum* (18) SA : *u-ḳu-u* (19) [DI]R-DIR : *a-da-ru* (20) [DIR]-DIR : *a-ḫa-zu*. The text reads *ilāni u-taḳ-ḳu-u a-d*[*ir* . . . .]; the end of the line may perhaps be restored as *a-d*[*ir i-ḫu-us-su-nu-ti*]. Lines 21–22, the beginning of the commentary to l. 5 of the text, give the title [^{ilu}]AS[ARU]-ALIM-NUN-NA, and the explanation [. .]-*ru-bu*, which may be restored from the text as [*ka*]-*ru-bu*. The text reads ^{ilu}*Asaru-alim-nun-na ka-ru-bu nu-ur* [. . . .]; see further, p. 93, n. 6.

R. 366 + 80-7-19, 288 + 293, Obv., col. i (pl. lvi), ll. 1–4, corresponding to l. 9 of the text, read : (1) ^{ilu}TU-TU : *ba-a-nu* (2) TU : *ba-nu-u* (3) TU : *e-de-šu* (4) DA : *šu-u*. From this l. 9 may be restored as ^{ilu}*Tu-tu ba-an te-diš-ti-šu-nu* [*šu-u*], see above, p. 93, n. 10. Lines 5–9 (cf. also S. 1,416, col. i, pl. lv), corresponding to l. 10 of the text, read : (5) [ ] KU : *el-lum* (6) [D]U : *sa-gu-u* (7) [D]A : *šu-u* (8) [Š]A : *lu-u* (9) [. .] : *pa-ša-ḫu*. The text of the line reads *li-lil sa-gi-šu-nu-ma šu-nu lu-u* [. . . .]; the end of the line may be conjecturally restored as *lu-u* [*pa-aš-ḫu-ni*], see above, p. 94 f. Lines 10–13, corresponding to l. 11 of the text, read : (10) TU : [*ba-nu*]-*u* (11) MU : *šip-tum* (12) DINGIR : *i-l*[*um*] (13) TI : *na-a-ḫu* ; l. 11 may therefore be conjecturally restored as *lib-ni-ma šip-ti ilāni li*-[*nu-ḫu*], see above, p. 94 f. Lines 14–18, corresponding to l. 12 of the text, read : (14) IB : *a-ga-gu* (15) ŠA : *lu-u* (16) IB : *te-bu-u* (17) TU : *ni-'-u* (18) GABA : *ir-tum*, from which l. 12 may be restored as *ag-giš lu te-bu-u li-ni-'-u* [*i-rat-su-nu*], see above, p. 94 f. Lines 19–24, which form two sections upon the tablet, read : (19) DA : *lu-u* (20) DA : *ša-ḳu-u* (21) TA : *i-n*[*a*] (22) MU : *p*[*u-* . . . .] (23) DINGIR : [*i-lum*] (24) [. . . .] : [. . . .]. It will be seen that these two sections correspond to a single line (l. 13) of the text, which reads : *lu-u šu-uš-ḳu-u-ma ina puḫur ilāni* [. . . .]; from l. 22 of the commentary we therefore obtain the new value MU = *p*[*u-uḫ-ru*].

K. 2,053, Obv. (pl. lix), ll. 1–4 (cf. pl. li, S. 11 + S. 980, Obv., col. ii, l. 1), the commentary to l. 17 of the text, read: (1) ZI : [. . . .] (2) ZI : [. . . .] (3) ZU : [. . . .] (4) NA : [. . . .]. The text reads *al-kat-su-un iṣ-ba-tu-ma u-ad-du-u* [. . . .]; l. 2 of the commentary may therefore be restored as ZI : [*ṣa-ba-tu*], cf. Br., No. 2,330; ZU in l. 4 is the equivalent of *u-ad-du-u*, and the equivalent of NA in l. 4 may possibly be restored as *šu-nu*, the 3 m. pl. pron. suffix (but cf. p. 95, n. 15). S. 11 + S. 980, Obv., col. ii, ll. 2–7 (cf. also K. 2,053, Obv., ll. 5–10), which form two sections upon the tablet, correspond to l. 18 of the text and read: (2) TA : *a*[. . .] (3) KU : *ba*[. . .] (4) TA : *i-*[*na*] (5) UKKIN : *a-p*[*a-ti*] (6) IB : *ip-še-*[*ti*] (7) GAB : *ku-u*[*l-* . . .]. The text reads *ai im-ma-ši i-na a-pa-ti ip-še-ta-*[. . . . .]; it is clear therefore from l. 3 that the commentary gives a slightly variant text, or at any rate a variant reading for the second word in the line. Lines 8–13 (cf. also K. 2,053, Obv., l. 11), corresponding to l. 19 of the text, read: (8) *ilu*do. *ilu* NA-ZI-AZAG-G[A] (9) RU : *ba-nu-*[*u*] (10) RU : *ni-bu-*[*u*] (11) ZI : *ka-a-nu* (12) AZAG : *el-lum* (13) AZAG : *te-lil-tum*. The text reads *ilu Tu-tu ilu Zi-azag šal-šiš im-bu-u mu-kil te-lil-ti*; the commentary thus gives a variant form of the title, and presupposes a longer (or an alternate) form of the line, for no equivalents occur in the text to ll. (9) and (12); while for *mu-kil* the text of the commentary read *mu-kin* (as in l. 21 of the text, cf. l. 23 of the commentary). Lines 14–19, corresponding to l. 20 of the text, read: (14) DINGIR : *i-lum* (15) TU (so glossed) : *ša-a-ri* (16) DU (so glossed) : *ṭa-a-bi* (17) DINGIR : *be-lum* (18) ZI : *še-mu-u* (19) ZI : *ma-ga-ru*. The text reads *il ša-a-ri ṭa-a-bi be-el taš-me-e u ma-ga-ri*. Lines 20–24, corresponding to l. 21 of the text, read: (20) ZI : *ba-šu-u* (21) AZAG : *ṣi-im-ru* (22) ḪA : *ku-bu-ut-te-e* (23) ZI : *ka-a-n*[*u*] (24) [. .] : *ḫeg*[*allu*]. The text reads *mu-šab-ši ṣi-im-ri u ku-bu-ut-te-e mu-kin ḫegalli*.

S. 1,416, col. ii (see pl. lv), joining S. 11, etc., gives traces of two sections of the commentary which should correspond to about l. 25 of the text. S. 11 + S. 980, Obv., col. iii (pl. li) gives traces of three sections of the commentary. The third section (l. 9) begins with a title of Marduk; this may possibly refer to l. 33 or l. 35 of the text, but the traces of the preceding section do not appear to correspond to l. 32 or l. 34. According to its position in the commentary, however, this fragment should refer to about that portion of the text. The fragment 82–3–23, 151 (pl. liv) includes traces of the right half of three sections of the commentary; the second section consists of the following words: *um-mu*, *ir-pi-e-tu*, *ma-lu-u*, *ka-ṣi-pu*, *ni-ši*, *ti-'-u-tu*, and *na-da-nu*. The signs *um-mu*, taken in conjunction with *ir-pi-e-tu*, may perhaps be compared with the phrase *Mu-um-mu ir-pi-e-tu ut-taḳ-ṣi-ba-am-ma*, which occurs in the explanatory text S. 747, Rev., l. 10 (see below, p. 170), where it is followed by the comment *Mu-um-mu* = *rig-mu*. We might perhaps restore the first line of the section as *ilu Mu-um-mu*, running across the column; but Mummu, explained as *rigmu*, is certainly not the title of Marduk, but the name of Apsū's minister; it is therefore possible *um-mu* in the commentary refers to Tiamat, and may perhaps be regarded as a title (cf. Ummu-Ḫubur). The sense of the second half of the line appears to be that Marduk is the guardian of mankind and gives them nourishment.

K. 8,299, Obverse (pl. lx) gives traces of the right half of three sections of the commentary. The Reverse, ll. 3–14 give the right half of the commentary to the first two lines preserved by the fragment K. 12,830 (see the block on p. 163). Lines 3–6 read: (3) [. . .]: *ni*(?)-*bu*-[*u*] (4) [. . .]: *kib-ra-a-te* (5) [. . .]: *ṣal-mat ḳaḳḳadi* (6) [. . .]: *ba-nu-u*. The first line preserved by K. 12,830 reads [. . . . . .] *ṣal-mat* [. . . . . .]; this may conjecturally be restored as [*ib-bi kib-ra-a-te*] *ṣal-mat* [*ḳaḳḳadi ib-ni-ma*]. The first sign in l. 3 of K. 8,299 is broken and its reading as *ni* is not certain; *ir* is possible, as suggested in the copy on pl. lx. Lines 7–14, from the right half of the commentary to the second line preserved by K. 12,830, read: (7) [. . .]: *e-li* (8) [. . .]:

ša-a-šu (9) [. . . .] : *ṭe-e-mu* (10) [. . . .] : [. . .]-*mu* (11) [. . . .] : [*l*]*a-a* (12) [. . . .] : [*i*]-*du-u* (13) [. . . .] : [. . .]-*lum* (14) [. . . .] : [. . . .]-*an*. The text reads [. . . . . . .]-*a-šu* *ṭe*-[. . . . . . .]; the first part of the line may therefore be restored as [*e-li ša*]-*a-šu* *ṭe*-[*e-mu* . . . . . .], but the restoration of the second half of the line is not certain.

K. 4,406, Reverse,[1] col. i (pls. liv f.), corresponding to the fourth line preserved by the fragment K. 13,761 (see the

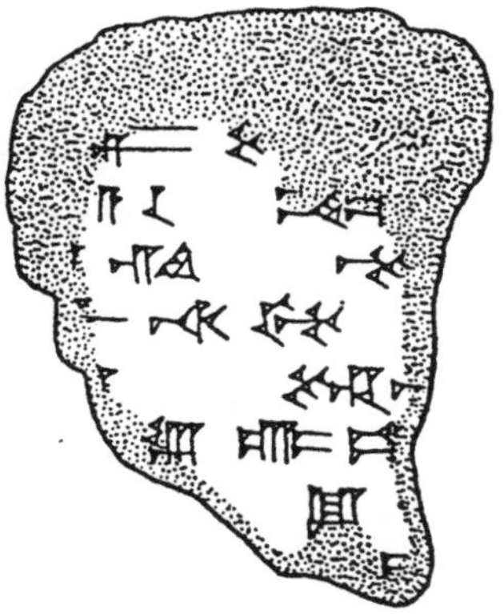

Fragment of the Seventh Tablet of the Creation Series (K. 12,830).

block on p. 164), read : (1) ^{ilu}GIL : *ma*-[. .] (2) IL : *ša-ḳu*-[*u*] (3) MA : *na-sa*-[*ḳu*(?)] (4) GIL : *a-gu*-[*u*] (5) GIL : *a-ša*-[*ru*] (6) GIL : *šal-t*[*um*(?)] (7) *šar a-gi-e* : *šar-ra*-[. .]. Of the text only the beginning of the title is preserved, ^{ilu}*A-gi*[*l* . . . . .]; in l. 1 of the commentary the sign A is omitted before GIL, and it is possible that *ma*-[. .] in the right half of the line is not to be taken as an explanation of the title, but as part of the title itself. Lines 8–13, corresponding to the next line of the text, read :

[1] It is possible that the text of K. 4,406 is from the obverse and not from the reverse of the tablet; see above, p. 104, n. 2.

(8) MA : *ba-nu-u* (9) IM : *ir-ṣ[i-tu]* (10) AN : *e-[lu-u]* (11) GIŠ : *mu-*[. . .] (12) GIN : *ḳ[a-a-nu*(?)] (13) DINGIR : [*i-lum*(?)]. Of the text only the first word, *ba-nu-u*, has been preserved. Lines 14–25 correspond to the next two lines of the text, and the title in l. 14 may be restored from the text as *ilu* ZU-[LUM-MU]. The next line of the text reads *ilu Mu-um-mu ba-a[n* . . . . . .]; the commentary, ll. 26–29, evidently presupposes a variant reading for this line, for it does not begin with the title *ilu* MU-UM-MU, although MU-UM-M[U], without the determinative, occurs in ll. 27 and 29.

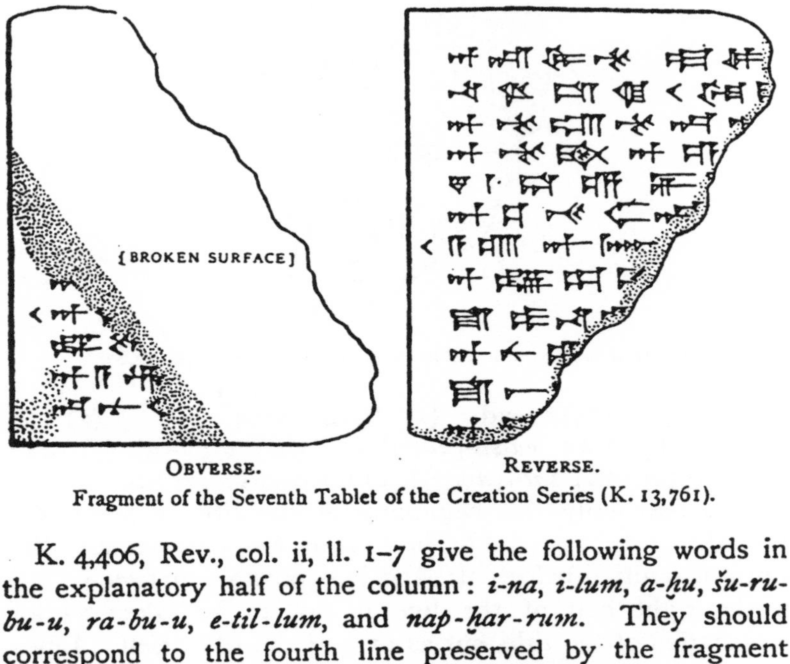

OBVERSE. REVERSE.

Fragment of the Seventh Tablet of the Creation Series (K. 13,761).

K. 4,406, Rev., col. ii, ll. 1–7 give the following words in the explanatory half of the column: *i-na*, *i-lum*, *a-ḫu*, *šu-ru-bu-u*, *ra-bu-u*, *e-til-lum*, and *nap-ḫar-rum*. They should correspond to the fourth line preserved by the fragment K. 8,519 (see the blocks on p. 165), which reads [. . . . *ša-ḳa*]-*a e-mu-ḳa-šu*. It is clear therefore that they presuppose a variant reading for the line, which may perhaps be conjecturally restored as *i-na ilāni a-ḫi-e-šu šur-bu-u ra-bu-u e-til nap-ḫa-ri*, "He is mighty among the gods his brethren, great is the lord of all!" With *e-til-lum* and *nap-ḫar-ru* may be compared [*n*]*ap-ḫar be-lim*, which occurs at the end of the preceding line preserved by K. 8,519. Lines 8–13,

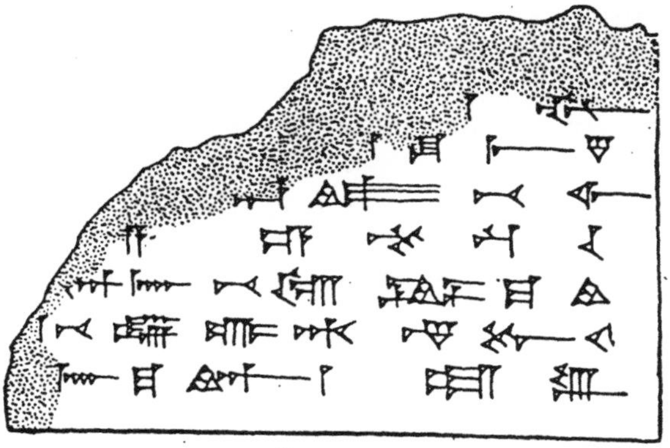

OBVERSE.

Fragment of the Seventh Tablet of the Creation Series (K. 8,519).

he commentary to the following line on K. 8,519, read: (8) [[ilu]] LUGAL-DUR-MAḪ (9) LUGAL : *šar-ru* (10) DUR : *nar-ka-su* (11) DINGIR : *i-lum* (12) LUGAL : *be-lum* (13) DUR-

REVERSE.

Fragment of the Seventh Tablet of the Creation Series (K. 8,519).

MAḪ : *dur-ma-ḫu*. The text of K. 8,519 and its duplicate K. 13,337 (see the block on p. 166) may be restored as [ilu]*Lugal-dur-maḫ šar m*]*ar*-[*k*]*as ilāni*[pl] *be-el dur-ma-ḫi*. Lines

14–22, the commentary to the following couplet on K. 8,519, read: (14) LU : *ša-a* (15) KU (DUR ?) : *i-na* (16) DUR : *šub-tum* (17) LUGAL : *šar-ru* (18) MAḪ : *ru-bu-u* (19) KU (DUR ?) : *a-na* (20) DINGIR : *i-lum* (21) MAḪ : *ma-'-du* (22) MAḪ : *ṣi-i-ru*. The text of the two lines reads *ša ina šu-bat šarru-u-ti šur-bu-u* and [*ša*] *ina ilāni*^{pl} *ma-'-diš ṣi-ru*. Lines 23–28, the commentary to the following line on K. 8,519, read: (23) ^{ilu}A-DU-NUN-NA (24) A-DU : *mil-ku* (25) NUN : ^{ilu}*E-a* (26) RU (so glossed) : *ba-nu-u* (27) DINGIR : *i-lum* (28) A : *a-bu*. The text may therefore be restored as [^{ilu}*A-du-nun-na*] *ma-lik* ^{ilu}*E-a ba-an ilāni*^{pl} *abē*^{pl}*-šu*. Lines 29–35, the

Fragment of the Seventh Tablet of the Creation Series (K. 13,337). Duplicate of K. 8,519.

commentary to the following couplet on K. 8,519, read: (29) RA : *ša-a* (30) RA : *a-na* (31) A-[D]U : *a-lak-tu* (32) [. .] : [*ru*][1]*-bu-u* (33) NU : *la-a* (34) RU (?) : [*ma-ša-lu* (?)] (35) DIN[GIR] : [*i-lum*]. The text of the two lines may therefore be restored as *ša a-*[*na*] *tal-lak-ti ru-bu-ti-šu* and *l*[*a-a u*]*-maš-ša-lu ilu ai-um-ma*.

K. 4,406, Rev., col. iii (pls. liv and lv) gives traces of four sections of the commentary. Of the first section only the ends of words in the right half of the column remain. The second section reads: (9) [. . .] - SIGIŠŠE - SIGIŠŠE

[1] The sign is much defaced (cf. the traces given on pl. lv), but is probably *ru*.

(10) UD-DU: *ša-ḳu-u* (11) RA: *i-na* (12) E: *bi-i-tu* (13) SIGIŠŠE-SIGIŠŠE: *ik-ri-bu* (14) RA: *ra-mu-u* (15) RA: *a-ša-bu.* Line 9 appears to give the end of a title of Marduk, which is perhaps explained as *ša-ḳu-u ina bītāti*[pl], "Who is exalted in the temples"; the second half of the line probably contained a second explanatory phrase. Lines 16–19 read: (16) DINGIR: *i-lum* (17) IGI: *maḫ-ru* (18) [T]U: *e-ri-bu* (19) [. . .]: *ḳat-ru-u*; from this it is possible to build up the line as *ilāni ma-ḫar-šu li-še-ri-bu ḳat-ra-šu-un*, "Let the gods bring their gifts into his presence"; a reference to this line is possibly contained in the explanatory text, S. 747, Rev., l. 6, which begins [. . . . . *l*.]*i-še-ri-bu ḳat-ra-šu-un* (see below, p. 170); the fourth section gives the first word of the next line as *a-di.*

S. 11 + S. 980, Rev., col. i (pls. lii f.), and its duplicates, K. 2,053, Rev., col. i (pls. lix f.), and R. 366 + 80–7–19, 293, Rev., col. i (pl. lvii), give traces of seven sections of the commentary, which appear to correspond to a portion of the text between ll. 90 and 100. S. 11 + S. 980, Rev., col. ii (pl. lii), ll. 1–6, corresponding to l. 106 of the text, read: (1) [. . . .]: [. . .]-*ru* (2) [. . . .]: [*ka*]*k*-[*k*]*a-b*[*u*] (3) [R]A: *ša-*[*a*] (4) RA: *i-na* (5) AN: *ša-me-e* (6) DU-DU: *šu-pu-u.* The text reads [. . . . -*r*]*u kakkaba š*[*a* . . . .], so that the end of the line may be conjecturally restored as *š*[*a i-na ša-me-e šu-pu-u*]. Ll. 7–12, corresponding to l. 107 of the text, read: (7) RA: *lu-u* (8) RA: *ṣa-ba-tu* (9) KUN-SAG-GE: *ri-e-šu ar-kat* (10) AN: *ri-e-šu* (11) RU: *ar-kat* (12) [. .]-ŠA-A-RU: *pa-la-su.* The text reads *lu-u ṣa-bit rēšu-arkāt šu-nu ša-a-šu lu-u pal-su* [. .], see above, p. 106 f. Lines 13–21 (cf. pl. lix for the duplicate commentary, K. 2,053, Rev., col. ii, ll. 1–5), corresponding to l. 108 of the text, read: (13) [ ] MA: *ma-a* (14) [ ] MA: *ma-ru* (15) RA: *ša-a* (16) RA: *i-na* (17) IR (so glossed on S. 11, etc., cf. l. 26): *kir-bu* (18) NE-RU (possibly ERIM, cf. Brünnow, No. 4,603): *tam-tim* (19) GID: *e-bi-ru* (20) RA: *la-a* (21) NE: *na-a-ḫu.* The text reads *ma-a ša kir-biš Ti-amat i-tib-bi-*[. . . . .], and from the commentary the end of the line may conjecturally be restored as *i-tib-bi-[ru la a-ni-ḫu]*. Lines 22–26 (K. 2,053, ll. 6–10), corresponding to l. 109 of the text, read: (22) NE: *šu-uš-šu* (23) RA: *lu-u* (24) NI-BI-RU: *Ni-bi-ru* (25) RA: *a-ḫa-zu* (26) IR (so glossed): *kir-bu*. The text reads *šum-šu lu* [ilu]*Ni-bi-ru a-ḫi-zu kir-bi-šu*. Lines 27–31 (K. 2,053, ll. 11–14), corresponding to l. 110 of the text, read: (27) RA: *ša-a* (28) AN: *kak-ka-bu* (29) AN: *šamē(e)* (duplicate *ša-me-e*) (30) RA (so glossed): *a-la-ku* (31) RA (so glossed): *ka-a-nu*. The text reads *ša kakkabāni*[pl] *ša-ma-me al-kat-su-nu li-ki-il-lu*; for *li-ki-il-lu* the commentaries thus give the variant reading *likīn*, "he ordained." Lines 32–38 (K. 2,053, ll. 15–21), corresponding to l. 111 of the text, read: (32) ḪAR: *ki-ma* (33) RI: *ṣi-e-nu* (34) RI: *ri-'-u* (35) DINGIR: *i-lum* (36) ḪAR: *lib-bi* (37) ŠAG: *lib-bi* (38) ŠAG: *pu-uḫ-ru*. The text reads *kīma ṣi-e-ni li-ir-ta-a ilāni gim-ra-šu-un*; thus for *gim-ra-šu-un* the text of the commentaries evidently gave a variant reading. Lines 39–44, corresponding to l. 112 of the text, read: (39) IR: *ka-mu-u* (40) NE-RU (see above): *tam-tim* (41) IR: *ši-*[. .] (42) ŠI: *na-p[iš-tu]* (43) KIR: *sa-[a-ku]* (44) KIR: [. . .]. The text reads: *lik-me Ti-amat ni-ṣir-ta-ša* (var. *na-piš-ta-šu*) *li-si-iḳ u lik-ri*; the commentary thus supports the variant reading to the text.

R. 366 + 80-7-19, 293, Rev., col. ii (pl. lvii), l. 1, which reads [. . .]: [*ṣa*]*-a-t*[*i*], corresponds to the last word of l. 114 of the text. Lines 2–8, corresponding to l. 115 of the text, read: (2) IR: *šu-u* (3) AN: *aš-ru* (4) *aš-ru*: *ša-mu-u* (5) RU (so glossed): *ba-nu-u* (6) RU: *pa-ta-ḳu* (7) RU: *dan-ni-ni* (8) *dan-ni-nu*: *irṣitim(tim)*. The text reads *aš-šu aš-ri ib-na-a ip-ti-ḳa dan-ni-na*; ll. 4 and 8 of the commentary explain *ašru* as referring to heaven, and *danninu* as referring to the earth; a reference to this line also possibly occurs in the explanatory text, S. 747, Rev., l. 10 (see below, p. 170). Lines 9–13, corresponding to l. 116 of the text, read: (9) EN KUR-KUR (i.e. *bēl mātāti*): *šum-šu* (10) MA: *šu-mu* (11) MA: *na-bu-u* (12) A: *a-bu* (13) EN KUR-KUR: [ilu]EN-LIL (i.e. [ilu]*Bēl*); l. 9 thus explains *bēl mātāti* as "his name," i.e. Marduk's name, and l. 13 gives it as the title of Enlil, or the elder Bēl, who in the text transfers it to Marduk. The text of the line reads *be-el mātāti šum-šu it-ta-bi a-bi* *ilu**Bēl.* Lines 14–17, corresponding to l. 117 of the text, read: (14) MA: *zik-ri* (15) AN: *ilu**Igigi* (16) MA: *ni-bu* (17) UZU: *nag-bu.* The text reads *zik-ri* (var. *ina zik-ri*) *ilu**Igigi im-bu-u na-gab-šu-un.* Lines 18–23, corresponding to l. 118 of the text, read: (18) [. . .]: *še-mu-u* (19) [. . .]: *ilu*[*E-a*] (20) [. . .]: *k*[*a-bit-tu*] (21) [ ] LI: *ra-*[. . .] (22) [ ] LI: *na-g*[*u-u*] (23) [ ] LI: *ḫi-*[. . .]. The text of the line reads *iš-me-ma ilu**E-a ka-bit-ta-šu i-le-en-gu*; the text of the commentary therefore gave a fuller form for the second half of the line. Lines 24–27, corresponding to l. 119 of the text, read: (24) A: *ma-*[*a*] (25) A: *a-*[*bu*] (26) A: *šur-r*[*u-ḫu*] (27) MA: *zik-*[*ri*]. The text of the line reads *ma-a ša abē**pl**-šu u-šar-ri-ḫu zik-ru-u-šu.*

At this point the scribe of R. 366, etc., ceases to give the commentary in the form of a bilingual list, and in ll. 28–34 he writes out the text of the Assyrian version of ll. 120–124 of the composition. Then follows a colophon of three lines which read: (35) *an-nu-u-tu* (?) *ul kalū u* [. . . . .] (36) *ša* LI *šumē**pl* *ša* [. . . . .] (37) *ša ina libbi* *ilu**Asar-ri* [. . . . .], "These are not all (?) and [. . . . .] of the fifty-one names of [. . . . .] which are in (the composition entitled) 'Asari [. . . . .].'" The reading of l. 35 is not certain, but the colophon seems to imply that the commentary was not complete, or else that the fifty (or fifty-one) names of Marduk were not all given in the composition itself. Two important facts may be deduced from the colophon. The first is that the Seventh Tablet of the Creation Series is here treated as an independent composition which takes its title from its opening line. The second is that in this independent form the composition ended with l. 124 of the tablet. It is clear, therefore, that ll. 125–142 of the Seventh Tablet are in the nature of an epilogue, which was added to the composition at the time it was incorporated as the concluding tablet in the series *Enuma eliš.*

The supposition that the text of the Seventh Tablet ended originally at l. 124 receives additional support from the explanatory text S. 747 (see *Cuneiform Texts*, pt. xiii, pl. 32).[1] When complete it is probable that the tablet, of which S. 747 formed a part, contained a kind of running commentary to the whole of the Creation Series; only fragments of the beginning and of the end of the commentary are preserved by S. 747, and these refer to the First Tablet and to the Seventh Tablet of the Series respectively. Thus, S. 747, Obv., l. 1, which reads [. . . . . .] *riš-tu-u za-ru-šu-un*, followed by the comment *za-ru-u* = [. . . . . .], refers to Tablet I, l. 3; l. 3, which reads [. . . . . . . -*t*]*i* *ṣu-ṣu-u nap-pa*-[. . .], refers to Tablet I, l. 6; and the mention of *Ēa* in l. 5 is in accordance with the prominent part which the god plays in Tablet I, in detecting and defeating the plot of Apsū and Tiamat. On the other hand, the reverse of S. 747 appears to deal with the Seventh Tablet of the Series; thus, l. 3 may perhaps be compared with the equation NUN = ^{ilu}*E-a*, given by K. 4,406, Rev., col. ii, l. 25, in the commentary to a line of the Seventh Tablet (see above, p. 166); l. 6 possibly contains a reference to the line of the Seventh Tablet to which the commentary K. 4,406, Rev., col. iii, ll. 16–19, corresponds (see above, p. 167); the words in l. 10, [. . .] *dan-ni-na* (or [. . . *u*]-*dan-ni-na*) *ir-ṣi-tum*, possibly refer to l. 115 of the Seventh Tablet, while the second half of the same line perhaps contains a reference to the line of the Seventh Tablet, to which the commentary 82–3–23, 151, section 2, corresponds (see above, p. 162, and for the verb *ut-taḳ-ṣi-ba-am-ma*, cf. Tablet V, l. 20); and the words *ri-e-šu ar-ka-tu* in l. 11 clearly refer to l. 107 of the Seventh Tablet. Line 12 of S. 747 quotes l. 124 of the Seventh Tablet, followed by the explanatory equations L (i.e. "Fifty") = *Ḫa-an-ša-a* (i.e. Marduk's last title) and L = ^{ilu}*Bēl*. Now, as l. 12 is the last line of S. 747, it is not unreasonable to suppose that the

[1] See above, p. 157.

portion of text it explains came at the end of the composition to which the commentary refers.

The tablet K. 2,107 + K. 6,086 (pls. lxi f.), which has already been referred to,[1] is not strictly a commentary to the Seventh Tablet of the Creation Series, but is of value for explaining some of the titles of Marduk which occur therein. The second column is subdivided by a perpendicular line; in the left half of the column are inscribed the titles of Marduk, and in the right half the explanations are set opposite them. Lines 9–18 form a single section, and probably give a number of alternative explanations referring to a single title which was written in the left half of l. 9. In the following transliteration of the text a translation of each Assyrian rendering in the right half of the column is added beneath it:—

	Title.		Explanation.
1.	[Wanting.]	:	[. . . . .]-*ni ma-tim ali u ni-ši* "[The . . .] of land, city, and people."
2.	[Wanting.]	:	[. . . *ma-ti*]*m ali u ni-ši* "[The . of la]nd, city, and people."
3.	[Wanting.]	:	[. . . . .] *maš-ki-ti ana ali u ni-ši* "[The . . . .] of drink unto city and people."
4.	[Wanting.]	:	[. . . . .] *a-li-id* ^{ilu}*Sin u* ^{ilu}*Šamaš* "[The . . .] Begetter of the Moon and the Sun."
5.	[Wanting.]	:	[. . .] *nap-ḫar be-li a-ša-rid nap-ḫar be-li* "[The . . .] of all lords, the Chief of all lords."
6.	[Wanting.]	:	[. . . . . . *-n*]*i ka-la ti-me-a-ti* "[The Creator(?)] of all words(?)."

[1] See above, p. 157.

	Title.	Explanation.
7.		[. . . . . *-n*]*i* *nap-ḫar* *ti-me-a-ti*[1] "[The Creator(?)] of all words(?)."
8.	[Wanting.] :	[. . .]^{pl} *šar* *ka-la* *ili* *u* *šarri* "[The . . .] of the [. . .], the King of all gods and kings."
9.	[Wanting.] :	[. . .] *ilāni*^{p} "[The . . .] of the gods."
10.		[. . . *šam*]*ē*(*e*) *u* *irṣitim*(*tim*) "[The . . . of hea]ven and earth."
11.		[. . . *šamē*](*e*) *u* *irṣitim*(*tim*) "[The . . . of heaven] and earth."
12.		[. . . . .] ^{ilu}*Bēl* "[The . . . . . .] of Bēl."
13.		*be-lum* [. . . *šam*]*ē*(*e*) *u* *irṣitim*(*tim*) "The Lord [. . .] of heaven and earth."
14.		*be - lum* *a - ši - ir* *ilāni*^{pl} "The Lord, the Blesser of the gods."
15.		*be - lum* *ga - me - il* *ilāni*^{pl} "The Lord, the Benefactor of the gods."
16.		*be - lum* *ša* *e - mu - ḳa - a - šu* *ša - ḳa - a* "The Lord, whose might is supreme."
17.		*be - el* *Bābili*^{KI} "The Lord of Babylon."
18.		*mud - diš* *Bābili*^{KI} "The Renewer of Babylon."

[1] This line gives a slightly variant explanation of the title in l. 6.

TITLE.	EXPLANATION.
19. ^{ilu}LUGAL-EN-AN-KI-A	: *be-el ilāni*^{pl} *ša šamē u irṣiti šar ilāni*^{pl} *ša šamē u irṣiti* "The Lord of the gods of heaven and earth, the King of the gods of heaven and earth."
20. ^{ilu}A-DU-NUN-NA	: *ma-lik* ^{ilu}*Bēl u* ^{ilu}*E-a* "The Counsellor of Bēl and Ea."
21. ^{ilu}TU-TU	: *mu-al-lid ilāni*^{pl} *mu-ud-di-iš ilāni*^{pl} "The Begetter of the gods, the Renewer of the gods."
22. ^{ilu}GU-GU	: *mu-tak-kil ilāni*^{pl} "The Strengthener of the gods."
23. ^{ilu}MU-MU	: *mu-uš-pi-iš ilāni*^{pl} "The . . . of the gods."
24. ^{ilu}DU-ṬU	: *ba-ni ka-la ilāni*^{pl} "The Creator of all the gods."
25. ^{ilu}DU-DU	: *mu-ut-tar-ru-u ilāni*^{pl} "The Leader of the gods."
26. ^{ilu}MU-AZAG	: *ša ši-pat-su el-lit* "Whose Incantation is pure."
27. ^{ilu}MU-AZAG	: *ša tu-u-šu el-lit* "Whose Spell is pure."
28. ^{ilu}ŠAG(-SUD)-ZU	: *mu-di-e libbi ilāni*^{pl} *lib-bu ru-u-ḳu* (*ḫi-bi eš-šu*)[1] "Who knoweth the heart of the gods, the wide heart (recent break)."

[1] The note *ḫi-bi eš-šu*, which is written in smaller characters, signifies that the end of the line was broken in the original tablet from which the scribe was copying.

	Title.	Explanation.
29.	Zi (-*do.*)-ukkin	: *nap-šat nap-ḫar ilāni* "The Life of all the gods."
30.	^{ilu}Zi (-*do.*)-si	: *na-si-iḫ ša-bu-ti* "The Remover[1] of the mighty."
31.	^{ilu}Suḫ (-*do.*)-kur	: *mu-bal-lu-u ai-bi* "The Destroyer of the foe."
32.	^{ilu}[. . .](-*do.*)-kur	: *mu-bal-lu-u nap-ḫar ai-bi na-si-iḫ rag-gi* "The Destroyer of all foes, the Remover of the wicked."
33.	[Wanting.]	: *na-si-iḫ nap-ḫar rag-gi* "The Remover of all the wicked."
34.	[Wanting.]	: [. . . *ra*]*g-gi e-šu-u rag-gi* "[The . . . of the] wicked; the Annihilator of the wicked."
35.	[Wanting.]	: [. . . *rag*]-*gi e-šu-u nap-ḫar rag-gi* "[The . . . of the wick]ed; the Annihilator of all the wicked."
36.	[Wanting.]	: [. . . . .]-*ti* "[. . . . .]."

In the earlier part of the text the titles which were given on the left side of the column in ll. 1–6 and 8 and 9 are wanting, but the explanations on the right side recall many phrases of the Seventh Tablet, from among which we may compare those given in l. 5 with the end of the 3rd line preserved by the fragment K. 8,519 (see above, p. 104 f.), and that in l. 16 with the 4th and 14th lines of the same fragment. Of the

[1] I.e., "Destroyer."

titles given in ll. 19 ff., compare l. 20 with ^{ilu}*A-du-nun-na* and its explanation in the 8th line preserved by K. 8,519; l. 21 with ^{ilu}*Tu-tu* in l. 9 of the Seventh Tablet (see above, p. 92 f.); l. 27 with ^{ilu}*Mu-azag* in l. 33 (see above, p. 98 f.); l. 28 with ^{ilu}*Šag-zu* in l. 35 (see above, p. 98 f.); l. 29 with ^{ilu}*Zi-ukkin-na* in l. 15 (see above, p. 94 f.); l. 30 with ^{ilu}*Zi-si* in l. 41 (see above, p. 100 f.); and l. 31 with ^{ilu}*Suḫ-kur* in l. 43 (see above, p. 100 f.). It is possible that col. i of the Obverse of K. 2,107 + K. 6,086 (see pl. lxi) also contained explanations of the Seventh Tablet, or at any rate referred to the Creation Series, as l. 4 reads [. . . . . .] *Apsū* and l. 15 [. . . . . *Ti* (?)]-*amat*.

It was stated on p. 157 that fragments exist of compositions very similar in character to the Seventh Tablet of the Creation Series. Remains of one such composition are preserved by the fragment of a Neo-Babylonian tablet, No. 54,228, the text of which is published in vol. ii, pl. lxiii, and by its two Assyrian duplicates, R. 395 (see vol. ii, pl. lxii) and R. 2, 538 (see the block on p. 176). R. 2, 538 is a duplicate of No. 54,228, Obv., ll. 6–15; R. 395, Rev., ll. 3–5 correspond to No. 54,228, ll. 8, 10, and 12. The Obverse of R. 395, which does not correspond to any portion of the text preserved by the other two fragments, reads as follows:—

1. [. . . . . .] 2. [ ] ^{ilu}[. . . . . .]
3. *ai ib - ba - ši - [m]a* ^{ilu}[. . . . . .]
4. *ip-te-ma ina inā*^{II} *ša nārāti*[^{pl} . . . . . .]
5. *e - piš zib - bat - sa tur - ma* [. . . . . .]
6. *ri - eš ta - mar - ti it - b*[*a -* . . . . . .]
7. *iš - mi - ma* ^{ilu}*Bēl pā - šu* [. . . . . .]
8. *iš - ši - ma miṭ - ṭa i*[*m -* . . . . . .]
9. *iš - tu* [. . . . . .] 10. ^{ilu}[. . . . . .]

If this fragment is in the form of narrative, it follows that ll. 1–6 are the concluding lines of a speech, since l. 7 reads

"Bēl hearkened and his mouth [. . . . .]." Bēl did not answer, however, for l. 8 reads "He raised the club [. . . .]." Now the phrase *iš-ši-ma miṭ-ṭa* occurs in Tablet IV of the Creation Series, l. 37, but the context on this fragment does not suggest a variant account either of the arming of Marduk for battle or of the actual fight with Tiamat. Moreover, the Reverse of the fragment, which is in part a duplicate of No. 54,228 and R. 2, 538 (see above), is inscribed with addresses in honour of Marduk under some of the titles

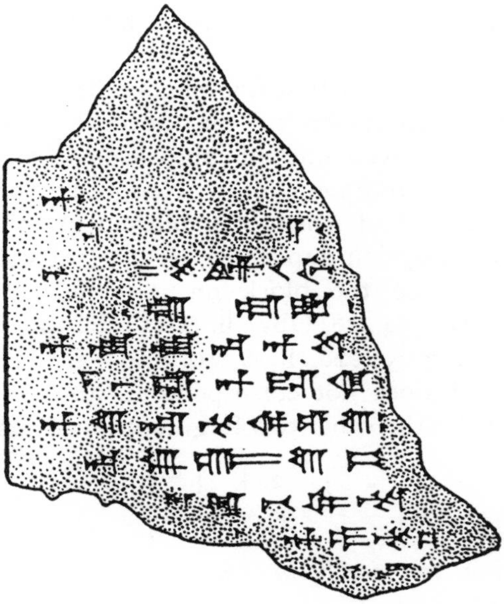

Fragment of a parallel text to the Seventh Tablet of the Creation Series (R. 2, 538). Duplicate of No. 54,228.

which occur on the Seventh Tablet of the Creation Series. It is therefore probable that the Obverse of R. 398 contains a part of the same composition. Line 4, which reads "He opened [. . . .] at the sources of the rivers [. . . .]," would in that case refer to some act of creation on the part of Marduk, and the lines which follow would celebrate incidents in the battle with Tiamat.

Only a few traces of characters are preserved on the Reverse of R. 395, but enough is left to prove that ll. 3, 4, and 5 are duplicates of No. 54,228, Obv., ll. 8, 10, and 12. The following is the text of No. 54,228 with restorations and variants from R. 395 and R. 2, 538 :—

OBV.

1\. [. . . .] *ḫa* [. . . .] 2. [. . . .] ^{ilu}*Ea ib*-[. . . .],

3\. *li - pu - uš iz - ri* - [. . . . .]

4\. *iṣu a - rik iš - kur*(?) *nu*[1] - [. . . . . .]

5\. GIŠ - GID - DA *a - rik* [. . . . .][2]

6\. ^{ilu}*Asar - ri ša - rik me* - [*riš - ti*[3] . . . . . .]

7\. *iz - ra - tum a* - [. . . . .]

8\. *ba - nu - u še - im u gu - e* [. . . . . .]

9\. *g*[*u*] - *u*[4] *ṣi - ḫir - t*[*u* . . . .]

10\. ^{ilu}*Tu - tu ba - an*[5] *te - diš* - [*ti - šu - nu* . . . .]

11\. *šum ilāni*^{pl} *ša ma - ḫa - zi*[6] [. . . .]

12\. ^{ilu}*Šag - zu mu - di - e lib - bi il*[*āni*^{pl}[7] . . . .]

13\. ^{ilu}*Šag - gar*(?)[8] *ba - ru - u lib - bi* [. . . .]

---

[1] Possibly *ḫ*[*a*- . . .].

[2] It will be noticed that ll. 4–17 are written in couplets, the second half of each couplet being set back a little from the edge of the tablet. It is just possible that these second lines give explanations of phrases in the lines which precede them. It appears on the whole more probable, however, that they form part of the actual text; in that case the couplets in ll. 8 f., 10 f., and 12 f. are written as single lines on the fragment R. 395.

[3] Restored from Tablet VII, l. 1, see above, p. 92.

[4] So the traces upon No. 54,228 appear to read; R. 2, 538 [*g*]*u-um*.

[5] R. 395, *ni*.

[6] For l. 11, R. 2, 538 reads *ša ina Bābili*^{KI}[. . . . . .].

[7] The traces of the following lines upon R. 395 do not correspond to the portions of the text preserved by No. 54,228.

[8] R. 2, 538 omits the title at the beginning of the line.

14. ^{ilu}*En-bi-lu-lu be-lum mu-diš māti - šu* [. . . .]

15. *na - mad šu - ' - u*[1] *mu - šab - šu* [. . . . .]

16. ^{ilu}*Tutu*[2] *ša pi - ti - iḳ māti i* - [. . . . . .]

17. ^{ilu}*Tutu* ^{ilu}*Marduk tam - tum b*[*a* (?) · . . .]

18. *Ti - amat iddu*(*du*) *šu - lu* - [. . . . .]

19. *ša ina ri - e - ši u ar - ka* - [*ti*[3] . . . .]

20. ^{ilu}*Nabū ina* BAR - NAM^{pl}[4] *ūmu VI*^{KAN} [. . . .]

21. ^{ilu}*A - du - nun - na ma - lik* ^{ilu}[. . . . . .]

22. ^{ilu}*Ninib* ^{ilu}*Ḫanšā ib* - [. . . . .]

23. [. . .] *a - lak - ti ru* - [. . . . .]

24. [. . .] *ṣilli* [. . .] 25. [. . . . . .]

REV.

1. [. . . . .] 2. *mu* - [. . . . . .]

3. *gi - pa - ri* [. . .] 4. *mi* - [. .] - *ri* (?) - [. . . .]

5. *ir - ṣi - tum* [. . .] 6. [. . . .]-*ma* [. . . .]

Fragmentary as the text of No. 54,228 is, a glance at the above transliteration will suffice to show that it preserves part of a composition which is very similar in character to the Seventh Tablet. That it does not form a missing portion of the text of that composition, is clear from the occurrence of certain phrases and titles of Marduk found in parts of the text of the Seventh Tablet which have already been identified; moreover, they are here arranged in a different order and with a different context. Thus, l. 6 f. correspond to the

---

[1] R. 2, 538, *i*.

[2] In this and the following line TU + TU is written as a conflate sign.

[3] Conjectural restoration.

[4] Possibly *ina parakki šīmāti*^{pl}.

opening line of Tablet VII; l. 8 corresponds to Tab. VII, l. 2[1]; l. 10 corresponds to Tab. VII, l. 9; l. 12 corresponds to Tab. VII, l. 35,[2] and l. 13 may be compared with the second half of the same line; l. 19 is clearly parallel to Tab. VII, l. 107; l. 21 corresponds to the line of Tab. VII preserved by K. 8,519, l. 8 (see above, p. 104); with *ilu Ḫanšā* in l. 22, cf. Tab. VII, l. 123; and with l. 23, cf. K. 8,519, l. 8, and the commentary to this line, K. 4,406, Rev., col. ii, l. 31 (see above, p. 166, and vol. ii, pl. lv), which gives the reading *a-lak-tu*. It may also be noted that in ll. 4 and 5 we have a reference to *iṣu arik*, "Long-bow," the first name given by Anu to Marduk's bow upon K. 3,449*a*, which probably forms part of the Fifth Tablet (see above, p. 82 f.); GIŠ-GID-DA in l. 5 is evidently the Sumerian form of the name. The title of Marduk, En-bilulu, which occurs in l. 14, and is there explained as "the Lord who hath renewed his land," is found also upon the fragment K. 5,233, which is described in the following paragraph.

[1] It may here be noted that on the fragment S. 298 occur the phrases [. . . . .] *ba-nu-u še-im u ki-e mu-diš-šu* [. . . . .], "[. . . .], Creator of grain and plants, Renewer of [. . . .]"; as two other lines of the same fragment read [. . . . .] *muš-te-ši-ru a-d*[*i-* . . . . .], "[. . . .] Director of the decrees of [. . . .]," and [. . . . . *ba*]*-nu-u te-ni-šit* [. . . . .], "[. . . . .] Creator of mankind [. . . . .]," it is clear that the fragment is part of a composition containing addresses to Marduk as lord of Creation. Too little is preserved to show whether in this text, as in the Seventh Tablet, he was addressed under his Sumerian titles.

[2] On an Assyrian fragment of a hymn, K. 12,582, occurs the following couplet:—

ilu Šag-zu mu-di-e lib-b[*i* . . . .]
a-pir a-gi-e bēlu-u-tu [. . . . .]
"Šag-zu, who knoweth the heart [of the gods . . . . .]
"Who weareth the crown of dominion [. . . . . . .]."

It is possible that this fragment also belonged to a composition, similar in character to the Seventh Tablet of the Creation Series.

It has already been remarked that the commentaries to the Seventh Tablet presuppose the existence of a Sumerian version of the text, and in the fragment K. 5,233, the text of which is given in the accompanying block, we may see a confirmation of this supposition. The fragment is part of an Assyrian tablet inscribed with a bilingual composition, and in each line of the Sumerian text which is preserved Marduk is addressed under a new title. In the following

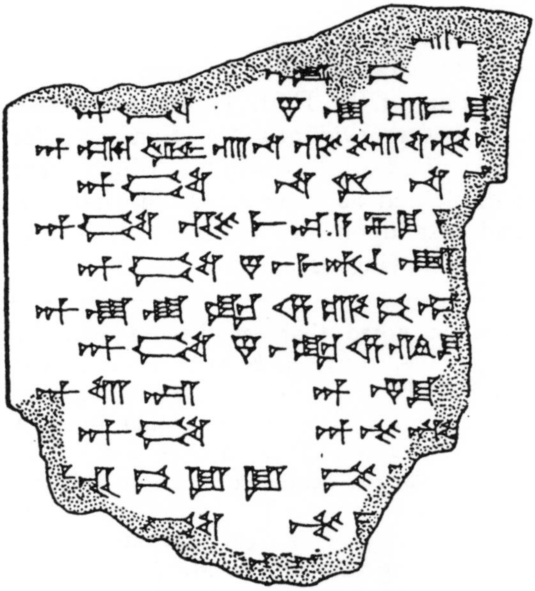

Fragment of a bilingual composition in honour of Marduk (K. 5,233).

transliteration and translation of the fragment the first couplet preserved is numbered "1," but it should be noted that it does not mark the beginning of the text :—

1. [DINGIR . . . . . .] MU - BI [. . . . .]

ilu Marduk ša tu - u - šu [. . . . .]

Marduk, whose spell [. . . . .]!

2. DINGIR ASARU-ALIM-NUN-NA ZI SU-UD-GAL-[. . . .]
   ilu Marduk na - din na - p[iš - ti (?) . . . .]
   Marduk, the giver of [life . . . .]!

3. DINGIR . . . NAM-IŠIB-BA-A-NI-KU GA[R- . . . .]
   ilu Marduk ša ina šip - ti - šu li - [. . . .]
   Marduk, who by his incantation [. . . .]!

4. DINGIR TU - TU SAR - AZAG - GA - BI [. . . . .]
   ilu Marduk ša ina SAR-AZAG-*gi-šu* [. . . .]
   Marduk, who by his . . . [. . . . .]!

5. DINGIR ŠAG - ZU DINGIR SUḪ - [KUR . . . .]
   ilu Marduk ilu Mu - bal - [*lu - u ai - bi* . . . .]
   Marduk, the Destroyer [of the foe . . . .]!

6. DINGIR EN - BI - LU - LU GAB - [. . . . .]
   ilu Marduk mu - [. . . . .]
   Marduk, who [. . . . .]!

It is possible that the title in l. 1 may be restored as DINGIR MU-AZAG from Tab. VII, l. 33. Of the other titles under which Marduk is here addressed, ASARU-ALIM-NUNA (l. 2) occurs in Tab. VII, l. 5, TUTU (l. 4) in Tab. VII, l. 9, ŠAG-ZU (l. 5) in Tab. VII, l. 35, and SUḪ-KUR in Tab. VII, l. 43. The restoration of the Assyrian version of l. 5 is taken from K. 2,107 + K. 6,086, Obv., col. ii, l. 31 (see above, p. 174, and vol. ii, pl. lxii). The title EN-BILULU also occurs in the parallel text to the Seventh Tablet preserved by No. 54,228 and R. 2, 538 (see above, p. 178 f.).

II.

On some fragments of the Series "Enuma eliš." and on some texts relating to the History of Creation.

IN this appendix some unpublished fragments of tablets of the Creation Series are given, which I came across after the lithographed plates of vol. ii had been printed off. At the beginning of the present year, while engaged on making a hand-list of the smaller fragments in the various collections from Kuyunjik, I identified ten such fragments as belonging to copies of the First, Second, Fifth, and Seventh Tablets of the Creation Series. The texts of five of these (KK. 2,854, 12,830, 13,761, 8,519, and 13,337), which belong to copies of the Seventh Tablet, are included in Appendix I under the sections dealing with those portions of the commentary which rendered it possible to identify them.[1] The texts of the remaining five fragments (KK. 7,871, 4,488, 10,008, 13,774, and 11,641), belonging to copies of the First, Second, and Fifth Tablets, are given in the following sections which are marked A, B, and C. In section D two small Assyrian fragments (K. 12,000*b* and 79-7-8, 47) are described, which possibly contain portions of the text of the Creation Series. In section E the text is given of the fragment (S. 2,013), which contains a reference to *Ti-amat e-li-ti* and *Ti-amat šap-li-ti*. Section F deals with the fragments K. 3,445 + R. 396 and K. 14,949, which probably contain an account of the creation of the world by Anšar, in place of Marduk. In section G the text is given of an address to the River of Creation which occurs in the opening lines of incantations upon the fragments S. 1,704 and 82-9-18, 5,311. Finally, in

[1] It may be noted that all of them have been used for the text of the Seventh Tablet as transliterated and translated on pp. 92 ff.

section H the tablet K. 3,364, which has been supposed to contain the instructions given by Marduk to man after his creation, is shown to be part of a long text containing moral precepts.

A. TWO FRAGMENTS OF THE FIRST TABLET OF THE CREATION SERIES.—The fragment K. 7,871, the text of which is given in the accompanying block, is from the right-

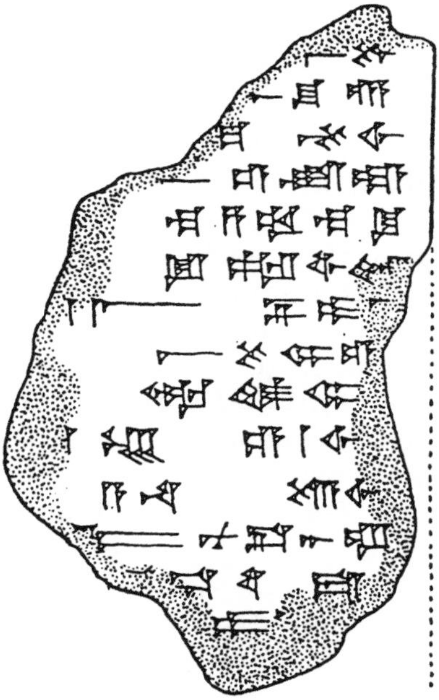

Creation Series, Tablet I, ll. 33–47 (K. 7,871).

hand edge of the obverse of a tablet, and the ends of lines which it preserves correspond to Tablet I, ll. 33–47. As the first sheet of this volume had been printed off at the time I came across it, the information it supplies as to this imperfectly preserved portion of the text of the First Tablet[1] may be briefly noted.

[1] See above, pp. 6–9.

In l. 33 the new fragment supports the reading *sak-pu* at the end of the line; in l. 34 it confirms the suggested restoration [*ma-ri-e-šu-un*], probably reading [*mārē*]*pl*-*šu-un*; the couplet, ll. 35 and 36, which may be conjecturally restored as *Ap*[*sū pa*]-*a-šu i-pu*-[*šam-ma i-ḳab-bi*], *a-na* [*T*]*i-am*[*at*] *el-li-tu-ma i-za*[*k-kar a-ma-tum*], it condenses into a single line which may probably be restored as [*Apsū pa-a-šu i-pu-šam*]-*ma izakkar-ši*, "[Apsū opened his mouth] and spake unto her"; the end of l. 37 may now be restored as *al-kat-su-nu e-li-ia*, i.e. "their way [is . . . .] unto me"; the suggested restoration of the end of l. 38 as *mu-ši* [*la ṣal-la-ak*] is confirmed, the fragment reading [. . . . .] *la ṣa-al-la-ku*; the end of l. 39 may now be restored as *lu-šap-pi-iḫ*, i.e. "Their way will I destroy and cast down"; the suggested restoration of the end of l. 40 as [*ni-i-ni*] is confirmed, the fragment reading *ni-i-n*[*i*]; the suggested restoration of the end of l. 41 as *i-na* [*še-mi-ša*] is confirmed, the fragment reading *ina še-mi-e*-[*ša*]. The suggested restoration (from Tab. IV, l. 89 and Tab. III, l. 125) of the phrase *il-ta-si e-li*-[*ta*] in l. 42 is shown to be incorrect, the fragment reading [. . . . .] *eli ḫar-mi*-[. .]; the line should run *i-zu-uz-ma* (var. [*e*]-*ziz-m*[*a*]) *il-ta-si e-li* (var. *eli*) *ḫar-mi*-[*ša*(?)]. For the end of l. 43 K. 7,871 reads [. . . . .]-*gat e-diš-ši*-[. .], and the verb preserved by No. 45,528 + 46,614 (see vol. ii, pl. iii) may probably be read *ug*-[*g*]*u-ga*[*t*]; the line may thus be partly restored as [. .] *mar-ṣi-iš*[1] *ug*-[*g*]*u-ga*[*t*] *e-diš-ši*-[. . . . .], "[. .] she was grievously angered, alone [she . . . .]"; K. 7,871 probably gave a variant reading for the verb, as the traces it gives of the sign before *gat* (or *kat*) are not those of *gu*.[2] The suggested restoration of the end of l. 44 as *a-na* [*Apsū i-zak-ḳar*] is shown by K. 7,871 to be incorrect, the fragment reading [. . . . .] *a-na kar-ši*-[. .]; the

[1] It may here be noted that the principal traces of this line upon the obverse of 81–7–27, 80 (see *Cun. Txts.*, part xiii, pl. 2) probably represent the word *mar-ṣi-iš*.

[2] The restoration of the line as [. . .] *mar-ṣi-iš ug*-[*g*]*u-gat e*-[. . .]-*kat e-diš-ši*-[. .] is also possible.

line may probably be restored as *li-mut-ta* (var. *ti*) *it-ta-di a-na kar-ši-*[*ša* (?)], "She plotted evil in [her] heart (?)." The end of l. 45, according to the fragment, reads [. . . . .]-*u nu-uš-ḫal-laḳ* ; it is possible that we may restore the line as [*mi*]-*na-a ni-i-nu ša ni-i*[*p-pu-uš lu*]-*u nu-uš-ḫal-laḳ*, "What, then, shall we do? Let us destroy!" The end of l. 46, according to the fragment, reads [. . . . .]-*du-tu da-* [. .] ; unless this represents a variant reading, the suggested restoration *i ni-*[*iṣ-lal ni-i-ni*] is incorrect. For

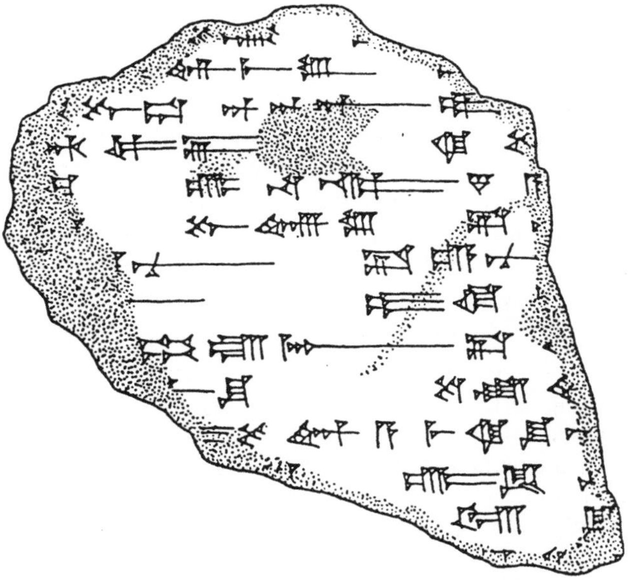

Creation Series, Tablet I, ll. 50–63 (K. 4,488).

l. 47 the fragment reads [. . . . .] *i-*[. . . . .], which corresponds to *i-ma-al-*[*li-ku*] at the end of the line.

Another new fragment of the First Tablet is K. 4,488, which gives portions of the second halves of ll. 50–63 ; for the text see the accompanying block. For ll. 50 and 51 the fragment reads [. . . . . *m*]*u-šiš l*[*u* . . . . .] and [. . . . .] *im-me-ru p*[*a-* . . . . .], and gives no variants to the text as known from other tablets ;

for l. 52 the fragment reads [. . . . . . *i*]*k-pu-du an ilāni mār*[. . .], which gives the variants *an* for *a-na* and *mār*[*ē pl -šu*] for *m*[*a*]*-ri-e-šu*; the fragment reads [. . . . .]-*ti-di-ir ki-šad-*[. .] for l. 53, which may probably be restored as [. . . .] *i-te-dir* (var. [.]-*ti-di-ir*) *ki-šad-*[*su*], "[. . . . his] neck was troubled." For l. 54 the fragment reads [. . . . . . -*š*]*u u-na-šaḳ ša-a-*[. .]; it is clear, therefore, that for the restoration [*i*]*-na-ša-ḳu* we should read [*u*]*-na-ša-ḳu*, and that the duplicate 81-7-27, 80 reads *u-na-aš-ša*[*ḳ*], as suggested on p. 11, n. 8. For l. 55 the fragment reads [. . . . .] *pu-uḫ-ru-uš-*[. .]; for the suggested reading (upon 81-7-27, 80 and No. 46,803) *bu-*[*u*]*k-ri-šu-un*, "their first-born," we should read *pu-*[*u*]*ḫ-*[1] *ri-šu-un*, "they all," or "their assembly," and the line may be translated "[Because of the evil] which they had planned together." For l. 56 the fragment reads [. . . . . -*š*]*u-nu uš-tan-nu-*[. .], and gives no variants to the text; the verb at the end of l. 57 may be restored from the fragment as *i-dul-lu*, "they lay in wait."[2] For l. 58 the fragment reads [. . . . .]-*ḳu-um-meš uš-*[. .], and confirms the

[1] The traces of this sign upon No. 46,803 are those of *uḫ*, rather than *uk* (see vol. ii, pl. ix).

[2] This verb occurs also in Tablet I, l. 89, which reads [. . . .] *i-du-ul-*[*li*], i.e. "[. . . .] he lay in wait," and again in l. 99, which reads [. . . . .]-*ḫi-iš ta-du-ul-l*[*i*], i.e. "[. . . .] thou hast lain in wait." The meaning of the verb *dālu* has been pointed out by Thompson in *Hebraica*, vol. xvii, p. 163, note 3, where he shows that its participle occurs in an Assyrian letter in the sense of "scout"; he also cites IV R, pl. 30*, Obv., l. 16, where *i-du-*[*ul*] (var. *i-dul*) may well have the meaning "to prowl" or "to lie in wait." On p. 13, note 11 and p. 66, note 5 it was suggested that the verb *i-ṭul-lu-šu*, which occurs in Tablet IV, ll. 63 and 64, should be transliterated *i-dul-lu-šu* and connected with the verbs in Tablet I, ll. 89 and 99. The reading *i-ṭul-lu-šu*, suggested by Delitzsch, gives good sense, but is not quite satisfactory from the omission of the doubled dental. Jensen (cf. K.B., vi, pp. 24 f., 334) reads *i-dul-lu-šu*, and also suggests for

suggested restoration of the second half of the line as [*ša-ḳu-um*]-*mi-iš uš-bu.* Of l. 59 the fragment gives the end as [. . . . . .]-*šu te-li*-[’(?)], the traces of the last sign reading HI[.]; in l. 60 it gives the variant *me-ki-šu-n*[*u*] for *me-ki-šu-un* ; of l. 61 it gives the last word as [. . . . .] *u-ḳi-š*[*u*], "[. . . .] he watched him"; in l. 62 it gives the variant *el-lu* for *el-lum*, and of l. 63 it only gives slight traces of two signs.

B. A FRAGMENT OF THE SECOND TABLET OF THE CREATION SERIES.—The fragment K. 10,008 is probably a fragment of the Creation Series, and if this is so the only place to which it is possible to assign it is the gap between ll. (85) and (104) of the Second Tablet (see above, p. 32 f.); this will be clear for the following reasons. It will be seen that the greater part of the fragment is inscribed with part of a speech of Anšar. Lines 10 and 11 read [. . . . . *ilu*]*A-nam ul i-li-’*-[. . . . .] and [. . . . .]-*mud i-dur-ma i-t*[*u-* . . . . .], and may be restored as [*aš-pur-ma ilu*]*A-nam ul i-li-’*-[*a ma-ḫar-ša*], [*ilu Nu-dim*]-*mud i-dur-ma i-t*[*u-ra ar-kiš*], "[I sent] Anu, but he could not [withstand her]; [Nudim]mud was afraid and turned [back]." Now these lines occur in Tablet III, l. 53 f., in the course of Anšar's instructions to Gaga, and again in l. 111 f., in Anšar's message as delivered by Gaga to Laḫmu and Laḫamu. Now, although the phrase *ilu Marduk abkal ilāni* occurs in the following line in each of these passages, the rest of the context upon K. 10,008 shows that it is not a duplicate of the Third Tablet. It therefore follows that the fragment cannot belong to a later tablet than the Second.

Now ll. (72)–(82) of the Second Tablet describe how Anšar sent Anu against Tiamat, and it is probable that in the gap

---

dālu the meaning "to run round," "to prowl round." In view of the use of the participle in the sense of "scout," we may perhaps render the phrase in Tablet IV, ll. 63 f. as "the gods watched him from hiding"; the repetition of the phrase emphasises Marduk's courage in setting out alone to do battle with Tiamat.

after l. 58 occurred the account of how Nudimmud was sent against Tiamat and how he turned back.[1] It therefore follows that the text of K. 10,008 must be put in the gap between ll. (85) and (104). On this assumption the greater part of the fragment (at least down to l. 12) carries on the speech of Anšar, which begins at l. (85). In this speech Anšar refers to the fate of Apsū (K. 10,008, l. 2), and the subsequent appointment of Kingu by Tiamat to lead the rebel forces[2]

[1] In view of the fact that in Tablet III, ll. 53 f. and 111 f. Anšar refers first to Anu's attempt to oppose Tiamat, and then to that of Nudimmud, it might legitimately be urged that this represents the order in which the events took place. And, as Anu's attempt is described in Tablet II, ll. (72)–(82), I was inclined, before I came across K. 10,008, to put Nudimmud's attempt in the gap between ll. (85) and (104). But the order in which Anšar refers to the setting out of Anu and Nudimmud is not necessarily chronological. Moreover, as Nudimmud had already overcome Apsū, and as it was he who brought the news of Tiamat's revolt to Anšar, it would be only natural that he should be the first to be sent against her; in support of this view it may be further noted that Nudimmud's name occurs in l. 58. On the other hand, if it be insisted that Anšar's references in Tablet III must be taken to imply that Nudimmud's setting out against Tiamat followed that of Anu, it is necessary to place the account referring to Nudimmud after the line conjecturally numbered as (85). And, as the earlier lines of K. 10,008 do not appear to refer to this episode, it follows that the gap after l. 58 is less than ten lines and that after l. (85) is greater than twenty lines; or else that K. 10,008 does not belong to the series *Enuma eliš*, but contains a variant account of the story of Creation. On the whole it appears to me preferable to suppose that the order in which the events are referred to in Anšar's speech is not to be taken as chronological, but as leading up to a climax; he says, "Anu I sent, but he could not withstand her; and even Nudimmud was afraid and turned back."

[2] With the phrase *mi-lam-mi eš-rit* in l. 4 may be compared Tablet I, ll. 118 and 126, and the parallel passages. The apparent reference to ten in place of eleven monsters is noteworthy.

and carry on the war against the gods (l. 7 f.); he then describes how he sent Anu and Nudimmud against Tiamat, and how they could not withstand her and turned back (l. 10 f.), and in the following line (l. 12) he either begins his appeal to Marduk, or, as appears to me more probable,

Fragment of the Second Tablet of the Creation Series (K. 10,008).

states his intention of appealing to Marduk to become the champion of the gods. The fragment may be transliterated as follows:—

1. [. . . . . . . *i*]*š* - [*pu*]*r* [. . . . .]
2. [. . . . . . .] *Apsû* *u*-[. . . . .]
3. [. . . . .] *it - tar - ru - šu* [. . . . .]

4. [. . . . .] *mi - lam - mi eš - ri*[*t* . . . . .]
5. [. . .]-*ku* (?) -*ma-'-ni ḫum* (?) -*mu-r*[*a-* . . .]
6. [. . . .]-*bi ap-ša-na la sa-ki-pa* [. . . .]
7. [. . . . . -*n*]*u* ^{ilu}*Kin-gu šu-uš-*[*ḳu-u* . . . .]
8. [. . . . . .] - *ma Ti - a - ma - t*[*i* . . . . .]
9. [. . . . . .] - *ak lib - bi - šu i* - [. . . . . .]
10. [*aš - pur - ma* ^{ilu}]*A - nam ul i - li - ' -* [*a ma - ḫar - ša*]
11. [^{ilu}*Nu - dim*] - *mud i - dur - ma i - t*[*u - ra ar - kiš*]
12. [. . . ^{ilu} *Mardu*]*k abkal ilāni*^{pl} [. . . . . .]
13. [. . . . . .] *ip - ti - ḳu k*[*u -* . . . . . .]
14. [. . . . . .] *u - sa - an - ni* [. . . . . .]
15. [. . . . .] *irpitu* [. . . . . . .]
16. [. . . . .] *bul - li -* [. . . . .]
17. [. . . . .] *ma - lu -* [. . . . . . .]
18. [. . . . .]

With l. 13 we may compare *lip-ti-ḳu ku-ru-na* in Tablet III, l. 9, and *ip-ti-ḳu* [*ku-ru-na*] in l. 134; and with *u-sa-an-ni* we may compare Tablet III, l. 135. These phrases upon K. 10,008 may be explained by supposing that Anšar's appeal to Marduk was accompanied by the mixing and drinking of wine.

C. TWO FRAGMENTS OF THE FIFTH TABLET OF THE CREATION SERIES.—The first eleven lines of the fragment K. 13,774 correspond (with some interesting variants) to the text of the Fifth Tablet, ll. 6–16; while the last three lines of the fragment give a variant text to that found in ll. 17–19 upon other copies of the Fifth Tablet. The unimportant variants may be first noted as follows: in l. 6 K. 13,774 gives the variant *ru* as the last syllable of ^{ilu}*Ni-bi-ri*, and for *ana* reads *a-na*; in l. 10 it reads *u-dan-ni-na* for *ud-dan-ni-na*; in l. 13 it reads *šuk-nat* for *šu-uk-nat*; in l. 14 it reads *ag*[*ī*] for *a-gi-*[*e*]; and in l. 16 it reads *a-na* for *ana*. In l. 8 it gives a more interesting variant, reading ^{ilu}*A-num* in place of *ilu E-a*; that is to say, l. 8, according to this version, would read, "He set the station of Bēl and Anu along with him," in place of "He set the station of Bēl and Ea along with him." For a further discussion of this reading, see the Introduction.

In l. 12 occurs a still more interesting variant; according to K. 13,774 the first half of the line runs [. . . *kak*]*kaba-šu uš-te-pa-a*, "[. . . .] his star he caused to shine forth," in place of *ilu Nannar-ru uš-te-pa-a*, "The Moon-god

Creation Series, Tablet V, ll. 6–19 (K. 13,774).

he caused to shine forth." As the beginning and end of the line are wanting, it would be rash to conjecturally restore them; but it may be regarded as certain that the phrase *šuk-nat mu-ši*, "a being of the night," in l. 13 refers to the Moon-god, and that the lines which follow contain Marduk's charge to him. In the course of Marduk's address to the Moon-god, in ll. 17 and 18, which upon other copies of the Fifth Tablet contain directions with regard to the 7th and 14th days of the month, K. 13,774 gives the variant readings

(17) [. . . . . .] *IV*^{KAN} *V ūmu* [. . . . . .] and (18) [. . . . . .] ^{KAN} *V ūmu* [. . . . . .]. The traces of l. 19 upon K. 13,774 do not correspond to the text of this line as already known.

K. 11,641 is part of another copy of the Fifth Tablet, and contains on its obverse parts of ll. 14–22, and on its reverse

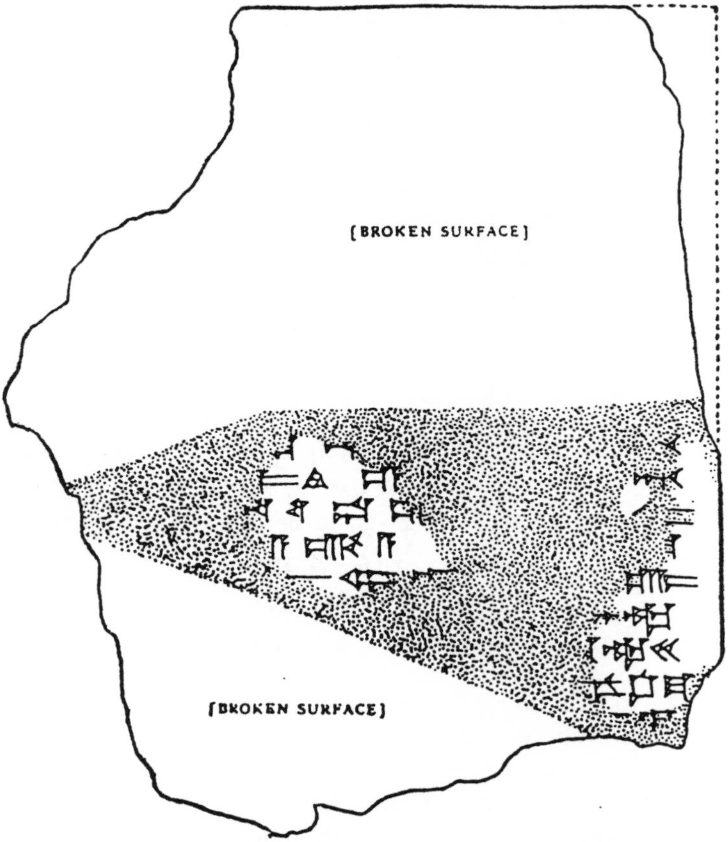

Creation Series, Tablet V, ll. 14–22 (K. 11,641, Obverse).

parts of lines which may be conjecturally numbered as ll. (128)–(140). The information which the obverse of the fragment supplies with regard to the text of the Fifth Tablet is not very great, and may be noted as follows: the traces of ll. 14 and 17 upon K. 11,641 give no variants nor restorations; for l. 15 the fragment reads [. . . . . . -*p*]*a-ḫi e-* [. . . . .]-*ti*, and proves that the suggested restoration

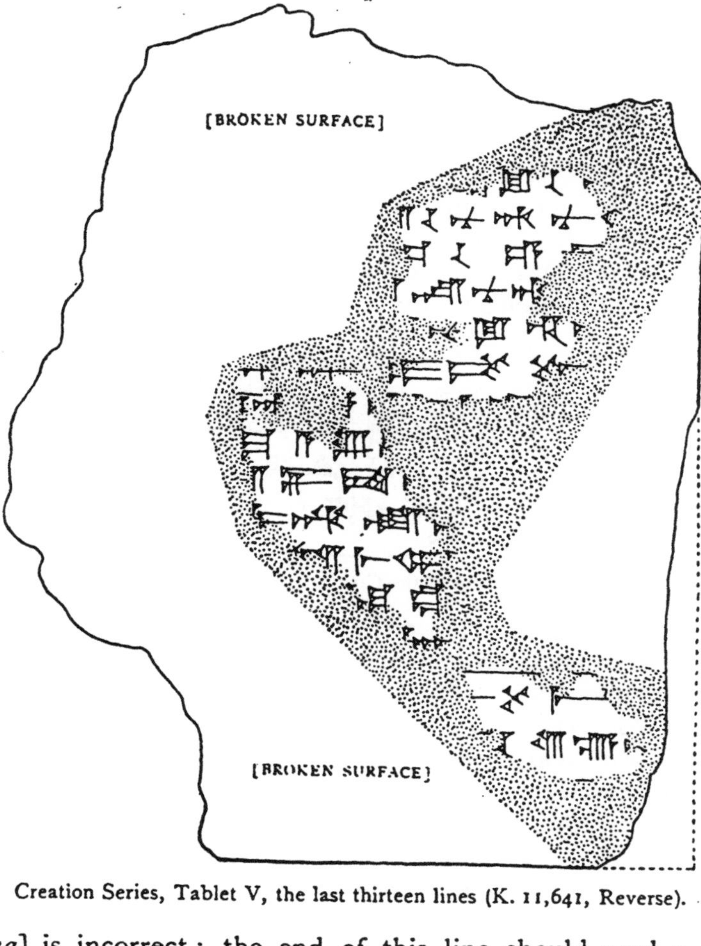

Creation Series, Tablet V, the last thirteen lines (K. 11,641, Reverse).

i-na] is incorrect; the end of this line should read *e*-[*li*] *na-a-ti*, which gives the same sense as before. In l. 16 the ragment gives the variant [*a*]-*na* for *ana*; in l. 18 for *meš-l*[*i*] t gives the variant *mi-i* (?)-[. . . . .]; in l. 19 it gives traces of the last character but one in the line, which does not correspond to those given by K. 3,567 + K. 8,588; at the end of l. 20 it gives the variant reading [*a*]*r-ka-niš*, and it is possible that K. 3,567, etc., read *ar-k*[*a-nu*]*-uš*; in l. 21 it confirms the suggested restoration of the sign *ma* at the end of the line; and in l. 22 it gives slight traces of the last two characters in the line.

The reverse of K. 11,641 has already been used on p. 84 f., in the transliteration and translation of the end of the Fifth Tablet. On p. 85, note 3, it is pointed out that the last six lines contain the complaint of the gods to Marduk in consequence of which he conceived the plan of creating mankind. It may here be noted that of the last line of the tablet, K. 11,641 seems to give traces of MEŠ, the plural sign;

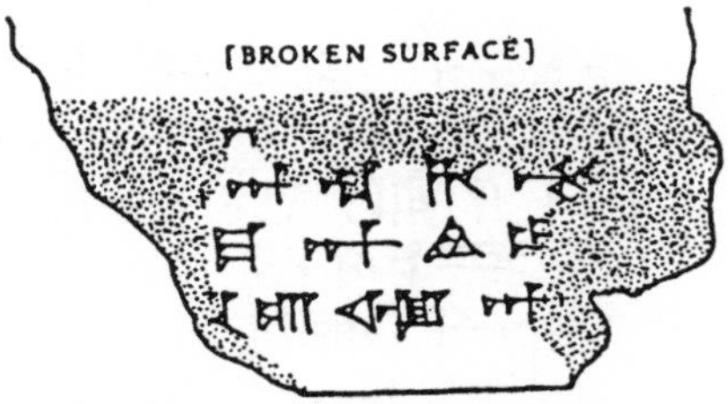

A possible fragment of the Creation Series (79-7-8, 47).

this may have been followed by a pronominal suffix, *ka*, or may have immediately preceded the word *ni-i-nu* preserved by the fragment K. 8,526.

D. TWO POSSIBLE FRAGMENTS OF THE CREATION SERIES.—In *Cuneiform Texts*, part xiii, pl. 24, the text is given of a small fragment, K. 12,000 *b*, of which the following is a transliteration: (1) [. . . . . . .] (2) [. . .] *a-n*[*a* . . . . .] (3) [. . .] *um-ma* [. . .] (4) [. . . . .] *Ti-amat uš*-[. . . . . .] (5) [. . .] *in-na-at*-[. . . . .] (6) [*a*]*r-nu-uš-šu lu*[. . . . . .] (7) [*i-p*]*u-lu-šu* [. . . . .] (8) [. . . . .]. From the style of the writing and the mention of Tiamat, it is possible that the fragment belongs to the Creation Series.

Another possible fragment of the Creation Series is 79-7-8,

47, the text of which is given in the block on p. 194. In the character of the clay and the style of writing it closely resembles K. 11,641, which is a fragment of a copy of the Fifth Tablet (see above, pp. 192 ff.); while the mention of the gods *ilu La-ḫa-mu* in l. 2, *An-šar* in l. 3, and [*ilu B*]*ēl* in l. 4 is in favour of its being a fragment of a tablet of the series.[1]

[1] Reference may also be made to the fragment R. 982 + 80-7-18, 178, of which the first few lines of the obverse are given in transliteration by Delitzsch, *Weltschöpfungsepos*, p. 110 f., note 1; for the text, see *Cuneiform Texts*, part xiii, pl. 31. In the character of its clay and in its style of writing this fragment resembles tablets of the Creation Series; cf. also l. 2 f. of the reverse, *ina ki-rib apsī ib-n*[*a* . . . . .], *ib-ni-šu-ma ilu E-a* [. . . . .]. The fragments of legends, K. 7,067 and K. 8,572 have been catalogued by Bezold as possibly belonging to tablets of the series *E-nu-ma e-liš*, and their texts are therefore given in *Cun. Txts.*, part xiii, pl. 31; the first line preserved by K. 7,067 probably reads *ilu E-a ina* [*ap*]*sī* [. . . . .], followed by the line *ilāni pl rabūti pl im-tal-ku-ma* [. . . . .], while the first line of K. 8,572 reads [. . . . .]*-da a-me-lu šum-šu i-*[. . . . .], but the grounds are slender for assigning them to the Creation Series. To this series the minute fragment K. 11,048 (see *Cun. Txts.*, part xiii, pl. 31) is assigned (with a query) by Bezold in the *Catalogue*, vol. v, p. 2,078, presumably from the character of the writing, unless K. 11,048 is a misprint. The fragment K. 12,000*c* (*Cun. Txts.*, part xiii, pl. 31) is also assigned by Bezold to the series (see *Catalogue*, vol. v, p. 2,078). Its colophon states that it is the First Tablet of a series styled *E-n*[*u-ma* . . . . .], but as the traces of the last four lines of the text do not correspond to the last four lines of the First Tablet of the series *Enuma eliš*, and as the catch-line does not correspond to the first line of the Second Tablet, it is clear that K. 12,000*c* is a fragment of the First Tablet of some other series. K. 10,791 (*Cun. Txts.*, part xiii, pl. 31) is another fragment which Bezold suggests may belong to the series *Enuma eliš*, presumably from the occurrence of the verbs *ib-ba-ni* in ll. 2 and 3 and *ib-ba-nu-u* in l. 4. As, however, it belongs to a text which is arranged in columns and divided into sections, it is clear that it does not belong to the Creation Series.

E. A REFERENCE TO "THE WATERS THAT WERE ABOVE" AND "THE WATERS THAT WERE BENEATH" THE FIRMAMENT.—The text may here be given of an interesting fragment, S. 2,013, which has been copied by Bezold (cf. Jensen in Schrader's *Keilins. Bibl.*, vi, p. 307) and by Delitzsch (cf. *Handwörterbuch*, p. xii), but has, I believe, not yet been published. If it is part (as is hardly probable) of the Creation Series, the reference to the upper and the lower Tiamat in l. 10 f. shows that it cannot belong to an earlier tablet than the Fifth; while in general style it appears to resemble the addresses found on the Seventh Tablet, rather

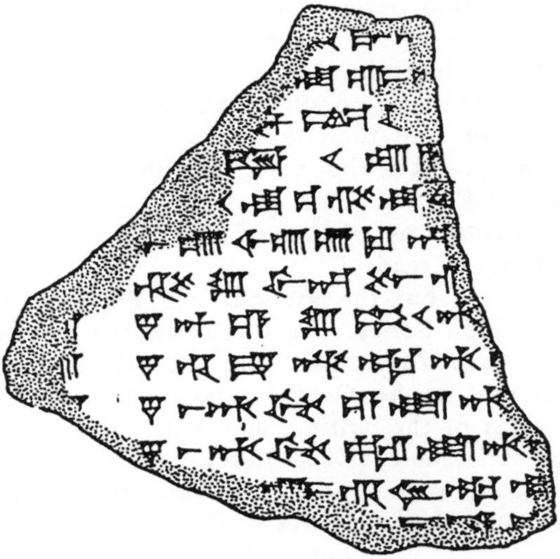

Fragment referring to the Upper Tiamat and the Lower Tiamat (S. 2,013).

than to be in narrative form. It will be seen, however, from the accompanying block that the lines are divided in writing into halves; this is characteristic of several neo-Babylonian copies of tablets of the Creation Series, but does not occur upon any of the Assyrian copies that have yet been identified. The text of the fragment may be transliterated as follows:—

1. [. . . . .] [. . . . .] *rabīti*[(*ti* ?) . . . .]
2. [. . . . .] [. . . . .] *tu u* [. . . . .]
3. [. . . . .] [. . . . *a*]*g ne šu* [. . . . .]
4. [. . . . .] [. . . .] *ḳabli u ta-ḫa-*[*ẓi* . . .]
5. [. . . . .] [. . . .]-*tu iz-zi-tu* [. . . . .]
6. [. . . . .] [*ma*]*ḫar bīt ziḳḳurrati*[1] *ib-ba-*[. . .]
7. [. . . . .] *nam - ru šal - ba - bu* [. . . . .]
8. [. . . . .] *ša šamē*(*e*) *ru-ḳu-u-ti* [. . . . .]
9. [. . . . .] *ša Ḫu - bur pal-ka-ti* [. . . . .]
10. [. . . . .] *ša ina Ti-amat e-li-ti* [. . . .]
11. [. . . . .] *ša ina Ti-amat šap-li-ti* [. . . .]
12. [. . . . .] [. . . .] *u-ri-kis ka-l*[*a-mu* (?) . .]
13. [. . . . .] [. . . . .] *s*[*a* (?)]-*k*[*ip* . . . . .]

For a discussion of the title *Ḫubur* and of the phrases *Ti-amat e-li-ti* and *Ti-amat šap-li-ti*, see the Introduction.

F. ANŠAR AND THE HISTORY OF CREATION.—A fragment, which it has been thought may perhaps belong to one of the later tablets of the Creation Series,[2] is K. 3,445 + R. 396 (cf. *Cun. Texts*, part xiii, pl. 24 f.)[3]; the smaller fragment K. 14,949 (op. cit., pl. 24) is a duplicate. Lines 1–26 of the obverse contain only traces of the beginnings of lines, among

---

[1] Possibly read [*ma*]*ḫar E-igi-e-nir*.

[2] Cf. George Smith, *Chaldean Account of Genesis*, pp. 67 ff., Bezold, *Catalogue*, vol. ii, p. 534, and Delitzsch, *Weltschöpfungsepos*, pp. 19, 51 ff., 87 f., 109 f. The text of the reverse of K. 3,445 was given by S. A. Smith in *Miscellaneous Texts*, pl. 10.

[3] In shape and writing the fragment resembles some of the tablets of the Creation Series. It may be noted that each tenth line of the text is indicated in the margin of the tablet by the figure "10." Thus, on the Obv., ll. 2, 12, 22, and 32 are so marked, and on the Rev., ll. 7, 16, 25, and 35; on the Rev. sometimes two lines of the text are written in one line of the tablet.

which it may be noted that l. 11 possibly begins with the name of Marduk. From l. 27 onwards the obverse reads: (27) *ul-tu u-me u-*[. . . . . .] (28) *ma-aṣ-rat mu-ši u im-*[*mi* . . . . .] (29) *ru-pu-uš-tu ša Ti-a*[*mat* . . . . .] (30) *Anšar ip-ta-*[1][. . . . . .] (31) *ik-ṣur-ma ana* [. . . . .] (32) *te-bi ša-a-ri* [. . . . .] (33) *šu-uk-tur im-*[. . . . .] (34) *u-ad-di-ma r*[*a-* . . . . . .] (35) *iš-kun ḳaḳḳada* [. . . . .] (36) *naḳ-bu up-te-it-* [. . . . .] (37) *ip-te-e-ma n*[*a-* . . . . .] (38) *na-ḫi-ri ša up-*[. . . . .] (39) *iš-pu-uk n*[*a-* . . . . . .] (40) *nam-ba-'-*[. . . . .]. The occurrence of the names of Anšar (l. 30) and possibly of Marduk (l. 11), the reference to "the slayer," or "the breadth," of Tiamat (l. 29) and possibly to her head (l. 35), and the mention of "springs" (l. 36f.), "deeps" (l. 40), and monsters of the deep ("dolphins?") in l. 38, would not be inconsistent with the fragment forming part of the Fifth Tablet of the Creation Series.

The reverse of the fragment reads as follows:—(1) [. . . . .] (2) *ḫa-šur-ru* [. . . . .] (3) [. . . . .]*-ki-ik-ma* [. . . . .] (4) [. . . . .]*-me šar-*[. . . . .] (5) [. . . . .] *ilu Adad* [. . . . .] (6) *iš-kun eli* [. . . . .] (7) *uš-bar šul-me* [. . . . .] (8) *ul-tu me-lam-me* [. . . . . .] (9) *a-za-mil-šu apsū ra-šub-*[*bu* . . . . .] (10) [2] *ina e-ma-ši aš-ša*[*k-* . . . . .] (11) *ina si-ma-ak-ki-šu* [. . . . .] (12) *ilāni pl ma-la ba-šu-*[*u* . . . . .] (13) *ilu Laḫ-mu u*[3] *ilu*[[4] . . . . . .] (14) *i-pu-šu-ma pa* (?)-[. . . . .] (15) *pa-na-a-ma An-šar* [. . . . .] (16) *i ilu Sin ša*[*r-* . . . . . .] (17) *ša-nu-u iz-zak-ru* [. . . . .] (18) *ilu*[. . . . . .] (19) *e-nu-ma a-na*

[1] The sign following *ta* is not *ni*, so that the reading *ib-ta-ni* is impossible.

[2] The duplicate K. 14,949 gives a variant reading for this line: *šu-*[. . . . .].

[3] Omitted by K. 14,949.

[4] The traces of the first sign of the name upon K. 14,949 suggest *La*, i.e. *ilu L*[*a-ḫa-mu*].

[. . . . . .] (20) *pī(?)-ka ma-ak-tum ki-*[. . . . . .] (21) *ul-tu u-me at-ta* [. . . . . .] (22) *mim-mu-u at-ta ta-ḳab-bu* [. . . . . .] (23) *An-šar pa-a-šu epuš(uš)-ma i-ḳab-bi : a-na* ^ilu^[. . . . . .] (24) *e-li-nu ap-si-i šu-bat* [. . . . . .] (25) *mi-iḫ-rit E-šar-ra ša ab-nu-u a-na-ku :* [. . . . . .] (26) *šap-liš aš-ra-ta u-dan-ni-n*[*a* . . . .] (27) *lu-pu uš-ma bīta lu šu-bat* [. . . . . .] (28) *kir-bu-uš-šu ma-ḫa-za-šu lu-šar-šid-ma :* [. . . . . .] (29) *e-nu-ma ul-tu apsī i-be-*[. . . . . .] (30) *aš-ru* [. . . . . .] *nu-bat-ta* [. . . . . .] (31) *e-*[. . . . . .]*-pat ṣilli* [. . . . . .] (32) *aš-r*[*u* . . . . . . *n*]*u-bat-ta kun-*[. . . . . .]*-ku-nu* [. . . . . .] (33) *ḳ*[*i-* . . . .]*-ki bītāti ilāni*^pl^ *rabūti*^pl^ [. . . . . .] *ni-ip-pu-*[. . . . . .] (34) [. . . . . .] *abu-šu an-na-a* [. . . . . .]*-a-šu* [. . . . . .] (35) ^ilu^[. . . . . .]*-lu-ka-ma : eli mimma ša ib-na-a ḳa-ta-a-ka* [. . . . . .] (36) *man-*[*nu* . . .]*-ka i-ši: eli ḳaḳ-ḳa-ru ša ib-na-a ḳa-ta-a-*[*ka* . . . .] (37) *man-*[*nu* . . . . . .]*-ka i-ši :* ^alu^*Aššur*^KI^ *ša taz-ku-ra mu(?)-*[. . . . . .] (38) *aš-*[. . . . . .]*-ta-ni i-di da-ri-šam* [. . . . . .] (39) [. . . . . .]*-tuk-ka-ni li-bil-lu-ni* [. . . . . .] (40) *ṣ*[*i-* . . . . . .]*-ni : ma-na-ma šip-ri-ni ša-ni* (41) *aš-ru* [. . . . . .]*-na-aḫ ur-*[. . . . . .] (42) *iḫ-du-*[. . . . . .] (43) *ilāni*^pl^ *šu-*[. . . . . .] (44) *ša i-du* [. . . . . .] (45) *ip-te-e-*[. . . . . .].

The mention of Laḫmu in l. 13 of the reverse may also be cited in favour of the fragment belonging to the Creation Series, while the references to Adad (l. 5) and to the city of Aššur (l. 37) are not necessarily inconsistent with this view. Lines 23 ff., however, can scarcely be reconciled with the end of the Fourth Tablet of the Creation Series. These lines read: "(23) Anšar opened his mouth and spake, and unto the god [. . . . he addressed the word]: (24) 'Above the Deep, the dwelling of [. . . .], (25) opposite E-šara which I have created, [. . . .] (26) I have strengthened the regions in the depth [. . . .] (27) I will build a house that it may be a dwelling for [. . . .] (28) In the midst thereof will I found his district (lit. city, cf. Tabl. IV, l. 146) and [. . . .].'" In this speech Anšar, and not Marduk, appears as the god of creation, which is scarcely in harmony with the general tenour of the Creation Series. Moreover, in l. 25 Anšar definitely states that he created E-šara, whereas in Tablet IV, ll. 144-146, it is related that Marduk, and not Anšar, created E-šara. Until more of the text of the Fifth and Sixth Tablets is recovered, it would be rash to assert that the fragment cannot belong to the Creation Series; meanwhile, in view of the inconsistencies noted, it is preferable to assume that it does not form part of that work, but is a fragment of a closely parallel version of the story in which Anšar plays a more prominent part.

G. The River of Creation.—On p. 128 f. a transliteration and translation are given of an address to a mystical

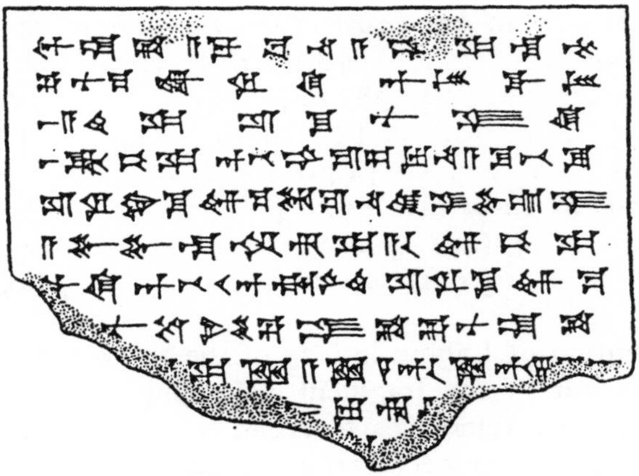

Fragment of an incantation-tablet containing an address to the River of Creation (82-9-18, 5,311, Obverse).

river of creation, which forms the opening lines of incantations upon the reverse of S. 1,704 and the obverse of 82-9-18, 5,311. As the text of these fragments has not been previously published, the obverse of the one and the reverse of the other are given in the accompanying blocks. It will be noted that ll. 1-8 of 82-9-18, 5,311 correspond to ll. 1-7 of

S. 1,704. The eighth line of S. 1,704, which concludes the direct address, or invocation, to the river, is omitted by 82-9-18, 5,311, and from this point onward it would seem that the tablets cease to be duplicates. The insertion of the common formula, given in the ninth line of 82-9-18, 5,311, would not by itself prove this, but what remains of the tenth line of 82-9-18, 5,311 does not correspond to the ninth line

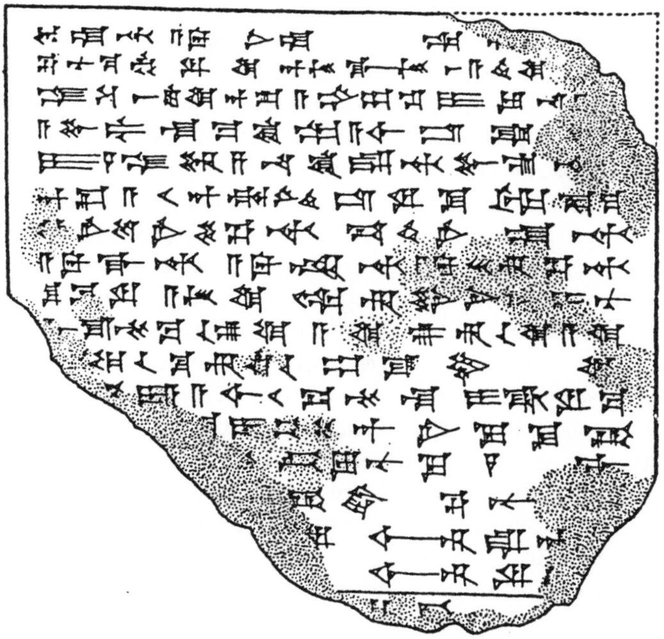

Fragment of an incantation-tablet containing an address to the River of Creation (S. 1,704, Reverse).

of S. 1,704. We are justified, therefore, in treating the address to the river as an independent fragment, which has been employed as the introduction to two different incantations.

H. THE SUPPOSED INSTRUCTIONS TO MAN AFTER HIS CREATION.—The tablet K. 3,364 (*Cun. Txts.*, pt. xiii, pl. 29 f.) was thought by George Smith to contain the instructions given to the first man and woman after their creation. In

The Chaldean Account of Genesis, p. 80, he says, "The obverse[1] of this tablet is a fragment of the address from the deity to the newly created man on his duties to his god"; and a little later on he adds, "The reverse of the tablet appears, so far as the sense can be ascertained, to be addressed to the woman, the companion of the man, informing her of her duties towards her partner." In his *Babylonische Weltschöpfungsepos*, pp. 19 f., 54 f., 88 f., and 111 f., Delitzsch also treats the tablet as forming part of the Creation Series.[2] The recovered portion of the Sixth Tablet of the Creation Series, however, and the Neo-Babylonian duplicate of K. 3,364, the text of which is published in vol. ii, pls. lxiv–lxvi (No. 33,851), together disprove the suggested connection of K. 3,364 with the Creation Series. The reasons on which this conclusion is based may be briefly stated as follows:—(1) The recovered portion of the Sixth Tablet indicates that the description of the creation of man there given was very similar to the account furnished by Berossus; and it follows that the greater part of the text must have been in the form of narrative. If Marduk gave man any instructions after his creation, these can have occupied only a small part of the tablet. But both the obverse and reverse of K. 3,364 contain moral precepts, and the same is the case with columns ii and iii of the new duplicate No. 33,851.[3] For such a long series of moral instructions there is no room upon the Sixth Tablet of the Creation Series. (2) Col. ii of No. 33,851 refers to certain acts which are good, and to others which are not good,

[1] The side of the tablet which George Smith refers to as the obverse is really the reverse; this is rendered certain by the duplicate No. 33,851.

[2] In my *Babylonian Religion and Mythology*, p. 82 f., I also provisionally adopted this view.

[3] In col. i of this tablet only the ends of lines are preserved, and in col. iv a part of the colophon.

in the eyes of Šamaš.[1] This is quite consistent with the character of Šamaš as the judge of heaven and earth, but he does not appear in this character in the Creation Series, where he is referred to merely as the sun which Marduk created and set upon his course. (3) In the duplicate, No. 33,851, the text is arranged in columns, two on each side of the tablet. This fact in itself is sufficient to prove that the composition has nothing to do with the series *Enuma eliš*. The text upon tablets of the Creation Series is never arranged in columns, but each line is written across the tablet from edge to edge. This characteristic applies not only to the copies of the Creation Series from Kuyunjik, but also to the Babylonian copies of all periods, and even to the rough "practice-tablets" on which students wrote out extracts from the poem.

The text inscribed upon K. 3,364 and No. 33,851 is, in fact, a long didactic composition containing a number of moral precepts, and has nothing to do with the Creation Series.[2] The composition in itself is of considerable interest, however, for enough of it remains to show that it indicates a high standard of morality.

---

[1] Cf. l. 9, *ul ṭa-a-bi eli* [ilu] *Šamaš i-*[. . . . . .]; and l. 13, *ṭa-a-bi eli* [ilu] *Šamaš i-*[. . . . . .]. The signs AN-UD in these passages are clearly to be rendered [ilu] *Šamaš*, and not *ilu-tu*, "godhead," in the sense in which *ilu-u-ti* occurs in K. 3,364, Rev., l. 14.

[2] It may be noted that the phrase *a-kil kar-ṣi* (K. 3,364, Rev., l. 5, and No. 33,851, col. iii, l. 4), which has been thought by some to be the title of a power of evil termed "the Calumniator" (cf. Bezold, *Catalogue*, vol. ii, p. 526), is not a proper name or title, but should be rendered simply as "a slanderer."

III.

On some traces of the History of Creation in Religious and Astrological Literature.

THERE is abundant evidence to prove that under the late Assyrian kings, and during the Neo-Babylonian and Persian periods, the history of the Creation as told upon the Seven Tablets of the series *Enuma eliš* was widely read and studied, and there can be no doubt that it exercised a considerable influence on the religious literature which continued to gather around Marduk's name. In the fragmentary hymns and prayers which have come down to us, however, it is difficult to determine how far the priestly and popular conceptions of Marduk were influenced by the actual story of the Creation as we know it, and to what extent they were moulded by earlier legends and beliefs, and by Marduk's own position as the native god of Babylon. That actual phrases from the Seventh Tablet of the Creation Series were made use of in other similar compositions is sufficiently proved by the fragments published at the end of Appendix I; and in view of this fact we may perhaps hear echoes from the earlier tablets of the series in some of the phrases and attributes applied to Marduk in the contemporary religious texts. It would be impossible within the limits of the present work to attempt an exhaustive treatment of this subject, but, as a striking instance of such allusions to the Creation story, reference may here be made to the fragment K. 3,351, which, I believe, has not hitherto been translated.[1]

---

[1] A rather rough copy of this tablet is included in Craig's *Religious Texts*, pl. 43. As several signs, including l. 4, are there omitted, and others are incorrectly copied, the text of the obverse is given in the block on p. 205.

The upper part of the tablet is broken and rubbed, but the greater part of the text is well preserved and clearly written, and may be transliterated as follows :—

1. [. . . *e*]*-til-lum mār* ^{ilu} *E-a* [. . . . .] *mut-tal-lum*

2. [. . .] *k*[*iš-šat*] *šamē*(*e*) *u irṣiti*(*ti*) *m*[*u*]*-šim ši-ma-a-ti*

3. [. . . . .] *bi - nu - tu*

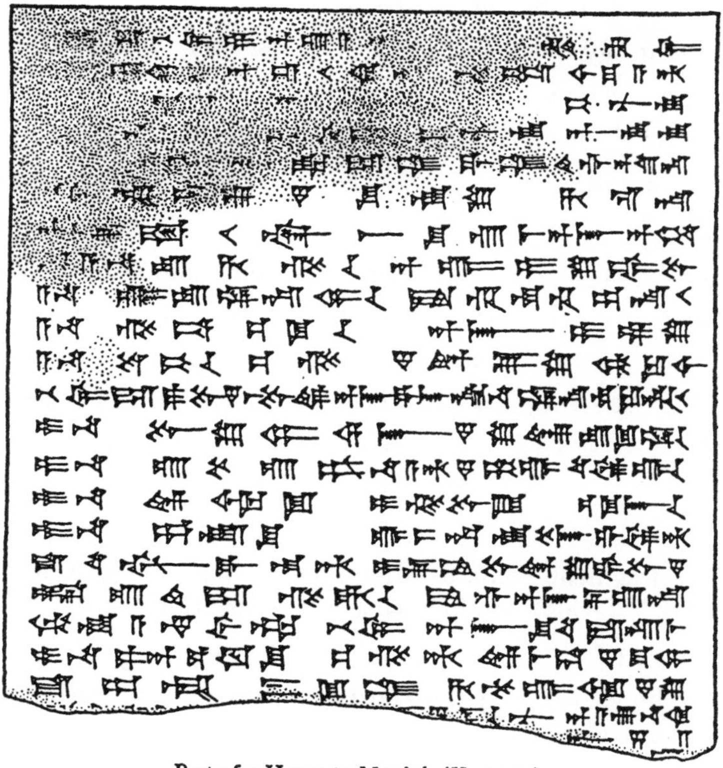

Part of a Hymn to Marduk (K. 3,351).

4. [. . . . .] *b*[*i*] *- n*[*u*] *- tu* ^{ilu} *Tu - tu*

5. [. . . . .] *šar-ra-tum rabītum*(*tum*) *ḫi-rat* ^{ilu} *Šag-zu*

6. [*b*]*e - l*[*um*] ^{ilu} *B*[*ēl ru*]*bū ša šu - tu - ru ḫa - si - su*

7. [. . .] *ḳabli u taḫāzi ina ḳāt abkalli ilāni*^{pl} ^{ilu} *Marduk*

8. *[š]a a - na ta - ḫa - zi - šu šamū(u) i - ru - ub - bu*
9. *a - na u - ta - az - zu - mi - šu id - dal - la - ḫu ap - su - u*
10. *a - na zi - ḳip kakki - šu ilāni*^{pl} *i - tur - ru*
11. *a - na te - bi - šu iz - zi ša - ' - ir - ru ul ib - ši*
12. *be-lum ra-aš-bu ša ina pu-ḫur ilāni*^{pl} *rabūti*^{pl} *šin-na-as-su la ib-ba-šu-u*
13. *i - na bu - ru - mi ellūti*^{pl} *ša - ru - uḫ ta - lu - uk - šu*
14. *i-na E-kur bīt tak-na-a-ti ša-ḳu-u par-ṣu u-šu*
15. *i - na im - ḫul - lu i - nam - bu - ṭu kakkē*^{pl} *- šu*
16. *i - na nab - li - šu u - tab - ba - tu šadāni*^{pl} *mar - ṣu - ti*
17. *ša tam - tim gal - la - ti i - sa - am - bu - ' ru - up - pu - ša*
18. *apil E-šar-ra zi-kir-šu ḳar-rad ilāni*^{pl} *ni-bit-su*
19. *ul-tu a-sur-rak-ka be-lum ilāni*^{pl} *šu-ut da-ad-me*
20. *i-na pa-an* ^{iṣu}*ḳašti-šu iz-zi-ti im-me-du ša-ma-mi*
21. *ša* AB - MAḪ *ṣal - lu - tum ḫa - mu - u u ša - ru*
22. [. . . . .] *š[a] ka[li]-šu-nu* ^{ilu}*A-nun-na-ki*
23. [. . . . . ! . . . .] ^{ilu}*Igigi*
24. [. . . .]

The fragment contains the opening lines of a hymn to Marduk,[1] of which the following is a translation:—

1. O lord [. . . .], son of Ea, the exalted [. . . .],
2. [Who . . . .] the [hosts] of heaven and earth, who ordaineth destinies!

---

[1] The composition is addressed to Marduk, who is named in l. 7 and is referred to in the three preceding lines under his titles Tutu, Šagzu, and Bēl; moreover, in l. 1 he is termed the "son of Ea." The Reverse of the tablet contains the last five lines of Ašur-bani-pal's common colophon.

3. [. . . . . the . . . .] offspring,
4. [. . . . . the . . . . off]spring is Tutu!
5. [. . . . .], the great queen, the consort of Sagzu!
6. O lord Bēl, thou prince, who art mighty in understanding!
7. [The . . . .] of war and battle is in the hand of Marduk, the director of the gods,
8. At whose battle heaven quaked,
9. At whose wrath the Deep is troubled!
10. At the point of his weapon the gods turned back!
11. To his furious attack there was no opponent!
12. O mighty lord, to whom there is no rival in the assembly of the great gods!
13. In the bright firmament of heaven his course is supreme!
14. In E-kur, the temple of true worship, exalted is his decree!
15. With the evil wind his weapons blaze forth,
16. With his flame steep mountains are destroyed!
17. He overwhelmeth the expanse of the billowing ocean!
18. The Son of E-šara is his name, the Hero of the gods is his title!
19. From the depth[1] is he lord of the gods of human habitations!
20. Before his terrible bow the heavens stand fast!
21. . . . plague and destruction, and tempest,
22. [. . . . .] of all the Aunnaki,
23. [. . . . .] the Igigi!
24. [. . . .]

[1] In this phrase we may probably see an antithesis to "the heavens" in the following line; for other passages in which the word *asurrakku* occurs, cf. Delitzsch, *Handwörterbuch*, p. 111, and Muss-Arnolt, *Concise Dict.*, p. 121.

It will be noticed that in ll. 8–11 the hymn describes the quaking of the heavens at Marduk's battle, the trouble of the Deep at his wrath, and the flight of the gods from the point of his weapon. We have here an unmistakable reference to the battle of Marduk with Tiamat, and the subsequent flight of the gods, her helpers. The reference in l. 12 to Marduk's supremacy in the assembly of the gods does not necessarily refer to the Seventh Tablet of the Creation Series, but the *imḫullu*, or "evil wind," in l. 15, and Marduk's "flame" in l. 16 are clearly reminiscences of the Fourth Tablet, ll. 45 and 96, and l. 40; and in "the billowing ocean (*tam-tim*)" in l. 17 we may possibly see a reference to Tiamat. Finally, the mention of Marduk's bow in l. 20 may be compared with the Fourth Tablet, l. 35, and with the fragment of the Fifth Tablet which describes the translation of the bow to heaven as the Bow-star (see above, p. 82 f.).

Such references to the Creation story are of considerable interest, but they do not add anything to the facts concerning Marduk's character which may be gathered from the Creation Series itself. An additional interest, however, attaches to some astrological fragments which I have come across, inasmuch as they show that at a late period of Babylonian history the story of the fight between Marduk and Tiamat had received a very definite astrological interpretation. One of the fragments exhibits Tiamat as a star or constellation in the neighbourhood of the ecliptic, and, moreover, furnishes an additional proof of a fact which has long been generally recognized, viz., the identification of the monster-brood of Tiamat with at any rate some of the signs of the Zodiak.

The most important of the astrological fragments above referred to is made up of three pieces, Nos. 55,466, 55,486, and 55,627, which I have rejoined, and its text is published in vol. ii, pls. lxvii–lxxii. It measures $5\frac{1}{4}$ in. by $3\frac{7}{8}$ in., and is part of a large tablet which was inscribed with two, or possibly three, broad columns of writing on each side. The fragment of the tablet recovered gives considerable portions of the first and last columns of the text, as well as traces of the second column on the obverse and of the last column but one on the reverse. The colophon, which possibly contained the date at which the tablet was inscribed, has not been preserved, but from the character of the writing and the shape of the tablet it may be concluded that it does not belong to an earlier period than that of the Arsacidæ; it may possibly be assigned to as late a date as the first century B.C.

From the first section which has been preserved of col. i it is clear that the text is closely connected with the story of the Creation. This will be apparent from the following transliteration and translation of the portions of ll. 1–7 which have been preserved: (1) [. . . . . .]-*nu ša ḳātē*[II]-*šu mul-mul is-si-ma* [. . . . . .] (2) [. . . . . . [ilu]*Kin*]-*gu ḫa-mi-ri-šu ina kakki la ga-ba-al i*[*t*]-*ta-kis-a*[*m*]-*m*[*a*] (3) [. . . . . .] *Ti-amat ik-mu-u il-ḳu-u šarru-us-su* (4) [. . . . . *dup*]*šīmāti*[pl] *ša* [ilu]*Kin-gu it-mu-ḫu ḳa-tu-uš-šu* (5) [. . . . . .]-*nu ib-ni-ma bāb ap-si-i u-ša-aṣ-bit* (6) [. . . . . .]-*mu ana la ma-ši-e ip-še-e-ti Ti-amat* (7) [. . . . . .] *u-kal-lam ab-bi-e-šu*, "(1) [. . . . . .] whose hands removed the Spear, and [. . . . . .] (2) [. . . . . . Kin]gu, her spouse, with a weapon not of war was cut off, and (3) [. . . . . .] Tiamat he conquered, he took her sovereignty. (4) [. . . . . .] the Tablets of Destiny from Kingu he took in his hand. (5) [. . . . . .] he created, and at the Gate of the Deep he stationed. (6) [. . . . . .] that the deeds of Tiamat should not be forgotten (7) [. . . . . .] he causeth his fathers to behold."

In the first line we may probably see a reference to Marduk's drawing forth of the *mulmullu*, or spear,[1] which we know from

[1] It is possible that *mul-mul* is here, not Marduk's actual weapon, but *Mul-mul*, the Spear-star of Marduk; and the verb *is-si-ma* may have the intransitive meaning, "disappeared." In view of the fact that the following lines refer to episodes in the Creation story, I think the rendering suggested above is preferable.

Tablet IV of the Creation Series, l. 101, he plunged into the belly of Tiamat, after he had filled her with the evil wind. Line 2 may be explained as referring to Marduk's conquest of Kingu after Tiamat's death, without further fighting, though it is possible that it has some connection with the obscure expression in Tablet IV, l. 120. In l. 3 the text returns to Marduk's defeat of Tiamat; and with the capture of the Tablets of Destiny from Kingu, referred to in l. 4, we may compare Tablet IV, l. 121 f. Line 5 possibly refers to an episode in the Creation which may have been recorded in the missing portion of Tablet V of the Creation Series. With it we may compare the fixing of a bolt by Marduk and the stationing of a watchman, in order to keep the waters above the firmament in their place (cf. Tablet IV, ll. 137 ff.); it is possible that a similar guardian was stationed by Marduk in order to restrain the waters of the Deep. Line 6 f. apparently refer to the instructions given by Marduk to the gods, "his fathers," in order "that the deeds of Tiamat (i.e. her revolt and subsequent conquest by himself) should not be forgotten."[1] It is possible that the instructions which Marduk is here represented as giving to the gods refer to their positions in heaven and to the heavenly bodies associated with them. If this interpretation is correct, it follows that the later Babylonians, at any rate, looked upon the astrological aspect of the Creation story as in accordance with definite instructions given by Marduk himself. While they believed that Marduk actually slew Tiamat and subsequently created the universe as narrated in the tablets of the Creation Series, they held that the association of the principal actors in the story with some of the more important stars and constellations was also Marduk's work, his object being to ensure that the history of the creation of the world should always be kept in remembrance.

The first section which is preserved of the text, referring

[1] This rendering appears preferable to the possible reading, *la ba-ši-e*, i.e. "that the deeds of Tiamat should be no more."

as it does to some of the most striking episodes recorded in the Creation Series, appears to be of the nature of an introduction to what follows. The second section reads: (8) [. . . . . . *ilu Marduk*](?) *u-kal-la-mu par-ṣi-šu-[nu]* (9) [. . . . . .]*-tim E-la-mu-u ša* [. . . . . .] *a-šak-[ku]* (10) [. . . . .] *Ti-amat itba-am-ma* [. . . . .] *ni[m* . . . . . .] (11) [. . *T]i-amat ina lib-bi ilu Sin in-n[am* (?)- . . . . . .] (12) [. .] *ilu Marduk ina lib-bi ilu Tam-tim* [. . . . . .] (13) *ki-i ša ru-bu-u ilu Marduk ana ša-kan a-b[u-bu* . . . . . .] (14) *i-na ri-kis si-pit-ti u me-lul-ti-šu i-ḳab-[* . . . . . .] (15) *e-liš u šap-liš li-mut-tum u-ša-tar-ma*[1] *i-kap-pu-du sur-ra-[a-tum]* (16) *ina u-mu šu-u agū taš-ri-iḫ-tum ša nu-uk-ku-ri šup-pal u-kal-l[i-* . . .] (17) *ana muḫ-ḫi paraṣ e-nu-tum ša la si-ma-a-tum i-šak-kan pa-ni*(?)-*[šu]* (18) *ilāni pl ma-ḫa-zi mâtu Akkadī KI amêlu nišē pl -šu-nu u-šaḫ-ḫa-su ul ul-la-a-tum*[2] (19) *a-mat su-uš-tum*(?) *i-dib-bu-bu i-ḳab-bu-u ma-ag-ri-tum* (20) *mi-il-ki la tuš-šir*(?) *im-tal-lik i-te-ip-šu sur-ra-a-tum* (21) *ig-ga-ag-ma ilu Bēl u-ḫal-laḳ eš-ri-e-tum* (22) *E-la-ma-a ṭi-e-mu i-šak-kan-ma i-sap-pan ma-a-tum* (23) *ana ku-um ša-kan a-bu-bu ana šul-mu* IZ-DIM-MU *epuš(uš)* NAM-BUL-BI.

In this section Marduk and Tiamat appear in their astrological characters, Marduk probably as Jupiter, and Tiamat as a constellation in the neighbourhood of the ecliptic. The approach of Tiamat and the Moon and of Marduk (i.e. Jupiter) and Tiamat would seem from ll. 13 ff. to portend the sending of an *abubu*, or deluge,[3] upon the earth, followed by rebellion and tumult among gods and men. If unchecked, the wrath of Bēl (i.e. Marduk) would result in the destruction of the temples and in the ruin of the land. To prevent the sending of a deluge and to change the omen to one of prosperity,

[1] The sign is MA, not IZ.

[2] For *ul ul-la-a-tum*, as parallel to *ma-ag-ri-tum* (cf. l. 19), see Jensen, *Kosmologie*, p. 121 f.

[3] Or, possibly, a thunderbolt.

the text enjoins the performance of certain NAM-BUL-BI prayers.[1]

The third and last section of the first column reads: (24) *ina* ^{arhu} *Dūzu ša ni-pi-šu ša sa-kap* ^{amēlu} *nakiri ina Bābili*^{KI} *i-pu-uš* (25) *ina lib-bi ša* ^{ilu} *Muštabarrū-mūtanu u* ^{ilu} *Sin bēlē*^{pl} *ni-ṣir-tum ša* ^{mātu} *Elamtu*^{KI} (26) NUM-LU^{pl} [2] ^{ilu} SAG-ME-GAR *u* ^{ilu} *Šamaš bēlē*^{pl} *ni-ṣir-tum ša* ^{mātu} *Akkadū*^{KI} (27) ŠU-[. .]-LU^{pl} *idāti*[^{pl}] *ša nu-uk-ku-ri palī Bābili*^{KI} *'-u-kal-lim-'* (28) NAM-BUL-BI *ina ali i-te-pu-uš* KI[3] *ni-ṣir-tum ša* ^{ilu} *Sin* (29) TE ŠU-GI *u Mul-mul* TE *ša Elamtu*^{KI} (30) KI *ni-ṣir-tum ša* ^{ilu} *Šamaš* ^{kakkabu} LU-KU-MAL ^{ilu} [. . . . . .] (31) KI *ni-ṣir-tum ša* ^{ilu} *Muštabarrū-mūtanu* ^{kakkabu} [. . . . .] (32) KI *ni-ṣir-tum ša* ^{ilu} SAG-ME-GAR ^{kakkabu} [. . . . . .] (33) *ina* ^{arhu} *Tap-pat-tum ina ḳar-nu-te di-*[. . . . . .] (34) [. . . . .]*-ba-ba-an paraṣ e-nu-tum* [. . . . . .] (35) [. . . . . .] *muḫ-ḫi šip*(?)*-tum* [. . . . . .]. This section is concerned with the positions of the planets *Muštabarrū-mūtanu* (Mercury) and SAG-ME-GAR (Jupiter) and of the moon and sun, and of the stars ŠU-GI and *Mulmul*; and it would seem that a change in the dynasty ruling at Babylon was portended by the relative positions of Mercury and Jupiter. To that extent this section resembles the one that precedes it, but there is little apparent connection between this portion of the text and the Creation Series. It is possible, however, that this section was continued in col. ii, and that the missing portion had some connection with the legend.[4]

[1] This may be the title of a special class of incantations (cf. my *Magic and Sorcery*, p. 129), or the expression may possibly be employed, as in some other passages, to indicate generally a class of incantations, or ceremonies, intended to avert the effects of an evil omen (cf. Thompson, *Reports of Magicians and Astrologers*, p. xlvii f.).

[2] Cf. Epping and Strassmaier, *Z.A.*, vii, p. 221 f.

[3] Possibly *ašar*.

[4] Of col. ii only traces of the beginnings of a few lines are preserved from the lower half of the column; they read: (1) *a-*[. . . . . .] (2) *ku-*[. . . . . .] (3) IT[I . . . . . .]

The greater part of the reverse of the fragment is inscribed with the upper half of the last column, which in some respects is the most interesting portion of the text. The lines that have been preserved read as follows: (1) *ina* *arḫu* *Tap-pat-tum ša ni-pi-šu an-nu-tu* [. . . . .] (2) *ana muḫ-ḫi* *ilu* *Marduk illiku(ku) ina ḳaḳ-ḳar* *arḫu* [. . . . . .] (3) *u* *ilu* *Kin-gu šu-u : ab-bi :* *arḫu* AB : *ab-*[. . . . . .] (4) TE BIR[1] *Ti-amat pu-uḫ-ri ana ṣal-tum ki-i* [. . . . . .] (5) *epuš(uš) Ti-amat u* *ilu* *Kin-gi ana iš-ten itūrū* *pl*-*ma* [. . . . . .] (6) *a-ḫa-meš in-nam-mar-ru-' aš-šu an-ni-i* TE *Enzu ša* KI TE *Aḳrabu* PAD [. . . . . .] (7) *E-zi-da* : TE *Enzu* : *kakkabu* *Uḫ-zu šum-šu par-ṣi ša Ti-amat* (8) *kul-lu gi-iz-za-ni-tum u pu-uš-ša-ni-tum ša it-ti lib-bi* TE *pl* E(*u*) (9) *ana muḫ-ḫi* *kakkabu* *Enzu u* TE MULU-BAD[2] *ina lib-bi* TE BIR KA-BI *Ti-amat u* *ilu* *Kin-gi* (10) *šu-nu : gi-iz-za-ni-tu : ki-iz-za-ni-tu šum-šu ana muḫ-ḫi* TE BIR *ki-iz-zu* (11) *pu-uš-ša-ni-tum pu-u-za-ni-tum šum-šu ana muḫ-ḫi* TE KA *ḳa-bi* (12) TE KA : TE MULU-BAD *Ti-amat tu-ra-am-tum šum-šu šanū pa-nu-šu zikru u sinništu šu-u* (13) *ina lib-bi ki-i i-kat ša* TE *Aḳrabu it-ti* *ilu* *Nin-lil u* *ilu* *Nin-ki-gal* (14) *bašū(u) ina muḫ-ḫi par-ṣa ša Ti-amat aš-ba-' Gud u Aḳrabu iš-ten šu-u* (15) GIR : *zu-ḳa-ki-pu* : GIR *lu-u* : *II . . . -pi aš-šu an-ni-i ina* *arḫu* *Tap-pat-tum* (16) KI *a-šak-ku* TE *Enzu ina* KI TE MULU-BAD *ina agī taš-ri-iḫ-tum illiku(ku)* (17) [. . . . .]*-da* TE UTU-KA-GAB-A *ina lib-bi te*

---

(4) *ilu* [. . . . . .] (5) *alu* [. . . . . .] (6) *ša* [. . . . .] (7) TE [. . . . . .] (8) *kakkabu* [. . . . . .] (9) *saḫ-*[. . . . . .] (10) *ul* [. . . . . .]. Similarly, only traces remain of the first column preserved upon the reverse of the tablet, which read: (1) [. . . . . .] (2) *ilu* *Na-na-*[*a* . . . . . .] (3) *ša ḫu-la-*[. . . . . .] (4) *ki-na-*[*a-* . . . . . .] (5, beginning a new section) *ina* *arḫu* [. . . . . .] (6) *ku-*[. . . . . .] (7) *a*[*lu* . . . . . .].

[1] I.e. Caper. The sign was read by Strassmaier and Epping as ŠAḪ, *šaḫū* (see *Astron. aus Bab.*, App., p. 7), but Jensen has shown that it is not ŠAḪ, but the sign Br. No. 2,024 (see *Kosmologie*, p. 313), which perhaps has the value BIR. As the tenth sign of the Zodiac it should possibly be read as *Lalū*.

[2] Explained as *pa-gar ašakki* (ID-PA) in VR., pl. 46, No. 1, Obv., l. 28.

BIR KI *ni-ṣir-tum ša* [mātu] *Elamtu* [[KI]] (18) [. . . . .]*-šu-ni u-tir-ru-nim-ma ana ṣal-tum iz-zi-zu-u* [ilu] *Šamaš ina lib-b* [. . . . .] (19) [. . . . .] *ša* [kakkabu] SAG-ME-GAI *ni-me-du* TE KAK-SI-DI *u* TE PAN *ina pa-ni* [kakkabu] [. . . . . (20) [. . . . .] *ta-ḫa-zi ki-ma iz-zi-zu ri-*[. . . . . (21) [. . . . .] *mi ba* [. . . . .] (22) [. . . . . [ilu] *Šamaš* [*bē*]*lu* [ilu] *Nin-ib šum-šu ana* . . . [. . . . . (23) [. . . . .]*-pu-šu* [amelu] TAB *i-sak-ki-pu* IGI MAF [ilu] *Nin-i*[*b* . . . . .] (24) [. . . . .] *kak-ku šu-u kak-ku a-bu-bu* [ilu] *Marduk ina šumi-šu ḳ*[*a-bi* (25) [. . . . . P]AN[1] *a-bu-bu kak-ka-šu rabā*(*a*) *aš-šu ša* [ilu] *Nin-ib a-ṣi aš-šu an-ni-i* [. . . . .] (26) [. . . . . *i-ḳab-bu-u* KI SIR NAM LUL *ša ūmu XVII*[KAN] *ina* ḲI SIG [. . . . .] (27) [. . . . .] [ilu] *Bēl ḳar-ra-du ša ina ag-gu lib-bi-šu a-šak-ku* [. . . . .] (28) [. . . . .]*-ri-šu i-si-ḫu tu-ḳu-un-tum* [ilu] *Nin-*[. . . . .] (29) [. . . . .]*-tum ina idi-šu* [*i*]*-lul*(*-*)*lu* (?) *E-kur* [. . . . .] (30) [. . . . .]*-ma-šu* [. . . . .]*-an-na ki* [. . . . .] (31) [. . . . .]*-ir ina* [. . . . .] *ik* [. . . . .] *u* [. . . . .] (32) [. . . . .] (33) [. . . . .].

It will be noticed that this portion of the text is in the main explanatory. Unlike col. i, these lines of the text do not run on in the form of connected sentences, but are broken up into a number of equations and explanations of terms and titles; thus, some terms are explained by a play upon words (cf. ll. 3 and 10 f.), while in other places the reason is given for certain titles (cf. ll. 6 and 7) or additional names (cf. l. 12). With regard to the connection of passages in this column with the Creation Series, it may be noted that Kingu, in addition to Marduk and Tiamat, is introduced. He is here associated in an astrological sense with Tiamat, and their alliance in opposition to Marduk is clearly referred to in ll. 4–6. Moreover, the fact that Caper and Scorpio are mentioned in close connection with this passage shows that

[1] Either the Bow-star, or, possibly, [IZ-B]AN, i.e. [ilu] *ḳaštu*, Marduk's bow.

they here occur, not only in their astronomical sense as constellations of the Zodiac, but also in their mythical character as monsters in the host of Tiamat. The reference to Marduk's "mighty weapon" in l. 24 f. is also noteworthy.

After the sheets of vol. ii had been printed off I came across two other fragments of somewhat similar astrological texts, which furnish additional illustrations of the manner in which the legends of the Creation were connected by the later Babylonians with astrological phenomena. The smaller of these fragments, No. 40,959, the text of which is given in

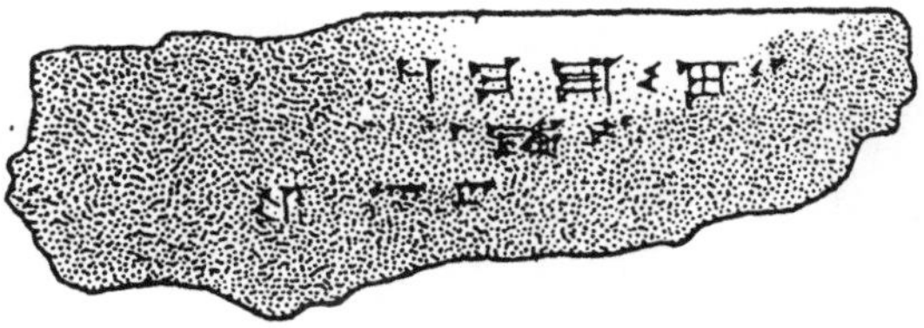

OBVERSE.

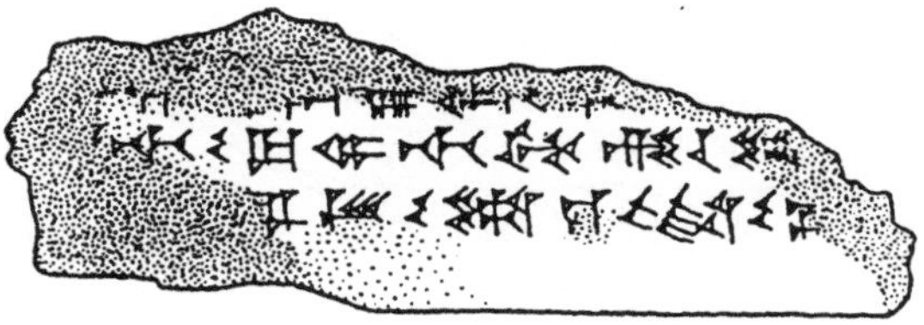

REVERSE.

Fragment of an astrological explanatory text (No. 40,959).

the accompanying block, preserves a few traces of signs from the beginning of the obverse and from the end of the reverse of the tablet. A few complete words occur in l. 2 of the reverse, which reads [. . . . .]-*ti*: *lik-mi Ti-amat napišta-šu* *l*[*i-* . . . . .]; l. 112 of the Seventh Tablet of the Creation Series reads *lik-me* (var. *li-ik-mi*) *Ti-amat ni-ṣir-ta-šu* (var. *na-piš-ta-šu*) *li-si-iḳ u lik-ri* (see above, p. 108 f.), and it is clear that this line is here quoted upon the fragment. Both the obverse and reverse of No. 40,959 resemble the last column of No. 55,466, etc, in being of an explanatory nature, and it is probable that the quotation from the Seventh Tablet is here introduced in an astrological context.

The larger of the two fragments is No. 32,574, and the text of its obverse is published in the accompanying block. This text also is explanatory, and of an astrological character, and, like No. 40,959, it has in some respects a close connection with the Creation Series. Thus l. 2 reads [. . . . . ALI]M-NUN-NA : *nu-ur ša* ^{ilu}*Anu* ^{ilu}*Bēl u* ^{ilu}[*E-a* :] A[SAR]U : [. . . . .]; now ^{ilu}*Asaru-alim-nun-na* occurs as one of the titles of Marduk in l. 5 of the Seventh Tablet of the

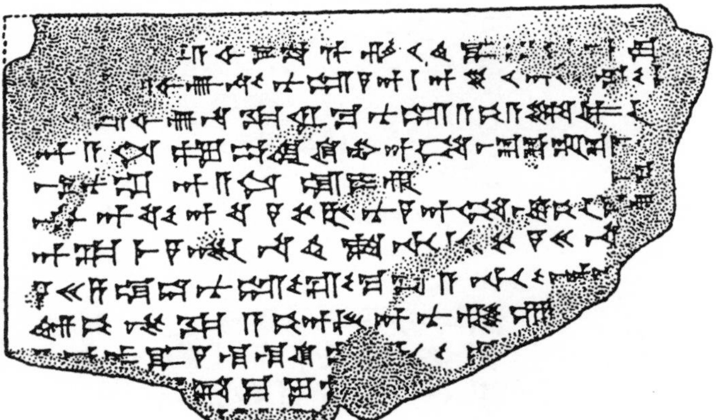

Fragment of an astrological explanatory text (No. 32,574, Obverse).

Creation Series, and with the explanation of the title here given as "the Light of Anu, Bēl, and Ea," we may compare the explanation in l. 6 of the Seventh Tablet, which reads *muš-te-šir te-rit* ^{ilu}*A-nim* ^{ilu}*Bēl* [*u* ^{ilu}*E-a*], "who directeth the decrees of Anu, Bēl, [and Ea]." Moreover, l. 3 of the fragment reads [. . . . . A]LIM-NUN-NA [1] *ka-ru-ba nu-ur a-bi*

[1] At the beginning of the line there is hardly room for the restoration [^{ilu} ASARU-A]LIM-NUN NA ; it is probable that the line read [^{ilu} A]LIM-NUN-NA, which may be regarded as a shorter form of the same title.

a-li-di-šu [. . . . . .]; now l. 5 of the Seventh Tablet reads ^{ilu}*Asaru-alim-nun-na ka-ru-bu nu-ur* [. . . . . . .], and the end of the line may probably be restored from the fragment as *nu-ur* [*a-bi a-li-di-šu*].[1] Line 9 of the fragment reads *im-bi šumu-ka a-bi ilāni*^{pl} ^{ilu}NU-NAM-NIR [. . . . .]; this also possibly refers to Marduk, and may be compared with the Seventh Tablet, l. 116 and ll. 118 ff.

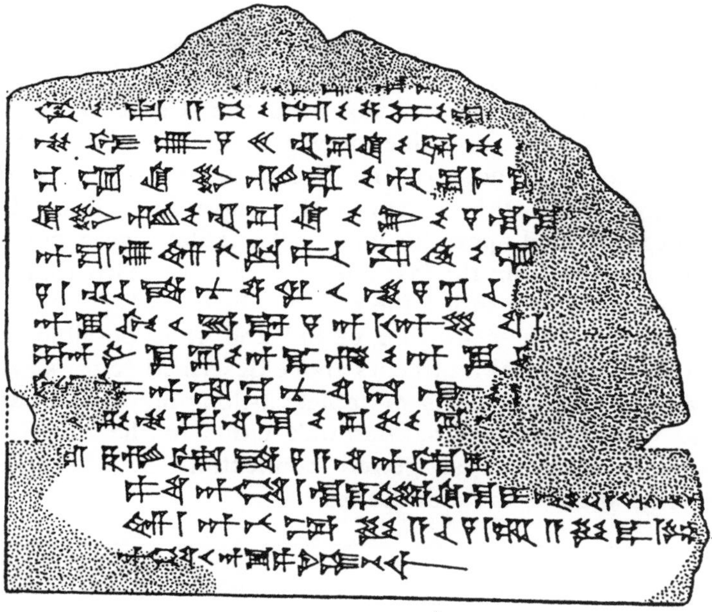

Fragment of an astrological explanatory text (No. 32,574, Reverse and Edge).

The text of the reverse of No. 32,574 (see the accompanying block) is also explanatory, and reads: (1) [. . . . . .] (2) SIGIŠŠE : *ṭa-a-bi* : UR : *zab-lum* : [. . . . .] (3) *mu-ṣu-u ša šar Nippuri*^{KI} : *šul-mu* [. . . . . .] (4) GIŠ-ŠID KI-IN-GI-RA : *ḫu-la me* [. . . . .] (5) KI-IN-GI : *Nippuru*^{KI} :

[1] See above, p. 92 f.

IR : *ša-la-la* [. . . . .] (6) *ilu Zu-u im-haṣ kap-pa-šu iš-bir* : ŠID [. . . . .] (7) *ša ana bēli-šu ḳar-nu ṣab-ru u mu-ša-kil-šu* [. . . . .] (8) *ilu Kin-gu u arhu Nisannu ša ilu Anu u ilu Bēl ūmu I* [. . . . .] (9) *kakkabu* LU - KU - MAL : *ilu Dumu-zi* : *ilu Kin-g*[*u* . . . . .] (10) [. . . . .] *ilu Al-ma-nu* UD-DU AG : [. . . . .] (11) [*ri*]-*ig-mu šak-na-at* : *E-kur* : *E*-[. . . . .]. In ll. 8 f. Kingu is introduced, but there is no other evidence of a connection between the Creation Series and this portion of the text; in fact, l. 6, beginning, "Zū smote and broke his wing," evidently gives a quotation from a legend of the Storm-god Zū, which has nothing to do with the Creation Series. Indirectly, however, this line proves that other Babylonian legends were, like those of the Creation, connected by the later Babylonians with certain of the heavenly bodies. The four lines inscribed upon the edge of the tablet give a portion of the colophon, from the last line of which we learn that the tablet belonged to a series, the title of which reads [. . . . . *ilu*]*Marduk u ilu Ṣar-pa-ni-tum* BE-ŠI,[1] and it is possible that the other astrological fragments above described (Nos. 55,466, etc., and 40,959) are parts of tablets belonging to the same series. The occurrence of Marduk's name in the title is in accordance with the suggested connection between these fragments and the Creation Series.

---

[1] The last two signs are not very carefully written, but they are distinctly BE-ŠI and not EŠ-BAR (i.e. *purussū*). With this title we may compare that which occurs at the beginning or upon the edge of many of the late Babylonian astronomical tablets, viz., *ina a-mat ilu Bēl u ilu Bēlti-ia purussū*, "At the word of the Lord and of my Lady, a decision!"; cf., e.g., Epping, *Astronomisches aus Babylon*, p. 153. The *Bēl* and *Bēlti-ia* are probably Marduk and Ṣarpanitum.

IV.

Supposed Assyrian Legends of the Temptation and the Tower of Babel.

IN vol. ii, pl. lxxiii f. the text is given of a fragment of a legend (K. 3,657), which was thought at one time by George Smith and others [1] to contain an Assyrian version of the story of the Tower of Babel (cf. Gen. xi, 1 ff.). The text is very broken, but from what remains of col. i it would appear to be part of a legend concerning a god, or possibly a king, who plotted evil in his heart and conceived a hatred against the father of all the gods. In col. i, ll. 5 ff. the passage occurs on which the supposed parallel with the story of the Tower of Babel was based, for these lines were believed to refer to the building of a tower at Babylon, and to describe how the tower erected by the builders in the day was destroyed in the night by a god, who confounded their speech and confused their counsel. There is, however, no mention of a tower or building of any sort, and Babylon is referred to as suffering through the evil designs of the god or king, described in ll. 2–4. Moreover, the lines supposed to recount the destruction of the tower by night really describe how the complaints of the oppressed people prevented the king, or possibly an avenger of the people, from getting any sleep at night upon his couch. The tablet is too broken to allow of a completely satisfactory explanation of the nature of the legend, but the rendering

[1] See *Chaldean Account of Genesis*, pp. 160 ff., German ed. (edited by Delitzsch), p. 122 f.; cf. also Boscawen, *T.S.B.A.*, v, pp. 304 ff., and *Records of the Past*, vol. vii, pp. 129 ff.

of ll. 1–14 given below[1] will suffice to show that the suggested connection between this legend and the story of the Tower of Babel was not justified.

As with the story of the Tower of Babel, so also has it been claimed that an Assyrian legend has been found which presents a close parallel to the story of the temptation of Eve in the garden of Eden, narrated in Gen. iii. That the description of paradise in Gen. ii shows traces of Babylonian influence is certain,[2] and it is not impossible that a Babylonian legend may at some future time be discovered which bears

[1] The first fourteen lines of col. i may be rendered as follows:— (1) [. . . . . *-s*]*u*(?)*-nu ab-*[. . . . .] (2) [. . . . .]*-ti-šu lib-ba-šu il-te-im-na* (3) [. . . . .]*a-bi ka-la ilāni^pl^ i-zi-ru* (4) [. . . . . *-t*]*i-šu lib-ba-šu il-te-im-na* (5) [. . . . . *Bābilu^KI^*] *ṣa-mi-id a-na il-ki-im* (6) [*ṣi-iḫ-ru u r*]*a-bu-u u-ba-al-lu dul-la* (7) [. . . . . *Bāb*]*ilu^KI^ ṣa-mi-id a-na il-ki-im* (8) [*ṣi-iḫ-ru*] *u ra-bu-u u-ba-al-lu dul-la* (9) [. . . . . *-i*]*m-ma-as-si-na ka-la u-mi i-šu-uš* (10) [*i*]*-na ta-az-zi-im-ti-ši-na i-na ma-ai-li* (11) *u-ul u-ḳat-ta ši-it-ta* (12) [*i-n*]*a ug-ga-ti-šu-ma te-me-ga-am i-sa-pa-aḫ* (13) [*a-na*] *šu-ba-al-ku-ut pa-li-e pa-ni-šu iš-ku-un* (14) [*uš*(?)*-t*]*an-ni ṭe-ma ut-tak-ki-ra mi-lik-šu-un* . . . . . . "(1) [. . . . .] their [. . . . .]; (2) [. . . . .] his heart plotted evil. (3) [. . . . .] the father of the gods he hated; (4) [. . . . .] his heart plotted evil. (5) [. . . . . Babylon] was yoked to forced labour; (6) [small and] great rendered(?) service. (7) [. . . . . Bab]ylon was yoked to forced labour; (8) [small] and great rendered(?) service. (9) [Through] their [. . . .], all day was he afflicted; (10) through their lamentation, upon (his) couch (11) he obtained no sleep. (12) [In] the anger of his heart he put an end to (?) supplication; (13) [to] overthrow the kingdom he set his face. (14) [He chan]ged (their) understanding, their counsel was altered . . . . . ." Too little is preserved of cols. ii and iii to allow of a connected translation, but it may here be noted that col. ii contains references to the gods ^ilu^ LUGAL-DUL (or DU)-AZAG-GA (l. 1) and ^ilu^ EN-ḪI (l. 2), and to the goddess ^ilu^ *Dam-ki-na* (l. 8), and col. iii to the god ^ilu^ NU-NAM-NIR (l. 5).

[2] For a further discussion of this subject, see the Introduction.

a close resemblance to the story of the temptation of Eve by the serpent.[1] The tablet which has been supposed to contain an Assyrian version of the story[2] is K. 3,473 + 79–7–8, 296 + R. 615, which is one of the principal copies of the Third Tablet of the Creation Series. The closing lines of the Third Tablet recount how the gods gathered to a feast at Anšar's bidding before they decreed the fate for Marduk, their avenger[3]; the passage which recounts how the gods ate bread (l. 134) was believed to contain a reference to man's eating the fruit of the tree of knowledge, and Marduk was supposed to be described in l. 138, not as the avenger of the gods, but as the "Redeemer" of mankind. This suggestion was never widely adopted and has long been given up, but it had meanwhile found its way into some popular works; and, as enquiries are still sometimes made for the Assyrian version of the story of the Temptation, it is perhaps not superfluous to state definitely the fact of its non-existence.

[1] The cylinder seal, Brit. Mus., No. 89,326, has been thought to furnish evidence of the existence of such a legend, as it represents a male and a female figure seated near a sacred tree, and behind the female figure is a serpent. George Smith published a woodcut of the scene in *The Chaldean Account of Genesis*, p. 91; for a photographic reproduction of the impression of the seal, see my *Bab. Rel. and Myth.*, p. 113.

[2] The suggestion was first made in the *Bab. and Or. Rec.*, iv (1890), pp. 251 ff.

[3] See above, p. 56 f., ll. 129–138.

V.

A "Prayer of the Raising of the Hand" to Ishtar.

In the following pages a transliteration and a translation are given of a remarkable "Prayer of the Raising of the Hand" to Ištar, No. 26,187, the text of which is published in vol. ii, pls. lxxv ff. An explanation is perhaps necessary of the reasons which have led to the publication of this tablet in a book dealing with legends of Creation and with texts connected therewith. In a previous work, entitled "Babylonian Magic and Sorcery," I had collected all the texts belonging to the series of "Prayers of the Raising of the Hand" which were known to me at the time; when later on I came across the text of No. 26,187 it followed that it must necessarily be published by itself, apart from other tablets of its class. It would, of course, have been possible to delay its publication until it could be included in a work dealing with a number of miscellaneous religious compositions, but, in view of the

Obv.

1. *šiptu u-sal-li-ki be-lit be-li-e-ti i - lat i - la - a - ti*
2. *ilu Ištar šar-ra-ti kul-lat da-ad-me muš-te-ši-rat te-ni-še-e-ti*
3. *ilu Ir - ni - ni*[1] *mut - tal - la - a - ti ra - bit ilu Igigi*
4. *gaš - ra - a - ti ma - al - ka - a - ti šu - mu - ki ṣi - ru*
5. *at-ti-ma na-an-na-rat šamē(e) u irṣitim(tim) ma-rat ilu Sin ḳa - rit - ti*

[1] Ištar, to whom the prayer is offered (cf. l. 106), is in this line and in l. 105 addressed by the title Irnini; in l. 12 she is addressed as Gutira. It is well known that in course of time Ištar was identified by the Babylonians and Assyrians with other goddesses,

interesting nature of its contents, it has seemed preferable to make it available without further delay for students of Babylonian religion, by including it as an appendix to the present work. It will be seen that the text, both from the beauty of its language and from its perfect state of preservation, is one of the finest Babylonian religious compositions that has yet been recovered. The tablet measures $6\frac{7}{8}$ in. by $2\frac{7}{8}$ in., and is of the long narrow shape which is one of the characteristics of the larger tablets of the series to which it belongs. From the colophon (cf. Rev., ll. 111 ff.) we gather that it was copied from an original at Borsippa by a certain Nergal-balāṭsu-iḳbi, who deposited it as a votive offering in E-sagila, the temple of Marduk at Babylon, whence it was probably removed before the destruction of the temple. The text is addressed to Ištar in her character as the goddess of battle, and she is here identified with Irnini and with Gutira (see below, note). Lines 1–41 contain addresses to the goddess, descriptive of her power and splendour, and at l. 42 the suppliant begins to make his own personal petitions, describing his state of affliction and praying for deliverance. A rubric occurs at the end of the text (cf. ll. 107 ff), giving directions for the performance of certain ceremonies and for the due recital of the prayer.

1. I pray unto thee, lady of ladies, goddess of goddesses!
2. O Ishtar, queen of all peoples, directress of mankind!
3. O Irnini,[1] thou art raised on high, mistress of the Spirits of heaven;
4. Thou art mighty, thou hast sovereign power, exalted is thy name!
5. Thou art the light of heaven and earth, O valiant daughter of the Moon-god.

---

e.g., Ninni, Nanā, Anunitum, and Bêlit; and when so identified she absorbed their names, titles, and attributes. In these passages we have two additional instances of her identification with other deities.

Obv.

6. *mut-tab-bi-la-at kakkē^{pl} ša-ki-na-at tu - ḳu - un - ti*
7. *ḫa-mi-mat gi-mir par-ṣi a-pi-rat a - gi - e be - lu - ti*
8. *^{ilu}bēlti*[1] *šu - pu - u nar - bu - ki eli ka-la ilāni^{pl} ṣi-ru*

9. *mul-ta-nu-ḳa-a-ti muš-tam-ḫi-ṣa-at aḫē^{pl} mit - gu - ru - ti*

10. *mut - ta - ad - di - na - at it - ba - ru*[2]
11. *it - bur - ti be - lit tu - ša - ri mut-tak-ki-pat*[3] *erišti-ia*

12. *^{ilu}Gu-tir-a*[4] *ša tu-ḳu-un-ta ḫal-pat la - bi - šat ḫar-ba-ša*

13. *gam-ra-a-ti šib-ṭa u purussā liḳ-ti irṣitim(tim) u ša-ma-mi*[5]

14. *suk-ku eš-ri-e-ti ni-me-da u parakkē^{pl} u - tuḳ - ḳu ka-a-ši*

15. *e-ki-a-am la šumu-ki e-ki-a-am la par - ṣu - ki*

16. *e-ki-a-am la uṣ-ṣu-ra uṣurâti^{pl}-ki e-ki-a-am la innadū^{pl} parakkē^{pl} - ki*
17. *e-ki-a-am la ra-ba-a-ti e-ki-a-am la ṣi - ra - a - ti*
18. *^{ilu}A-num ^{ilu}Bēl u ^{ilu}E-a ul-lu-u-ki ina ilāni^{pl} u-šar-bu-u be-lu-ut-ki*

---

[1] As the determinative AN is employed before the ideogram, it is possible that here and in ll. 29 and 104 it should be rendered as the proper name, or title, *Bēlit* (cf. the preceding note). Elsewhere in the prayer, however, the word takes in addition the 1 s. pron. suffix (cf. ll. 43, 56, 59, 72, 73, 79, 93, and 94); it seems more probable, therefore, that the ideogram is employed for the substantive *bēltu*, "lady."

[2] This line probably continues the class of attributes ascribed to the goddess in the preceding line, and does not form a contrast to it; the meaning "strength" rather than "friendship" is

6. Ruler of weapons, arbitress of the battle!
7. Framer of all decrees, wearer of the crown of dominion!
8. O lady,[1] majestic is thy rank, over all the gods is it exalted!
9. Thou art the cause of lamentation, thou sowest hostility among brethren who are at peace;
10. Thou art the bestower of strength![2]
11. Thou art strong, O lady of victory, thou canst violently attain[3] my desire!
12. O Gutira,[4] who art girt with battle, who art clothed with terror
13. Thou wieldest the sceptre and the decision, the control of earth and heaven![5]
14. Holy chambers, shrines, divine dwellings, and temples worship thee!
15. Where is thy name not (heard)? Where is thy decree not (obeyed)?
16. Where are thine images not made? Where are thy temples not founded?
17. Where art thou not great? Where art thou not exalted?
18. Anu, Bēl, and Ea have raised thee on high, among the gods have they made great thy dominion,

---

therefore to be assigned to *il-ba-ru*. In support of this view, cf. the attributes in the following lines, and the occurrence of *il-bur-ti* in l. 11, where any other meaning but "Thou art strong" is out of the question.

[3] It is clear that in this passage we must assign some such active meaning to the Ifteal of *nakāpu*.

[4] See above, p. 222 f., n. 1.

[5] The second half of the line is in apposition to the phrase *šibṭa u purussā*, "the sceptre" representing the control of earth and "the decision" that of heaven.

Obv.

19. *u-ša-aš-ḳu-ki ina nap-ḫar* ilu *Igigi u-ša-ti-ru man-za-az-ki*

20. *a-na ḫi-is-sat šu-me-ki šamū(u) u irṣitim(tim) i-ru-ub-bu*[1]

21. *ilāni* pl *i-ru-bu i-nar-ru-ṭu* ilu *A-nun-na-ki*
22. *šumu-ki ra-aš-bu iš-tam-ma-ra te-ni-še-e-ti*
23. *at-ti-ma ra-ba-a-ti u ṣi-ra-a-ti*
24. *nap-ḫar ṣal-mat ḳaḳ-ḳa-di*[2] *nam-maš-šu-u te-ni-še-e-ti i-dal-la-lu ḳur-di-ki*
25. *di-in ba-ḫu-la-a-ti ina kit-ti u mi-ša-ri ta-din-ni at-ti*

26. *tap-pal-la-si ḫab-lu u šaḳ-šu*[3] *tuš-te-eš-še-ri ud-da-kam*

27. *a-ḫu-lap-ki be-lit šamē(e) u irṣitim(tim) ri-e-a-at nišē* pl *a-pa-a-ti*
28. *a-ḫu-lap-ki be-lit E-an-na*[4] *ḳud-du-šu šu-tum-mu el-lu*

29. *a-ḫu-lap-ki* ilu *bēlti*[5] *ul a-ni-ḫa šēpā* II*-ki la-si-ma bir-ka-a-ki*

30. *a-ḫu-lap-ki be-lit ta-ḫa-zi ka-li-šu-nu tam-ḫa-ri*

31. *šu-pu-u-tum la-ab-bat* ilu *Igigi mu-kan-ni-šat ilāni* pl *šab-su-ti*

32. *li-'-a-at ka-li-šu-nu ma-al-ku ṣa-bi-ta-at ṣir-rit šarrāni* pl

33. *pi-ta-a-at pu-su-um-me*[6] *ša ka-li-ši-na ardâti* pl

---

[1] The verb *rābu* is here used of the "quaking" of the heaven and earth (see above, p. 206 f., l. 8), and in the following line of the "trembling" of the gods; for its use in the former sense in the astrological reports, cf. Thompson, *Reports of the Magicians and Astrologers*, vol. ii, p. 129.

[2] Literally "the black-headed," i.e. mankind.

19. They have exalted thee among all the Spirits of heaven, they have made thy rank pre-eminent.
20. At the thought of thy name the heaven and the earth quake,[1]
21. The gods tremble, and the Spirits of the earth falter.
22. Mankind payeth homage unto thy mighty name,
23. For thou art great, and thou art exalted.
24. All mankind,[2] the whole human race, boweth down before thy power.
25. Thou judgest the cause of men with justice and righteousness;
26. Thou lookest with mercy on the violent man, and thou settest right the unruly[3] every morning.
27. How long wilt thou tarry, O lady of heaven and earth, shepherdess of those that dwell in human habitations?
28. How long wilt thou tarry, O lady of the holy E-anna,[4] the pure Storehouse?
29. How long wilt thou tarry, O lady,[5] whose feet are unwearied, whose knees have not lost their vigour?
30. How long wilt thou tarry, O lady of all fights and of the battle?
31. O thou glorious one, that ragest among the Spirits of heaven, that subduest angry gods,
32. That hast power over all princes, that controllest the sceptre of kings,
33. That openest the bonds[6] of all handmaids,

---

[3] The word *šaḳ-šu* is practically synonymous with *ḫab-lu*, and conveys the meaning of "destruction" or "violence," rather than "wrong."

[4] I.e., the temple of Ištar in the city of Erech.

[5] See above, p. 224, n. 1.

[6] The rendering of the word *pusummu* is conjectural.

OBV.

34. *na-an-še-a-at na-an-di-a-at ḳa-rit-ti* ^{ilu}*Ištar ra-bu-u ḳur-di-ki*

35. *na-mir-tum di-par šamē(e) u irṣitim(tim) ša-ru-ur kal da-ad-me*

36. *iz - zi - it ḳab - lu la ma - ḫar a - li - lat tam-ḫa-ri*

37. *a-ku-ku-u-tum*[1] *ša ana ai-bi nap-ḫat ša-ki-na-at šul-lu-uḳ-ti ik-du-ti*

38. *mu - um - mil - tum* ^{ilu}*Iš - tar mu-paḫ-ḫi-rat pu-uḫ-ri*

39. *i-lat ziḳrūti*^{pl} ^{ilu}*Iš-tar sinnišāti*^{pl} *ša la i-lam-ma-du mi-lik-šu ma-am-man*

40. *a-šar tap-pal-la-si i-bal-luṭ* ^{amelu}*mītu i - te - ib - bi mar-ṣu*

41. *iš - ši - ir la i - ša - ru a-mi-ru pa-ni-ki*

42. *ana-ku al-si-ki an-ḫu· šu-nu-ḫu šum-ru-ṣu arad-ki*

43. *a-mur-in-ni-ma* ^{ilu}*bēlti-ia li-ki-e un - ni - ni - ia*

44. *ki-niš nap-li-sin-ni-ma ši-mi-e tas - li - ti*

45. *a-ḫu-lap-ia ki-bi-ma ka-bit-ṭa-ki lip - pa - aš - ra*

46. *a-ḫu-lap zumri-ia na-as-si ša ma-lu-u e-ša-a-ti u dal-ḫa-a-ti*

47. *a-ḫu-lap lib-bi-ia šum-ru-ṣu ša ma-lu-u dim-ti u ta-ni-ḫi*

48. *a-ḫu-lap te-ri-ti-ia na-as-sa-a-ti e-ša-a-ti u dal-ḫa-a-ti*

49. *a-ḫu-lap bīti-ia šu-ud-lu-bu ša u-na-as-sa-su nissati*^{pl}

---

[1] For the meaning of the word *akukūtum*, cf. II R, pl. 39, K. 2,057, Obv., col. ii, l. 5, where *a-ku-ku-t*[*um*] and *a-šam-šu-tum*

34. That art raised on high, that art firmly established,—
O valiant Ištar, great is thy might!

35. Bright torch of heaven and earth, light of all dwellings,

36. Terrible in the fight, one who cannot be opposed, strong in the battle!

37. O whirlwind,[1] that roarest against the foe and cuttest off the mighty!

38. O furious Ishtar, summoner of armies!

39. O goddess of men, O goddess of women, thou whose counsel none may learn!

40. Where thou lookest in pity, the dead man lives again, the sick is healed;

41. The afflicted is saved from his affliction, when he beholdeth thy face!

42. I, thy servant, sorrowful, sighing, and in distress cry unto thee.

43. Look upon me, O my lady, and accept my supplication,

44. Truly pity me, and hearken unto my prayer!

45. Cry unto me "It is enough!" and let thy spirit be appeased!

46. How long shall my body lament, which is full of restlessness and confusion?

47. How long shall my heart be afflicted, which is full of sorrow and sighing?

48. How long shall my omens be grievous in restlessness and confusion?

49. How long shall my house be troubled, which mourneth bitterly?

---

occur as equivalents of two ideograms which form a section by themselves; see also Delitzsch, *Handwörterbuch*, p. 53.

OBV.

50. *a-ḫu-lap kab-ta-ti-ia ša uš-ta-bar-ru-u dim-ti u ta-ni-ḫi*

51. ^{ilu}*Ir-ni-ni* [. .][1]*-i-tum la-ab-bu na-ad-ru lib-ba-ki li-nu-ḫa*

52. *ri-i-mu šab-ba-su-u ka-bit-ta-ki lip - pa - aš - ra*
53. *damḳāti*^{pl} *īnā*^{II} *- ki lib - ša - a e - li - ia*
54. *ina bu-ni-ki nam-ru-ti ki-niš nap-li-sin-ni ia-a-ši*
55. *uk-ki-ši u-pi-ša limnēti*^{pl} *ša zumri-ia nūru-ki nam-ru lu-mur*
56. *a-di ma-ti* ^{ilu}*bēlti-ia bēlē*^{pl} *da-ba-bi-ia ni-kil-mu-u-in-ni-ma*

REV.

57. *ina sur-ra-a-ti u la ki-na-a-ti i-kap-pu-du-ni lim-ni-e-ti*

58. *ri - du - u - a ḫa - du - u - a iš - tam - ma - ru eli - ia*

59. *a - di ma - ti* ^{ilu}*bēlti - ia lil - lu*[2] *a-ku-u i-ba-'-an-ni*

60. *ib-na-an-ni muk-ku*[3] *ar-ku-um-ma ana-ku am-mir-ki*[4]

61. *en - šu - ti id - ni - nu - ma ana - ku e - ni - iš*
62. *a - šab - bu - ' ki - ma a - gi - i ša up-pa-ku šāru lim-na*

63. *i - ša - ' it - ta - nap - raš lib - bi ki-ma iṣ-ṣur ša-ma-mi*

64. *a-dam-mu-um ki-ma su-um-ma-tum mu - ši u ur - ra*
65. *na - an - gu - la - ku - ma*[5] *a - bak - ki zar - biš*

---

[1] The scribe has erased the first character of the word and has not rewritten it.

[2] The meaning assigned to *lillu* in the translation is conjectural; among other passages in which the word occurs, cf. especially IV R, pl. 27, No. 4, l. 57, and its context; see also Delitzsch, *Handwörterbuch*, p. 377, and Muss-Arnolt, *Concise Dictionary*, p. 481.

[3] Some such general meaning is probably to be assigned to

50. How long shall my spirit (be troubled), which aboundeth in sorrow and sighing?
51. O [. . .][1] Irnini, fierce lioness, may thy heart have rest!
52. Is anger mercy? Then let thy spirit be appeased!
53. May thine eyes rest with favour upon me;
54. With thy glorious regard truly in mercy look upon me!
55. Put an end to the evil bewitchments of my body; let me behold thy clear light!
56. How long, O my lady, shall mine enemies persecute me?
57. How long shall they devise evil in rebellion and wickedness,
58. And in my pursuits and my pleasures shall they rage against me?
59. How long, O my lady, shall the ravenous demon[2] pursue me?
60. They have caused me continuous affliction,[3] but I have praised[4] thee.
61. The weak have become strong, but I am weak;
62. I am sated like a flood which the evil wind maketh to rage.
63. My heart hath taken wing, and hath flown away like a bird of the heavens;
64. I moan like a dove, night and day.
65. I am made desolate,[5] and I weep bitterly;

---

nukku in this passage; the subject of the verb is probably impersonal, and it may be taken as followed by the double accusative.

[4] It is clear that in this passage an active meaning is to be assigned to *namāru*; cf. *im-mir-šu-ma*, V R, pl. 55, ll. 27 and 37, and *u-mu-ka nam-mar*, 82–3–23, 4,344, etc. (*P.S.B.A.*, xviii, p. 258), cited by Muss-Arnolt, *Concise Dictionary*, p. 684.

[5] iv, 1 from *nagālu*, cf. Syr. *n'gal*.

REV.

66. *ina '-u-a a-a šum-ru-ṣa-at ka-bit-ti*
67. *mi-na-a e-pu-uš ili-ia u ^{ilu}iš-tar-ia a-na-ku*
68. *ki-i la pa-liḫ ili-ia u ^{ilu}ištari-ia ana-ku ip-še-iḳ*

69. *šak-nu-nim-ma mur-ṣu ṭi-'-i ḫu-lu-uḳ-ḳu-u u šul-lu-uḳ-ti*
70. *šak-na-ni ud-da-a-ti suḫ-ḫur pa-ni u ma-li-e lib-ba-a-ti*

71. *uz-zu ug-ga-ti me-nat*[1] *ilāni^{pl} u a-me-lu-ti*
72. *a-ta-mar ^{ilu}bēlti-ia ūmē^{pl} uk-ku-lu-ti arḫē^{pl} na-an-du-ru-ti šanāti^{pl} ša ni-zik-ti*
73. *a-ta-mar ^{ilu}bēlti-ia šib-ṭa i-ši-ti u saḫ-maš-ti*

74. *u-kal-la-an-ni mu-u-tu u šap-ša-ḳu*
75. *šu-ḫar-ru-ur sa-gi-e-a šu-ḫar-ru-rat a-šir-ti*
76. *eli bīti bābi u ḳar-ba-a-ti-ia ša-ḳu-um-ma-ti tab-kat*

77. *ili-ia ana a-šar ša-nim-ma suḫ-ḫu-ru pa-nu-šu*
78. *sap-ḫat il-la-ti ta-bi-ni pur-ru-ur*
79. *u-pa-ḳa a-na ^{ilu}bēlti-ia ka-a-ši ib-ša-ki uznā^{II}-ai*

80. *u-sal-li-ki ka-a-ši '-il-ti pu-uṭ-ri*
81. *pu-uṭ-ri ar-ni*[2] *šir-ti ḫab-la-ti. u ḫi-ṭi-ti*

82. *mi-e-ši ḫab-la-ti-ia li-ki-e un-ni-ni-ia*
83. *ru-um-mi-ia ki-rim-ia šu-bar-ra-ai šuk-ni*

84. *šu-te-ši-ri kib-si nam-riš e-til-liš it-ti amēlūti^{pl} lu-ba-' sūḳi*

85. *ki-bi-ma ina ki-bi-ti-ki ilu zi-nu-u li-is-lim*

---

[1] Literally, "numbers of, the host of."

[2] Under the line, and between the signs *ni* and *šir*, the scribe has written the division mark followed by the word *i-ši-ti*, "my

66 With grief and woe my spirit is distressed.
67. What have I done, O my god and my goddess?
68. Is it because I feared not my god or my goddess that trouble hath befallen me?
69. Sickness, disease, ruin, and destruction are come upon me;
70. Troubles, turning away of the countenance, and fulness of anger are my lot,
71. And the indignation and the wrath of all[1] gods and men.
72. I have beheld, O my lady, days of affliction, months of sorrow, years of misfortune;
73. I have beheld, O my lady, slaughter, turmoil, and rebellion.
74. Death and misery have made an end of me!
75. My need is grievous, grievous is my humiliation;
75. Over my house, my gate, and my fields is affliction poured forth.
77. As for my god, his face is turned elsewhere;
78. My strength is brought to nought, my power is broken!
79. But unto thee, O my lady, do I give heed, I have kept thee in my mind;
80. Unto thee therefore do I pray, dissolve my ban!
81. Dissolve my sin,[2] my iniquity, my transgression, and my offence!
82. Forgive my transgression, accept my supplication!
83. Secure my deliverance, and let me be loved and carefully tended!
84. Guide my footsteps in the light, that among men I may gloriously seek my way!
85. Say the word, that at thy command my angry god may have mercy,

confusion"; he probably had omitted the word by mistake and intended it to be inserted after *ar-ni*.

Rev.

86. *^{ilu}ištari ša is - bu - sa li - tu - ra*
87. *e - ṭu - u šu - šub lim-me-ir ki-nu-ni*

88. *bi - li - ti*[1] *li - in - na - pi - iḫ di - pa - ri*
89. *sa - pi - iḫ - tu il - la - ti lip - ḫur*
90. *tarbaṣu li-ir-piš liš-tam-di-lu su - pu - ri*
91. *mug - ri li - bi - en ap - pi - ia ši - me - e su-pi-e-a*

92. *ki - niš nap - li - sin - ni - ma* [erasure by the scribe][2]
93. *a-di ma-ti ^{ilu}bēlti-ia zi-na-ti-ma suḫ-ḫu-ru pa-nu-ki*

94. *a-di ma-ti ^{ilu}bēlti-ia ra-'-ba-ti-ma uz-zu-za-at kab-ta-at-ki*

95. *tir-ri ki-šad ki ša ištu ad-di-ia a-mat damiḳtim(tim) pa-ni-ki šuk-ni*
96. *ki-ma mē^{pl} pa-šir nāri ka-bit-ta-ki lip - pa - aš - ra*

97. *ik-du-ti-ia ki-ma ḳak-ḳa-ru lu - kab - bi - is*
98. *šab-su-ti-ia kun-nu-šim-ma šu-pal-si-ḫi ina šap-li-ia*

99. *su - pu - u - a u su - lu - u - a lil - li - ku eli - ki*
100. *ta - ai - ra - tu - ki rab - ba - a - ti lib - ša - a eli - ia*
101. *a-mi-ru-u-a ina sūḳi li-šar-bu-u zi - kir - ki*

102. *u ana-ku ana ṣal-mat ḳakḳadi ilu-ut-ki u ḳur-di-ki lu-ša-pi*

103. *^{ilu}Iš - tar - ma ṣi - rat ^{ilu}Iš-tar-ma šar-rat*
104. *^{ilu}bēlti*[3] *- ma ṣi - rat ^{ilu}bēlti - ma šar - rat*

---

[1] Probably Perm. Ḳal from *bēlu*; the word, however, is possibly the lengthened form of *bēlti*, its occurrence being due to the necessities of rhythm.

86. And that my goddess, who is wroth, may turn again!
87. The darkness hath settled down, so let my brazier be bright;
88. Thou art the ruler,[1] let then my torch flame forth!
89. May my scattered strength be collected;
90. May the fold be wide, and may my pen be bolted fast!
91. Receive the abasement of my countenance, give ear unto my prayer,
92. Truly pity me, and [accept my supplication]![2]
93. How long, O my lady, wilt thou be angry and thy face be turned away?
94. How long, O my lady, wilt thou rage and thy spirit be full of wrath?
95. Incline thy neck, which (is turned) away from my affairs, and set prosperity before thy face;
96. As by the solving waters of the river may thine anger be dissolved!
97. My mighty foes may I trample like the ground;
98. And those who are wroth with me mayest thou force into submission and crush beneath my feet!
99. Let my prayer and my supplication come unto thee,
100. And let thy great mercy be upon me,
101. That those who behold me in the street may magnify thy name,
102. And that I may glorify thy godhead and thy might before mankind!
103. Ištar is exalted! Ištar is queen!
104. My lady[3] is exalted! My lady is queen!

---

[2] The scribe has erased the second half of the line; we may probably restore some such phrase as *li-ki-e un-ni-ni-ia*, as suggested in the translation.

[3] See above, p. 224, n. 1.

REV.

105. [ilu]*Ir-ni-ni ma-rat* [ilu]*Sin ḳa-rit-ti ma-ḫi-ra ul išat*

---

106. INIM-INIM-MA ŠU-IL-LA [DINGIR] INNANNA(NA)-KAN [1]

---

107. *epuš annā* KI KIŠ TAR AD *gušuru arḳu mū ellu tasallaḫ*
IV *libnāti*[pl] *libbi ḫalāḳi* (?) [2] *tanaddi(di)*

108. *immeru telikē(e)* [iṣu]*ṣarbatu te-ṣi-en išatu tanaddi(di)*
rikkē[pl] *upuntu burašu*

109. *tattabak(ak) mi-iḫ-ḫa tanakki(ki)-ma lā tuš-kin*
mi-nu-tu an-ni-tu ana pān [ilu]*Iš-tar*

110. *šalultu šanitu tamannu(nu)* KI-ZA-ZA-*ma* [3] *ana arki-ka*
lā tabari

---

111. *šiptu ša-ḳu-tum* [ilu]*Iš-tar mu-nam-mi-rat kib-ra-a-ti* [4]

112. *gab-ri Bar-sip*[KI] *kīma labiri-šu* [m][ilu]*Nergal-balāṭ-su-iḳ-bi*
apil [m]*A-ta-rad-kal-me* [amêlu]*asipu*

113. *ana balāṭi-šu išṭur ibri-ma ina E-sag-ila u-kin*

---

[1] Line 106 gives the title of the prayer; then follows a rubric of four lines giving directions for the performance of certain ceremonies and for the due recital of the prayer.

[2] In the four bricks, which, if the suggested rendering is correct,

105. Irnini, the valiant daughter of the Moon-god, hath not a rival!

106. Prayer of the Raising of the Hand to Ištar.[1]

107. This shalt thou do . . . . a green bough shalt thou sprinkle with pure water; four bricks from a ruin[2] shalt thou set in place;

108. a lamb shalt thou take; with ṣarbatu-wood shalt thou fill (the censer), and thou shalt set fire (thereto); sweet-scented woods, some upuntu-plant and some cypress-wood

109. shalt thou heap up; a drink offering shalt thou offer, but thou shalt not bow thyself down. This incantation before the goddess Ištar

110. three times shalt thou recite, ... and thou shalt not look behind thee.

111. "O exalted Ištar, that givest light unto the (four) quarters of the world!"[4]

112. (This) copy from Borsippa, (made) like unto its original, hath Nergal-balāṭsu-iḳbi, the son of Atarad-kalme, the magician,

113. written for (the preservation of) his life, and he hath revised it, and hath deposited it within the temple of E-sagila.

'e here directed to be brought from a ruin, we may perhaps see symbolical offering to Ištar in her character of the goddess of attle and destruction.

[3] Possibly *ki za-za-ma*, but cf. Brünnow, No. 9,843.

[4] Line 111 gives the catch-line for the next tablet.

Indices, Glossary, etc.

I.

Index to Texts.

CUNEIFORM TEXTS FROM BABYLONIAN TABLETS, ETC., IN THE BRITISH MUSEUM, PART XIII (1901), PLATES 1–41.

ATE.		
1.	K. 5,419c, Obv. :	Cr. Ser., Tabl. I, ll. 1–16.
	„ Rev. :	Traces of catch-line to Tabl. II, and colophon.
	No. 93,015, Obv. :	Cr. Ser., Tabl. I, ll. 1–16.
2.	81–7–27, 80, Obv. :	„ „ ll. 31–56.
	„ Rev. :	„ „ ll. 118–142.
3.	K. 3,938, Obv. :	„ „ ll. 33–42.
	„ Rev. :	„ „ ll. 128–142.
	No. 93,015, Rev. :	„ „ ll. 124–142, and colophon.
4.	No. 38,396, Obv. :	„ Tabl. II, ll. 11–29.
	„ Rev. :	„ „ ll. (105)–(132).
5.	K. 4,832, Obv. :	„ „ ll. 32–58.
	„ Rev. :	„ „ ll. (104)–(138).
6.	79–7–8, 178, Obv. :	„ „ ll. (69)–(75).
	„ Rev. :	„ „ ll. (76)–(85).
	K. 292, Rev. :	„ „ ll. (131)–(140), catch-line to Tabl. III, and colophon.
7.	K. 3,473, etc., Obv. :	„ Tabl. III, ll. 1–56.
8.	„ Obv. (cont.) :	„ „ ll. 57–85.
	„ Rev. :	„ „ ll. 86–113.
9.	„ Rev. (cont.) :	„ „ ll. 114–138, and catch-line to Tabl. IV.
	K. 6,650 :	„ „ ll. 38–55, or 96–113.

PLATE.		
10.	No. 93,017, Obv. :	Cr. Ser., Tabl. III, ll. 47–77.
11.	,, Rev. :	,, ,, ll. 78–105.
12.	K. 8,575, Obv. :	,, ,, ll. 69–76.
	,, Rev. :	,, ,, ll. 77–85.
	K. 8,524 :	,, ,, ll. 75–86.
	83–1–18, 2,116 :	joined to 82–9–18, 5,448 ; see vol. ii, pl. xxxiv.
	83–1–18, 1,868 :	joined to 82–9–18, 6,950 ; see vol. ii, pl. xxix.
13.	82–9–18, 1,403 :	joined to 82–9–18, 6,316 ; see vol. ii, pls. xxv ff.
14.	No. 93,016, Obv. :	Cr. Ser., Tabl. IV, ll. 1–44.
15.	,, Rev. :	,, ,, ll. 116–146, catch-line to Tabl. V, and colophon.
16.	K. 3,437, etc., Obv. :	,, ,, ll. 36–59.
17.	,, Obv. (cont.) :	,, ,, ll. 60–83.
18.	,, Rev. :	,, ,, ll. 84–107.
19.	,, Rev. (cont.) :	,, ,, ll. 108–119.
	R. 2, 83 :	,, ,, ll. 117–129.
20.	No. 93,051, Obv. :	,, ,, ll. 42–54.
	,, Rev. :	,, ,, ll. 85–94.
	79–7–8, 251, Obv. :	,, ,, ll. 35–49.
	,, Rev. :	,, ,, ll. 103–107.
21.	K. 5,420*c*, Obv. :	,, ,, ll. 74–92.
	,, Rev. :	,, ,, ll. 93–119.
22.	K. 3,567, etc., Obv. :	,, Tabl. V, ll. 1–26.
	,, Rev. :	catch-line to Tabl. VI, and colophon.
23.	K. 8,526, Obv. :	Cr. Ser., Tabl. V, ll. 1–18.
	,, Rev. :	,, ,, ll. (138)–(140).
	K. 3,449*a*, Obv. :	,, ,, ll. (66)–(74).
	,, Rev. :	,, ,, ll. (75)–(87).
24.	K. 12,000*b* :	see Appendix II, p. 194.
	K. 14,949 :	see Appendix II, p. 197 f.
	K. 3,445, etc. :	see Appendix II, pp. 197 ff.
25.	,, Rev. (cont.) :	see Appendix II, pp. 198 ff.
26.	K. 8,522, Obv. :	Cr. Ser., Tabl. VII, ll. 15–45.
27.	,, Rev. :	,, ,, ll. 105–137.
28.	K. 9,267, Obv. :	,, ,, ll. 40–47.
	,, Rev. :	,, ,, ll. 109–138.

B. Supplementary Texts, published in Vol. II, Plates I–LXXXIV.

C. Supplementary Texts, published in Appendices I, II, and III.

II.

Index to Registration-Numbers.

REGISTRATION NO.	TEXT.	CONTENTS.
82–9–18, 6,950+ 83–1–18, 1,868.	Vol. II, pl. xxix.	Cr. Ser., Tabl. III, ll. 19–26 or 77–84.
83–1–18, 1,868.	see 82–9–18, 6,950.	
83–1–18, 2,116.	see 82–9–18, 5,448.	
88–4–19, 13.	see No. 93,017.	
No. 26,187.	Vol. II, pls. lxxv–lxxxiv.	see App. V, pp. 222 ff.
No. 32,574.	App. III, p. 216 f.	see pp. 216 ff.
No. 33,851.	Vol. II, pls. lxiv–lxvi.	see App. II, p. 202 f.
No. 35,134.	,, pl. vii.	Cr. Ser., Tabl. I, ll. 11–21.
No. 35,506.	,, pls. xlvi–xlviii.	Cr. Ser., Tabl. VII, ll. 14–36, 105–142.
No. 36,688.	,, pl. vii.	Cr. Ser., Tabl. I, ll. 38–43.
No. 36,726.	,, pl. viii.	Cr. Ser., Tabl. I, ll. 28–33.
No. 38,396.	Cun. Txts., XIII, pl. 4.	Cr. Ser., Tabl. II, ll. 11–29, (105)–(132).
No. 40,559.	Vol. II, pls. xiv–xxi.	Cr. Ser., Tabl. II, ll. 1–40, (111)–(140).
No. 40,959.	App. III, p. 215.	see p. 215 f.
No. 42,285.	Vol. II, pls. xxx–xxxiii.	Cr. Ser., Tabl. III, ll. 46–87.
No. 45,528+46,614.	,, pls. i–vi.	Cr. Ser., Tabl. I, ll. 1–48, 111–139.
No. 46,614.	see No. 45,528.	
No. 46,803.	Vol. II, pls. ix–xi.	Cr. Ser., Tabl. I, ll. 46–60, 62–67, 83–103.
No. 54,228.	,, pl. lxiii.	see App. I, pp. 175 ff.
No. 55,466+55,486+ 55,627.	,, pls. lxvii–lxxii	see App. III, pp. 208 ff.
No. 55,486.	see No. 55,466.	
No. 55,627.	see No. 55,466.	
No. 91,139+93,073.	Vol. II, pls. xxxviii–xlv.	Cr. Ser., Tabl. VII, ll. 3–40, 106–141.

REGISTRATION NO.	TEXT.	CONTENTS.
No. 92,629.	Vol. II, pls. xxxv–xxxvii.	Cr. Ser., Tabl. VI, ll. 1–21, 138–146.
No. 92,632+93,048.	,, pls. xxii–xxiv.	Cr. Ser., Tabl. II, ll. 14–29, (114)–(131).
No. 93,015 (82–7–14, 402).	Cun. Txts., XIII, pls. 1, 3.	Cr. Ser., Tabl. I, ll. 1–16, 124–142.
No. 93,016 (82–9–18, 3,737).	,, ,, pls. 14–15.	Cr. Ser., Tabl. IV, ll. 1–44, 116–146.
No. 93,017 (88–4–19, 13).	,, ,, pls. 10–11.	Cr. Ser., Tabl. III, ll. 47–105.
No. 93,048.	see No. 92,632.	
No. 93,051.	Cun. Txts., XIII, pl. 20.	Cr. Ser., Tabl. IV, ll. 42–54, 85–94.
No. 93,073.	see No. 91,139.	

III.

Glossary of Selected Words.

א

u, enclitic interrogative particle: *šab-ba-su-u*, p. 230, l. 52.

abubu, "deluge; thunder-bolt(?)": *a-bu-ba* (var. *bu*), Tabl. IV, l. 49 (p. 64); *a-bu-ba*, Tabl. IV, l. 75 (p. 68).

abāku, III 1, "to cause to bring, to cause to be brought": Imper. *šu-bi-ka*, Tabl. III, l. 6 (p. 38).

abālu, I 1, "to bring"; I 2, "to bring out, to proclaim(?)": *lit* (var. *li-it*)-*tab-bal*, Tabl. VII, l. 33 (p. 98); *lit* (var. *li-it*) -*ta-bal*, Tabl. VII, l. 122 (p. 110).

abāru, I 1, "to be strong"; I 2, do.: Perm. *it-bur-ti*, p. 224, l. 11.

itbaru, "strength": *it-ba-ru*, p. 224, l. 10.

ebēru, I 1: *e-bi-ru*, p. 167.

I 2, "to pass through, to force a way into": *i-tib-bi-ru*, Tabl. VII, l. 108 (p. 106).

abātu, II 2, "to be destroyed": *u-tab-ba-tu*, p. 206, l. 16.

agāgu, II 1, "to make angry": Perm. *ug-*[*g*]*u-ga*[*t*], Tabl. I, l. 43 (p. 184).

ugallu, "hurricane": Tabl. I, l. 122 (p. 18); Tabl. II, l. 28 (p. 26); Tabl. III, l. 32 (p. 42), l. 90 (p. 50).

adū, "age": plur. *a-di* (var. *a-di-i*), Tabl. I, l. 11 (p. 4).

ādū, "course, way, affair": *ad-di-ia*, p. 234, l. 95.

idu, "side"; *iduš*, "to the side of": *i-du-uš sa-pa-ra* (var. *ru*), Tabl. IV, l. 44 (p. 62).

idu, "to know; to choose (?)": *e-du-u*, Tabl. I, l. 135 (p. 20); Tabl. II, l. 41 (p. 26); Tabl. III, l. 45 (p. 44), l. 103 (p. 52).

uddu, "daylight."

uddakam, adv., "in the morning, every morning": *ud-da-kam*, p. 226, l. 26.

uddū, "trouble": plur. *ud-da-a-ti*, p. 232, l. 70.

edēlu, I 1, "to bolt."

III 2, "to be bolted": *liš-tam-di-lu*, p. 234, l. 90.

adāru, I 2, "to be troubled": Pret. *i-te-dir*, var. [. .]-*ti-di-ir*, Tabl. I, l. 53 (pp. 10, 186).

[**àzāmu**], II 2, "to be angry(?)": Inf. *u-ta-az-zu-mi-šu*, p. 206, l. 9.

aḫāzu, I 1, "to take; to undertake, to begin": *i-ḫu-zu*, Tabl. IV, l. 18 (p. 60).
IV 1, "to be taken": *in-ni-ḫaz*, Tabl. IV, l. 100 (p. 70).

aḫulap, interrog. adv., "how long?": *a-ḫu-lap*, p. 228, ll. 46, 47, 48, 49, p. 230, l. 50; with suffix, *a-ḫu-lap-ki*, p. 226, ll. 27, 28, 29, 30; with *ḳibū*, by transference of meaning, "to cry 'It is enough!'": *a-ḫu-lap-ia ki-bi-ma*, p. 228, l. 45.

eṭū, "to be dark"; Inf. "darkness": *e-ṭu-u*, p. 234, l. 87.

ekiām, interrog. adv., "where?": *e-ki-a-am*, p. 224, ll. 15, 16, 17.

akū, "hungry, ravenous": *a-ku-u*, p. 230, l. 59.

akukūtu, "whirlwind": *a-ku-ku-u-tum*, p. 228, l. 37.

[**akālu**], "to be afflicted": Pres. *a-ka-la*, p. 146, n. 4; p. 148, l. 22.
ukkulu, "afflicted": *uk-ku-lu-ti*, p. 232, l. 72.

[**akāšu**], II 1, "to put an end to": Imper. *uk-ki-ši*, p. 230, l. 55.

ali, interrog. adv., "where?": *a-li*, Tabl. II, l. 56 (p. 30).

elū, "high"; fem. plur. *elāti*, "the height; the zenith (?)": *e-la-a-ti*, Tabl. V, l. 11 (p. 78).

alādu, I, "to bear."
II 1, do.: Part. *mu-al-li-da-at*, var. *mu-um-ma-al-li-da-at* (= *muwallidat*), Tabl. I, l. 4 (p. 2).

alāku, "to go."
malaku, "going, gait": *ma-lak-šu*, Tabl. IV, l. 67 (p. 66).

ulinnu, "border (?) of a robe": *ulinni-šu*, p. 118, l. 16.

amu, "reed (?)": *a-mi*, p. 132, l. 18; *a-ma-am*, p. 132, l. 17.

[**amū**], "to speak."
amātu, "speech; thing, deed": *a-ma-tu-šu*, Tabl. VII, l. 31 (p. 98).

emū, I 1, "to be like."
III 1, "to make like; to create": *uš-ta-mu-u*, p. 126, l. 14; *šu-ta-mu-u*, p. 125, n. 5.

ūmu, "day"; *ištu ūmimma*, "henceforth": *iš-tu u-mi-im-ma*, Tabl. IV, l. 7 (p. 58).

ūmu, "tempest": Tabl. I, l. 123 (p. 18); Tabl. II, l. 29 (p. 26); Tabl. III, l. 33 (p. 42), l. 91 (p. 52); applied to Marduk's chariot, Tabl. IV, l. 50 (p. 64).

emēdu, IV 1, "to be established; to advance": *in-nin-du-ma*, var. [*in-nin-d*]*u u*[ ], Tabl. I, l. 21 (p. 4); *in-nin-du-ma*, Tabl. IV, l. 93 (p. 70).

imḫullu, "evil wind": *im-ḫul-lu* (var. *la*), Tabl. IV, l. 96 (p. 70); *im-ḫul-la*, Tabl. IV, l. 45 (p. 62), l. 98 (p. 70); *im-ḫul-lu*, p. 206, l. 15.

[**amālu**], II 1, intrans., "to be furious": Part. *mu-um-mil-tum*, p. 228, l. 38.

ammatu, "the sure earth": Tabl. I, l. 2 (p. 2).

unkennu, "might, strength, forces": *unken-na*, Tabl. I, l. 112 (p. 16); Tabl. II, l. 18 (p. 24); Tabl. III, l. 22 (p. 40), l. 80 (p. 50); *un-ki-en-na*, Tabl. III, l. 80 (var., p. 50, n. 5).

[**esēḫu**], "to despair": Pres. *is-si ḫu*, p. 146, n. 4; p. 148, l. 22; *te-si-iḫ-ḫu*, var. *te-iš*(sic)-*si-iḫ-ḫu*, p. 152, l. 16.

asurakku, "bed of a river; depth": *a-sur-rak-ka*, p. 206, l. 19.

apu, "swamp": *a-pa*, p. 134, l. 32; *a-pu-um-ma*, p. 134, l. 27.

appunu, "huge": [*a*]*p-pu-na-a-ta*, Tabl. I, l. 126 (var., p. 18).

appunama, adv., "of huge size": *ap-pu-na-ma*, Tabl. I, l. 126 (p. 18); Tabl. II, l. 32 (p. 26); Tabl. III. l. 94 (var., p. 52); *ap-pu-un-na-ma*, Tabl. III, l. 36 (p. 42), l. 94 (p. 52).

epēḳu, II 1, "to cause to rage": *up-pa-ḳu*, p. 230, l. 62.

apparu, "marsh": *ap-pa-ri*, p. 134, ll. 25, 27.

upišu, "bewitchment": *u-pi-ša*, p. 230, l. 55.

aṣu, I 1, "to go out"; III 1, "to cause to go out; to take oneself off, to take to flight": *u še-ṣu-ma*, Tabl. IV, l. 109 (p. 72).

iṣṣimtu, "bone": *iṣ-ṣi-im-*[*tu*]*m*, Tabl. VI, l. 5 (p. 86).

eṣēpu, "to add to; to bring upon": Pret. *e-ṣip*, p. 148, l. 24.

uḳū: *u-ḳu-u*, p. 160.

II 2, "to pay homage, to worship": *u-tak-ḳu-u*, Tabl. VII, l. 4 (p. 92); *u-tuk-ḳu*, p. 224, l. 14.

aḳrab-amēlu, "scorpion-man": Tabl. I, l. 122 (p. 18); Tabl. II, l. 28 (p. 26); Tabl. III, l. 32 (p. 42), l. 90 (p. 50).

'āru, āru, "to set out, to set out against, to attack": *'-ir*, Tabl. III, l. 55 (p. 46), l. 113 (p. 54); *ia-ar-ka*, Tabl. II, l. 122 (p. 34).

arāku, I 1, "to be long, to endure": [*li-r*]*i-ik*, Tabl. VII, l. 114 (var., p. 108 f.).

II 1, "to lengthen; to be long": *ur-ri-ku*, varr. *u-ur-ri-ku*, *u-ri-ki*, Tabl. I, l. 13 (p. 4); [*u*]*-ri-ku-ma*, Tabl. II, l. 7 (p. 22).

urriš, adv., "by day": [*ur-r*]*iš*, Tabl. I, l. 50 (p. 10).

erēšu, "to desire."
erištu, "desire": *erišti* (ŠA-DI)-*ia*, p. 224, l. 11.
ešū, "to rage, to be in confusion; to destroy": Imper. *e-ši*-[. . .], Tabl. I, l. 49 (p. 10).
ašābu, I 2, "to seat oneself": Imper. *tiš-ba-ma*, var. *ti-iš-b*[*a*]-*ma*, Tabl. II, l. 137 (p. 36); *taš-ba-ma*, var. *ta-aš-ba-ma*, Tabl. III, l. 61 (p. 46 f.), l. 119 (p. 54); *ti-šam-ma*, Tabl. IV, l. 15 (p. 58).
ešgallu, "mansion": *eš-gal-la*, Tabl. IV, l. 144 f. (p. 76).
ùšumgallu, "monster-viper": *ušumgallē*[pl], Tabl. I. l. 117 (p. 16); Tabl. II, l. 23 (p. 24); Tabl. III, l. 27 (p. 42), l. 85 (p. 50).
ašamšutu, "hurricane": *a-šam-šu-tum*, Tabl. IV, l. 45 (p. 62).
ašāru, "to humble oneself": Pret. *i-šir*, Tabl. III, l. 70 (p. 48).
aširtu, "humiliation": *a-šir-ti*, p. 232, l. 75.
ašru, "place"; employed as synonym for "heaven": *aš-ru* = *ša-mu-u*, p. 168; *as-ri* (varr. *ra*, *ru*), Tabl. VII, l. 115 (p. 108).
ašriš, "towards": *aš-riš*, Tabl. IV, l. 60 (p. 66).
ašru, "shrine, sanctuary": *aš-ru-uk-ka*, Tabl. IV, l. 12 (p. 58).
uššu, "grass": *uš-šu*, p. 134, l. 25.
etilliš, "gloriously": *e-til-liš*, p. 232, l. 84.
[**atāru**], II 1, "to make exceeding strong": *u-wa*(i.e. PI)-*at-te-ir*, p. 146, n. 4.
atta'u, "fang (?)": Tabl. I, l. 115 (p. 16); Tabl. II, l. 21 (p. 24); Tabl. III, l. 25 (p. 40), l. 83 (p. 50).

ב

bēlu, "to rule, control, hold sway": *li-bil-ma*, var. *li-bi-el-ma*, Tabl. VII, l. 122 (p. 110); (?) *li-bi-il*, Tabl. VII, l. 114 (p. 108).
[**barū**], III[II] 1, "to tend carefully": Inf. *šu-bar-ra-ai*, p. 232, l. 83.
III[II] 2, "to abound in": *uš-ta-bar-ru-u*, p. 230, l. 50.
burumu, "heaven": *bu-ru-mi*, p. 206, l. 13; [*bu*]-*ru-mi*, p. 122, l. 2.
bašmu, "viper": Tabl. I, l. 121 (p. 18); Tabl. II, l. 27 (p. 24); Tabl. III, l. 31 (p. 42), l. 89 (p. 50).
batnu: *ba*(?)-*at-nu*, Tabl. IV, l. 36 (p. 62).

ג

guḫḫu: *guḫḫē*[pl], p. 144, l. 8; p. 150, l. 20.

gallû, "devil": *gal-li-e*, var. *gallê*, Tabl. IV, l. 116 (p. 72).

gisgallu, "station": *gi-is-gal-la-ša*, Tabl. V, l. 83 (p. 84).

gipâru, "field (?)," or possibly a kind of tree: *gi-pa-ra*, var. *gi-par-ra*, Tabl. I, l. 6 (p. 2).

gašâru, I 1, "to strengthen."

II 1, "to make very strong": Perm. *gu-uš-šur*, Tabl. I, l. 19 (p. 4).

magšaru, "might": Tabl. I, l. 142 (p. 20); Tabl. II, l. 48 (p. 28); Tabl. III, l. 52 (p. 44), l. 110 (p. 54).

ד

dabru, "mighty (?)": Tabl. I, l. 123 (p. 18); Tabl. II, l. 29 (p. 26); Tabl. III, l. 33 (p. 42), l. 91 (p. 52).

dâlu, "to move about; to scout; to prowl round, to watch from hiding": Pret. *i-dul-lu*, Tabl. I, l. 57 (p. 186); *i-du-ul-[li]*, Tabl. I, l. 89 (p. 12); *ta-du-ul-l[i]*, Tabl. I, l. 99 (p. 14); *i-dul-lu-šu*, Tabl. IV, l. 63 f. (pp. 66, 186 f.).

dalâbu, III 1, "to trouble": Perm. *šu-ud-lu-bu*, p. 228, l. 49.

dullu, "service (of the gods)": *dul-lu*, Tabl. VI, l. 8 (p. 88).

danninu, "firmness; the firm earth": *dan-ni-nu* = *irṣitim(tim)*, p. 168; *dan-ni-na*, Tabl. VII, l. 115 (p. 108).

dupšîmtu, pl. *dupšîmâti*, "the Tablets of Destiny": Tabl. I. l. 137 (p. 20); Tabl. II, l. 43 (p. 28); Tabl. III, l. 47 (p. 44), l. 105 (p. 52); Tabl. IV, l. 121 (p. 74); p. 209, l. 4.

durmaḫu, "ruler (?)": *dur-ma-ḫi*, p. 104 (Tabl. VII); *dur-ma-ḫu*, p. 165.

[dašû], II 1, "to cause to be fruitful": *lid-diš-ša-a*, var. *li-id-[di]-eš-ša-a*, Tabl. VII, l. 130 (p. 112).

III[II], "to cause to abound in, to clothe with": Pret. *uš-daš-ša-a*, Tabl. I, l. 118 (p. 16); Tabl. II, l. 24 (p. 24); Tabl. III, l. 28 (p. 42), l. 86 (p. 50).

dittu, **udittu**, "rush": *di-il-ta*, p. 134, l. 25.

ז

zazâru: *i-za-az-ru-šu*, p. 134, l. 30.

zaḳâru, I 1, "to be high."

II 1, "to exalt": *u-zak-k[a-ru-šu]*, Tabl. VI, l. 146 (p. 90).

zaḳiḳu, "tempest": *za-ki-ḳu*, Tabl. I, l. 104 (p. 14).

[**zāru**], Pret. *izīr*, "to hate, to conceive a hatred for": Tabl. II, l. 11 (p. 22); Tabl. III, l. 15 (p. 40), l. 73 (p. 48).

[**zarbabu**], IV 1, "to fume, to rage": Perm. *na-zar-bu-bu*, Tabl. I, l. 111 (p. 16); Tabl. II, l. 17 (p. 24); Tabl. III, l. 21 (p. 40), l. 79 (p. 50).

ח

ḫabāṣu, "to be filled, to be bloated (?)": Perm. *ḫa-ba-ṣu*, Tabl. III, l. 136 (p. 56).

ḫalāḳu, III 1, "to destroy": Pres. (not as Prec.) *nu-uš-ḫal-laḳ* (= *nušaḫlaḳ*, Tabl. I, l. 45 (p. 185).

ḫamū, "to destroy (?)": *ḫa-mu-u*, p. 206, l. 21.

ḫasāsu, "to think, to know": Part. *ḫa-sis*, Tabl. I, l. 18 (p. 4), l. 60 (p. 12).

ḫipū, I 2, "to shatter, to burst": *iḫ-te-pi*, Tabl. IV, l. 101 (p. 70).

ḫāḳu, "to mingle together," intrans.: Pret. *i-ḫi-ḳu-u-ma*, Tabl. I, l. 5 (p. 2).

[**ḫarmamu**], III 1, "to destroy, to overcome (?)": *liš-ḫar-mi-im*, Tabl. I, l. 119 (p. 16); Tabl. III, l. 29 (p. 42).

IV 1, do. (?): *li-iḫ-ḫar-mi-im*, Tabl. II, l. 25 (p. 24); Tabl. III, l. 87 (p. 50).

ט

ṭābu, "to be sound, to be healed": Pres. *i-te-ib-bi*, p. 228, l. 40.

ṭubtu, "joy": plur. *tu-ub-ba-a-ti*, Tabl. II, l. 115 (p. 32).

כ

kabātu, II 1, "to make weighty; to oppress": *u-kab-bi[t]-ma*, Tabl. II, l. 1 (p. 22); *kub-bu-tu-ma*, Tabl. VI, l. 10 (p. 88).

kabittu, "midst (?)": *ka-bit-ti-ša-ma*, Tabl. V, l. 11 (p. 78).

kubuttū, "abundance": *ku-bu-ut-te-e*, Tabl. VII, l. 21 (p. 96); p. 161.

kālu, II 1, "to uphold, to hold, to bring": *li-ki-il-lu*, Tabl. VII, l. 110 (p. 108); *mu-kil*, Tabl. VII, l. 19 (p. 96).

kalū, II 1, "to make an end of": *u-kal-la-an-ni*, p. 232, l. 74.

II 2, "to cease (?)": (?) *uk-ta-li* (var. *lu*), Tabl. VII, l. 114 (p. 108).

[**kalāmu**], II 1, "to inform."

taklimtu, "instruction": *ta[k]-lim-ti*, Tabl. VII, l. 137 (p. 114).

[kalmū], IV 1, "to look with anger upon, to persecute": Perm. *ni-kil-mu-u-in-ni-ma*, p. 230, l. 56.

kamū, IV 1, "to be taken captive": Pret. *ik-ka-mu-u*, Tabl. I, l. 98 (p. 14).

kamāru, I 2, Inf. *kitmuru*, "battle": Tabl. I, l. 142 (p. 20); Tabl. II, l. 48 (p. 28); Tabl. III, l. 52 (p. 44), l. 110 (p. 54).

kamāru, "snare."

kamāriš, "in the snare": *ka-ma-riš*, Tabl. IV, l. 112 (p. 72).

kanū, II 1, "to tend carefully."

taknītu, "fostering care, true worship": *tak-na-a-ti*, p. 206, l. 14.

kinūnu, "brazier": *ki-nu-ni*, p. 234, l. 87.

kisukku, "bondage."

kisukkiš, "in bondage": *ki-suk-kiš*, Tabl. IV, l. 114 (p. 72).

kusarikku, "ram": Tabl. I, l. 123 (p. 18); Tabl. II, l. 29 (p. 26); Tabl. III, l. 33 (p. 42), l. 91 (p. 52).

kupu, "trunk (?)": *šir ku-pu*, Tabl. IV, l. 136 (p. 76).

kipdu, "plan": [*ki*]*p-di-šu-nu*, Tabl. VII, l. 44 (p. 100).

kirimmu, "love": *ki-rim-ia*, p. 232, l. 83.

karru, "costly raiment (?)": Tabl. I, l. 132 (p. 20); Tabl. II, l. 38 (p. 26); Tabl. III, l. 42 (p. 44), l. 100 (p. 52).

kašāšu, "to collect (?)": Pret. *ik-ša-šu-nim-ma*, Tabl. III, l. 129 (p. 56).

katāmu, III 1, "to overcome": Perm. *šuk-tu-mat*, Tabl. II, 119 (p. 32).

ל

[**li'ū**], "to be strong; to be able."

la'ātu, "full extent": *a-na la-'-a-ti-su*(var. *ša*), Tabl. IV, l. 97 (p. 70).

[**labābu**], "to rage": Tabl. II, l. 12 (p. 22), l. 17 (p. 24); Tabl. III, ll. 16, 21 (p. 40), l. 74 (p. 48), l. 79 (p. 50); p. 226, l. 31.

labbu, "lion, lioness": *la-ab-bu*, p. 230 (l. 51).

labbu, "dragon": *lab-bi*, p. 118, ll. 17, 20, 24; p. 120, ll. 7, 9; *lab-ba*, p. 120, l. 4.

labānu, **lebēnu**, "to abase": Inf. *li-bi-en*, p. 234, l. 91.

luddu, a weapon: *lu-ud-di*, p. 146, l. 17.

lalū, I 1, "to be full."

II 1, "to make full": Perm. *lul-la-a*, Tabl. IV, l. 72 (p. 66).

lillu, "demon": *lil-lu*, p. 230, l. 59.

lamū, "to surround."

limītu, "circumference, circuit": pl. *li ma-a-ti*, p. 118, l. 10.

limēnu, I 2, "to plan evil": *il-le-im-na*, p. 220, n. 1.

II 1, "to do evil, to plan evil": Pret. *u-lam-mi-in*, Tabl. II, l. 3 (p. 22).

lumašu, "zodiacal constellation": *lu-ma-ši*, Tabl. V, l. 2 (p. 78).

lasāmu, "to be vigorous": *la-si-ma*, p. 226, l. 29.

lapātu, "to place, to set out (?)": *al-pu-t[u]*, p. 144, l. 7; *al-p[u-t]u*, p. 150, l. 19.

מ

magāru, "to be favourable."

mitguru, "peaceful": *mit-gu-ru-ti*, p. 224, l. 9.

meḫū, "tempest": *me-ḫa-a*, var. *me-ḫu-u*, Tabl. IV, l. 45 (p. 62).

miḫḫu, "drink offering": *mi-iḫ-ḫa*, p. 236, l. 109.

maḫāṣu, III 2, "to render hostile, to cause hostility among": *muš-tam-ḫi-ṣa-at*, p. 224, l. 9.

maḫariš, "over against, before": *ma-ḫa-ri-iš* (var. *riš*), Tabl. II, l. 114 (p. 32); *ma-ḫa-ri-iš*, Tabl. IV, l. 2 (p. 58).

matū, I 1, "to lament"; *am-ṭi-ma*, p. 146, n. 4.

I 2, do.: *in-da-ṭa-a*, p. 116, l. 2.

miṭṭu, "club (?)": *iṣumiṭ-ṭa*, var. *miṭ-ṭa*, Tabl. IV, l. 37 (p. 62); *mi-ṭi-šu*, Tabl. IV, l. 130 (p. 74); *miṭ-ṭa*, p. 175.

meku, "snarling, muttering": *me-ki-šu-un* (var. *nu*), Tabl. I, l. 60 (pp. 12, 187); *me-ku-uš*, Tabl. II, l. 81 (p. 30); *me-ki-šu*, Tabl. IV, l. 66 (p. 66).

malū, "to fill; to be full."

tamlū, "dam": *tam-la-a*, p. 134, l. 31.

millu, "troop (?)": *mi-il-la*, Tabl. IV, l. 116 (p. 72).

malmališ, adv., "corresponding with": *mal-ma-liš*, p. 125, n. 5.

mulmullu, "spear": *mul-mul-lum*, var. *mul-mul*, Tabl. IV, l. 36 (p. 62); *mul-mul*, p. 209, l. 1.

mummu, "chaos": Tabl. I, l. 4 (p. 2); = *rig-mu*, p. 162.

[maṣāru], II 1, "to divide": *u-ma-aṣ-ṣir*, Tabl. V, l. 3 (p. 78).

miṣru, "section (?)": plur. *mi-iṣ-ra-ta*, Tabl. V, l. 3 (p. 78).

[maṣāru], IV 1, "to be banded together (?)": *im-ma-aṣ-ru-nim-ma*, Tabl. I, l. 109 (p. 16); Tabl. II, l. 15 (p. 24); Tabl. III, l. 19 (p. 40), l. 77 (p. 48).

mukku, "affliction (?)": *muk-ku*, p. 230, l. 60.

marāru, "to be bitter."
namurratu, "anger, terrible splendour; fear (?)": *na-mur-ra-ti*, p. 128, l. 6; *na-mur-ra-tu*, p. 148, l. 4.
[mēšu], "to forgive": Imper. *mi-e-ši*, p. 232, l. 82.
mūšiš, "by night": *mu-šiš*, Tabl. I, l. 50 (p. 10).
mašdū, "flat (?)": *maš-di-e*, Tabl. IV, l. 137 (p. 76).
mašālu, I 1, "to be like."
II 2, "to make like": Pret. *um-taš-šil*, Tabl. I, l. 118 (p. 16), Tabl. III, l. 28 (p. 42), l. 86 (p. 50); *um-taš-ši-il*, varr. *um-ta-aš-ši-il*, *um-taš-ši-ir*, Tabl. II, l. 24 (p. 24 f.); *um-taš-ši-il*, Tabl. III, l. 86 (var., p. 51).
muttiš, "before": *mut-tiš*, Tabl. II, l. 75 (p. 30); *mut-ti-iš*, Tabl. III, l. 131 (p. 56).
nabū, "to name, to proclaim": Imper. *i-ba-a*, Tabl. II, l. 136 (p. 36); Tabl. III, l. 60 (p. 46), l. 118 (p. 54).
nabāṭu, "to blaze forth": *i-nam-bu-ṭu*, p. 206, l. 15.
nagū, I 1: *na-g[u-u]*, p. 169.
IV 2, "to be rejoiced": *i-te-en-gu*, var. *it-ta-an-gu*, Tabl. VII, l. 118 (p. 110).
nagālu, IV 1, "to be made desolate": Perm. *na-an-gu-la-ku-ma*, p. 230, l. 65.
nadū, IV 1, "to be placed, to be established": Perm. *na-an-di-a-at* (fr. *nadū*, rather than IV 1, Perm. fr. *emēdu*), p. 228, l. 34.
[nadāru], "to rage."
nanduru, "afflicted, sorrowful": *na-an-du-ru-ti*, p. 232, l. 72.
niziḳtu, "misfortune": *ni-ziḳ-ti*, p. 232, l. 72.
niknaku, "censer": *nik-na-ki*, p. 138, l. 6.
nakāpu, I 2, "to violently attain": *mut-tak-ki-pat*, p. 224, l. 11.
namalu, "marsh (?)": *na-ma-la*, p. 134, l. 32.
namāru, "to be bright; to praise": *am-mir-ki*, p. 230, l. 60.
namurtu, "splendour": *na-mur-tum*, p. 129, n. 7.
nūn-amēlu, "fish-man": Tabl. I, l. 123 (p. 18); Tabl. II, l. 29 (p. 26); Tabl. III, l. 33 (p. 42), l. 91 (p. 52).
[nannartu], "light": *na-an-na-rat*, p. 222, l. 5.
nisū, I 1, "to remove, to carry away": *li-is-si-e-ma*, Tabl. VII, l. 114 (p. 108).
II 2, "to disappear, to depart": Pret. *ut-te-is-si* (var. *su*), Tabl. II, l. 116 (p. 34).
nasāḫu, "to carry off, to remove, to destroy": *is-su-ḫu*, Tabl. VII, l. 34 (p. 98).

nasāku, "to place; to place the hand upon, to grasp, to seize": *is-suk*, Tabl. IV, l. 101 (p. 70); *is-su-kam-ma*, p. 118, l. 7; *us-kam-ma*, p. 118, l. 4.

nasāsu, II 1, with *nissatu*, "to mourn bitterly": *u-na-as-sa-su*, p. 228, l. 49.

nassu, "sorrowful, grievous, lamenting": *na-as-si*, p. 228, l. 46; *na-as-sa-a-ti*, p. 228, l. 48.

nissatu, "mourning, lamentation": *nissati*pl, p. 228, l. 49.

napāḫu, "to flame out; to roar against (of a wind)": *nap-ḫat*, p. 228, l. 37.

nipru, "offspring, child": *ni-ip-ri-šu*, Tabl. II, l. 2 (p. 22).

napāšu, II 1, "to make broad, to make merciful": Part. *mu-nap-pi-šu*, Tabl. II, l. 110 (p. 32).

niṣirtu, "treasure"; employed as synonym for "life": *ni-ṣir-ta-šu*, var. *na piš ta-šu*, Tabl. VII, l. 112 (p. 108).

nāḳu, I 1, "to lament."

III 2, "to cause lamentation": *mul-ta-nu-ḳa-a-ti*, p. 224, l. 9.

naḳū, II 2, "to be poured out": Pres. *ul-tak-ka* (?), Tabl. II, l. 130 (p. 36).

narāṭu, "to become weak, to falter": *i-nar-ru-ṭu*, p. 226, l. 21.

našū, IV 1, "to be raised on high": Perm. *na-an-še-a-at*, p. 228, l. 34.

našaku, III 1, "to remove from": *u-ša-as-si-ku* (var. *ka*), Tabl. VII, l. 28 (p. 96).

našāḳu, I 1, "to kiss": [*i*]*š-ši-iḳ*, Tabl. II, l. 116 (p. 34).

I 2, do.: *it-ta-šiḳ*, Tabl. V, l. 79 (p. 82).

IV 1, "to kiss one another": Pret. *in-niš-ḳu*, Tabl. III, l. 132 (p. 56).

našāḳu, II 1, "to give way beneath (?)": [*u*]-*na-ša-ḳu*, varr. *u-na-aš-ša*[*ḳ* . .], *u na-šaḳ*, Tabl. I, l. 54 (pp. 10, 186).

našāru, "to diminish": Perm. *na-ši-ir*, Tabl. I, l. 25 (p. 6).

ס

sagū, "to want, lack, need": Inf. *sa-gu-u*, p. 160; *sa-gi-šu-nu*, Tabl. IV, l. 12 (p. 58); *sa-gi-šu-nu-ma*, Tabl. VII, l. 10 (p. 94); *sa-gi-e-a*, p. 232, l. 75.

[**siḫū**], "to cease": Perm. *si-ḫa-ti*, Tabl. IV, l. 68 (p. 66).

sakāpu, "to lie down, to rest": Part. *sa-ki-pu*, Tabl. I, l. 110 (p. 16), Tabl. II, l. 16 (p. 24), Tabl. III, l. 20 (p. 40), l. 78 (p. 50); Perm. *sak-pu*, Tabl. I, l. 33 (p. 6).

[salū], II 1: "to pray, to supplicate": Inf. *su-lu-u-a*, p. 234, l. 99.

sinništu, "female, woman": *si-in-ni-ša-tum*, var. *si-in-ni-ša-at*, Tabl. II, l. 122 (p. 34).

[sapū], II 1, "to pray": Inf. *su-pu-u-a*, p. 234, l. 99.

sapāḫu, II 1, "to make of no effect, to cast down": Prec. *lu-sap-pi-iḫ*, Tabl. I, l. 39 (p. 84).

saparu, "net."

saparis, "in the net": *sa-pa-riš*, Tabl. IV, l. 112 (p. 72).

supuru, "fold": *su-pu-ri*, p. 234, l. 90.

sarāru, "to oppose, to resist (?)": *sa-ra-ar*, Tabl. IV, l. 9 (p. 58).

sarru, f. plur. *sarrāti*, "rebellion": *sar-ra-a-ti*, Tabl. IV, l. 72 (p. 66).

פ

pagru, "body"; *pa-ag-ri*, "my body, myself," p. 146 f., n. 4; cf. also *pūtu*.

palū, symbol of royalty, "ring (?)": *palū(a)*, Tabl. IV, l. 29 (p. 60).

[pēlu], III[II] 2, "to alter, annul": *uš-te-pi-il*, var. *uš-te-pi-el-l[u]*, Tabl. VII, l. 132 (p. 112).

palāsu, "to pay homage to (?)": *pal-su*[. .], Tabl. VII, l. 107 (p. 106); *pa-la-su*, p. 167.

[palsū], IV 1: *ni-pil-su-u*, p. 148, l. 4.

[palsaḫu], III 1, "to crush": Imper. *šu-pal-si-ḫi*, p. 234, l. 98.

[paltū], IV 1, "to succumb, to be defeated (?)": *ip-pal-tu-u*, Tabl. IV, l. 16 (p. 58).

pusummu, "bond (?)": *pu-su-um-me*, p. 226, l. 33.

pisannu, "treasure-chest": *pi-sa-an-na-ti-ka*, p. 154, l. 22.

[pāḳu], II 1, "to give heed to": *u-pa-ḳa*, p. 232, l. 79.

[paršadu], IV 1, "to escape": *na-par-šu-diš* (var. *di-iš*), Tabl. IV, l. 110 (p. 72).

pašāḫu, III 1, "to pacify"; Perm. "to rest": *šu-up-šu-ḫa-ak* (var. *ku*), Tabl. I, l. 38 (p. 8); *šup-šu-ḫa-at*, Tabl. I, l. 50 (p. 10).

[pešēḳu], "to be in trouble": Pret. *ip-še-iḳ*, p. 232, l. 68.

pašāru, I 2, "to divulge (?)": *ip-ta-šar* (?): Tabl. II, l. 4 (p. 22).

pūtu, "front; person": *pu-ut-ka*, p. 154, l. 25; *pag-ri u pu-u-ti* (var. *pu-ti*), "my own person, myself," p. 140, l. 8, p. 148, l. 2.

pitḳu, "handiwork": *pi-ti-iḳ-šu*, Tabl. II, l. 1 (p. 22).

צ

ṣabātu, I 1, "to take."
I 2, Inf. *tiṣbutu*, "to begin": Tabl. I, l. 130 (p. 18); Tabl. II, l. 36 (p. 26); Tabl. III, l. 40 (p. 42), l. 98 (p. 52).
IV 1, "to be held fast, to be held in remembrance": *li-iṣ-ṣab-tu-ma*, var. [*li-iṣ*]-*ṣa-ab-tu*, Tabl. VII, l. 125 (p. 110).

ṣabāru, I 2, "to attain (?)," or "to understand (?)": Inf. *ti-iṣ-bu-ru*, Tabl. III, l. 5 (p. 38).
III 1, "to impart to, to make known to": Pret. *u-ša-aṣ-bi-ra-an-ni*, Tabl. III, l. 14 (p. 40), l. 72 (p. 48); *u-ša-aṣ-bir-an-ni*, Tabl. III, l. 72 (var., p. 48 f.).

ṣalālu, "to lie down, to lie down to rest": Pret. *ni-iṣ-lal*, Tabl. I, l. 40 (p. 8), l. 46 (but cf. p. 185), ll. 100, 102 (p. 14); Pres. *ni-ṣa-al-lal*, Tabl. I, l. 96 (p. 14); Perm. *ṣal-la*-[*at*], Tabl. I, l. 50 (p. 10); *ṣa-al-la-ku*, Tabl. I, l. 38 (p. 184).

ṣallūtu, "plague": *ṣal-lu-tum*, p. 206, l. 21.

ṣimru, "fulness": *ṣi-im-ri*, Tabl. VII, l. 21 (p. 96); *ṣi-im-ru*, p. 161.

ṣuṣū, "marsh": *ṣu-ṣa-a*, var. *ṣu-ṣa-'*, Tabl. I, l. 6 (p. 2).

[**ṣāru**?], II 1, "to cover (?)": *u-ṣir*, Tabl. V, l. 14 (p. 78).

ṣīriš, "unto": *ṣi-ri-iš*, var. *ṣi-riš*, Tabl. I, l. 32 (p. 6); *ṣi-ri-iš*, Tabl. IV, l. 128 (p. 74).

ṣirmaḫu, plur. *ṣirmaḫē*, "monster-serpent": Tabl. I, l. 114 (p. 16); Tabl. II, l. 20 (p. 24); Tabl. III, l. 24 (p. 40), l. 82 (p. 50).

ṣirritu, "sceptre": *ṣir-rit*, p. 226, l. 32.

ṣirruššu, "dragon": Tabl. I, l. 121 (p. 18); Tabl. II, l. 27 (p. 24); Tabl. III, l. 31 (p. 42), l. 89 (p. 50).

ק

ḳablu, "midst, inward parts": *ḳab-lu-uš Ti-a-ma-ti*, Tabl. IV, l. 65 (p. 66).

ḳudmiš, "before": *ḳu-ud-mi-iš*, var. *ḳud-meš*, Tabl. I, l. 33 (p. 6).

ḳuddušu, "pure, holy": *ḳud-du-šu*, p. 226, l. 28.

ḳāpu, I 2, "to entrust to": *iḳ-ti-pa*, Tabl. V, l. 12 (p. 78).

[**ḳaṣābu**], III 2: Imper. *šu-taḳ-ṣi-ba-am-ma*, Tabl. V, l. 20 (p. 80).

ḳaṣāru, I 1, "to collect, to take": *lu-uk-ṣur-ma*, Tabl. VI, l. 5 (p. 86).
I 2, "to make, to fix, to form, to contrive": Pret. [*iḳ*]-*ta-ṣar*, Tabl. II, l. 2 (p. 22); Perm. *ki-iṣ-ṣu-ra*, Tabl. I, l. 6 (p. 2).
II 1, do.: Perm. *ku-zu-ru*, Tabl. I, l. 6 (var., p. 2).

ḳarābu, I 2, Inf. *ḳitrubu*, "battle."
ḳitrubiš, "to the battle": [*ḳi*]*t-ru-bi-iš* (var. *biš*), Tabl. II, l. 111, p. 32.

ḳirbu, "midst, inward parts": *kir-biš* (var. *bi-iš*) *Ti-amat*, Tabl. IV, l. 41 (p. 62), l. 48 (p. 64); *kir-biš Tam-tim*, p. 106; *kir-biš* (var. *i-na kir-bi*) *Ti-amat*, Tabl. VII, l. 108 (p. 106); *a-ḫi-zu*(var. *iz*) *kir-bi-šu*, a title of Marduk, Tabl. VII, l. 109 (p. 108); *kir-bu*, pp. 107, 168.

ḳarbāti, plur., "fields": *ḳar-ba-a-ti-ia*, p. 232, l. 76.

ḳīšu, "forest": *ki-šu*, p. 134, l. 25.
ḳīštu, "forest": plur. *ki-ša-tu-ma*, p. 134, l. 29.

ר

ra'ābu, "to rage": Perm. *ra-'-ba-ti-ma*, p. 234, l. 94.

rābu, "to quake": *i-ru-ub-bu*, p. 206, l. 8; p. 226, l. 20; *i-ru-bu*, p. 226, l. 21.

rabū, III 2, "to make pre-eminent": Imper. *šu-te-ir-ba-'*, Tabl. II, l. 136 (var., p. 36 f.).

[rabābu], II 1, "to make great": *li-ra-ab-bi-ib*, Tabl. III, l. 52 (p. 45).
III[II] 1, do.: *liš-rab-bi-ib*, Tabl. I, l. 142 (p. 20); Tabl. II, l. 48 (p. 28); Tabl. III, l. 52 (p. 44), l. 110 (p. 54).

ridū, "to follow, pursue"; Inf. "pursuit, occupation": *ri-du-u-a*, p. 230, l. 58.

raṭu, "water-channel (on land); current, movement (in water)": *ra-ṭu-um-ma*, p. 132, l. 11.

rakābu, III 2, "to sling on (a spear)": *uš-tar-ki-ba*, Tabl. IV, l. 36 (p. 62).

rakāsu, "to fix, to lay": *ir-ku-us*, p. 132, l. 17.
riksu, "limit, bound (?)": *rik-si-šu-un*, Tabl. V, l. 6 (p. 78).
markasu, "band": [*m*]*ar-kas*, p. 104; *mar-ka-su*, p. 165.

ramū, II 1, "to set free": Inf. "deliverance": *ru-um-mi-ia*, p. 232, l. 83.

rēsu, II 1, "to smite, to crush (?)": *li-ra-i-su*, Tabl. IV, l. 16 (p. 58).

rūḳu, "distant; wide, compassionate (of the heart)": *ru-u-ḳu*, Tabl. VII, l. 135 (p. 112), p. 173.

rēšu-arkāt, "the Beginning and the Future": *rēšu-arkāt*, Tabl. VII, l. 107 (p. 106); *ri-e-šu ar-kat*, p. 167; cf. also *ša ina ri-e-ši u ar-ka-[ti . . .]*, p. 178, l. 19.

ש

šē'u, "to take wing, to fly": *i-ša-'*, p. 230, l. 63.

še'ū, "to seek, to look for: to perceive, to behold": *i-še'-a*, Tabl. I, l. 60 (p. 12), Tabl. IV, l. 66 (p. 66); *i-še-'-am-ma*, Tabl. II, l. 81 (p. 30); *te-še-'-e-ma*, var. *te-eš-[. . .]*, Tabl. IV, l. 83 (p. 68); Perm. *še-'* (= *še'i*), Tabl. I, l. 6 (p. 2).

ša'ālu, I 1, "to ask."

II 1, "to demand, to cry out for": *u-ša-'-lu*, var. *u-ša-'-a-lu*, Tabl. IV, l. 92 (p. 70).

šabū, I 2, "to overwhelm": *i-sa-am-bu-'*, p. 206, l. 17.

šabāšu, "to turn, to pervert (?)": *šab-šu*, p. 140, l. 7.

[**šudu**], con. st. *šud*, "height, supremacy"; *šud tamḫari*, "command in battle": Tabl. I, l. 131 (p. 20); Tabl. II, l. 37 (p. 26); Tabl. III, l. 41 (p. 42), l. 99 (p. 52).

šadādu, "to drag": Pres. *i-šad-da-[ad]*, p. 118, l. 12.

[**šaḫādu**], I 2, "to rear up": *liš-taḫ-ḫi-dam-ma*, Tabl. I, l. 120 (p. 16); Tabl. III, l. 30 (p. 42), l. 88 (p. 50); *liš-taḫ-ḫi-da-am* (var. *dam*)-*ma*, Tabl. II, l. 26 (p. 24).

šuḫarruru, "to be afflicted": Pret. *uš-ḫa-ri-ir-ma*, Tabl. II, l. 6 (p. 22); Perm. *šu-ḫar-ru-ur*, *šu-ḫar-ru-rat*, p. 232, l. 75.

šaḫātu, I 1, "to rage."

III 1, "to cause to rage, to stir up": *u-ša-aš-ḫi-it*, p. 120, l. 5; *šu-uš-ḫi-it*, p. 120, l. 2.

šiklu, "sense (?)": *ši-ik-la-šu*, p. 140, l. 7.

šikkatu, "supremacy, control"; *rab-šikkati*, "chief"; *rab-šikkatūtu*, "chieftain-ship": Tabl. I, l. 131 (p. 20); Tabl. II, l. 37 (p. 26); Tabl. III, l. 41 (p. 42), l. 99 (p. 52).

šakānu, "to set; to provide."

šukuttu, "provision": *šu-ku-us-su*, Tabl. VII, l. 8 (p. 92).

šakāru, "to drink"; Perm. "to be drunk (?)": *ši-ik-ru* (poss. subs., "carouse"), Tabl. III, l. 136 (p. 56).

šalummatu, "glory, pride": *ša-lum-mat*, p. 148, l. 3.

šalāḳu, "to cut out, to cut off."

šulluḳtu, "cutting off, destruction": *šul-lu-uḳ-ti*, p. 228, l. 37; p. 232, l. 69.

šumu, "name," plur. *šumē*: *šu-mi-e-šu*, Tabl. VII, l. 124 (var., p. 110).

šemû, I 1, "to hear."
IV 1, "to be heard": (?) *liš-ši-ma* (or *našû*, I 1; cf. var. fr. *nisû*, p. 109, n. 17), Tabl. VII, l. 114 (p. 108).
šamāru, I 2, "to rage": *is-lam-ma-ru*, p. 230, l. 58.
šumurratu, "confusion, rage, anger": *šu-mur-ra-tu*, Tabl. VII, l. 42 (p. 100).
šitmuriš, "wildly": *šit-mu-riš* (var. *ri-iš*), Tabl. IV, l. 89 (p. 70).
šanû, "to repeat"; Inf. *šanû*, "version": *š[a]-n[i]-[e]*, p. 126, l. 8.
šanānu, "to rival."
šinnatu, "rivalry": *šin-na-as-su*, p. 206, l. 12.
šasû, I 2, "to cry": *il-la-si*, Tabl. I, l. 42 (p. 8).
šipru, "business, occupation": *ši-pir*, p. 152, l. 19.
šuḳammumu, "to roar": Perm. [*šu*]-*ḳa-am-mu-m*[*a*]-*a*[*t*], Tabl. I, l. 26 (p. 6).
šaḳummiš, **šaḳummeš**, adv., "in sorrow": [*ša-ku-um*]-*mi-iš*, var. [*ša*]-*ḳu-um-meš*, Tabl. I, l. 58 (pp. 10, 186); *ša-ḳu-um-mi-iš*, Tabl. II, l. 6 (p. 22).
šaḳāšu, "to destroy."
šaḳšu, "violent, unruly": *šaḳ-šu*, p. 226, l. 26.
šāru, "wind": *šār arba'i*, "the fourfold wind"; *šār sibi* (var. VII-*bi-im*), "the sevenfold wind"; *šāra ešâ*, "the whirlwind"; *šāra la šanān*, "the wind which had no equal," Tabl. IV, l. 46 (p. 62).
[**šāru**], "to oppose (?)": Part. *ša-'-ir-ru*, p. 206, l. 11.
šērtu, "punishment": *še-rit-su*, Tabl. IV, l. 114 (p. 72).
šarbabu, "terror (?)": *šar-ba-ba*, Tabl. I, l. 119 (p. 16); Tabl. III, l. 29 (p. 42), l. 87 (p. 50); *šar-ba-bi-iš* (probably with pron. suff., not adv.), Tabl. II, l. 25 (p. 24).
šarāḳu, "to present, to furnish": *iš-ruk-*[*ku*], p. 128, l. 5; *iš-ru-uk-ku*, p. 129, n. 7; *iš-ru-ku-nik-kim-ma*, p. 128, l. 7.
šarûru, "light": *ša-ru-ur*, p. 228, l. 35.
šurišam, adv. (?): *šu-ri-šam*, Tabl. IV, l. 124 (p. 74).
šašmu, "battle, fight."
šašmeš, "to the fight": *ša-aš-meš*, Tabl. IV, l. 94 (p. 70).
šutummu, "storehouse": *šu-tum-mu*, p. 226, l. 28.

ת

tabinu, "power, might": *ta-bi-ni*, p. 232, l. 78.
tubuḳtu, "enclosing wall": *tub-ḳa-a-ti*, p. 154, l. 24.
taḫāzu, "battle."
taḫāziš, "to the battle": *ta-ḫa-zi-iš*, Tabl. IV, l. 94 (p. 70).

IV.

Index to names of Deities, Stars, Places, etc.

Adad, god: ^{ilu}*Adad*, p. 198, l. 5.

Adu-nuna, title of Marduk: ^{ilu}*A-du-nun-na*, Tabl. VII (K. 8,519 and comm. K. 4,406, Rev., col. ii, l. 23), pp. 104 f., 166; p. 173, l. 20; p. 178, l. 21.

Aga-azag, title of Marduk: ^{ilu}*Aga-azag*, Tabl. VII, l. 25 (p. 96 f.).

Agi[**l** . . .], title of Marduk: ^{ilu}*A-gi*[*l* . . .], Tabl. VII (K. 13,761), p. 102 f.; var. ^{ilu}GIL[ ], p. 163.

Akkadû, Akkad: *Ak-ka-di-i*, p. 147, note, l. 20; ^{mâtu}*Akkadû*^{KI}, p. 212, l. 26; ^{mâtu}*Akkadî*^{KI}, p. 211, l. 18; *ṣi-ri Ak-ka-di-i*, p. 147, note, l. 16.

Aḳrabu, Scorpio: *Aḳrabu*, p. 213, ll. 6, 13, 14.

Alim-nuna, possibly shorter form of *Asaru-alim-nuna*, title of Marduk: [. . . A]LIM-NUN-NA, p. 216.

Almanu, deity: ^{ilu}*Al-ma-nu*, p. 218, l. 10.

Ana, the god Anu: AN-NA, p. 124, l. 1; p. 126, l. 6; see also **Anu**.

Anbanini, mythical king: *An-ba-ni-ni*, p. 142, l. 18.

Anšar, god: *An-šar*, Tabl. I, ll. 12, 15 (p. 4 f.); Tabl. II, ll. 8, 9 (p. 22 f.), l. 49 (p. 28 f.), l. 72 (p. 30, restore *An-šar*), l. 79 (p. 30 f.), ll. 83, 114, 115 (p. 32 f.), l. 119 (p. 34 f.); Tabl. III, l. 1 (p. 38 f.), l. 13 (p. 40 f.), l. 71 (p. 48 f.), l. 131 (p. 56 f.); Tabl. IV, l. 125 (p. 74 f.); p. 195; p. 198, l. 30, l. 15 (Rev.); p. 199, l. 23; = 'Ασσωρός, see Introduction.

Anu, god: ^{ilu}*A-nu*, Tabl. I, l. 14 (p. 4 f.); ^{ilu}*A-num*, Tabl. I, l. 14 (var., p. 5), ll. 15, 16 (p. 4 f.), l. 85 (p. 12 f.); Tabl. II, l. 81 (p. 30 f.); Tabl. III, l. 53 (var., p. 46); Tabl. IV, ll. 4, 6 (p. 58 f.), l. 146 (p. 76 f.); Tabl. V, l. 8 (var. for ^{ilu}*E-a*, K. 13,774, p. 190 f.), l. 78 (p. 82 f.), p. 126, l. 8, p. 224, l. 18; ^{ilu}*A-nu-um*, Tabl. I, l. 16 (var., p. 5); Tabl. III, l. 53 (p. 46 f.), l. 111 (p. 54 f.); ^{ilu}*A-nim*, Tabl. IV, l. 44 (p. 62 f.); Tabl. VII, l. 6 (p. 92 f.); [^{ilu}] *A-nam*, Tabl. II, between ll. 85 and 104 (K. 10,008, p. 190); ^{ilu}*Anu*, p. 216, l. 2, p. 218,

l. 8; AN-NA = ^{ilu}*A-nu*, p. 138, l. 13 f.; ='Ανός, see Introduction.

Anunitu, goddess: ^{ilu}*A-nu-ni-tum*, p. 144, l. 10; p. 150, l. 22.

Anunnaki, the spirits of the earth: ^{ilu}*A-nun-na-ki*, Tabl. I, l. 136 (p. 20 f.); Tabl. III, l. 46 (p. 44 f.), l. 104 (p. 52 f.); Tabl. VI, l. 20 (p. 88 f.), p. 140, l. 5, p. 206, l. 22, p. 226, l. 21; [(DINGIR)A]-NUN-NA-GE-E-NE = ^{ilu}*A-nun-na-ki*, p. 132, l. 15; see also **Enukki**.

Anūtu, the power of Anu: ^{ilu}*A-nu-ti*, Tabl. I, l. 139 (p. 20 f.); Tabl. II, l. 45 (p. 28 f.); Tabl. III, l. 49 (var. *e-nu-ti*, "lordship," p. 44), l. 107 (p. 54 f.); ^{ilu}*An-nu-ti*, Tabl. IV, l. 82 (var. ^{ilu}*A*-[. . .], p. 68 f.).

Apsū, (1) primeval water-god: *Ap-su-u*, Tabl. I, l. 97 (p. 14 f.); *Ap*-[. . . .], Tabl. I, l. 47 (var., p. 9); *Apsū(u)*, Tabl. I, l. 3 (var., p. 2); *Apsū*, Tabl. I, l. 3 (p. 2 f.), ll. 22, 25, 29, 35 (p. 6 f.), l. 47 (p. 8 f.), l. 51 (p. 10 f.); Tabl. II, l. 3 (p. 22 f.), l. 55 (p. 28 f.), between ll. 85 and 104 (K. 10,008, p. 189), p. 175; = 'Απασών, see Introduction; (2) the Deep, not personified: *ap-su-u*, p. 206, l. 9; *ap-si-i*, p. 128, l. 4; *apsi*, Tabl. IV, ll. 142, 143 (p. 76 f.); ABZU = *ap-su-u*, p. 130, l. 8, p. 132, l. 13, p. 138, l. 8 f.; *bāb ap-si-i*, "the Gate of the Deep," p. 209, l. 5.

Aruru, goddess: (DINGIR)A-RU-RU, p. 134, l. 21.

Asari, title of Marduk: ^{ilu}*Asar-ri*, Tabl. VII, l. 1 (pp. 92 f., 158); p. 177, l. 6; in title of composition, p. 169.

Asaru-alim, title of Marduk: ^{ilu}*Asaru-alim*, Tabl. VII, l. 3 (pp. 92 f., 159).

Asaru-alim-nuna, title of Marduk: ^{ilu}*Asaru-alim-nun-na*, Tabl. VII, l. 5 (pp. 92 f., 160); ^{DINGIR}ASARU-ALIM-NUN-NA, p. 181, l. 2; [. . . . . ALI]M-NUN-NA, p. 216, l. 2.

Aššur, city: ^{alu}*Aššur*^{KI}, p. 199, l. 37.

Bābilu, Babylon: [*Bāb*]*ilu*^{KI}, p. 220, n. 1; *Bābili*^{KI}, p. 172, ll. 17, 18, p. 212, ll. 24, 27; [KA-DINGIR-RA](KI) = *Bābilu*^{KI}, p. 132, l. 14.

Barsip, Borsippa: *Bar-sip*^{KI}, p. 236, l. 112.

Bēl, Enlil, Illil, the elder Bēl: ^{ilu}*Bēl*, Tabl. IV, l. 146 (p. 76 f.); Tabl. V, l. 8 (p. 78 f.); Tabl. VII, l. 6 (p. 92 f.), l. 116 (p. 110), p. 116, l. 7, p. 126, l. 8, p. 172, l. 12, p. 195, p. 216, l. 2, p. 218, l. 8, p. 224, l. 18; ='Ιλλινος, see Introduction.

Supplementary Texts.

Preface.

In this volume is published for the first time the texts from a group of tablets, inscribed in the Neo-Babylonian character, and containing new portions of the great series of Creation Legends, to which the Assyrians and Babylonians gave the title *Enuma elish.* The group includes :—1. Portions of four copies of the First Tablet of the series, together with two extracts from the text, inscribed upon rough "practice-tablets" by the pupils of Babylonian scribes; 2. Portions of two copies of the Second Tablet of the series; 3. Part of a copy of the Third Tablet, and fragments of three "practice-tablets" inscribed with portions of the text, which I have joined to other similar fragments already published in *Cuneiform Texts from Babylonian Tablets, etc., in the British Museum*, Part XIII (1901); 4. Part of a copy of the Sixth Tablet, which is of peculiar interest inasmuch as it refers to the Creation of Man, and settles the disputed question as to the number of Tablets, or sections, of which the Creation Series was composed; and 5. Portions of two copies of the Seventh Tablet of the series.

A "practice-tablet," which is inscribed in the Sumerian and Babylonian languages with texts relating to the Creation of the Moon and of the Sun, is also included.

The Appendices contain texts which, for the most part, are closely connected with the interpretation of the Creation Legends. They include :—1. A number of Assyrian commentaries on the Seventh Tablet of the Creation Series, together with fragments of texts which are similar in character to that composition ; 2. A Neo-Babylonian duplicate of the tablet which has been supposed to belong to the Creation Series and to contain the instructions given to man after his creation, but which is now shown by the new duplicate to be part of a tablet of moral precepts and to have no connection whatsoever with the Creation Series ; 3. Part of a large astrological text of the period of the Arsacidae, in which some of the chief personages of the Creation-story appear in astrological characters, and the story itself is interpreted on astrological lines ; and 4. The text of the legend which was at one time commonly, but erroneously, believed to contain an Assryian version of the story of the Tower of Babel. The last appendix contains a "Prayer of the Raising of the Hand to Ishtar," which belongs to the series of similar compositions already published in my *Babylonian Magic and Sorcery* (1896); both from the beauty of its language and from its perfect state of preservation, it must be regarded as one of the finest and most complete Babylonian religious texts which have hitherto been recovered.

After the plates in this volume had been printed off, and whilst I was engaged in making a hand-list of the smaller fragments in the Kuyunjik Collections, I identified ten additional fragments of the Creation Series, belonging to copies of the First, Second, Fifth, and Seventh Tablets of the composition. The texts of these fragments, as well as those of some other closely allied Assyrian and Neo-Babylonian tablets, are published by means of outline blocks in the first volume of this work.

L. W. KING.

LONDON, July 29th, 1902.

45528 + 46614.

OBVERSE.

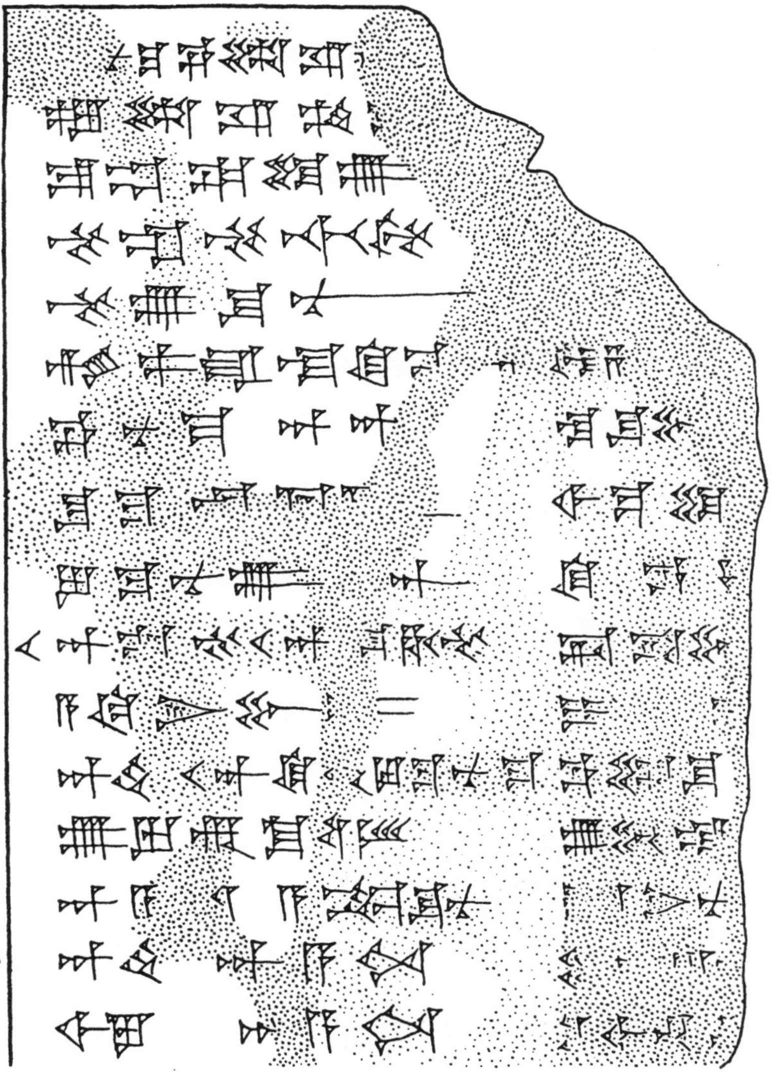

45528 + 46614.

OBVERSE (Cont.).

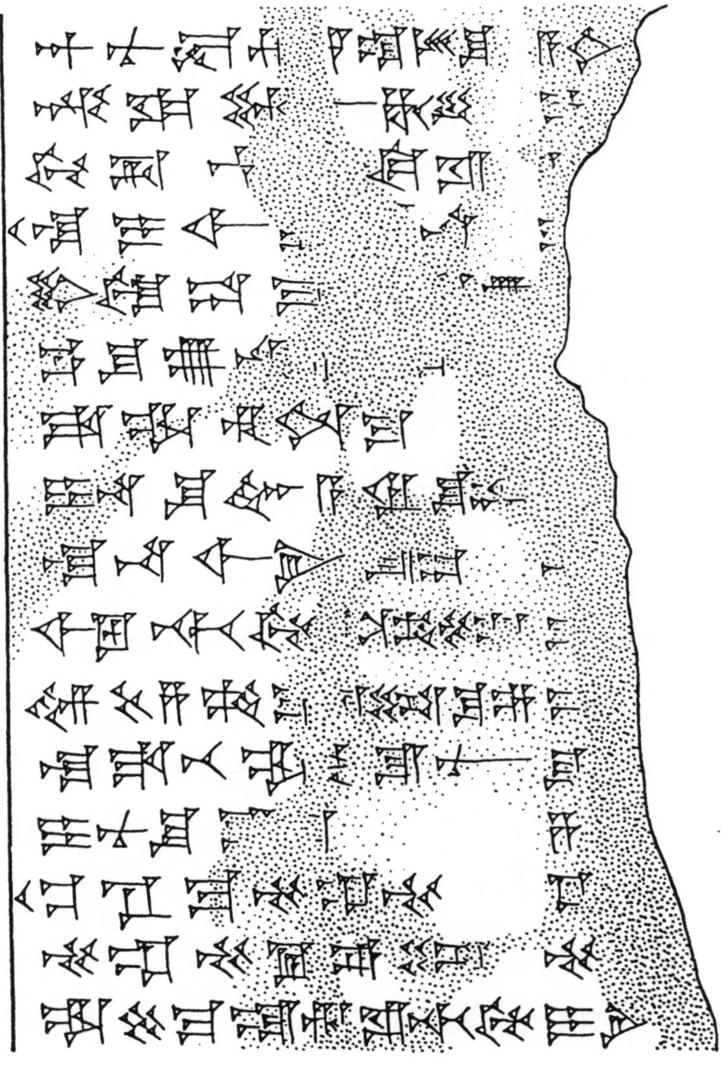

45528 + 46614.

OBVERSE (Cont.).

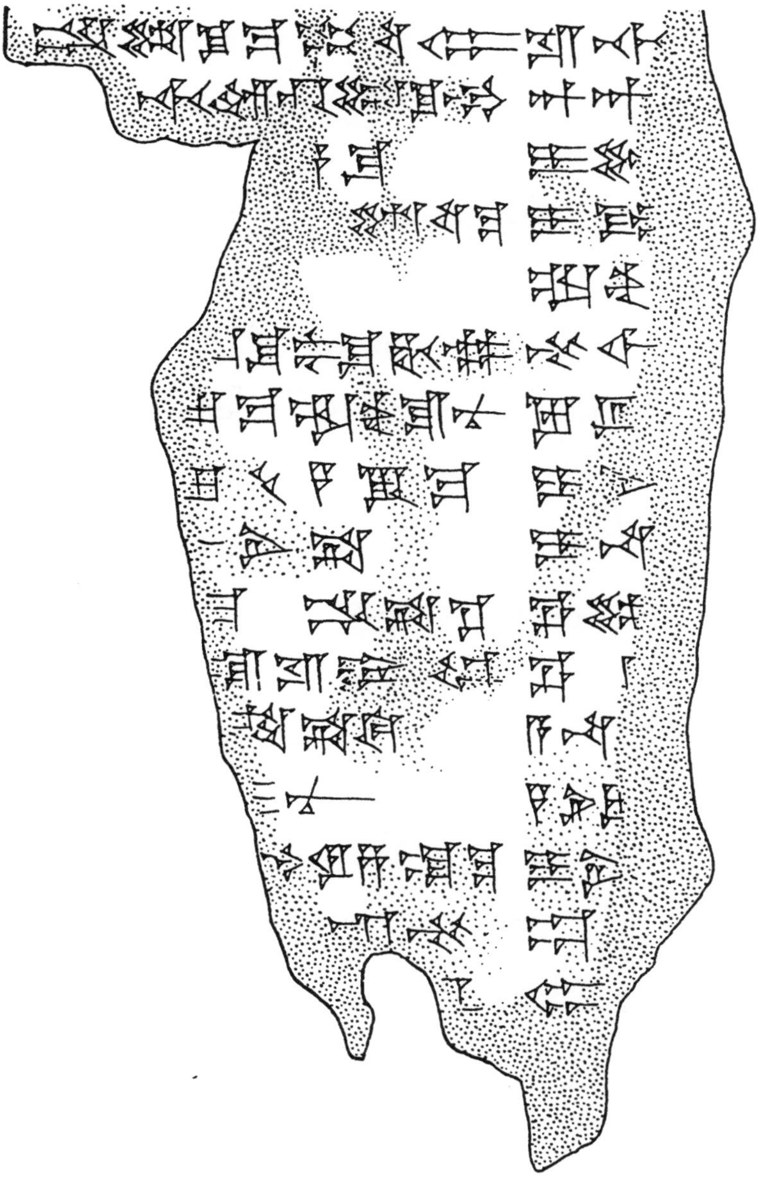

45528 + 46614.

REVERSE.

45528 + 46614.

REVERSE (Cont.).

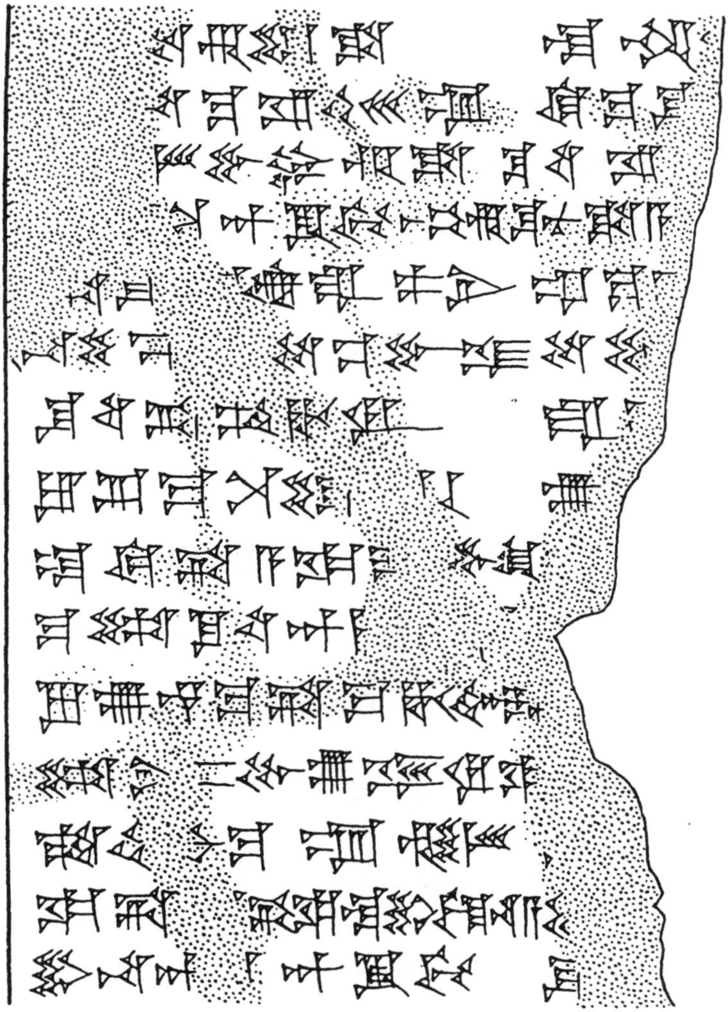

45528 + 46614.

REVERSE (Cont.).

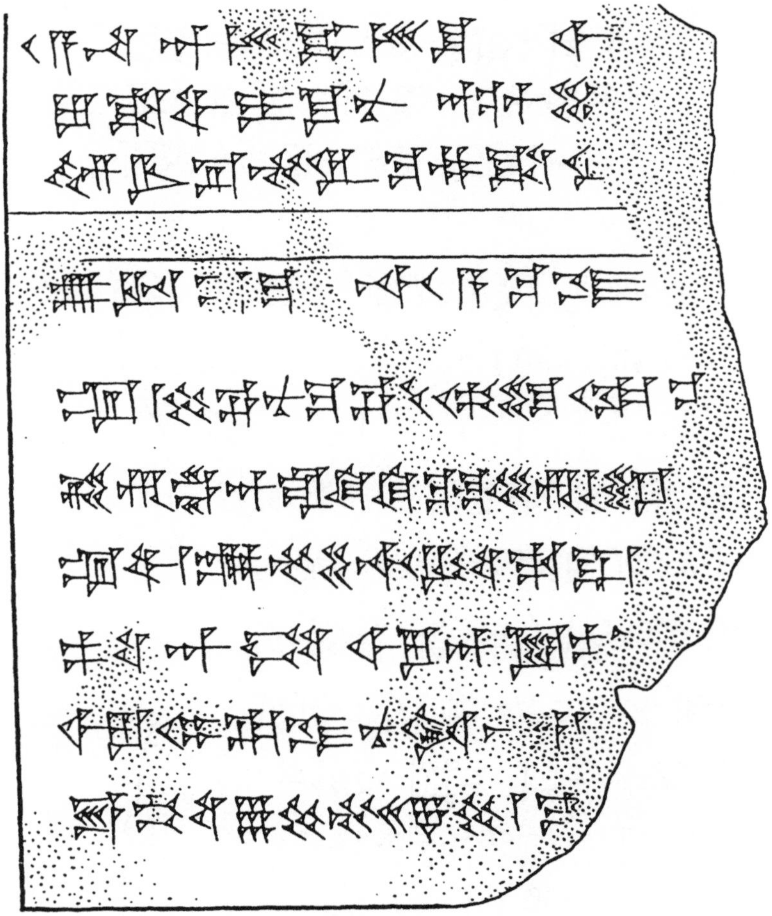

35134.

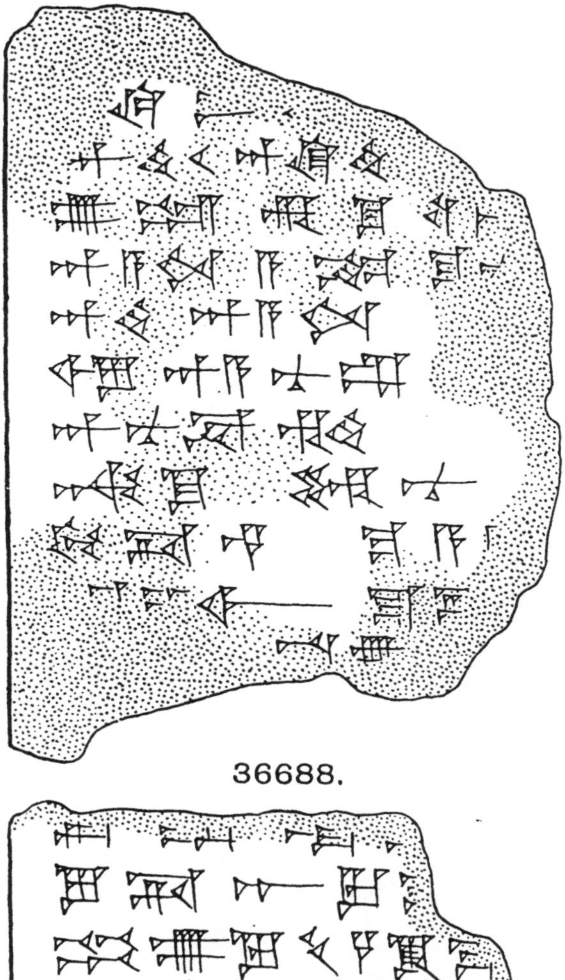

36688.

The text is an extract from a practice-tablet.

36726.

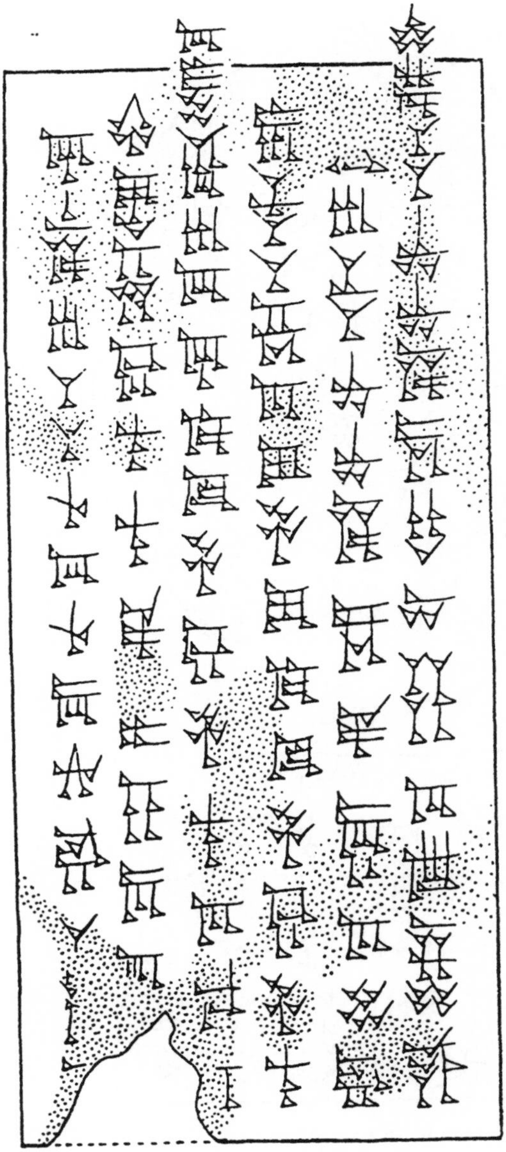

The text is an extract from a practice-tablet.

46803.

OBVERSE.

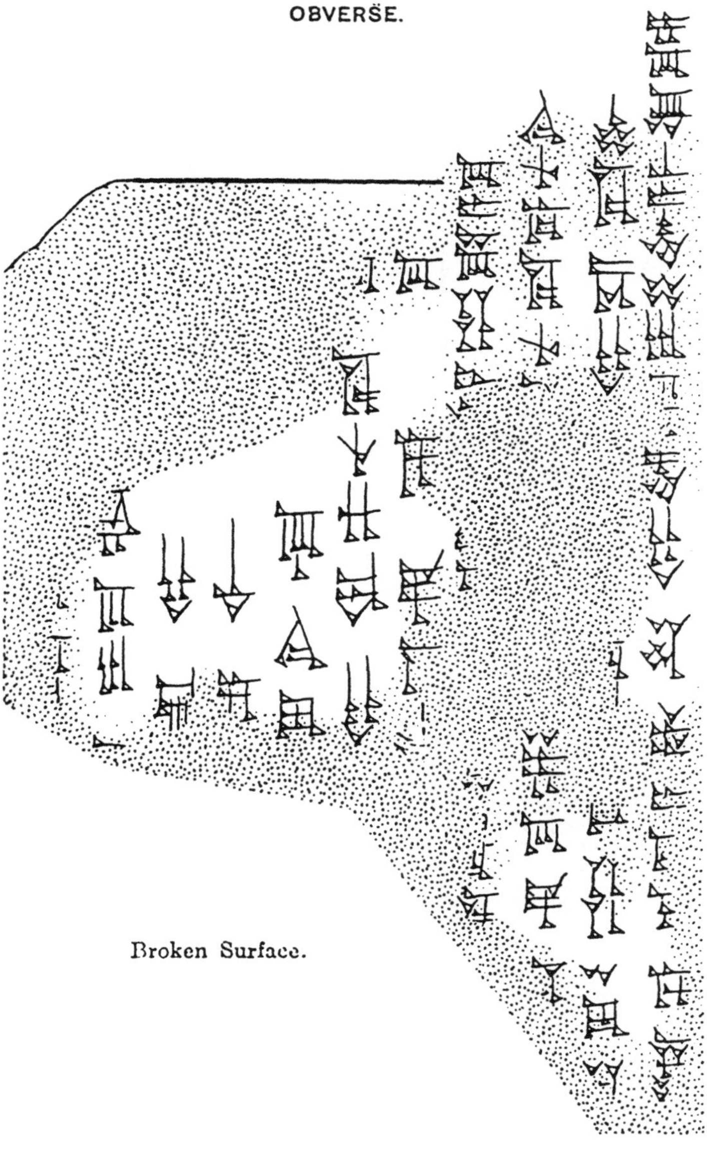

46803.

OBVERSE (cont.). & REVERSE

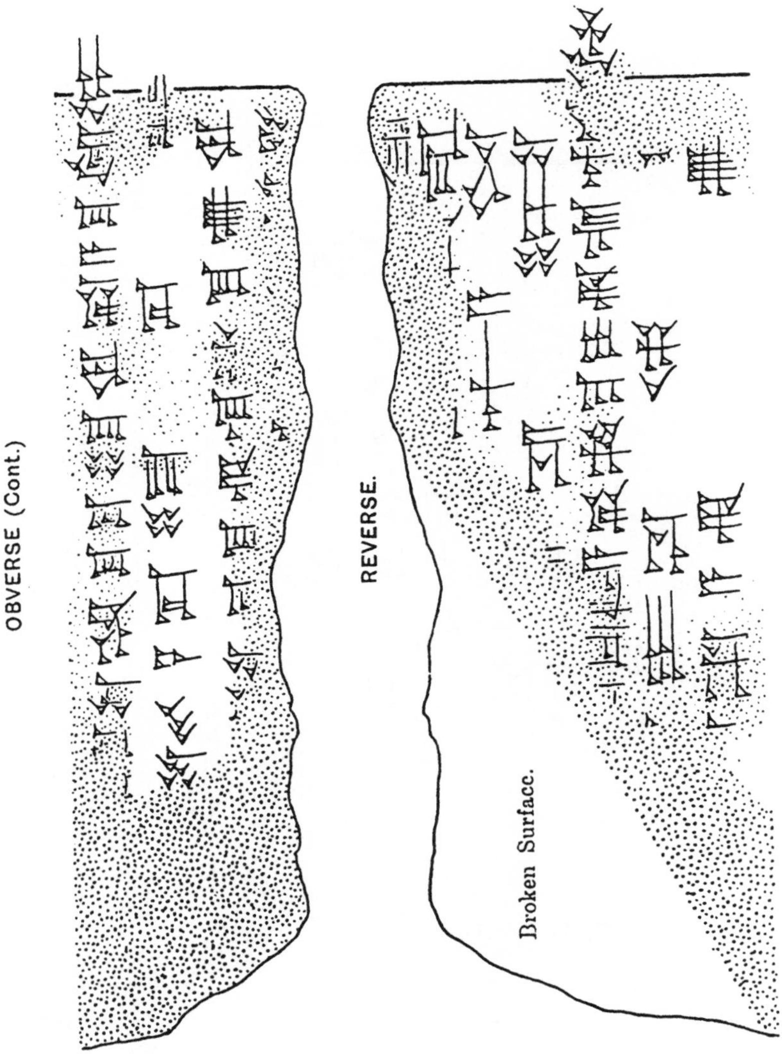

46803.

REVERSE (cont.).

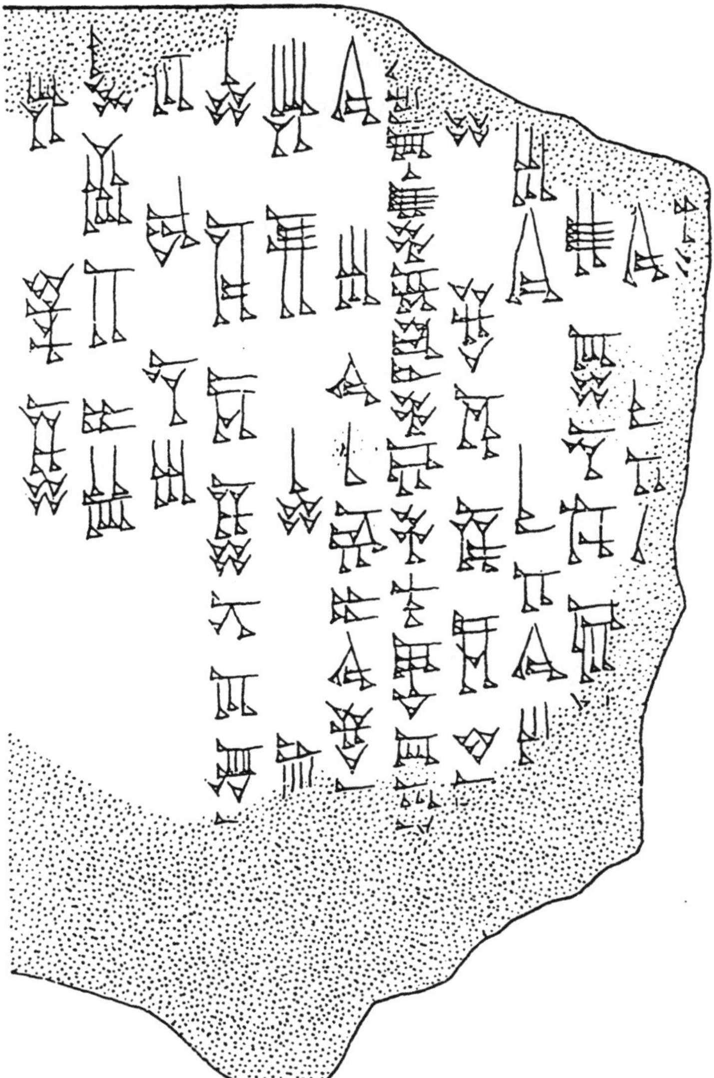

82-9-18, 6879.

REVERSE.

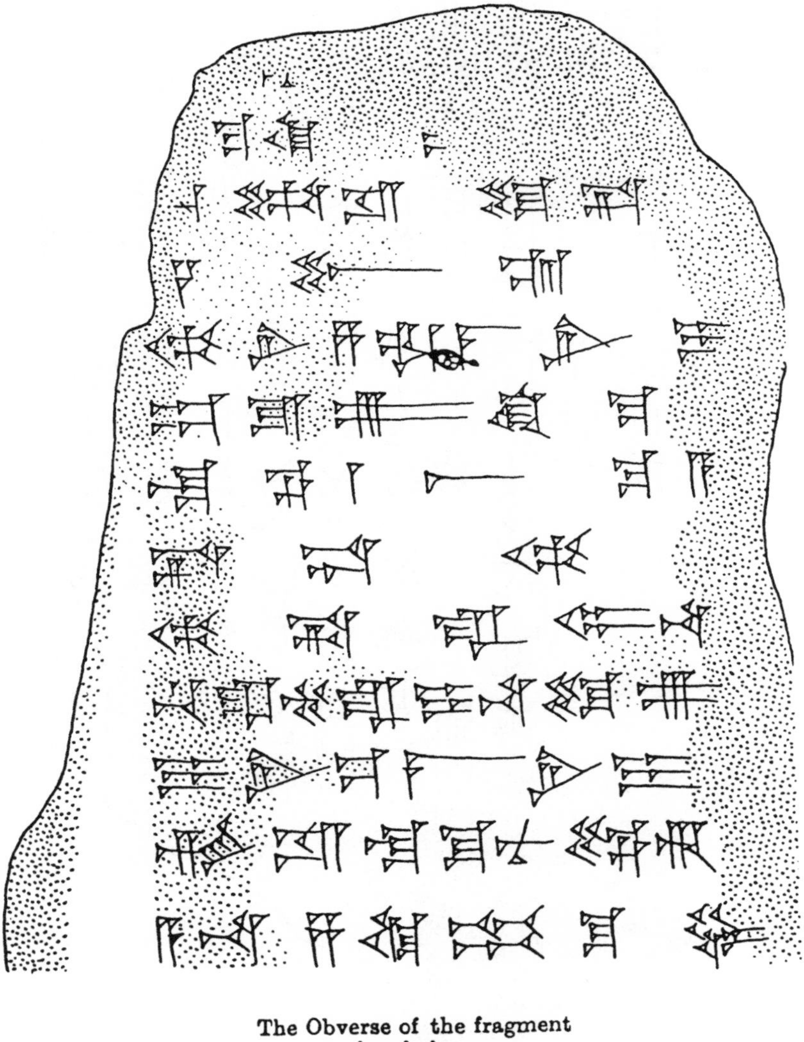

The Obverse of the fragment is missing.

82-9-18, 6879.

REVERSE (cont.).

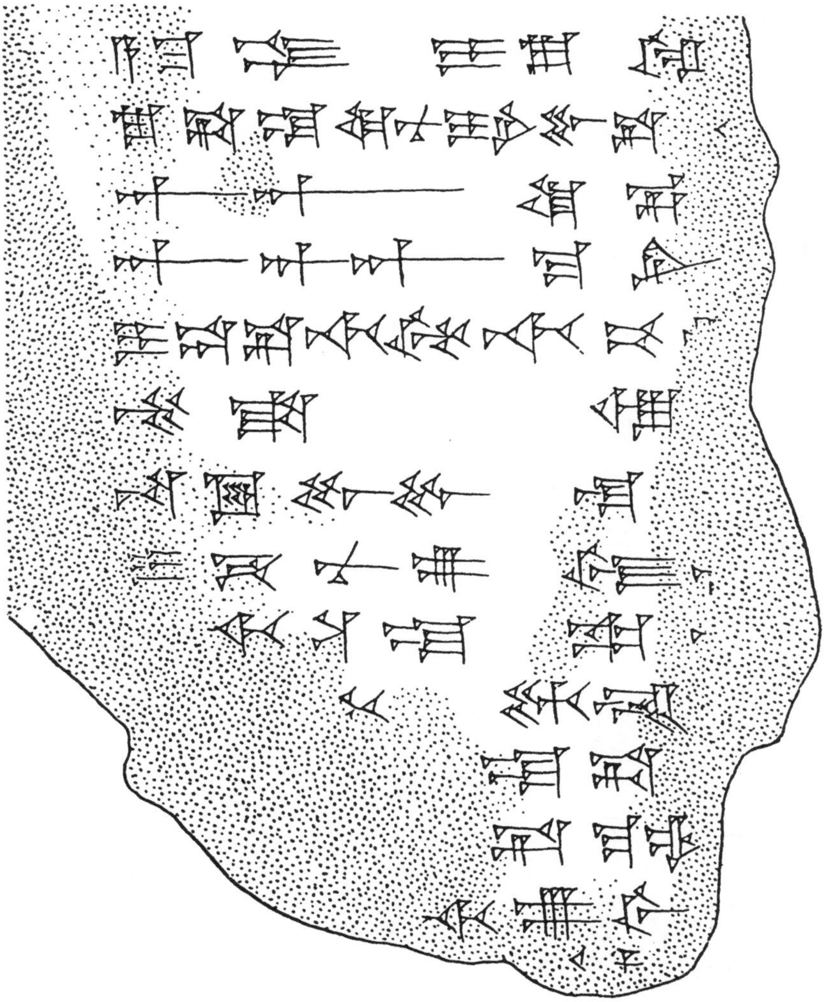

40559.

OBVERSE.

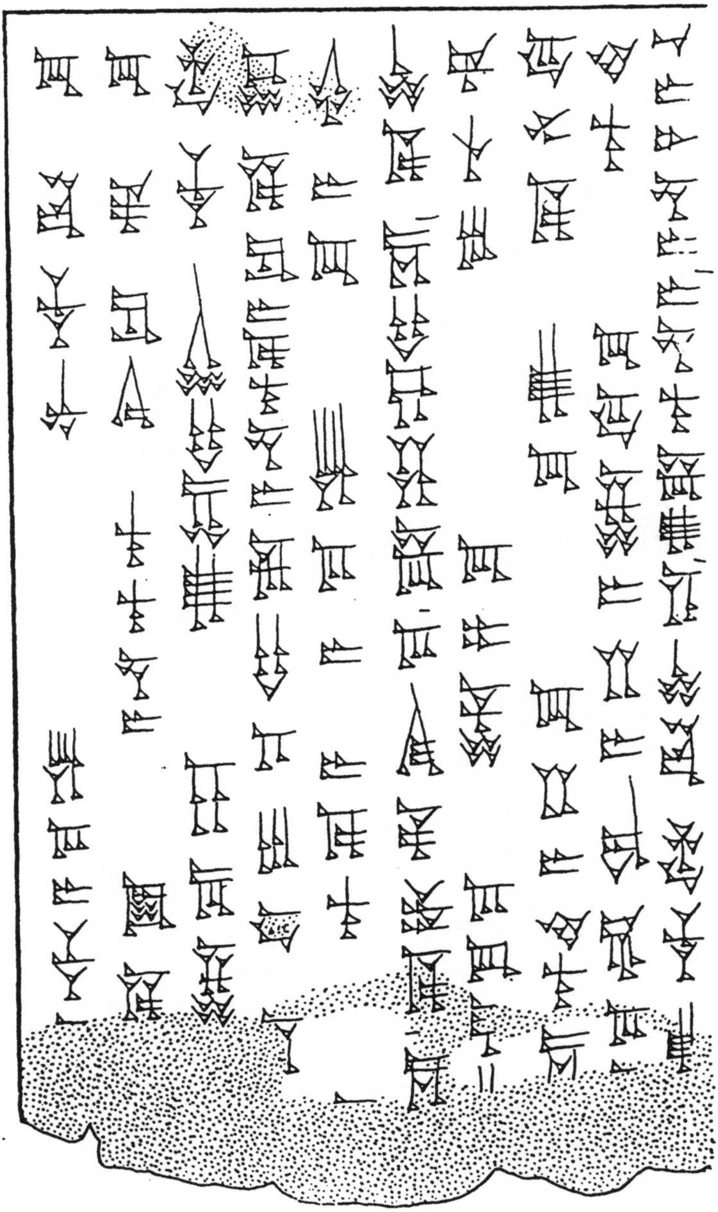

40559.

OBVERSE (cont.).

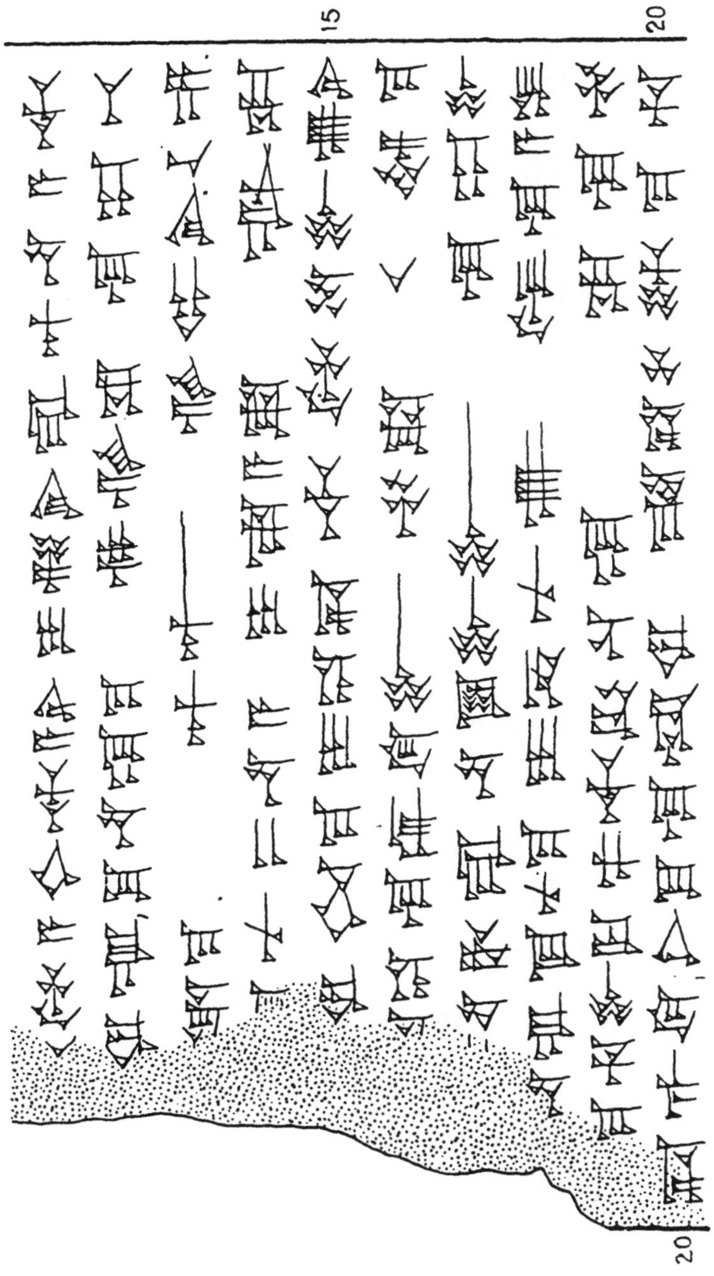

40559.

OBVERSE (cont.).

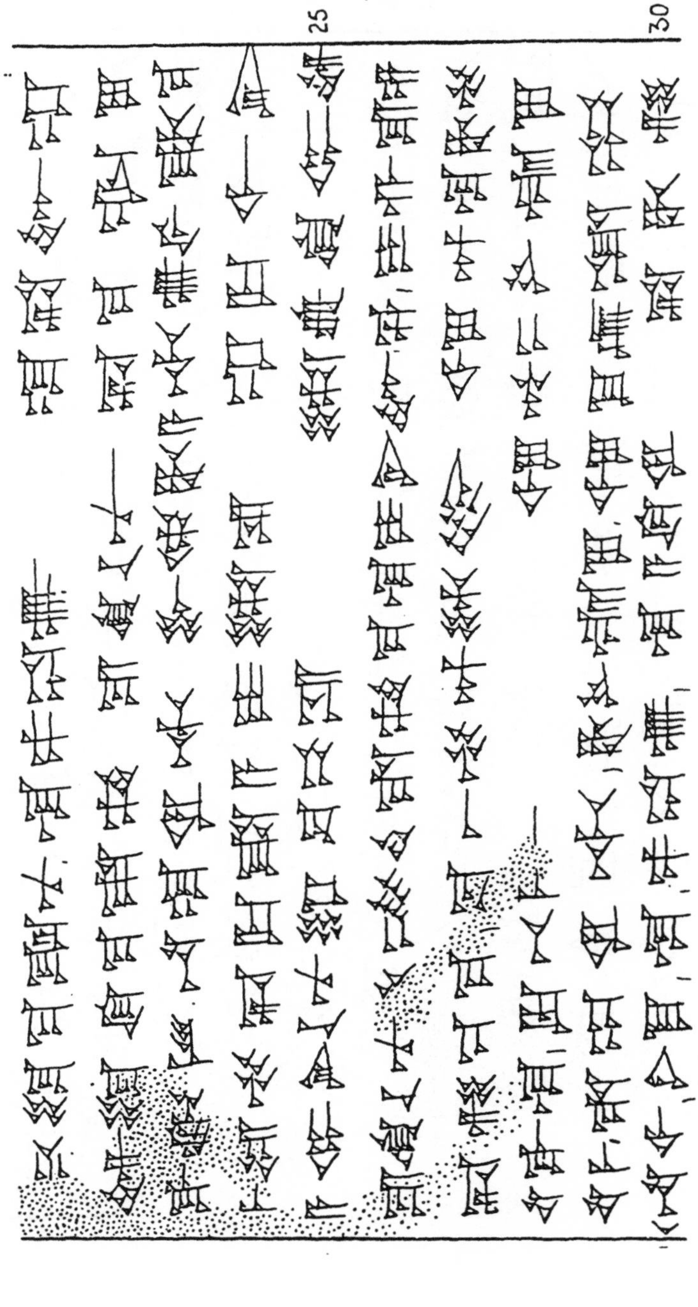

40559.

OBVERSE (cont.).

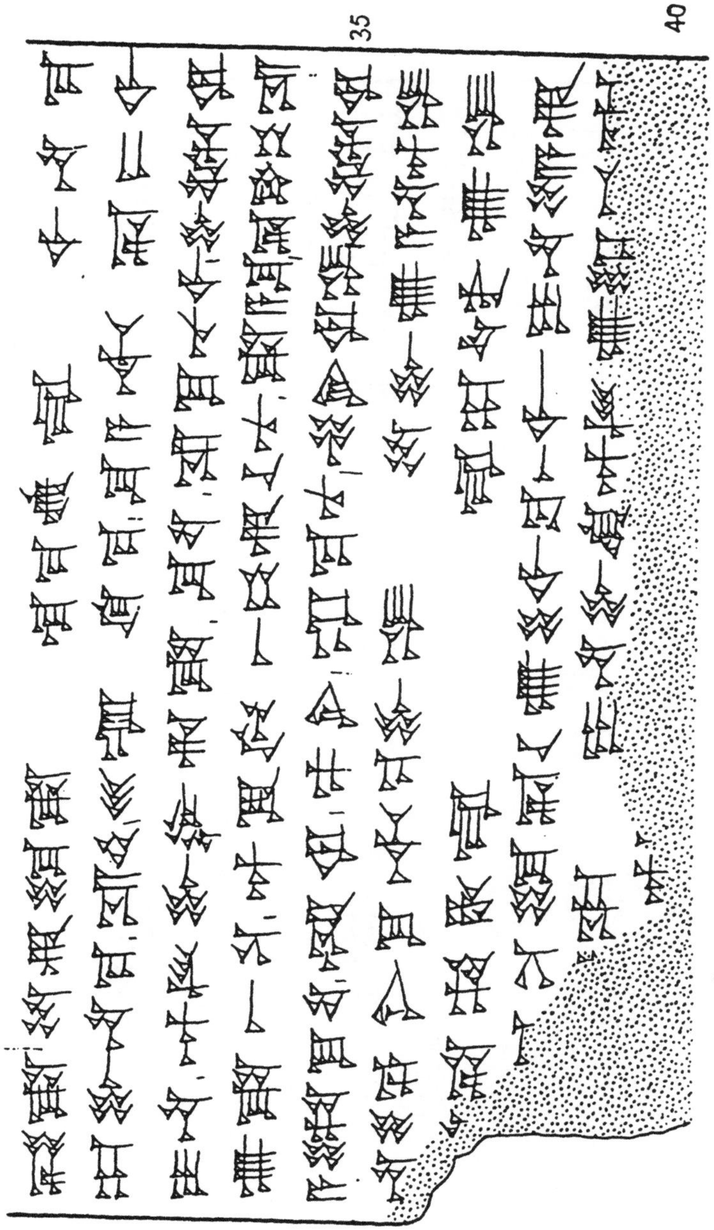

40559.

REVERSE.

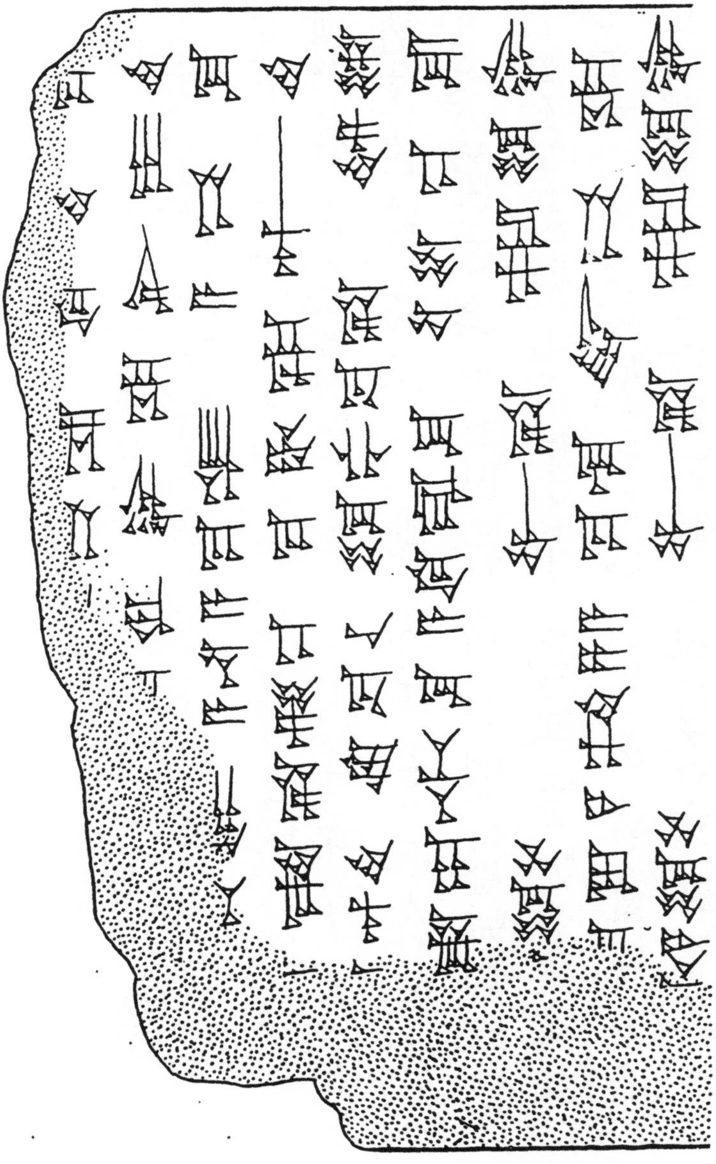

40559.

REVERSE (cont.).

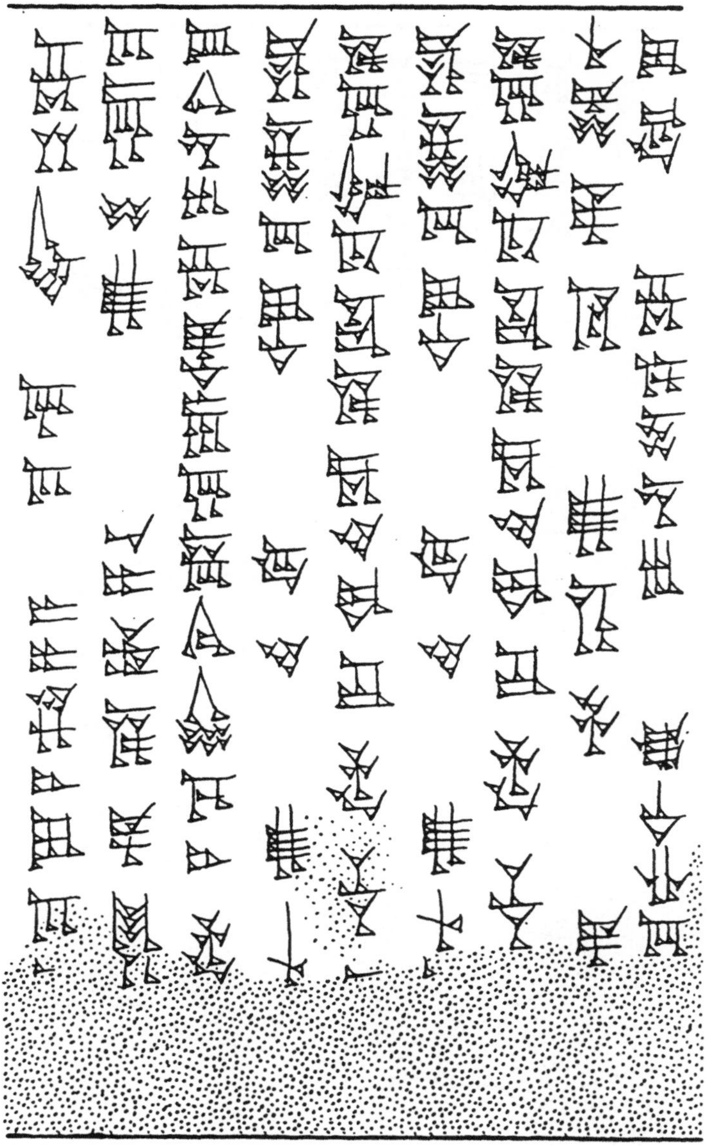

40559.

REVERSE (Cont.).

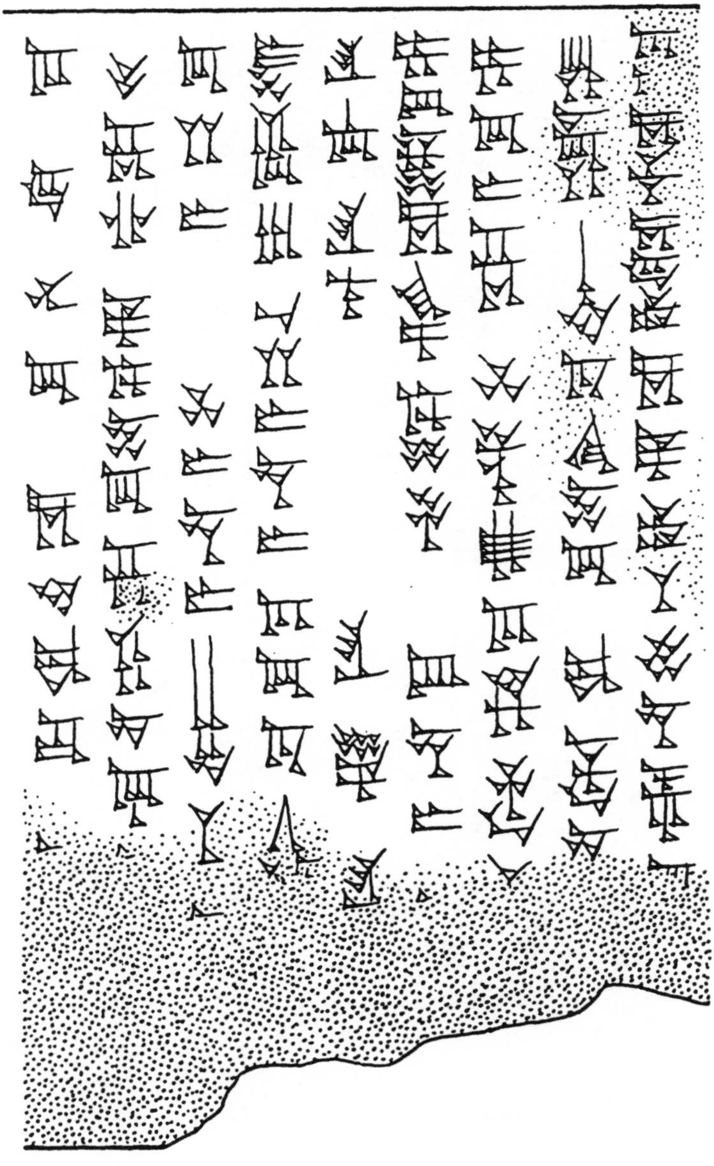

40559.

REVERSE (cont.).

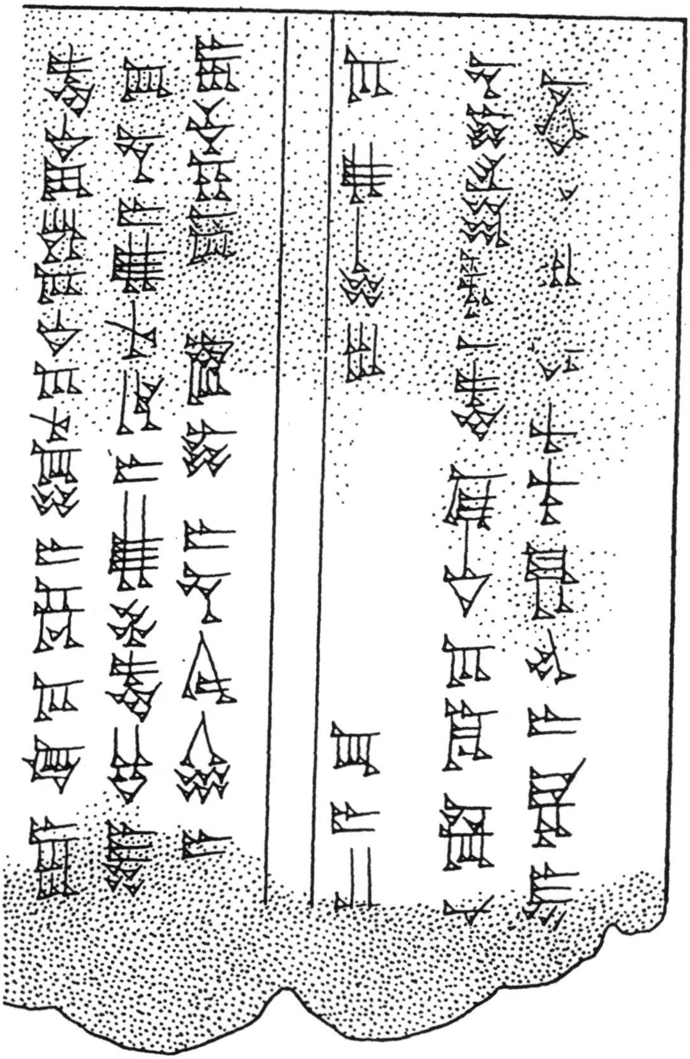

92632 + 93048.

OBVERSE.

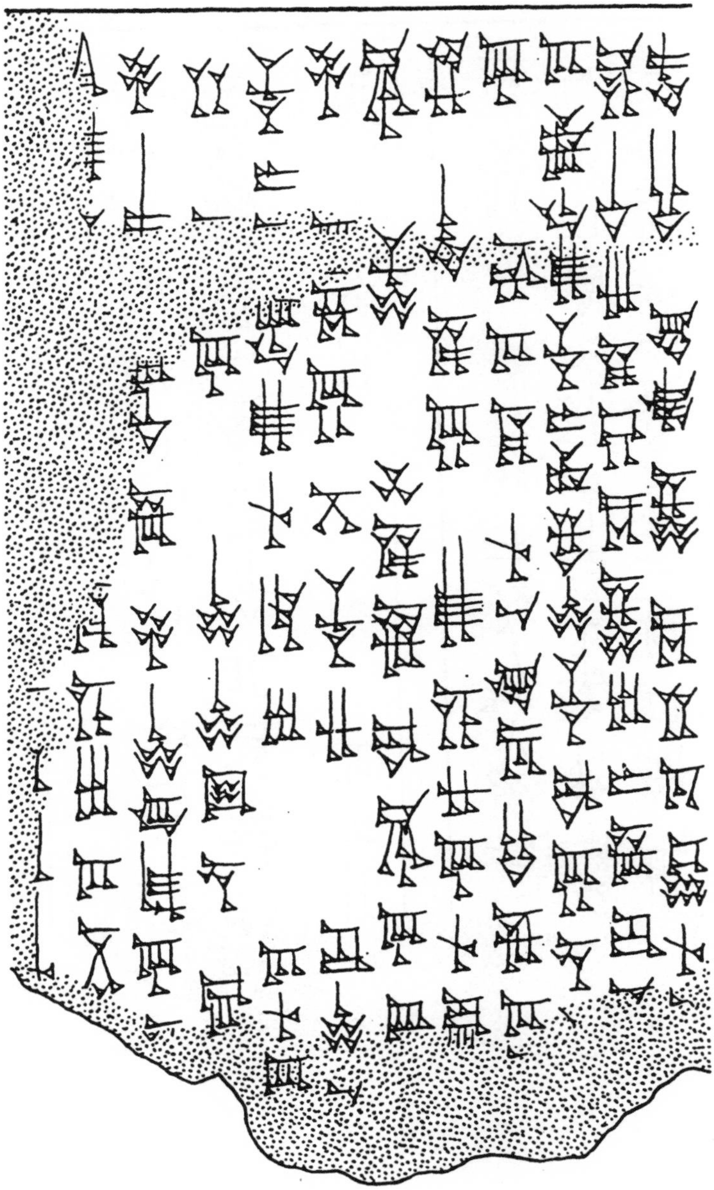

92632 + 93048.

OBVERSE (cont.).

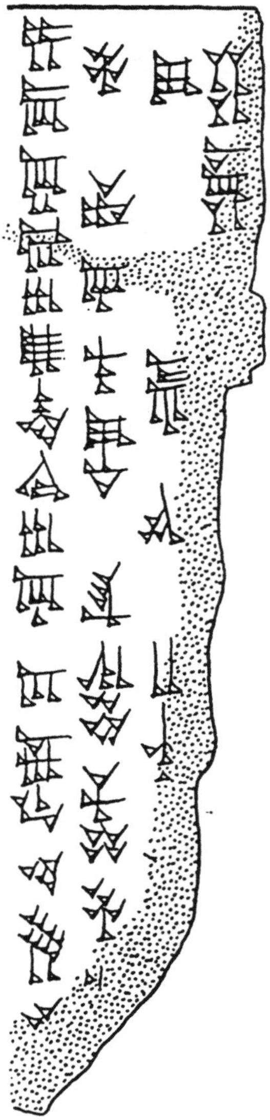

REVERSE.

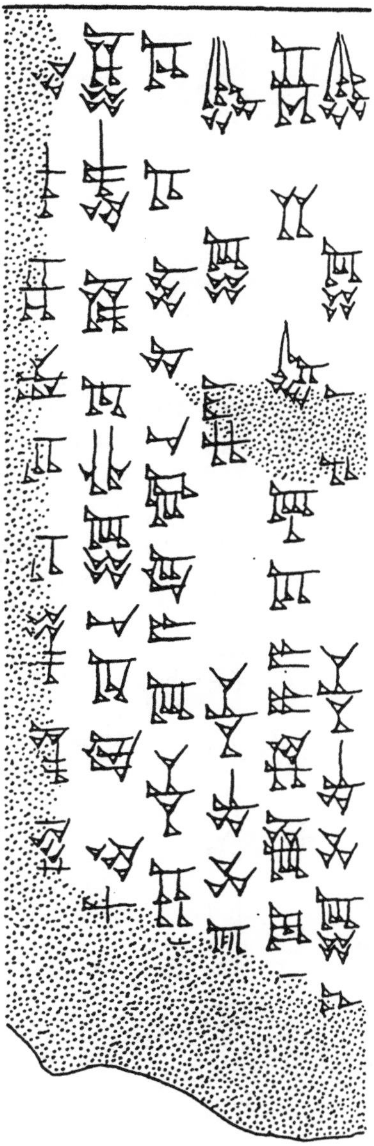

92632 + 93048.

REVERSE (cont.).

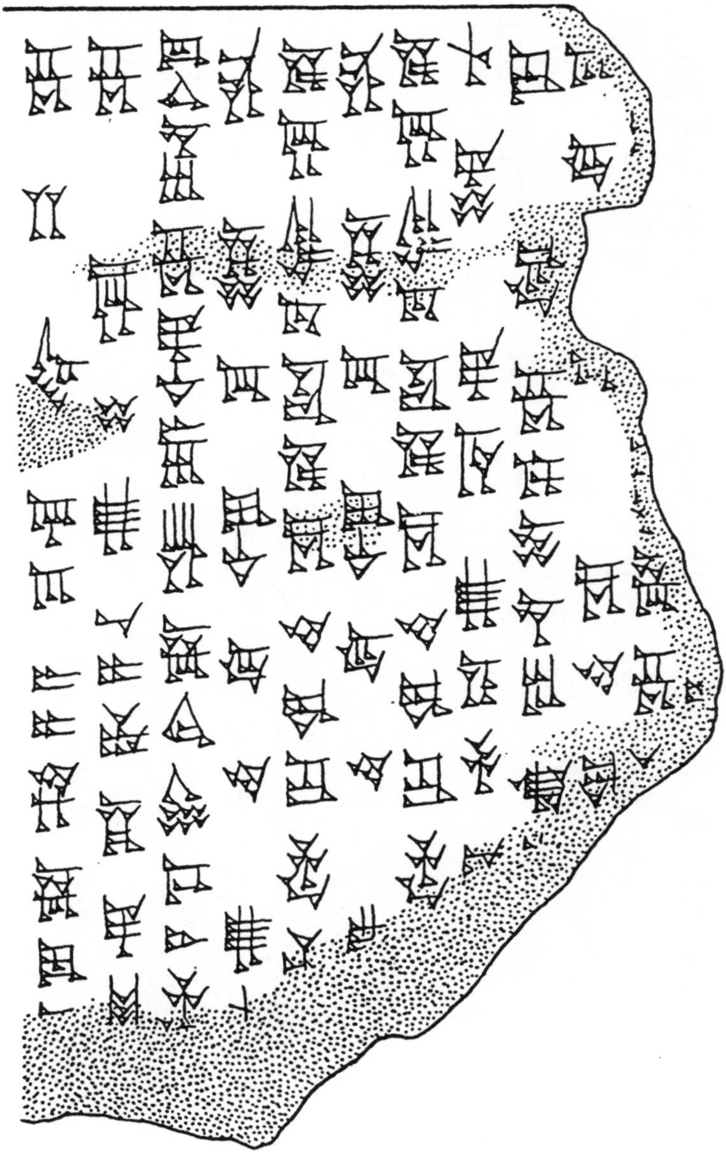

82-9-18, 1403 + 6316.

OBVERSE.

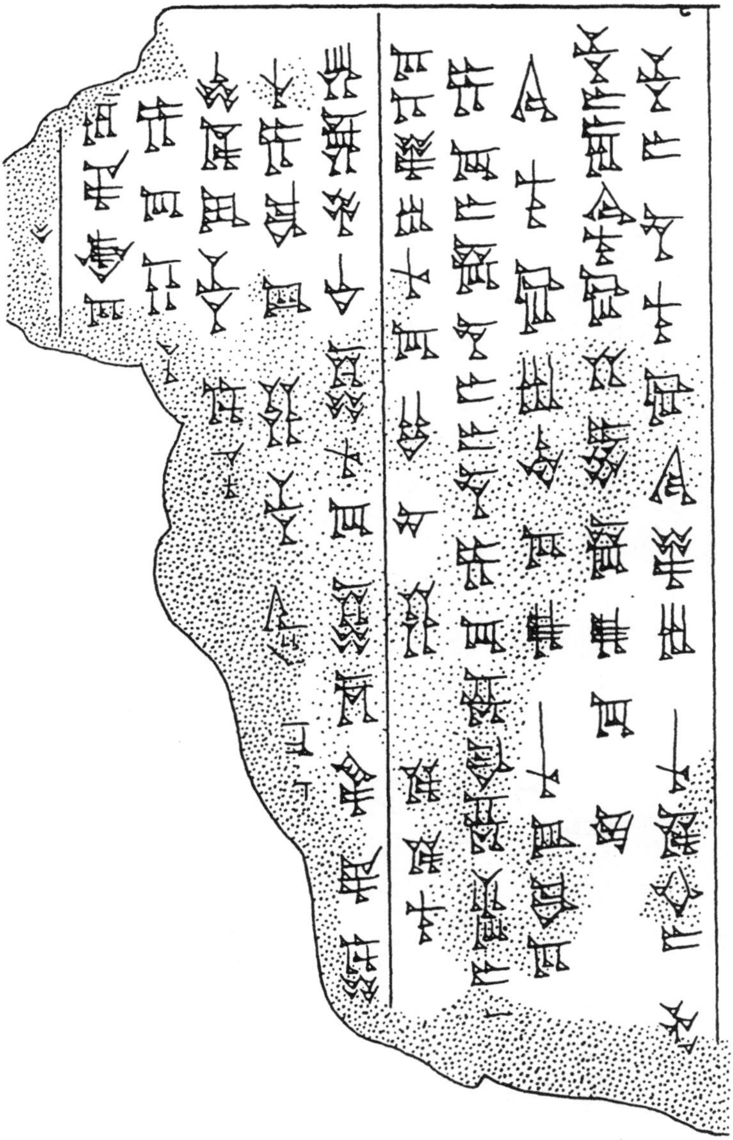

82-9-18, 1403 + 6316.

OBVERSE (Cont.).

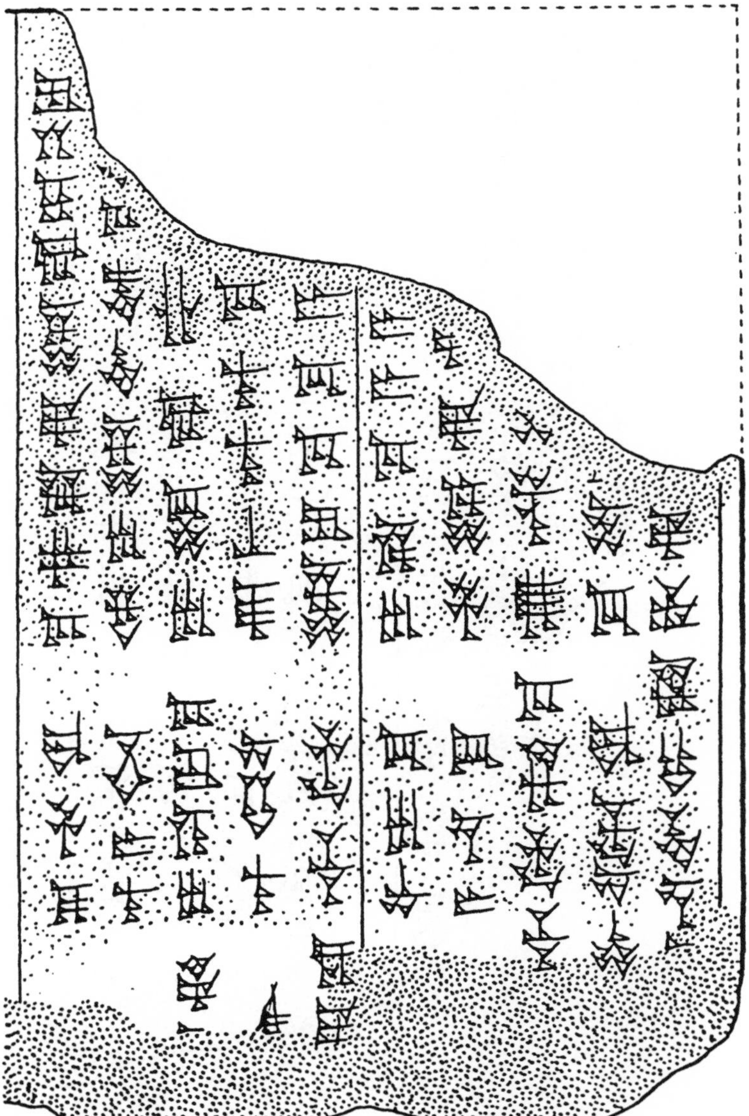

82-9-18, 1403 + 6316.

REVERSE.

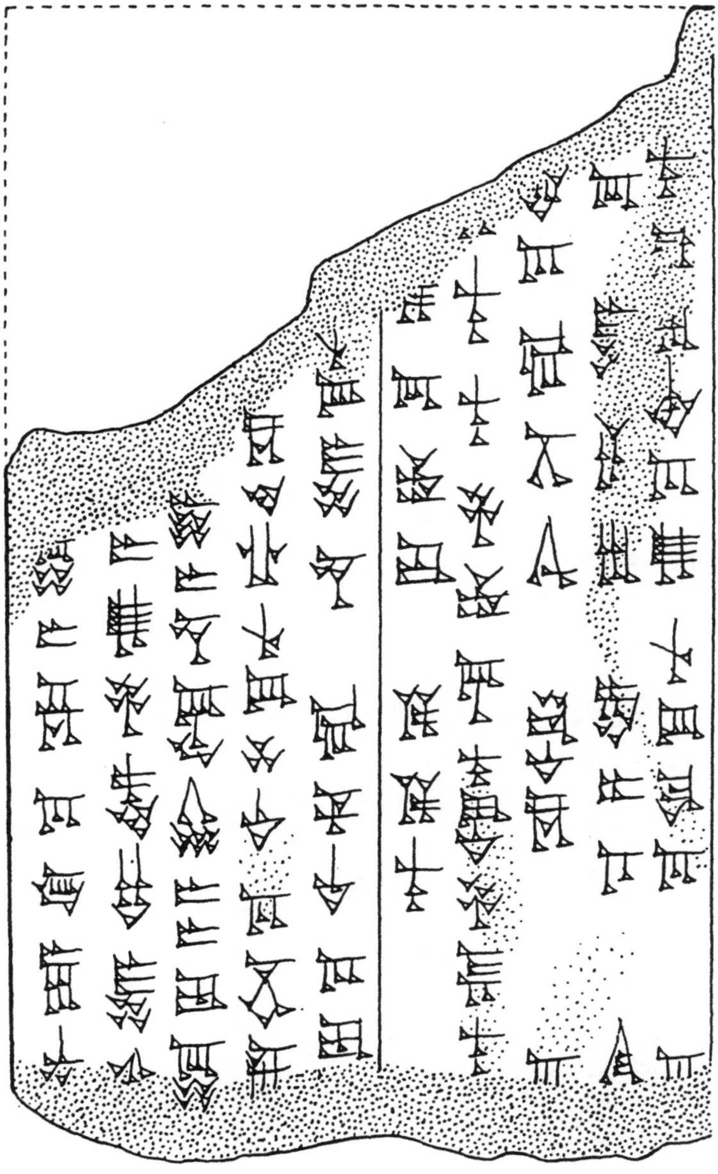

82-9-18, 1403 + 6316.

REVERSE (Cont.).

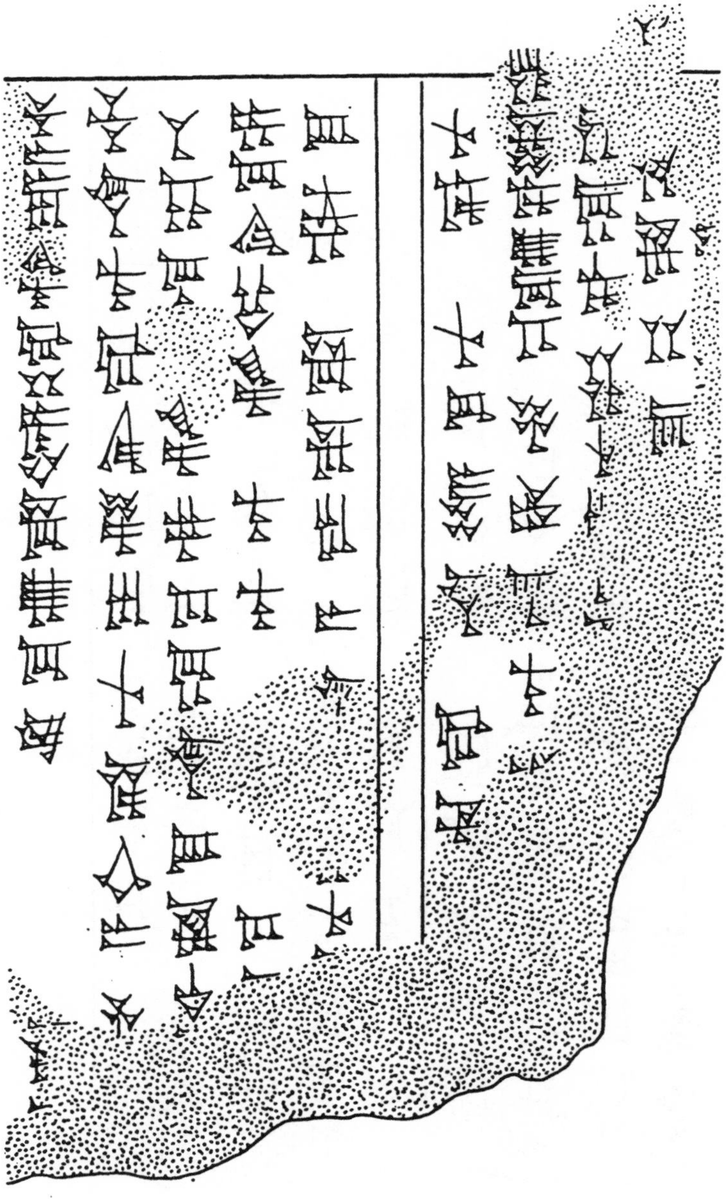

82-9-18, 6950 + 83-1-18, 1868.

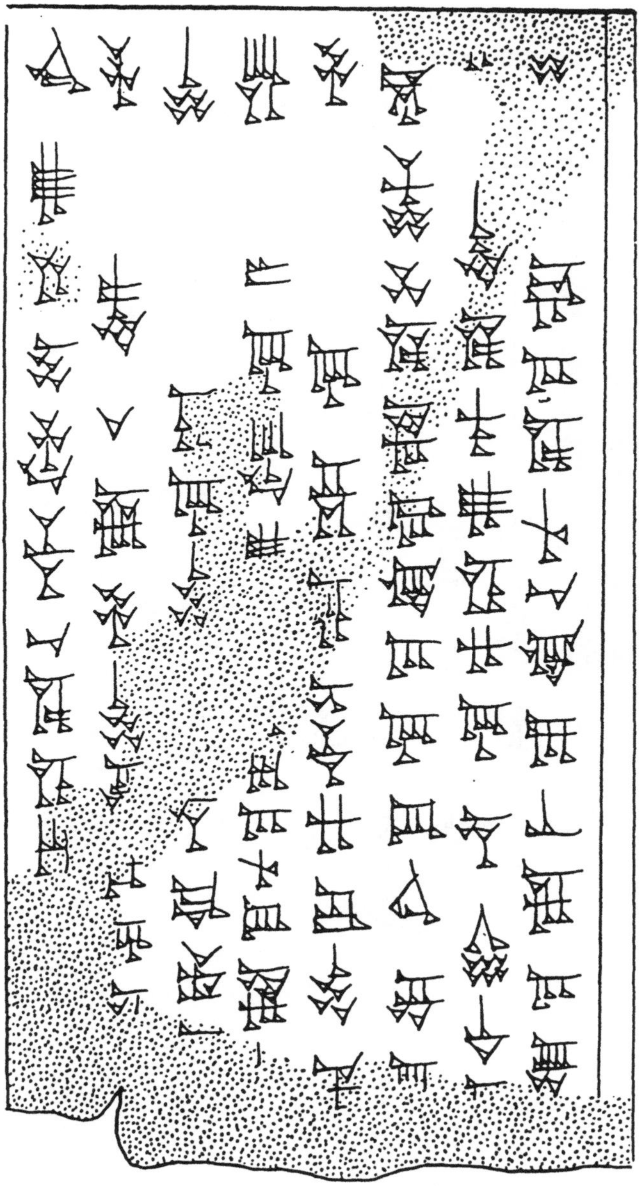

The text is an extract from a practice-tablet.

42285.

OBVERSE.

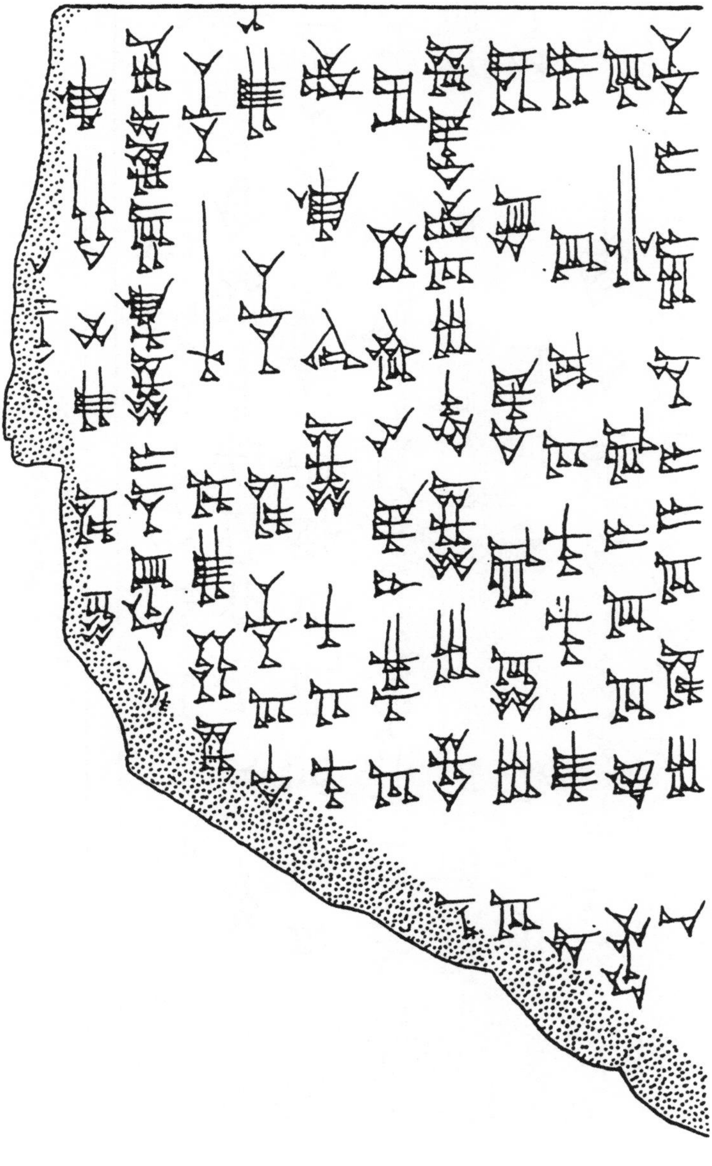

42285.

OBVERSE (Cont.).

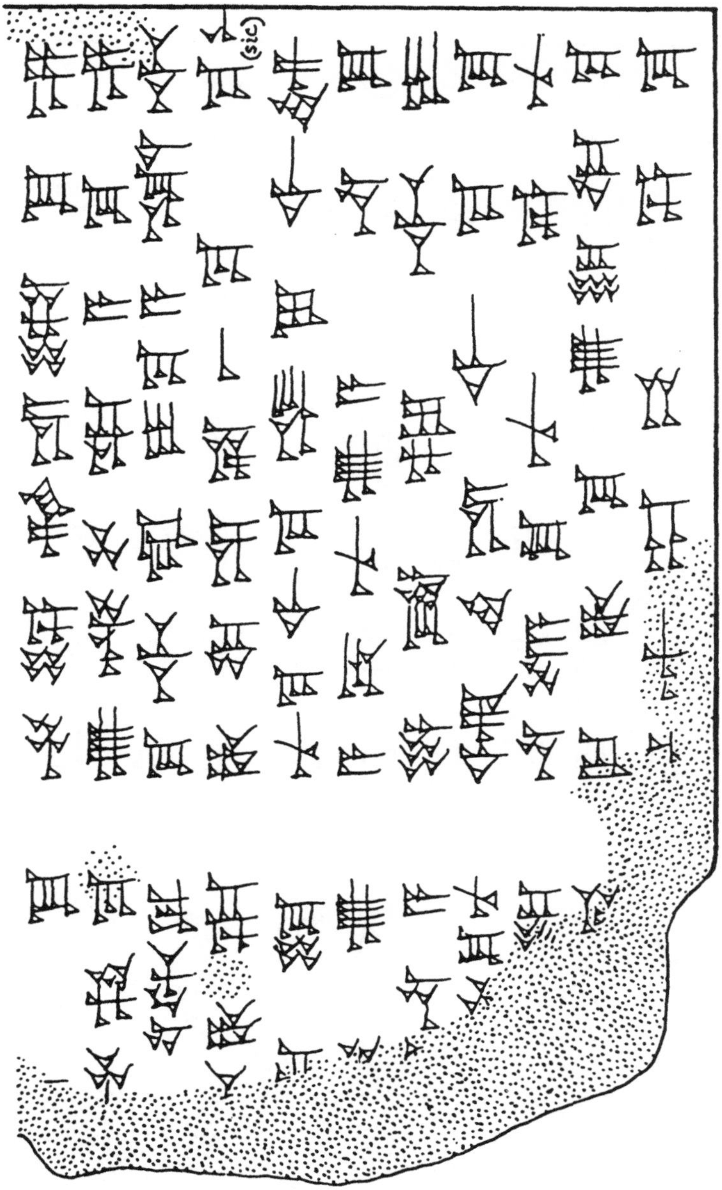

42285.

REVERSE.

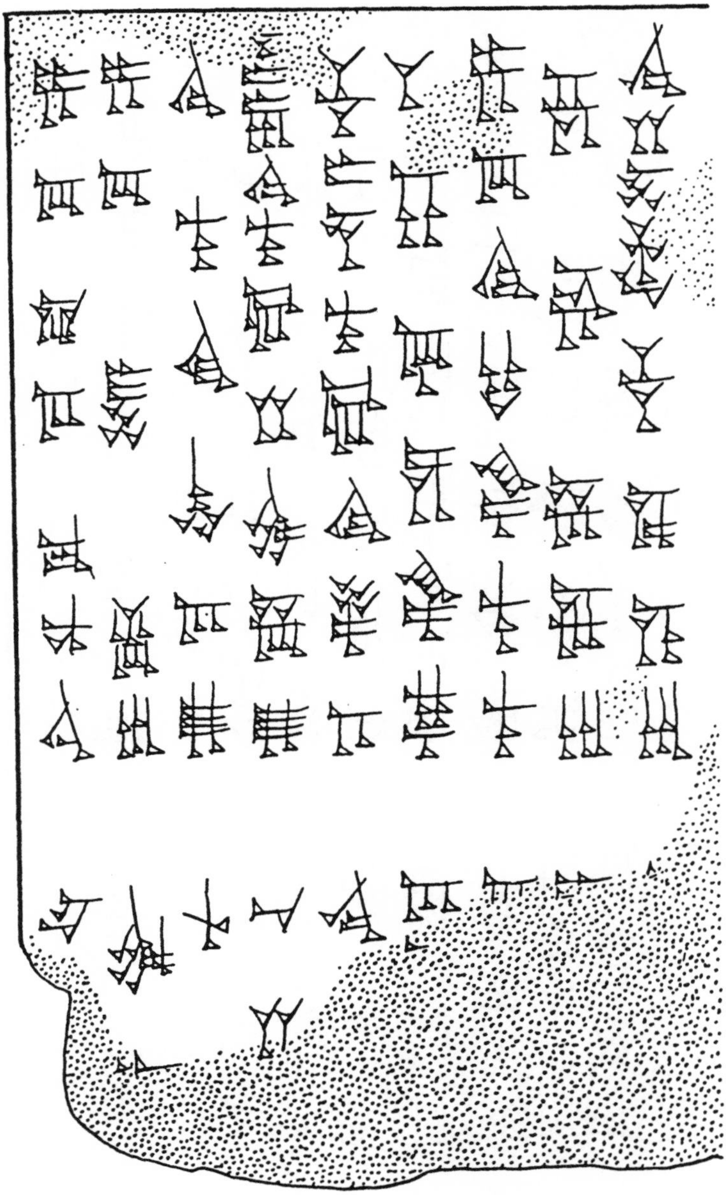

42285.

REVERSE (Cont.).

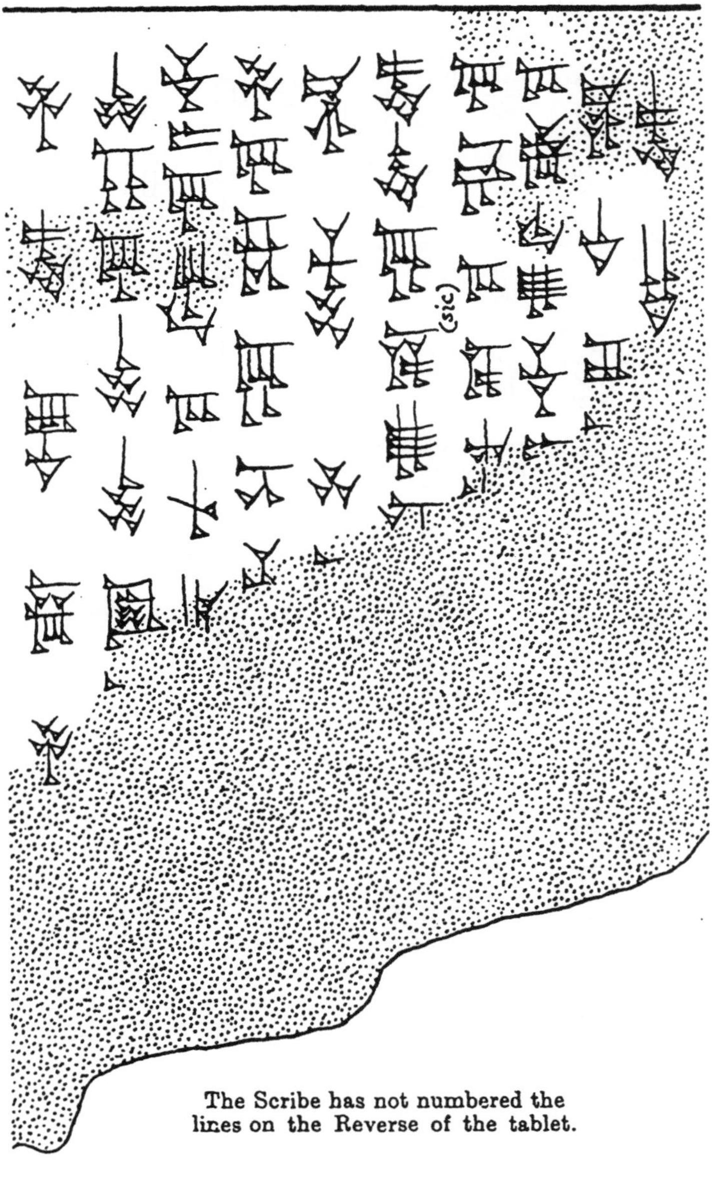

The Scribe has not numbered the
lines on the Reverse of the tablet.

82-9-18, 5448 + 83-1-18, 2116.

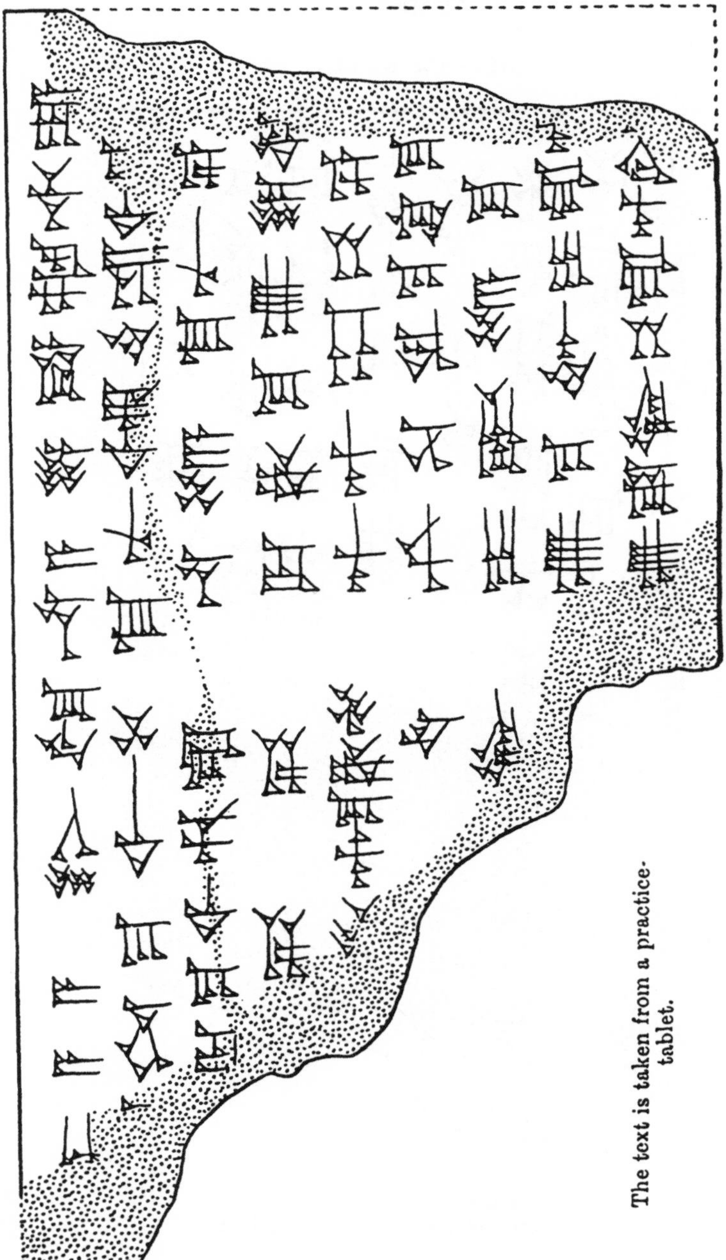

The text is taken from a practice-tablet.

92629.

OBVERSE.

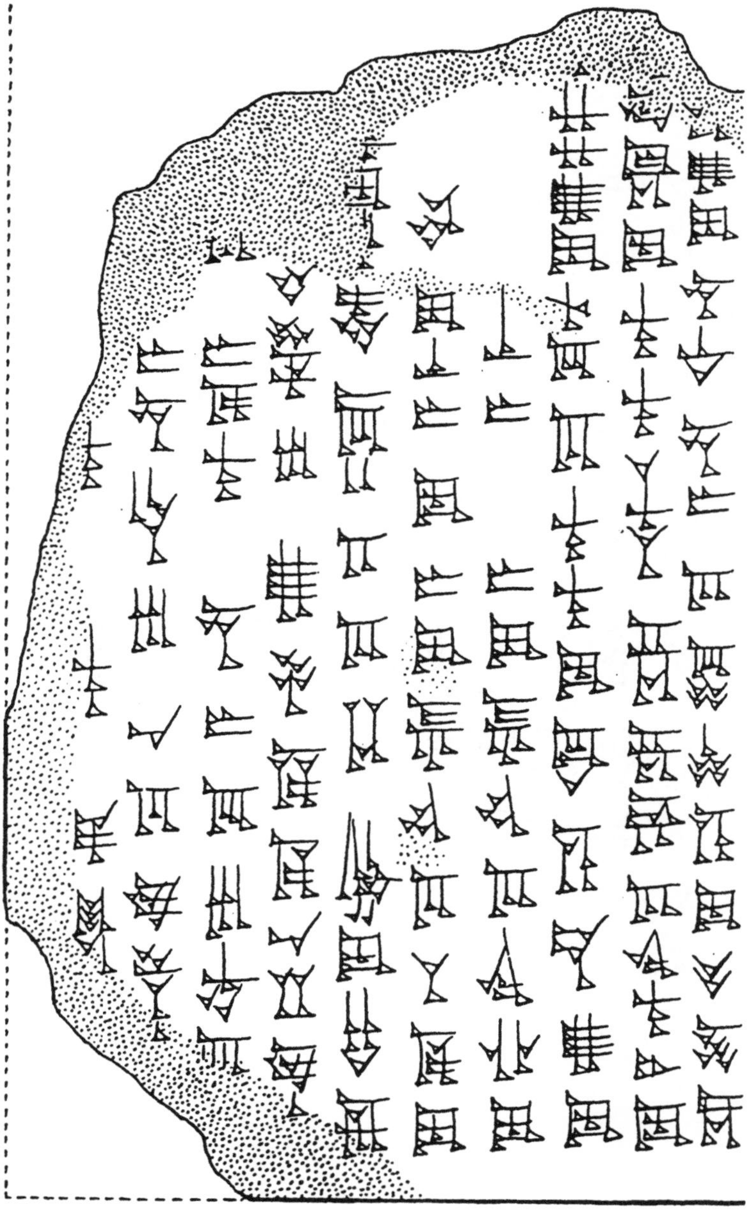

92629.

OBVERSE (cont.).

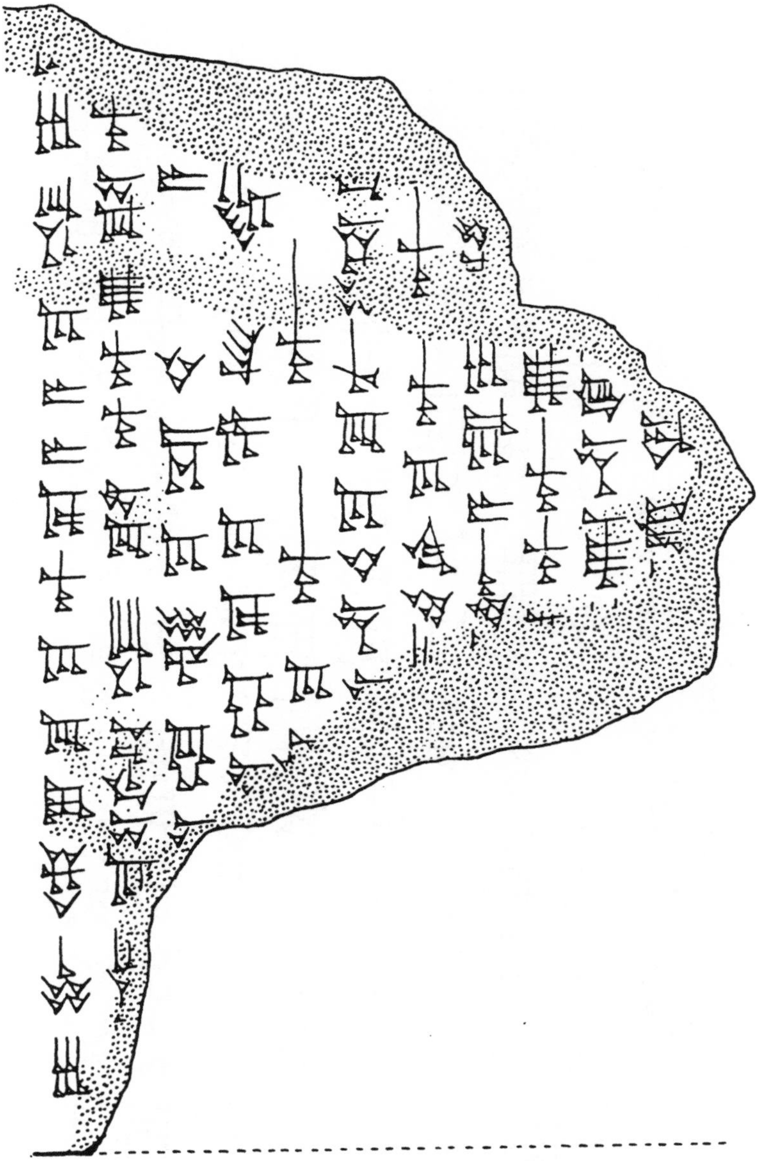

92629.

REVERSE.

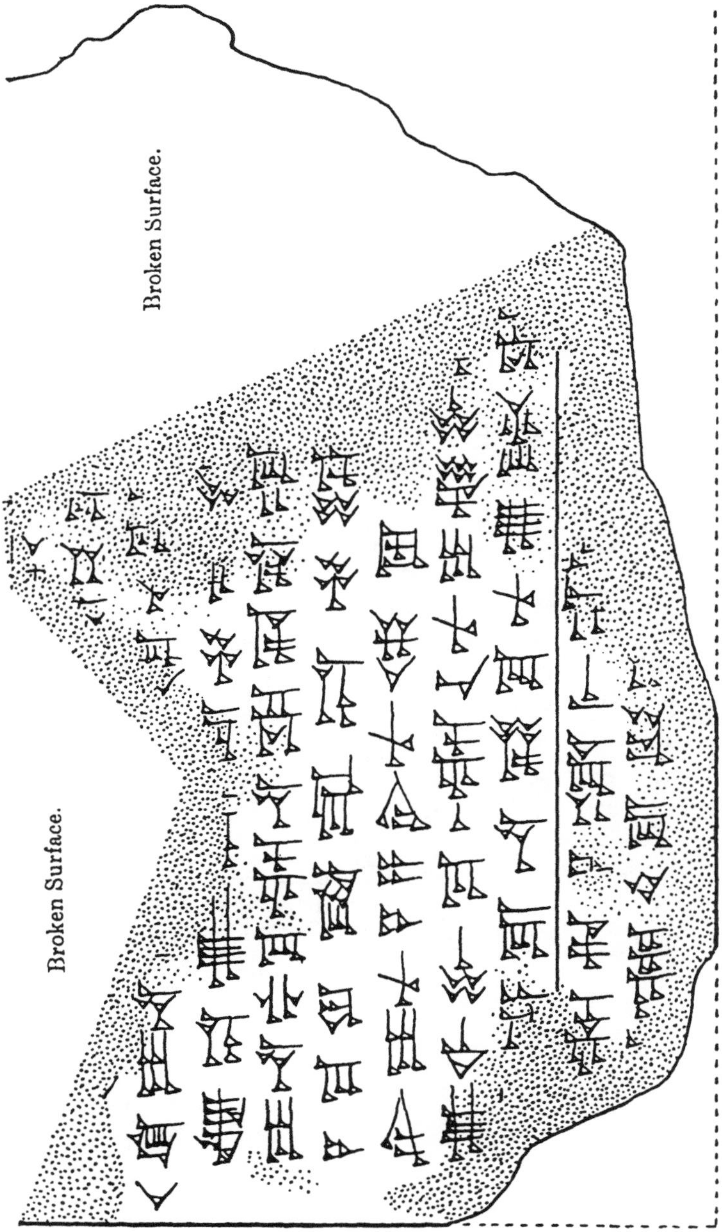

91139 + 93073.

OBVERSE.

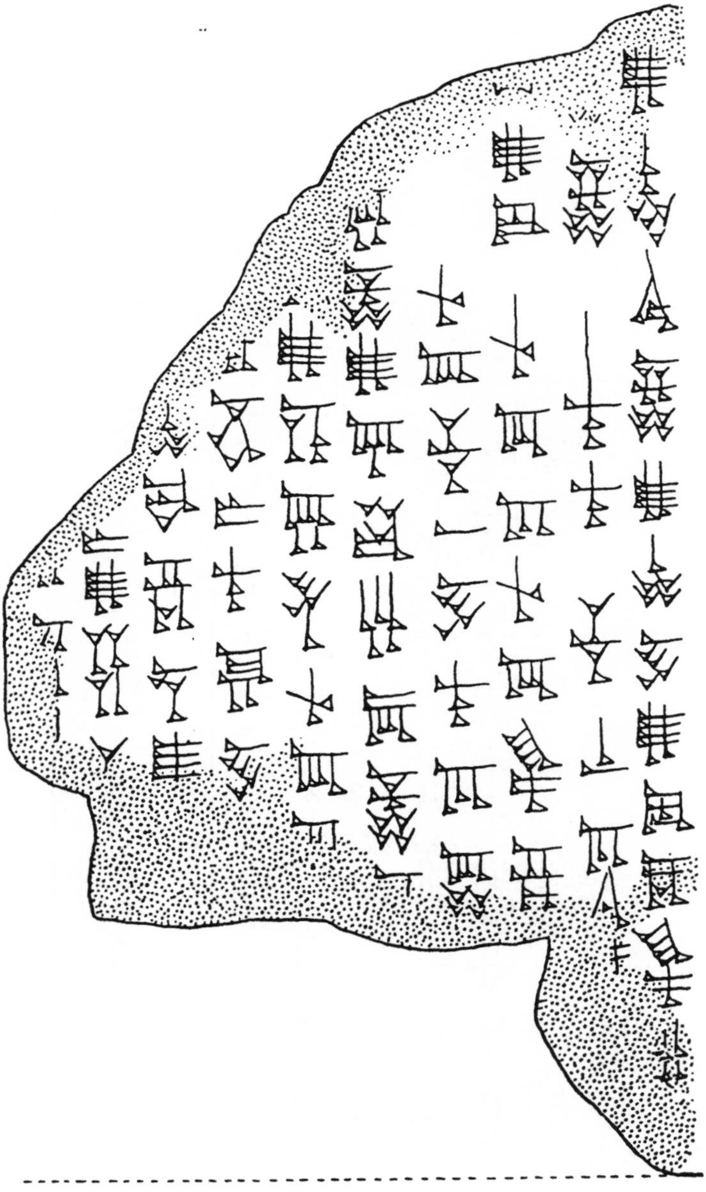

91139 + 93073.

OBVERSE (cont.).

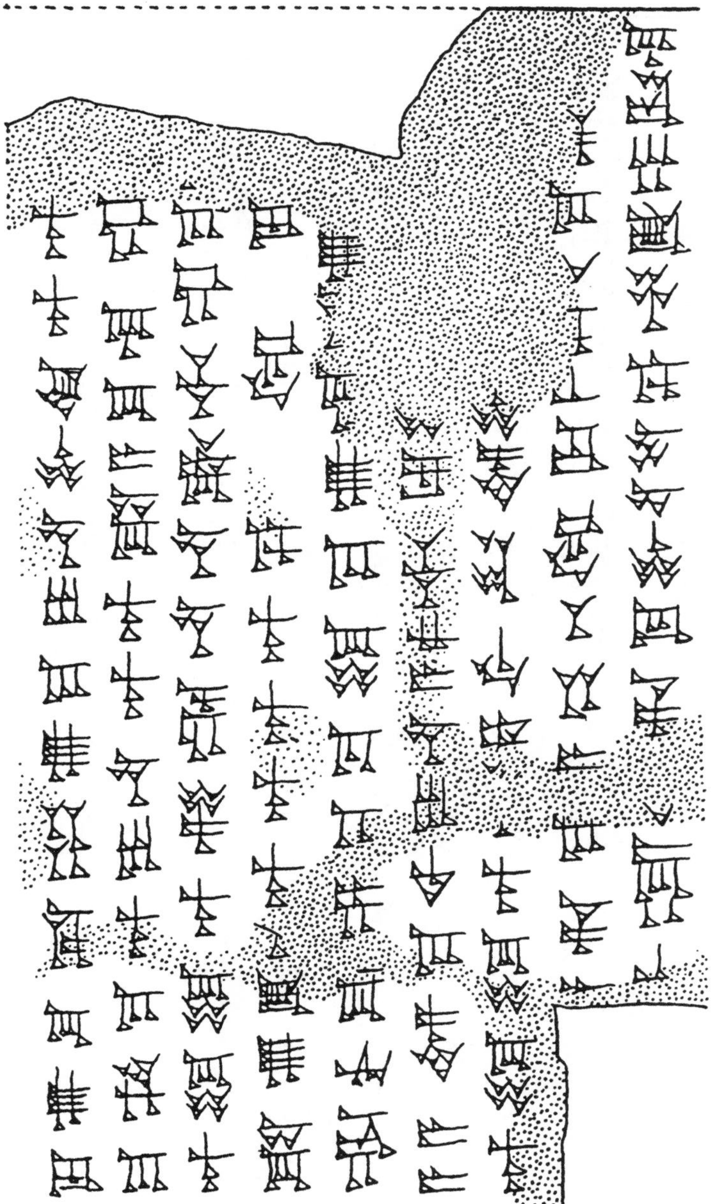

91139 + 93073.

OBVERSE (cont.).

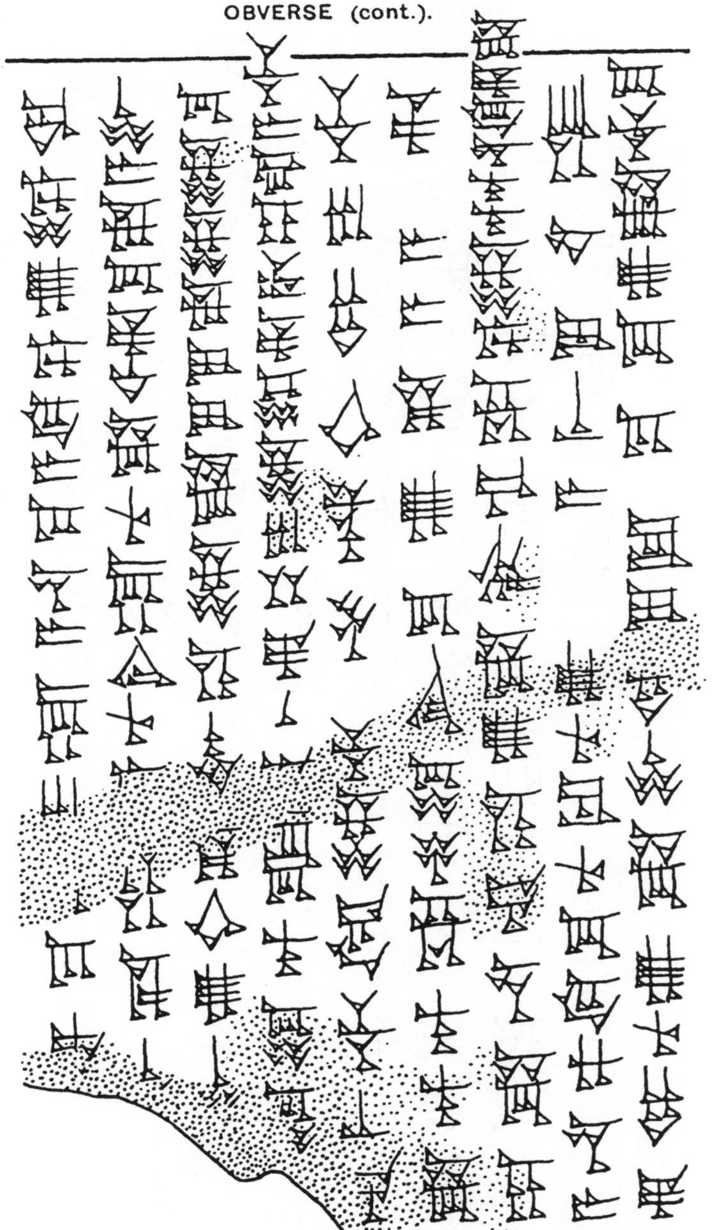

91139 + 93073.

OBVERSE (Cont.).

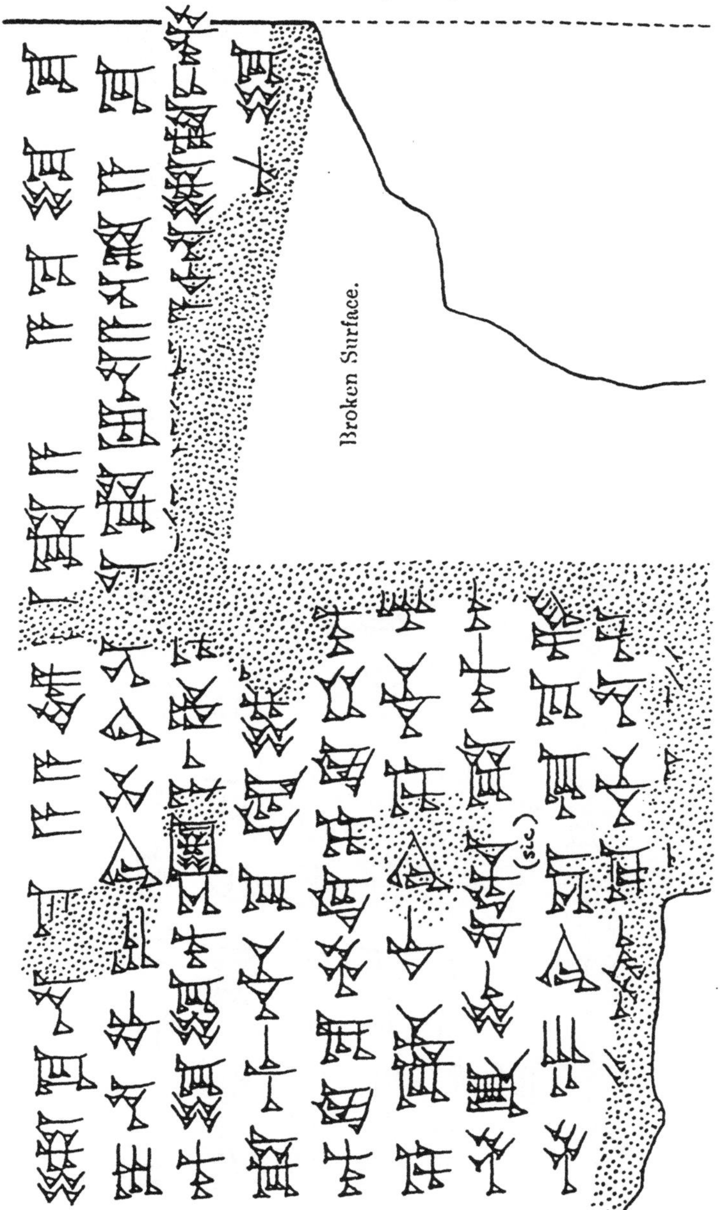

91139 + 93073.

REVERSE.

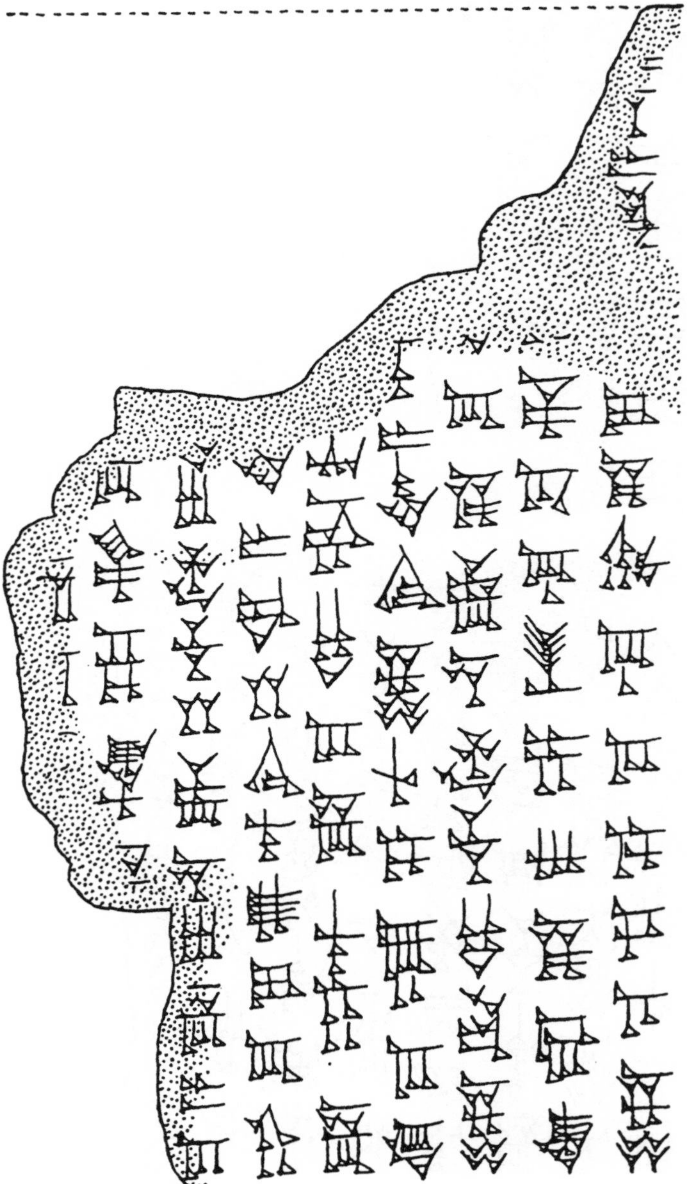

91139 + 93073.

REVERSE (cont.).

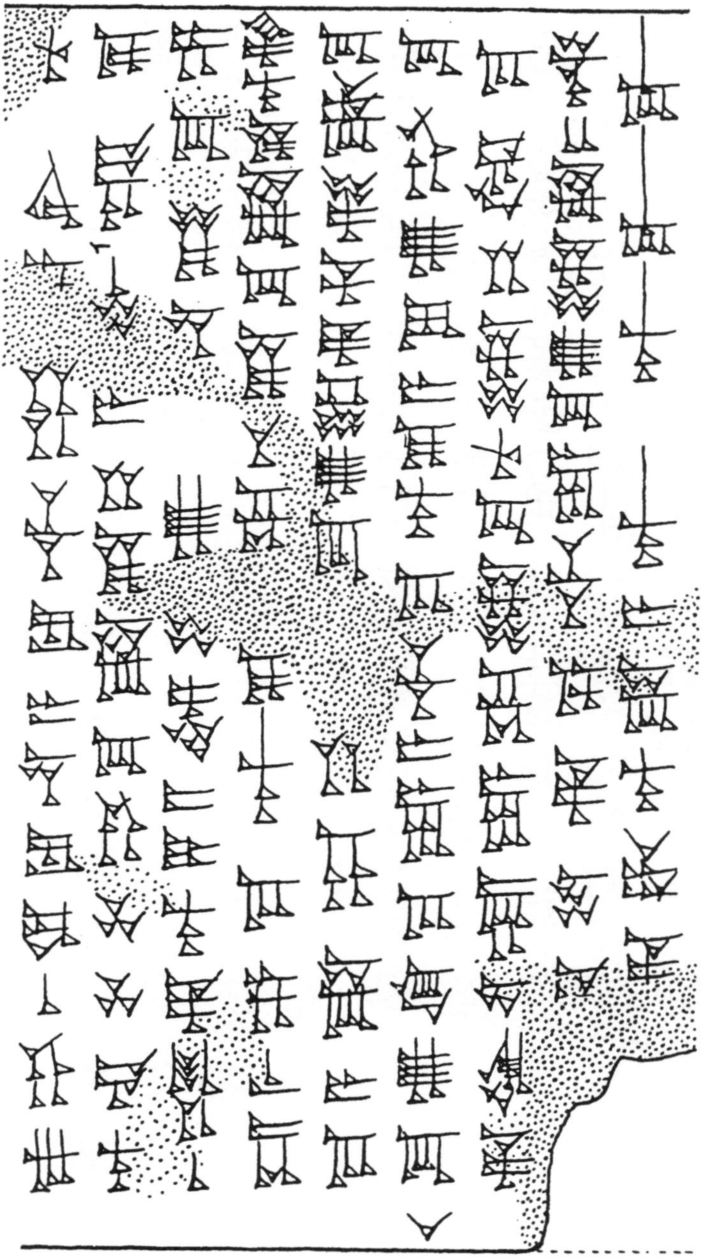

1. Erasure by the Scribe.

91139 + 93073.

REVERSE (cont.).

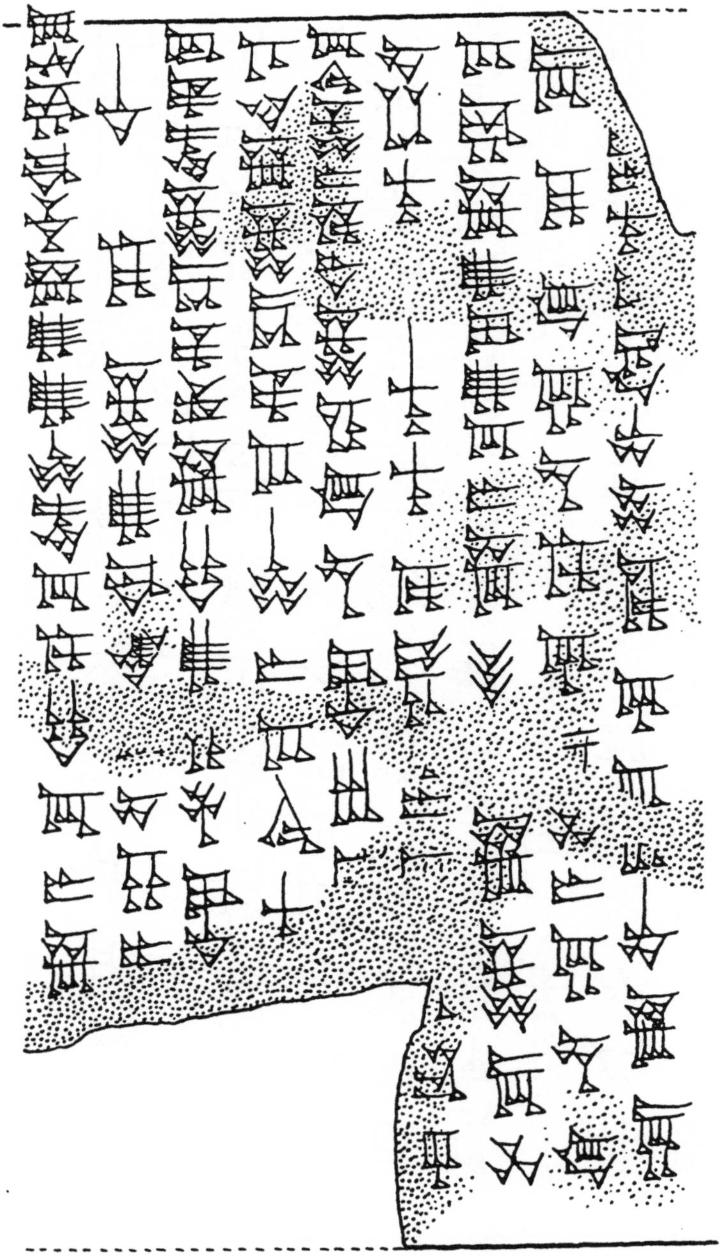

91139.+ 93073.

REVERSE (cont.).

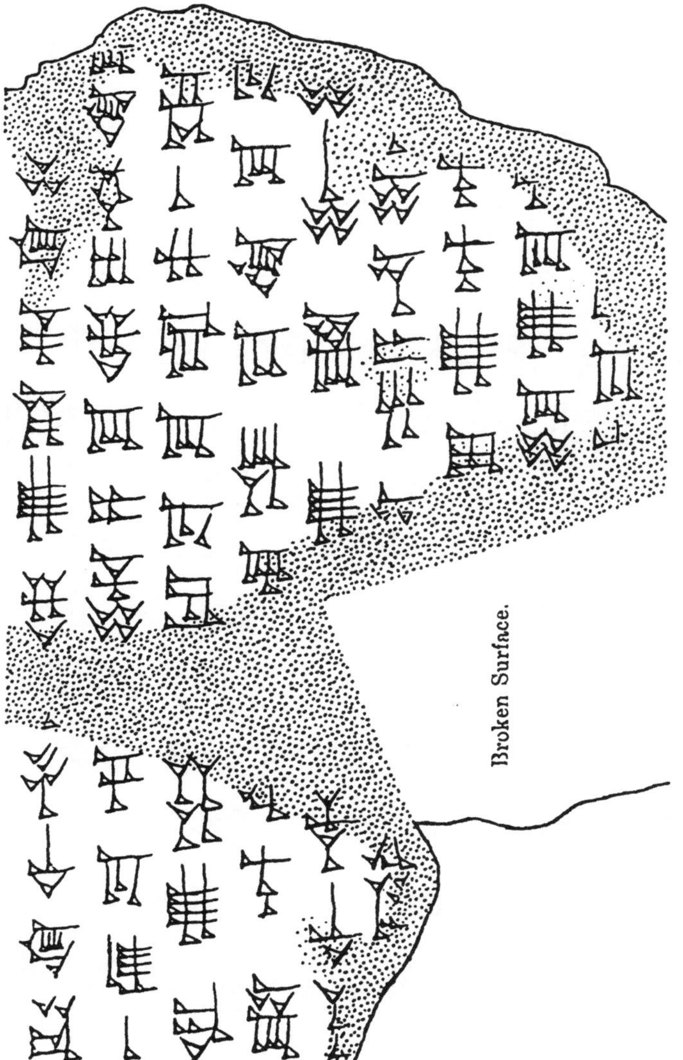

35506.

OBVERSE.

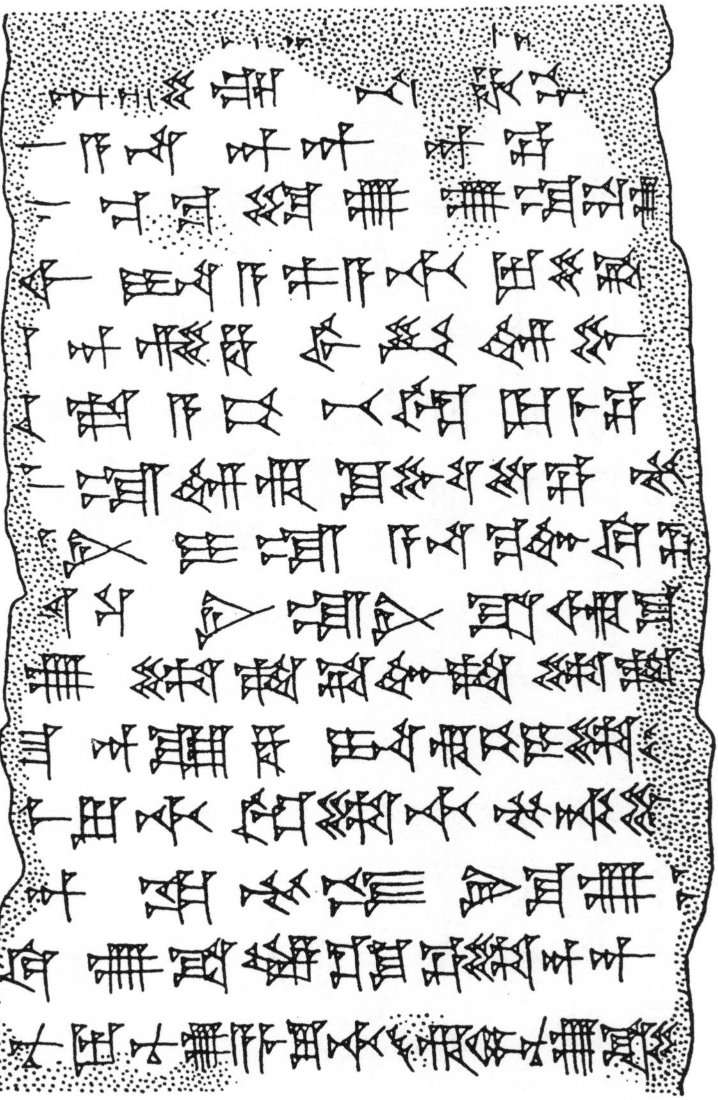

35506.

OBVERSE (Cont.).

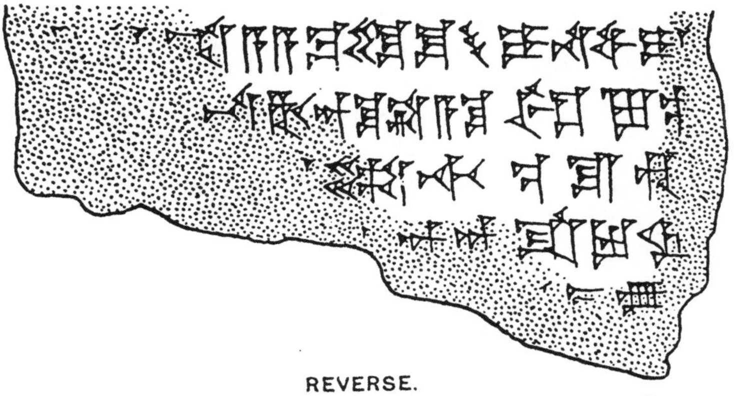

REVERSE.

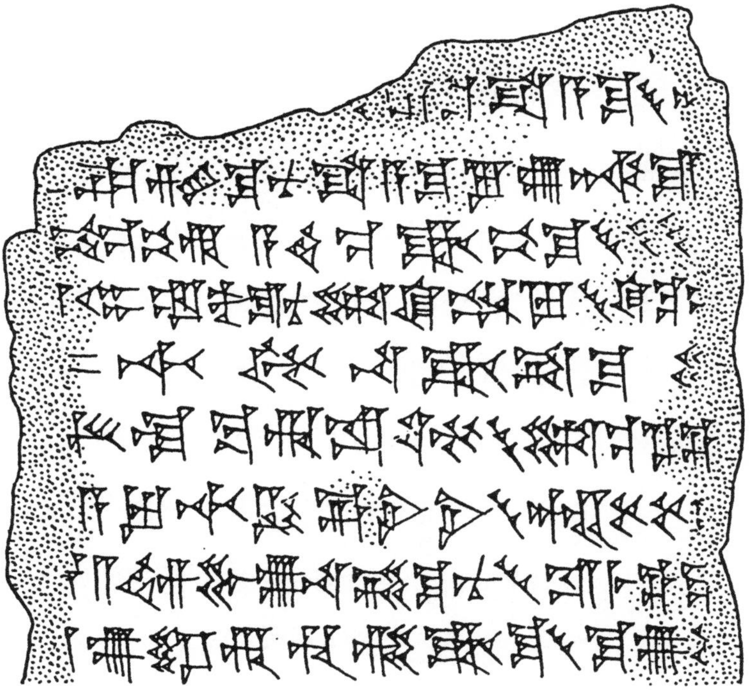

35506.

REVERSE (Cont.).

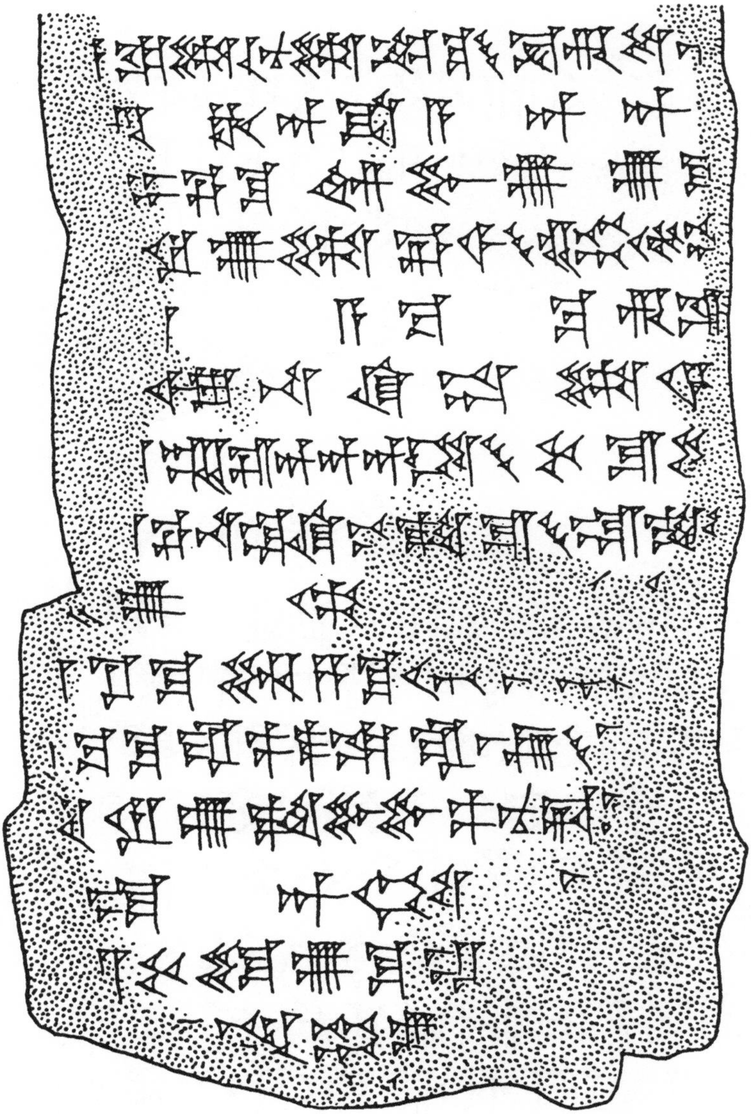

82-7-14, 4005.

OBVERSE.

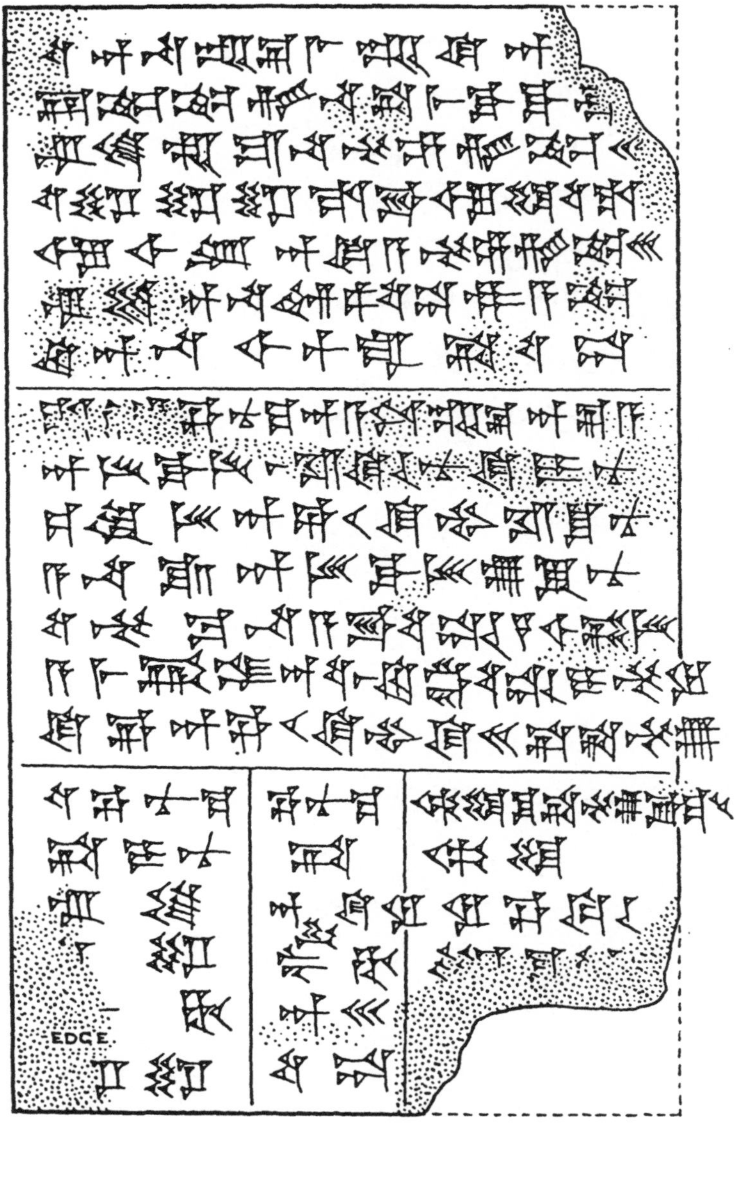

82-7-14, 4005.

REVERSE.

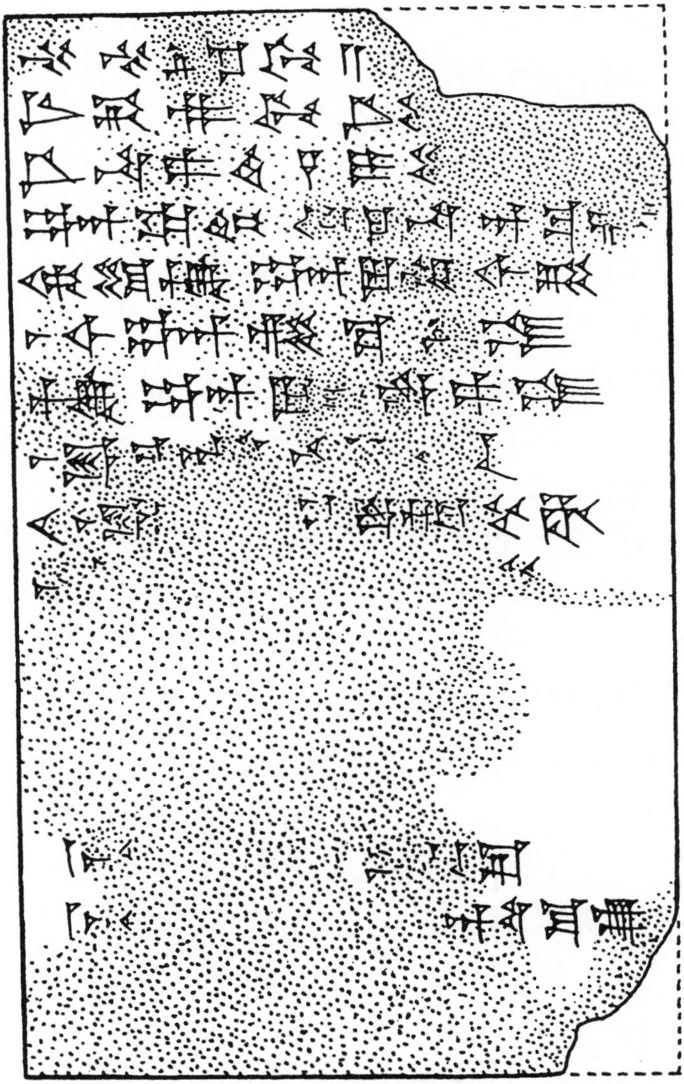

S. 11 + S. 980.

OBVERSE.

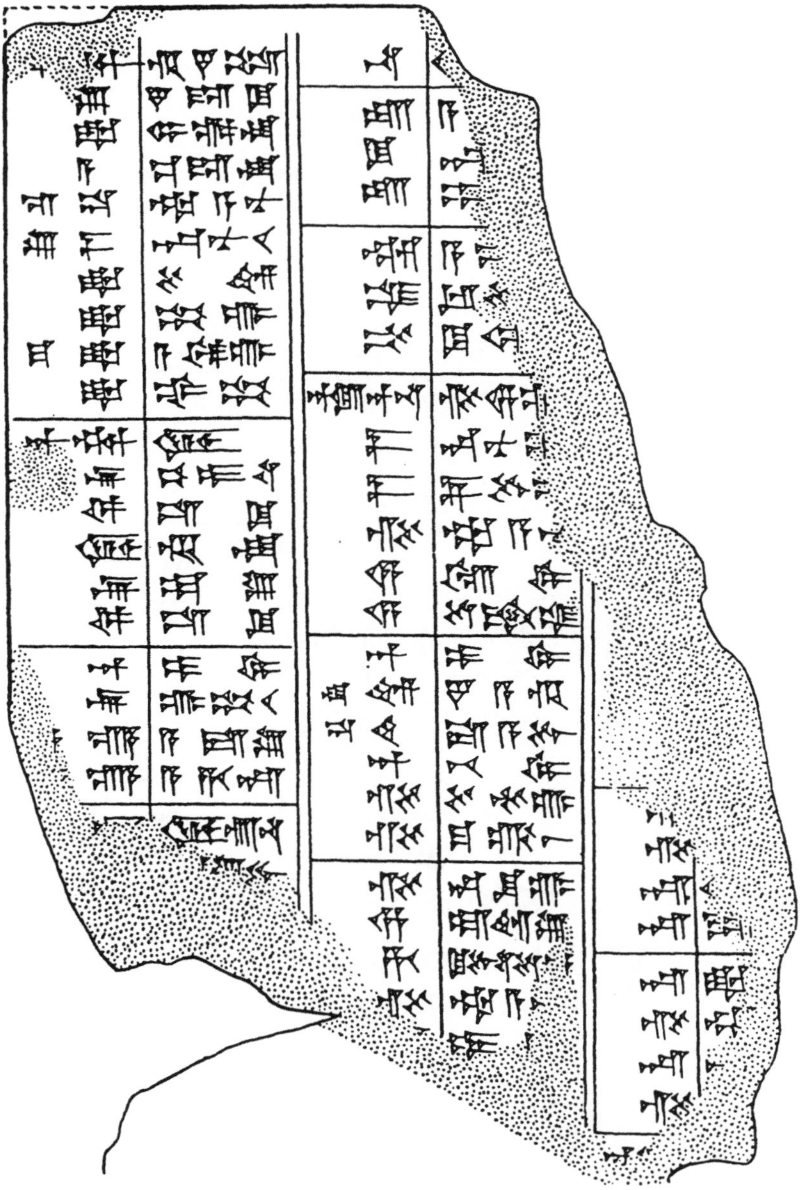

S. 11 + S. 980.

REVERSE.

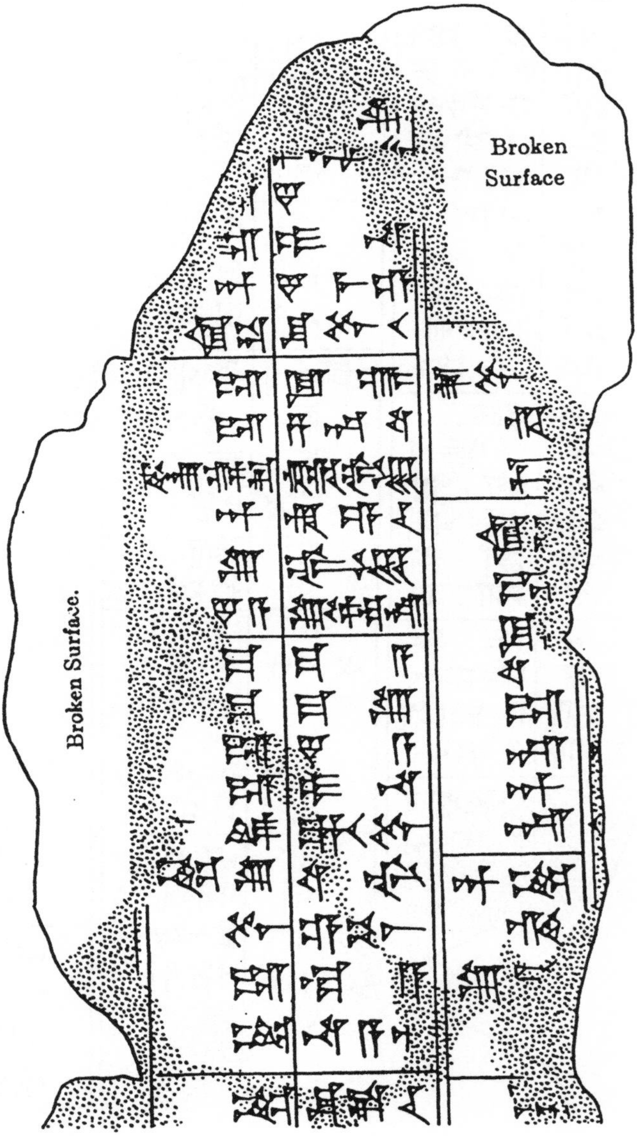

S. 11 + S. 980.

REVERSE (Cont.).

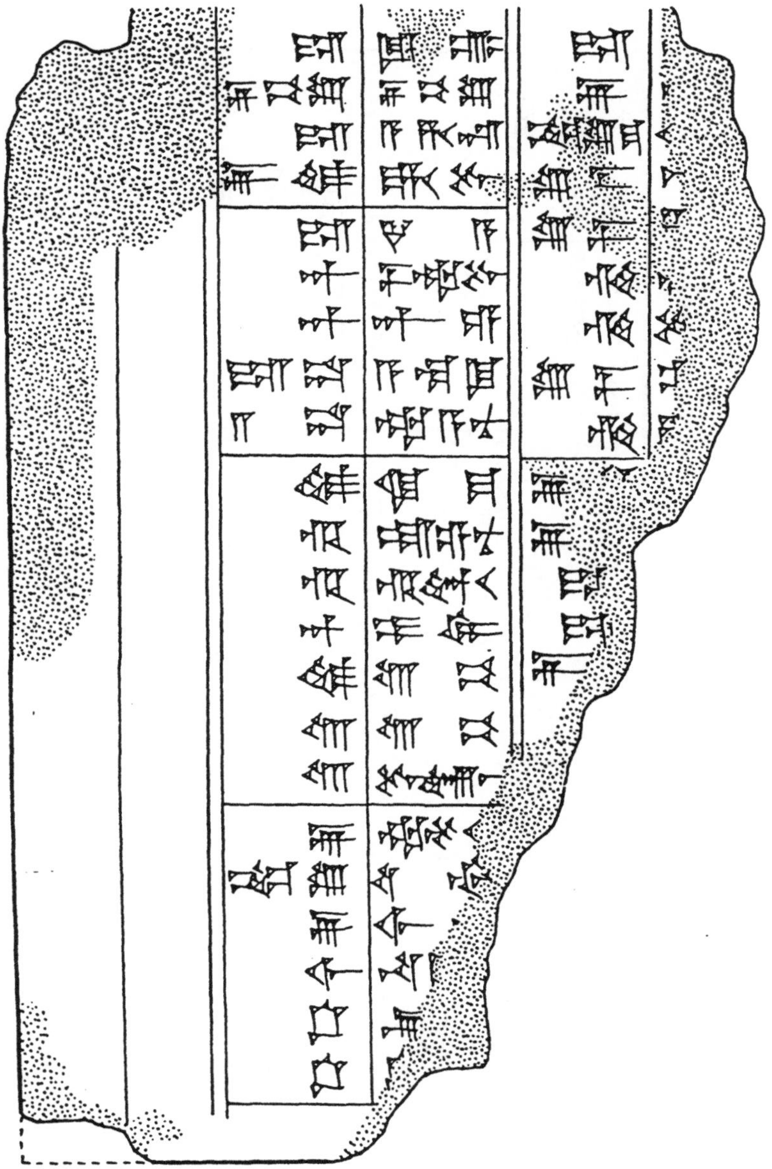

K. 4406.

REVERSE.

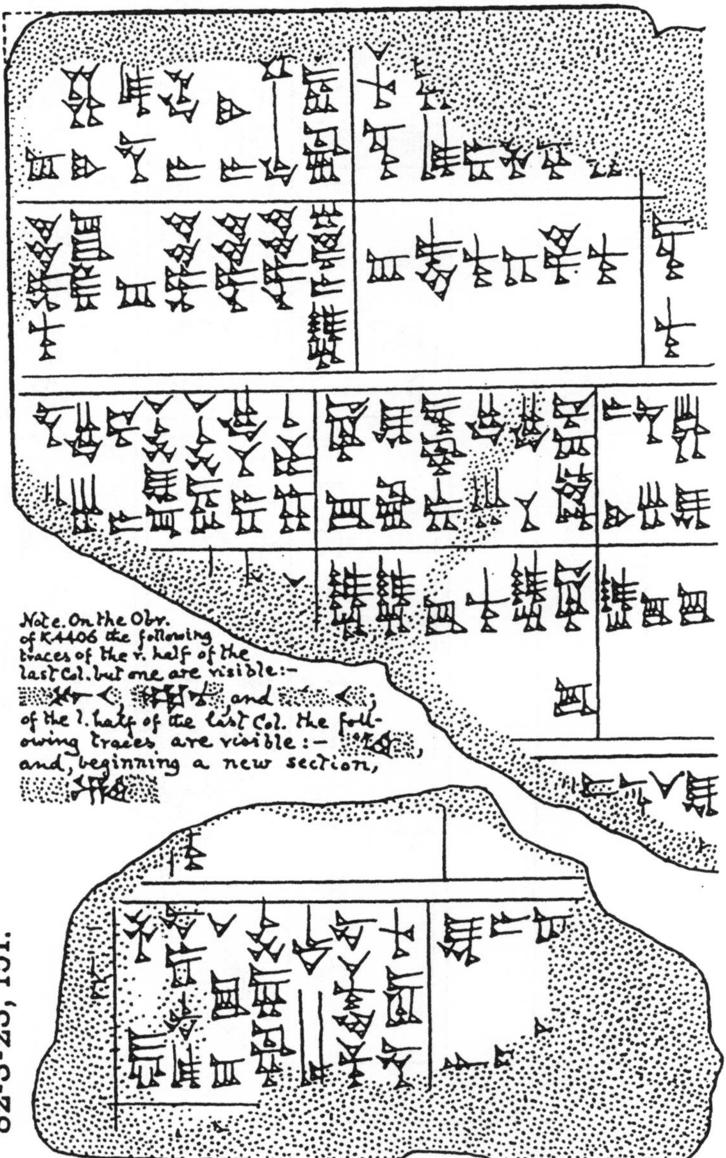
Note. On the Obv.
of K4406 the following
traces of the r. half of the
last Col. but one are visible:-
and ;
of the l. half of the last Col. the following traces are visible:- ,
and, beginning a new section,

82-3-23, 151.

K. 4406.

REVERSE (Cont.).

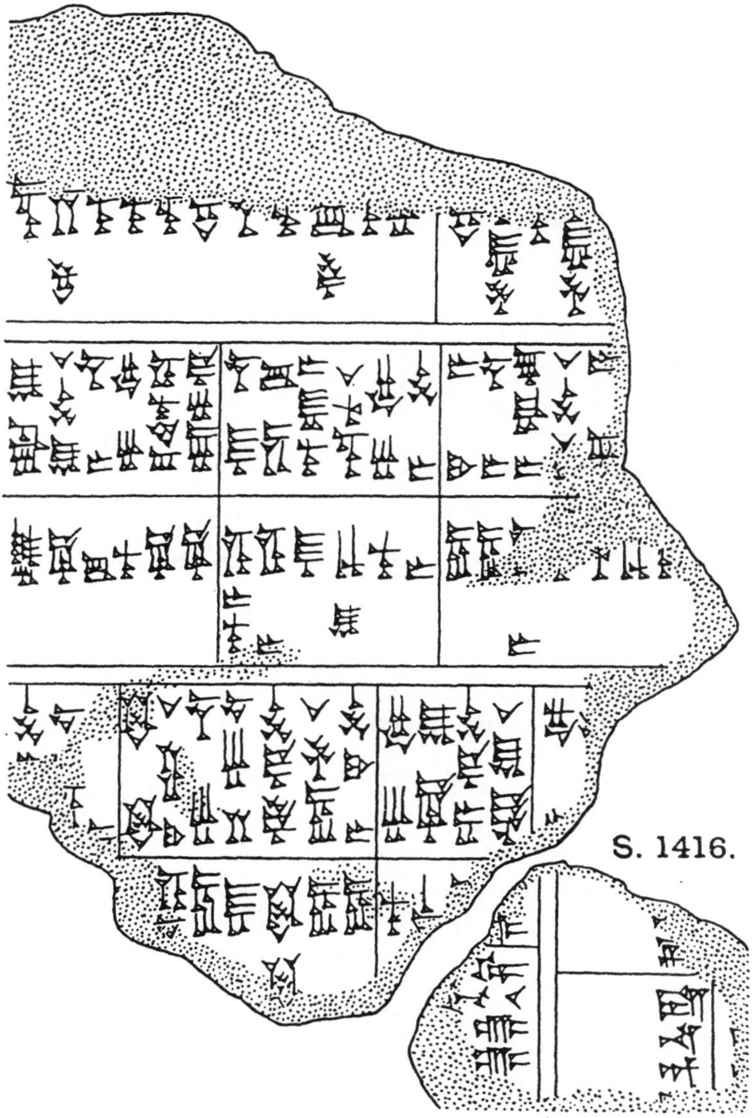

S. 1416.

R. 366 + 80-7-19, 293.

OBVERSE.

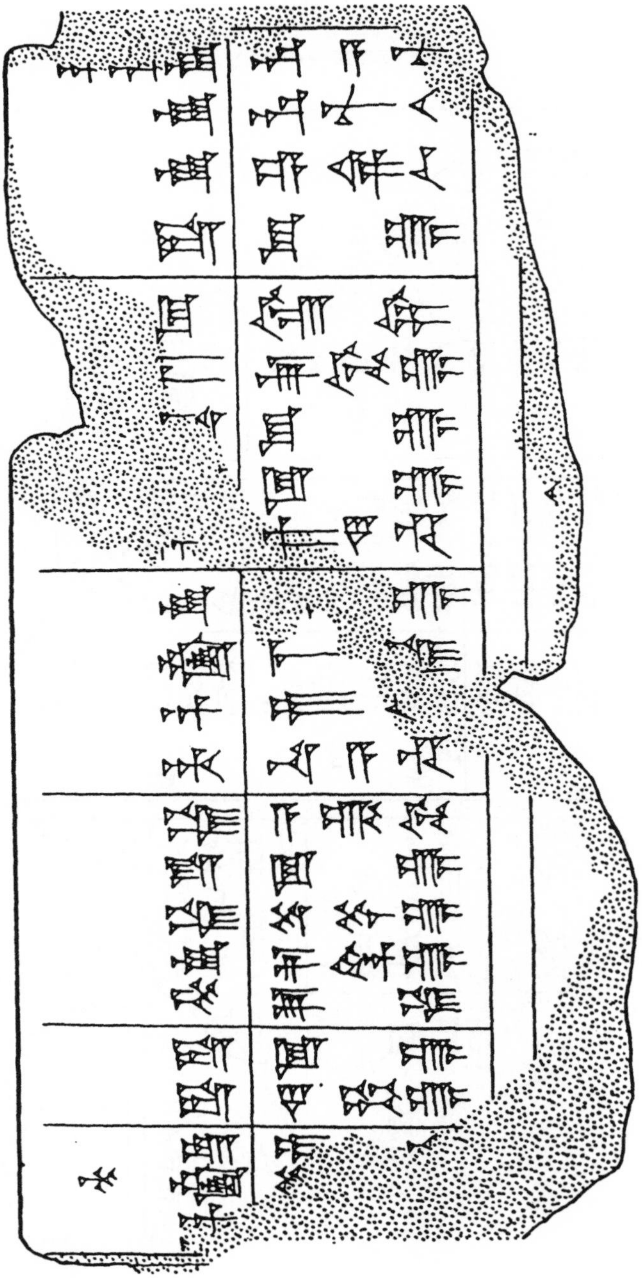

R. 366 + 80-7-19, 293.

REVERSE.

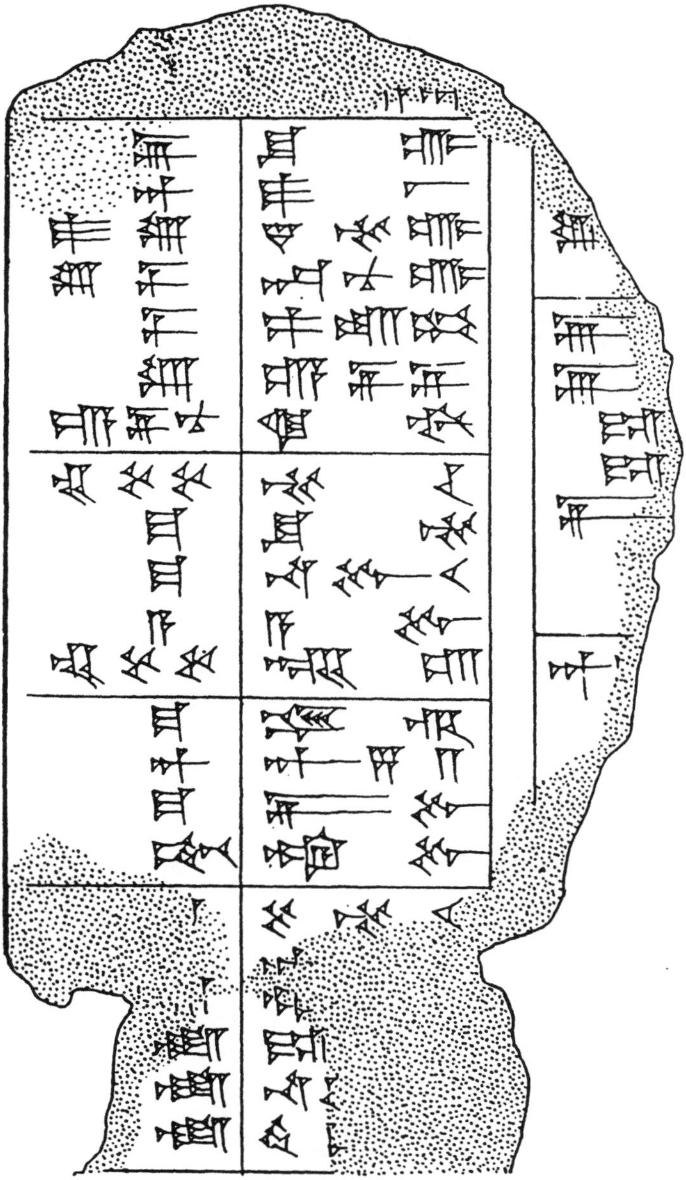

R. 366 + 80-7-19, 293.

REVERSE (cont.).

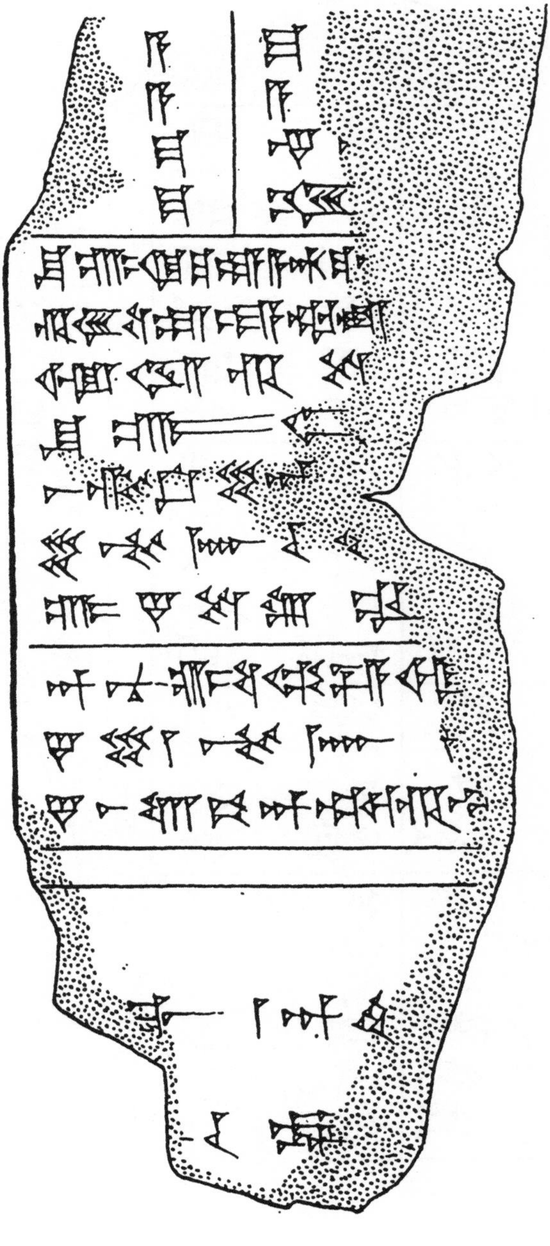

K. 2053.

OBVERSE.

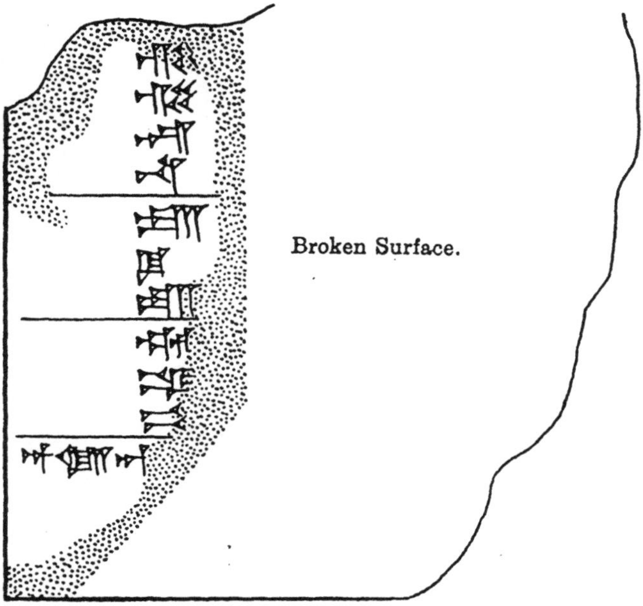

REVERSE.

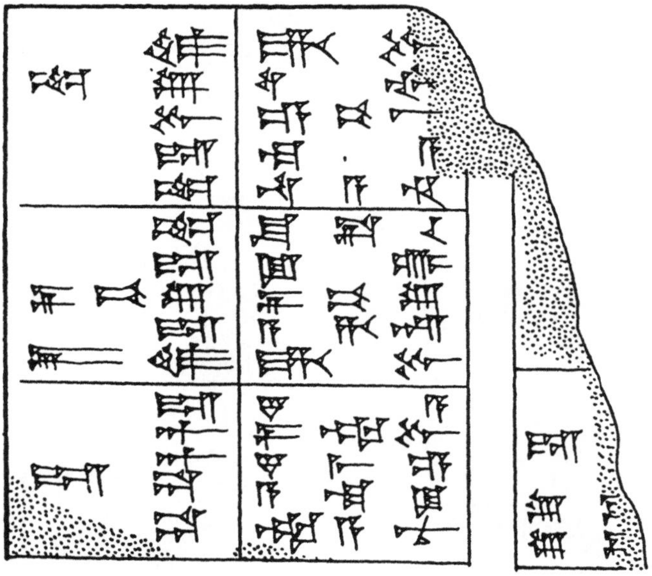

K. 2053.

REVERSE (cont.).

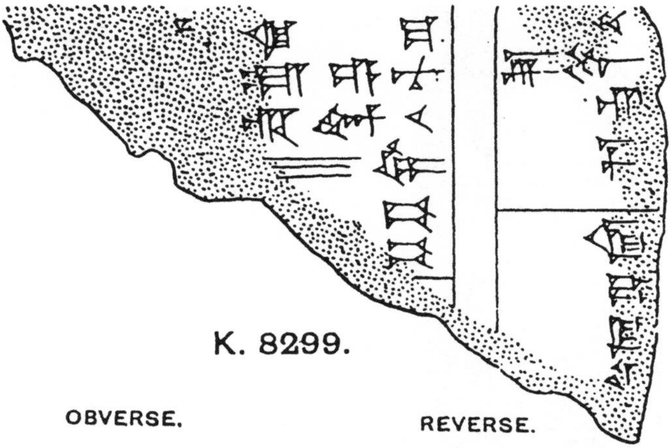

K. 8299.

OBVERSE.

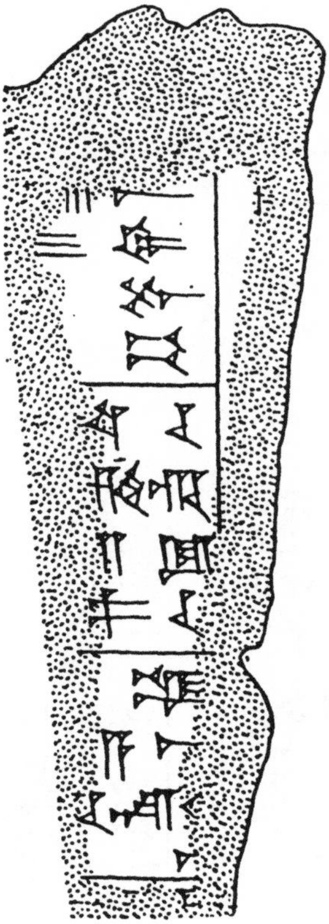

REVERSE.

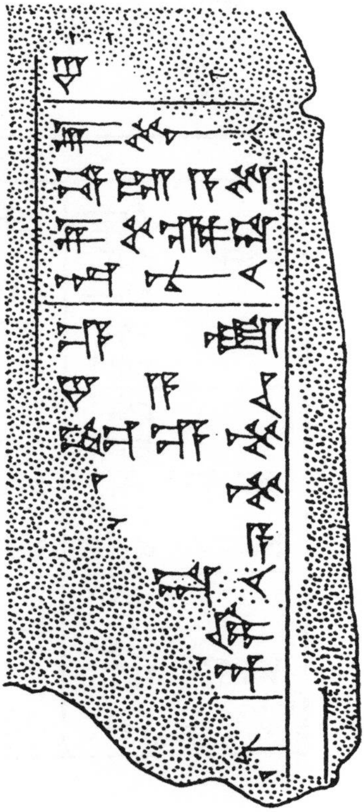

K. 2107 + K. 6086.

OBVERSE.

The Reverse of the Tablet is inscribed with a list of Temples.

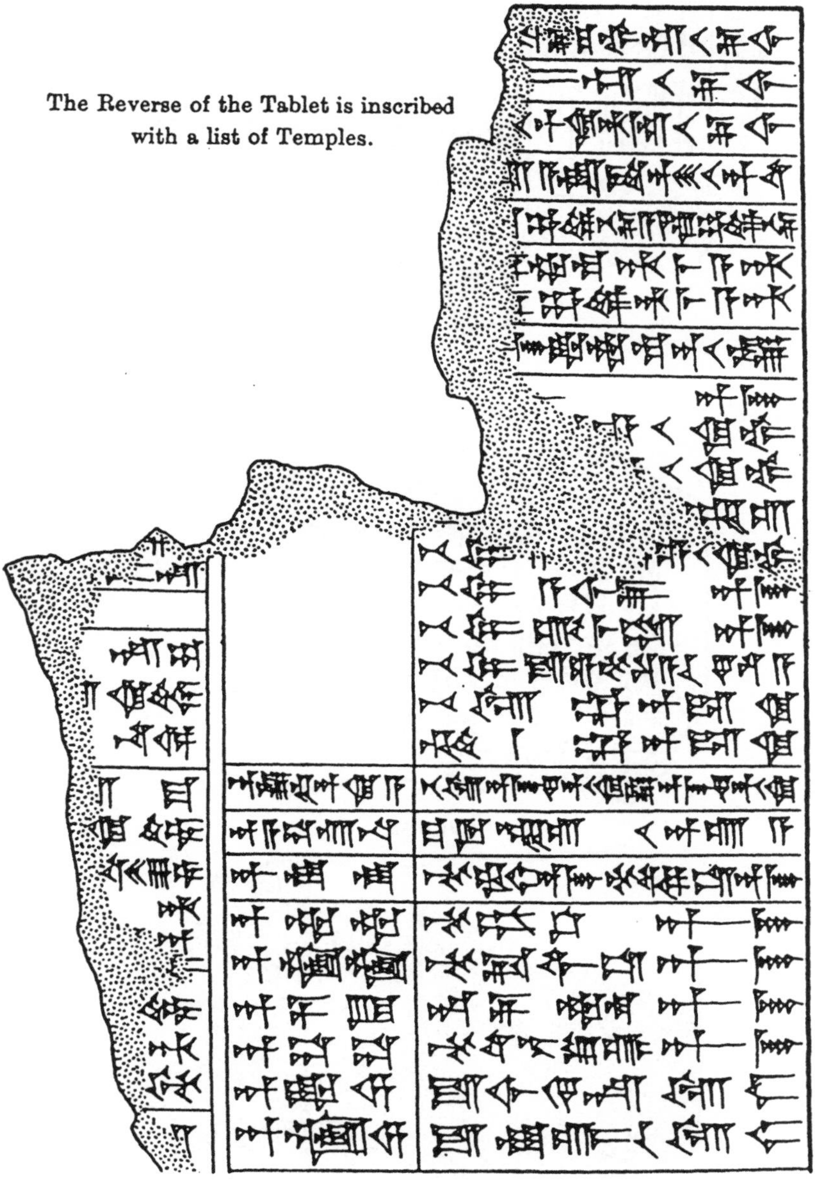

K. 2107 + K. 6086.

OBVERSE (Cont.).

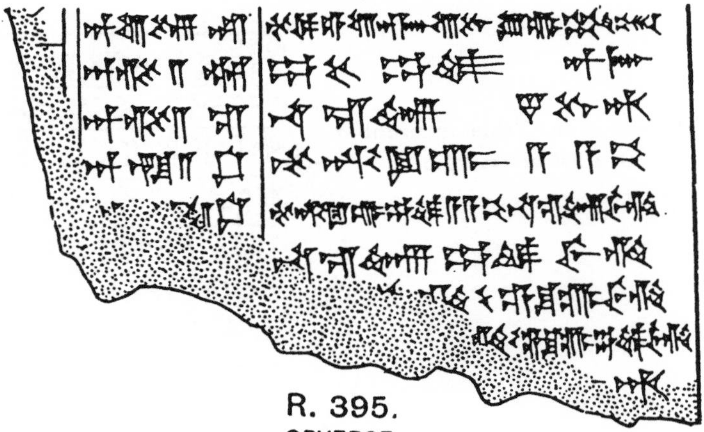

R. 395.

OBVERSE.

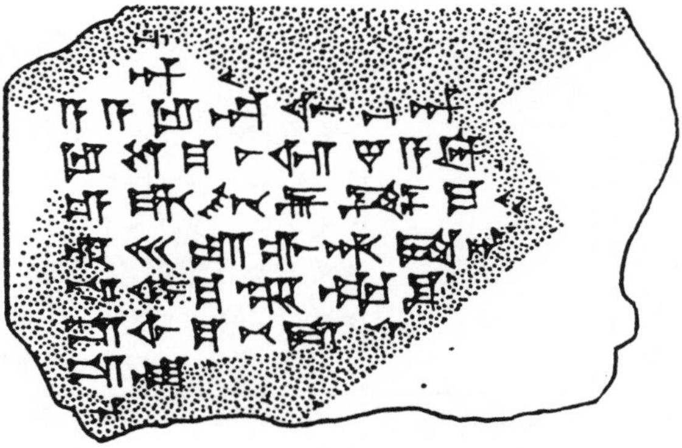

REVERSE.

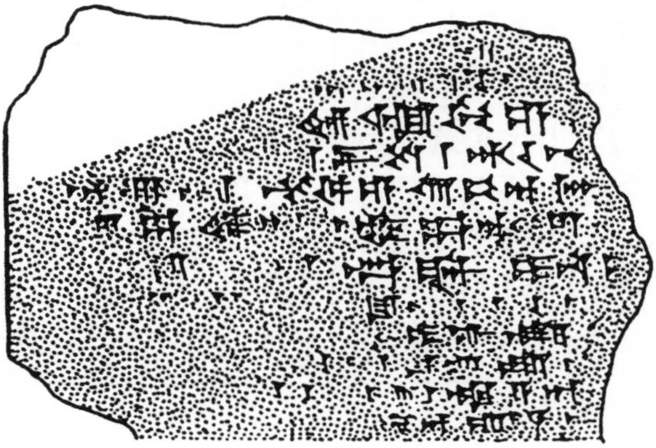

54228.

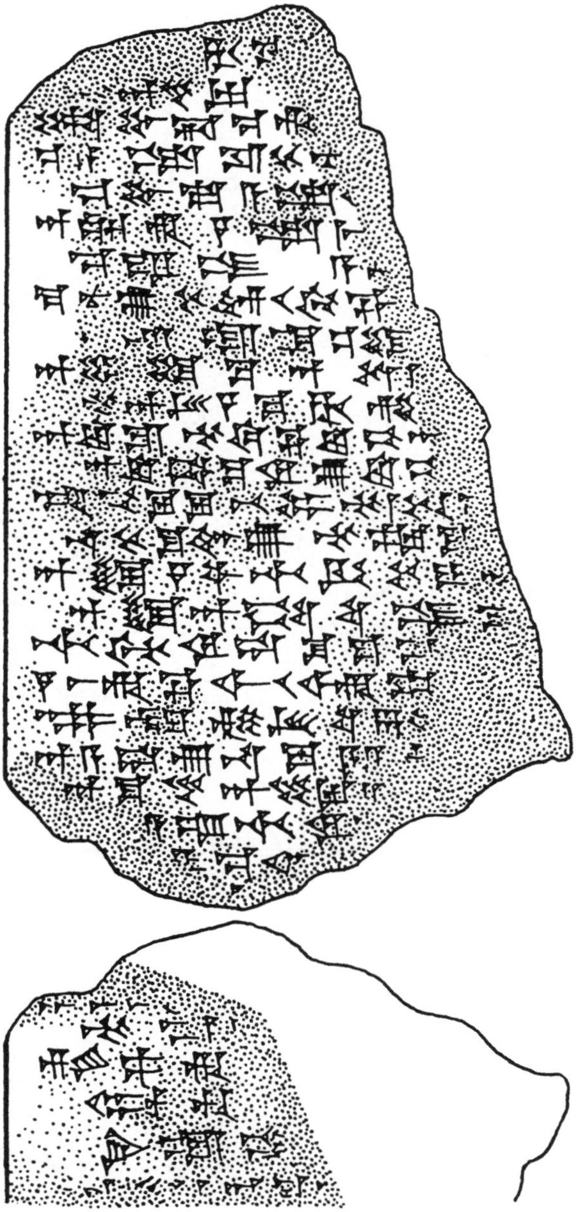

33851.

OBVERSE.

COL. II.

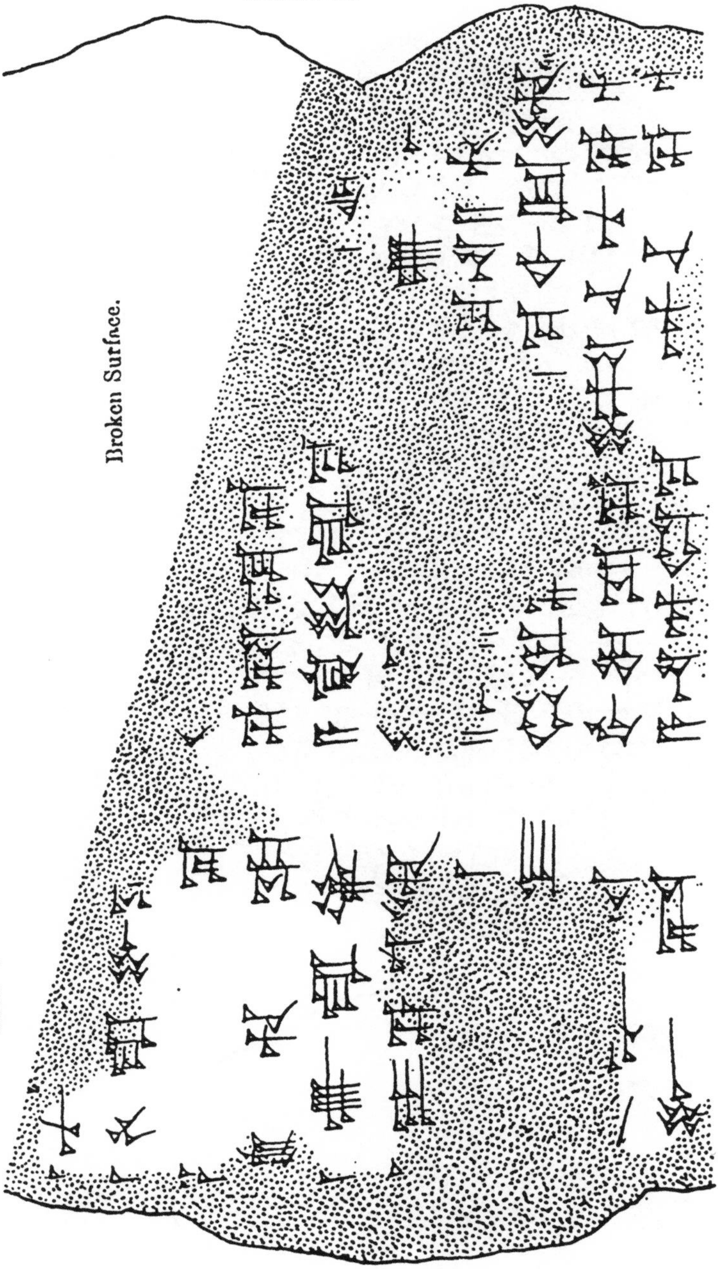

COL. I.

33851.

OBVERSE (Cont.).

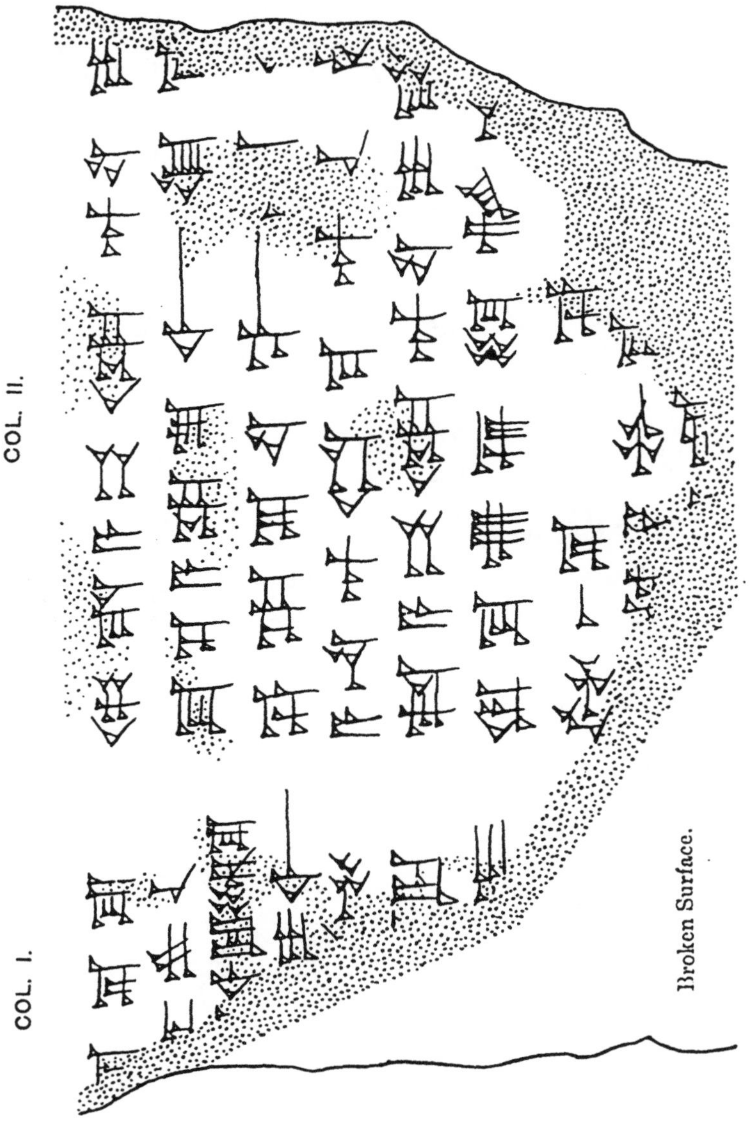

33851.

REVERSE.

COL. III.

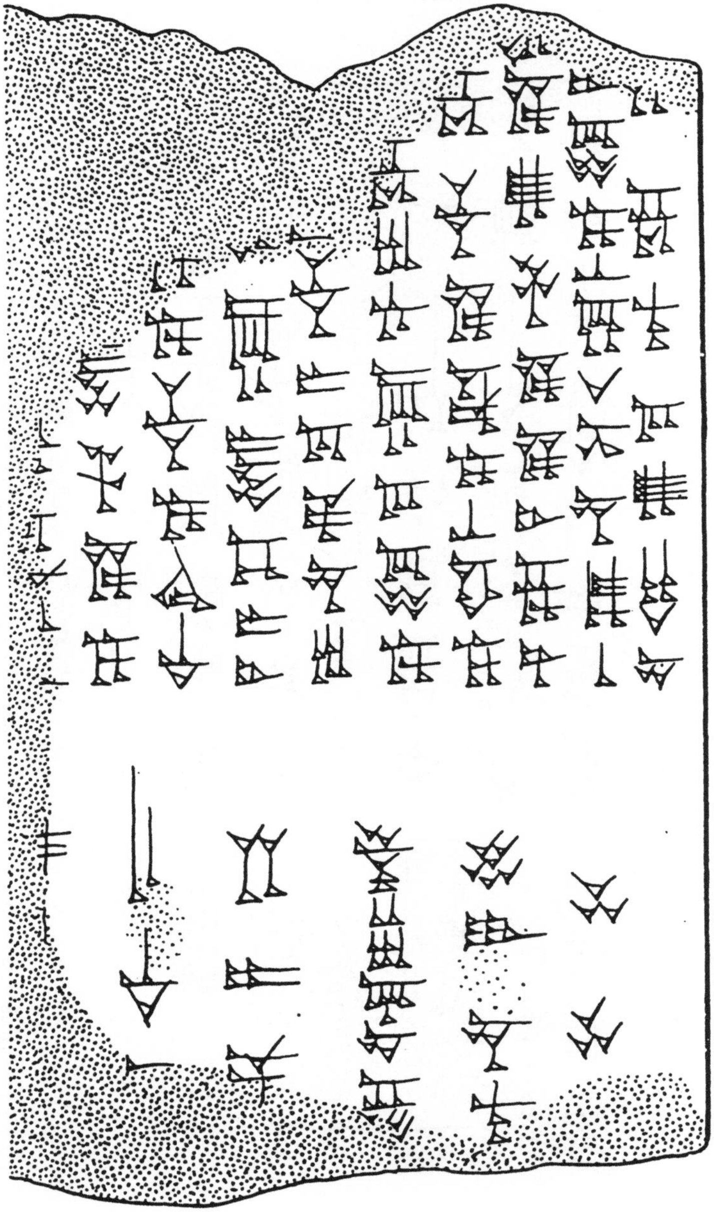

COL. IV.

55466+55486+55627.

OBVERSE.

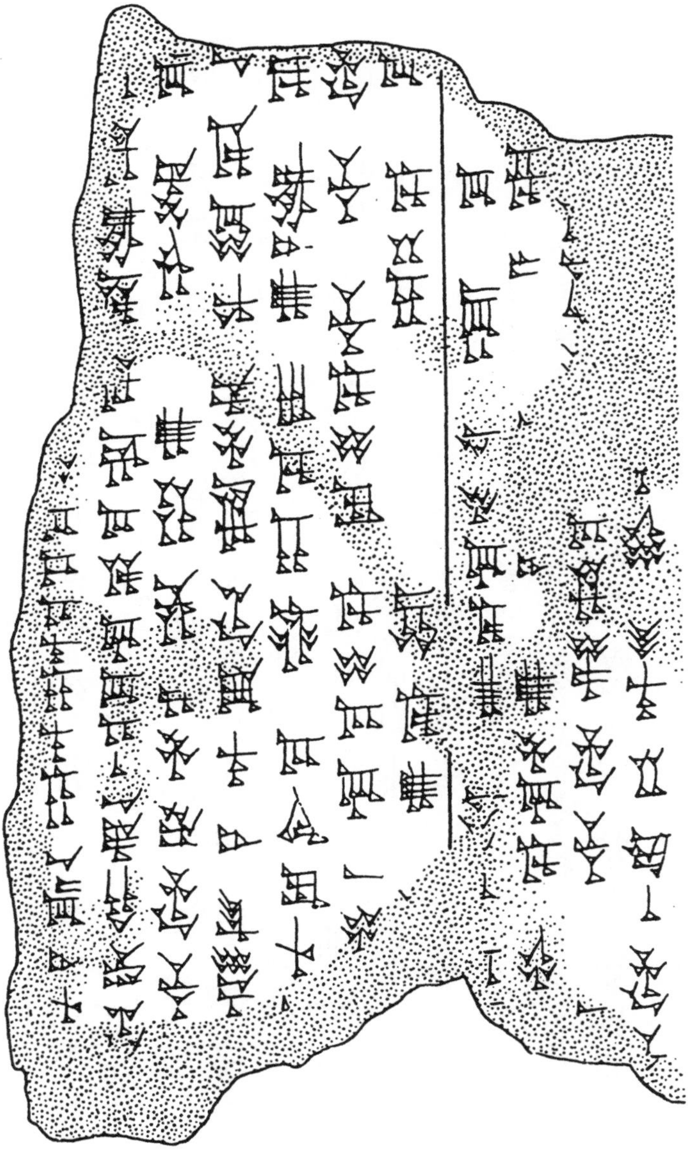

55466+55486+55627.

OBVERSE (Cont.).

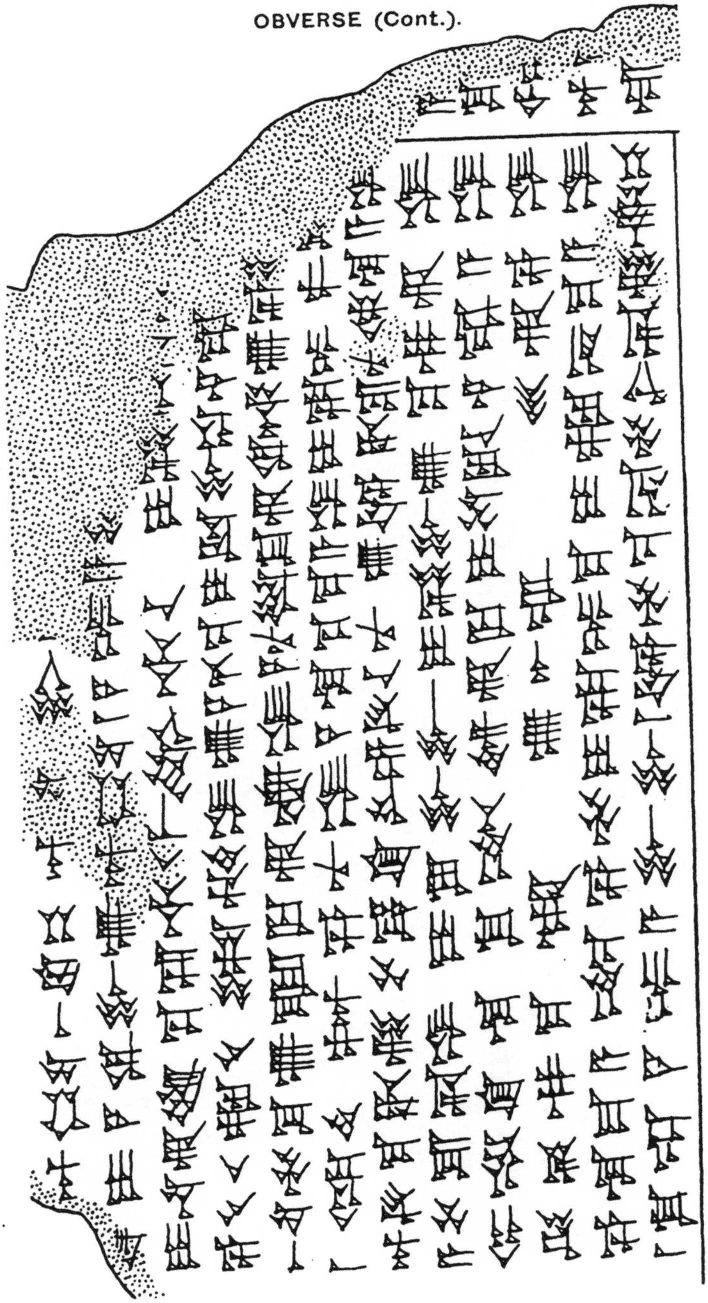

55466+55486+55627.

OBVERSE. (Cont.).

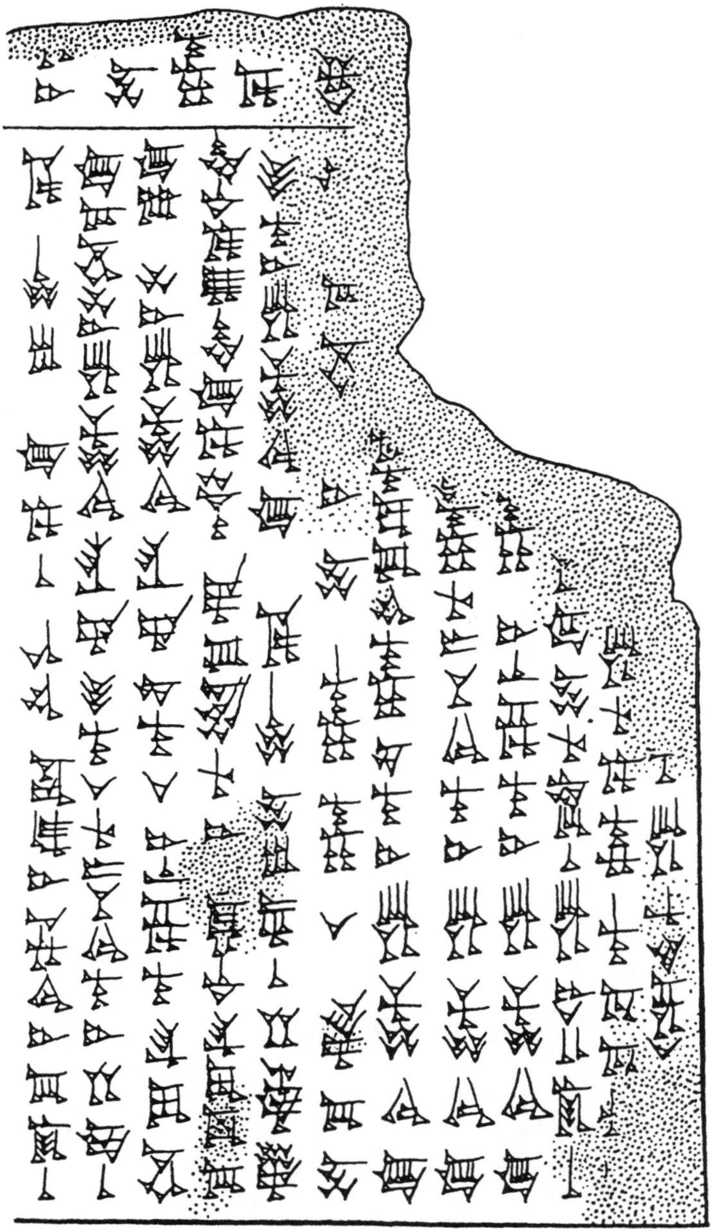

55466+55486+55627.

REVERSE.

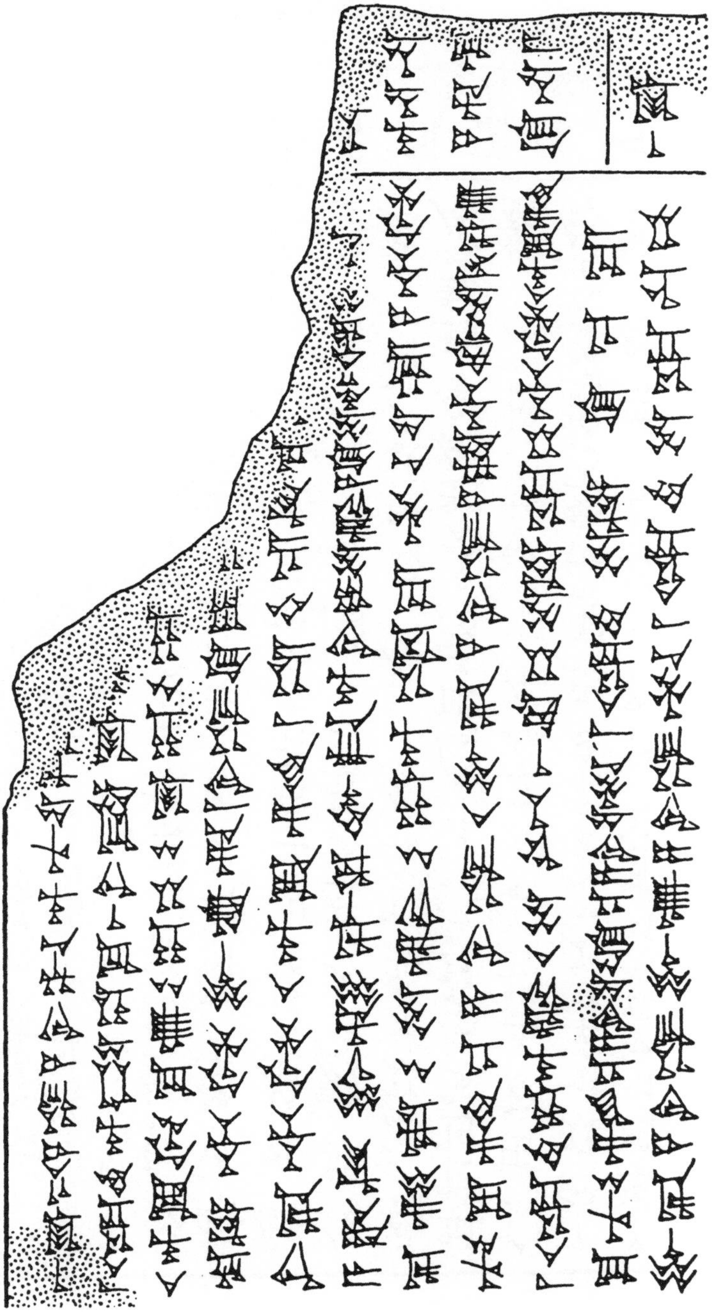

55466+55486+55627.

REVERSE (Cont.).

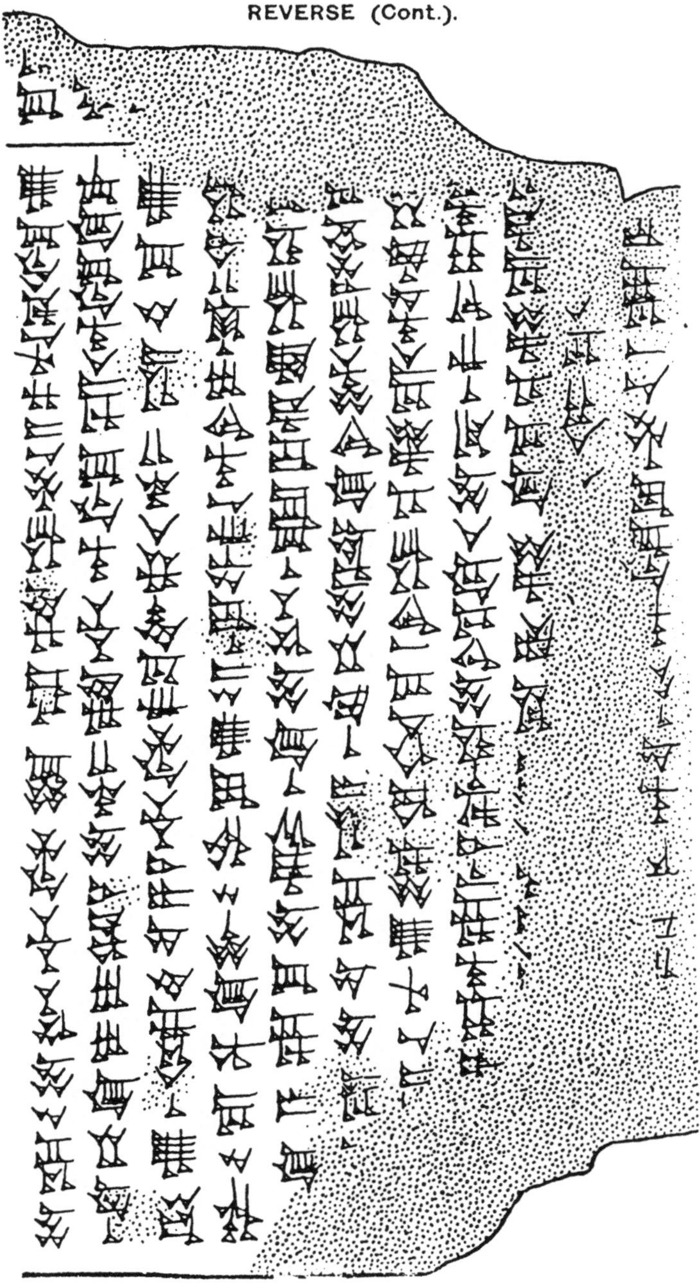

55466+55486+55627.

REVERSE (Cont.).

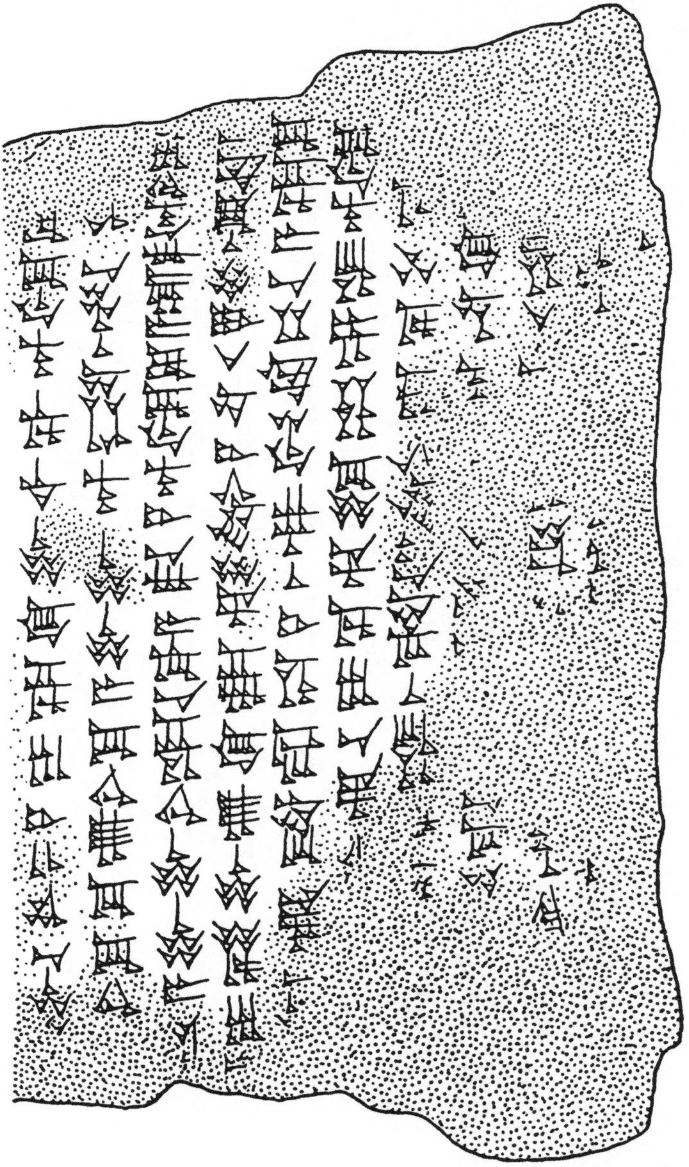

K. 3657.

OBVERSE.

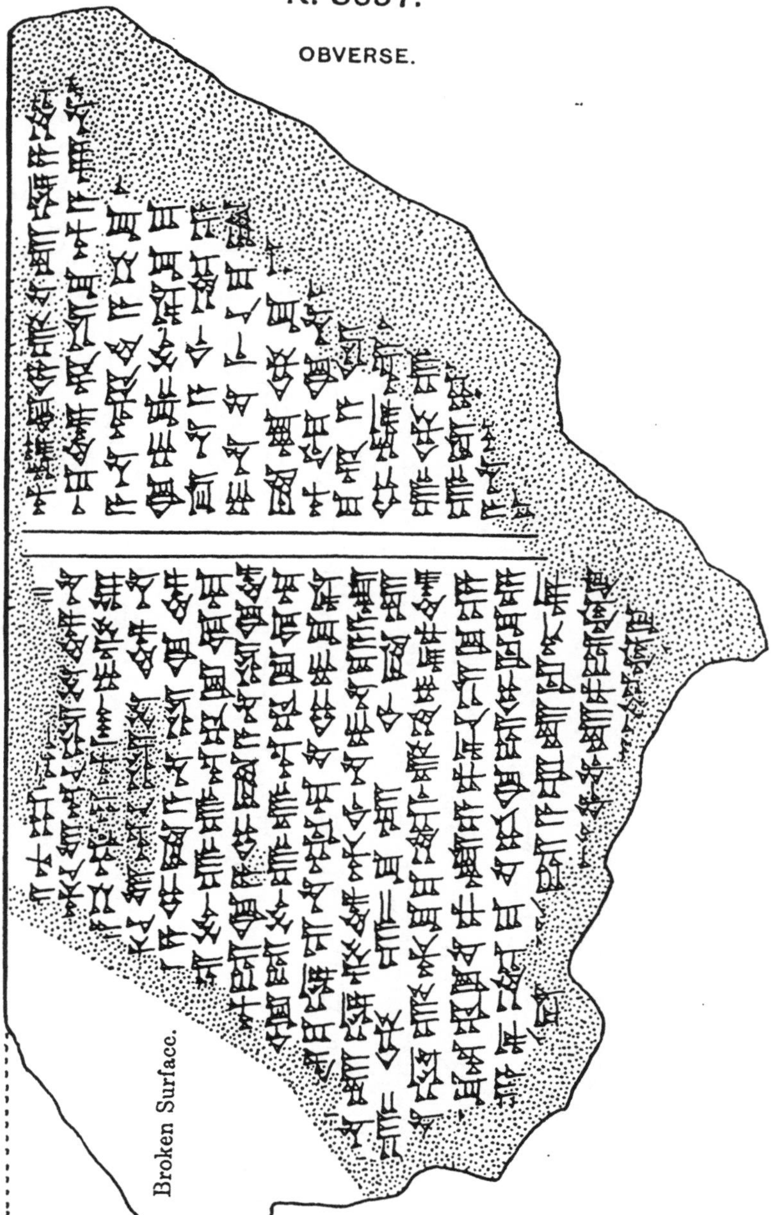

K. 3657.

REVERSE.

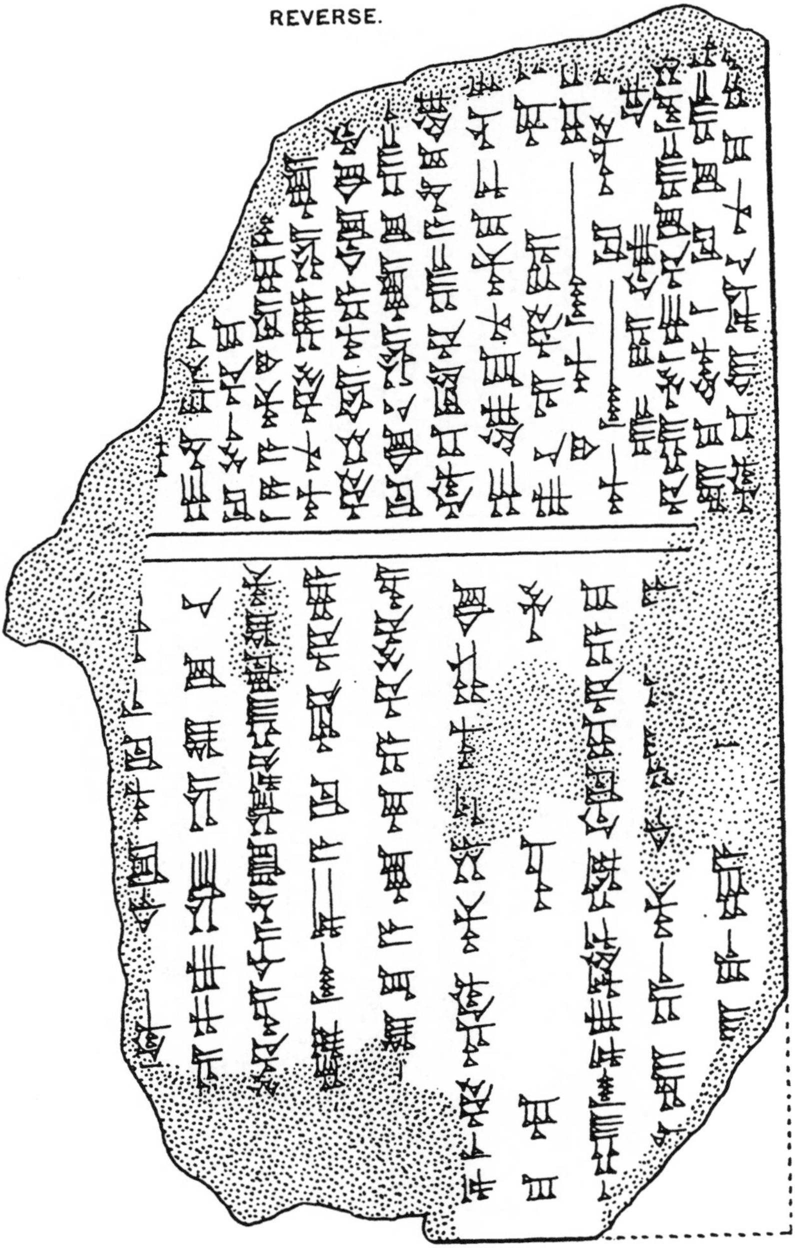

26187.

OBVERSE

APPENDIX V. PLATE LXXVI.

26187.

OBVERSE (cont.).

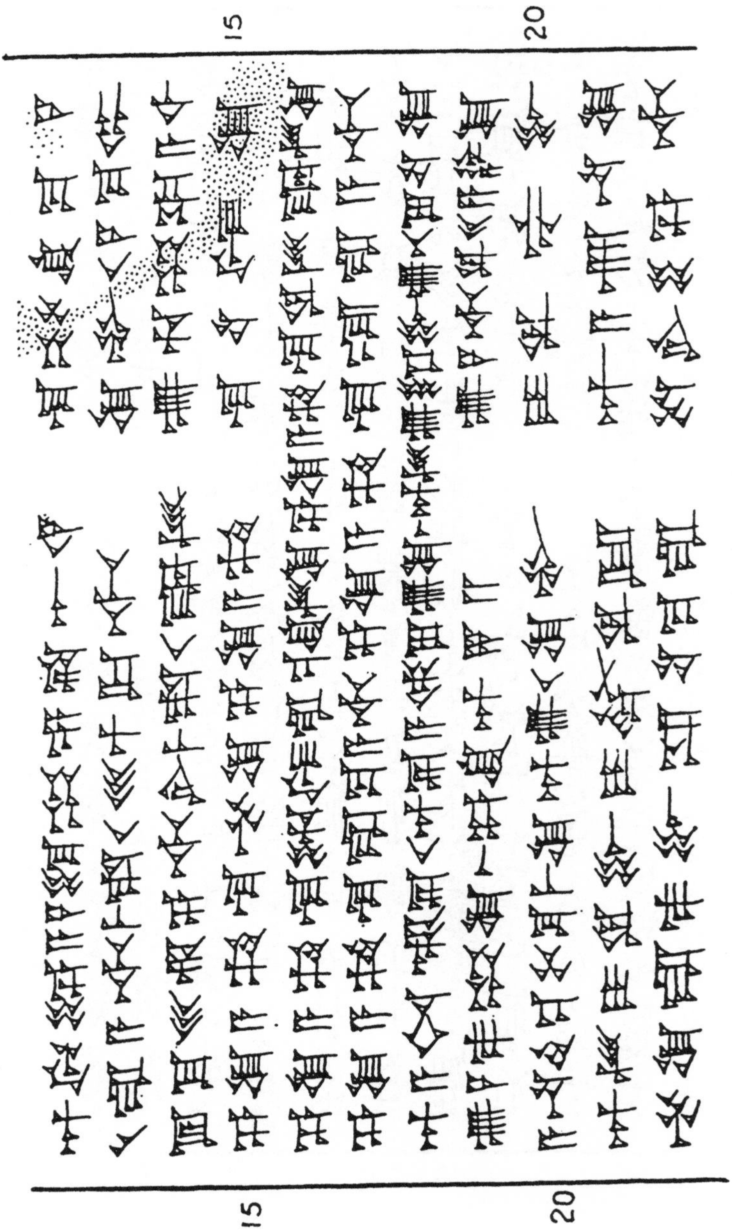

26187.

OBVERSE (Cont.).

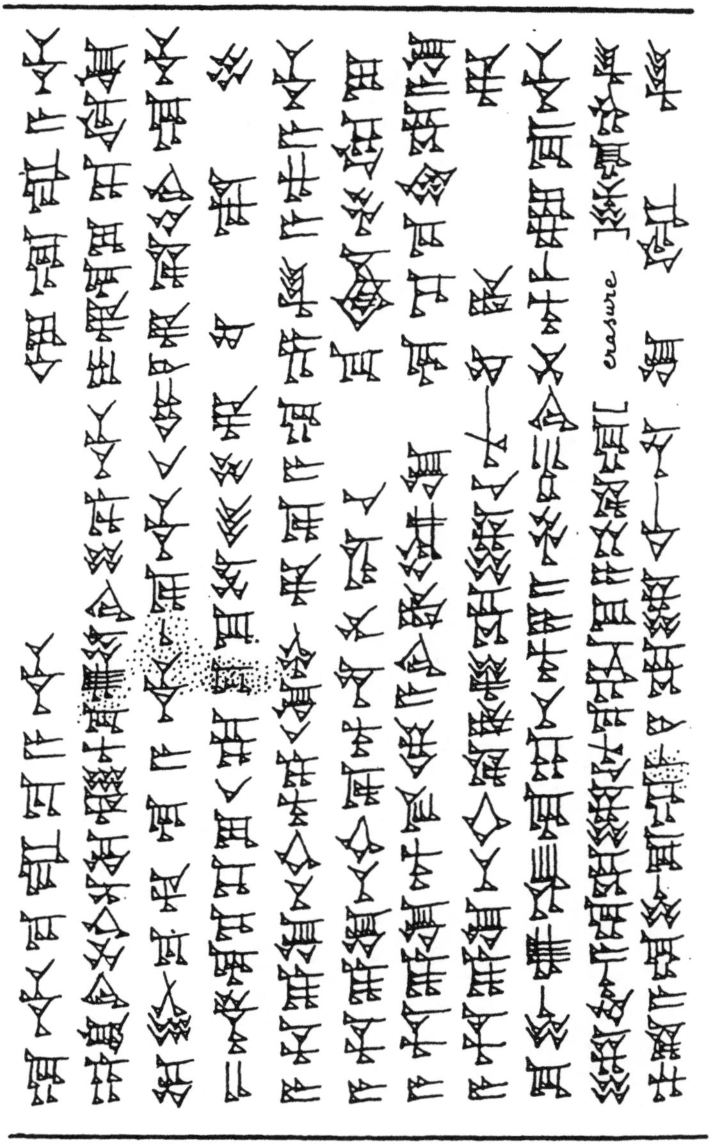

26187.

OBVERSE (cont.).

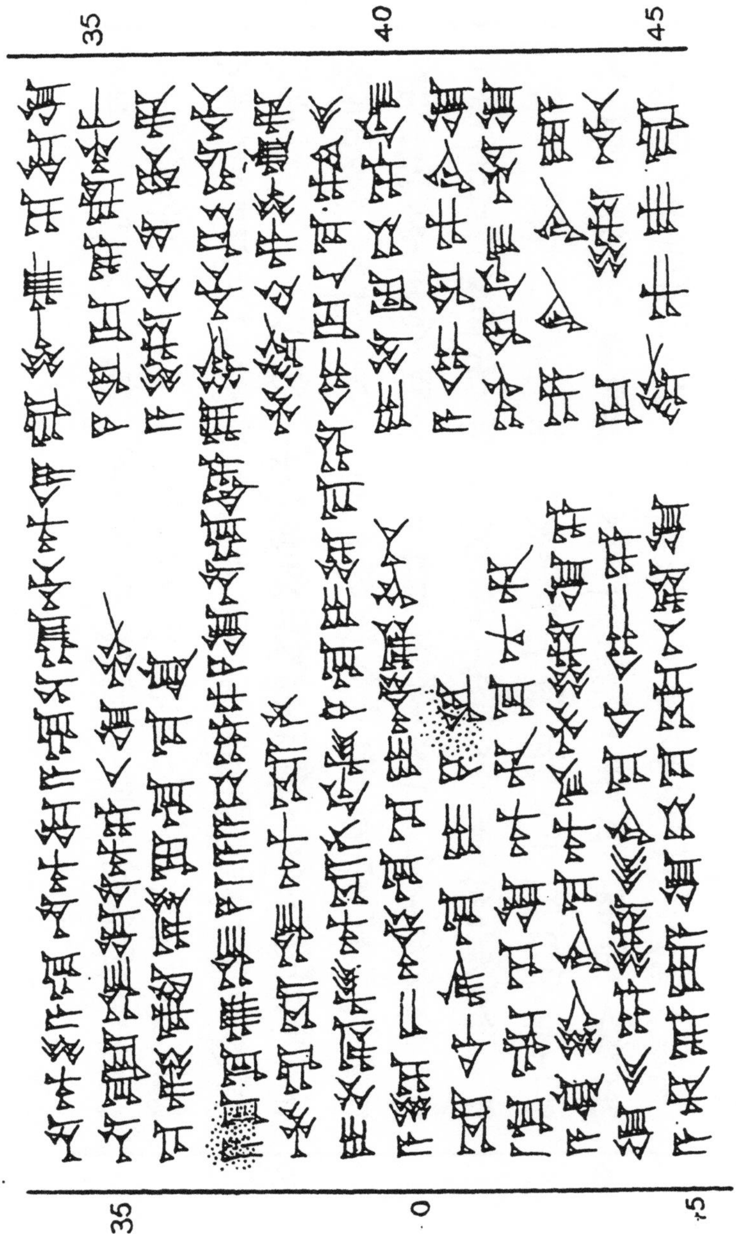

26187.

OBVERSE (cont.).

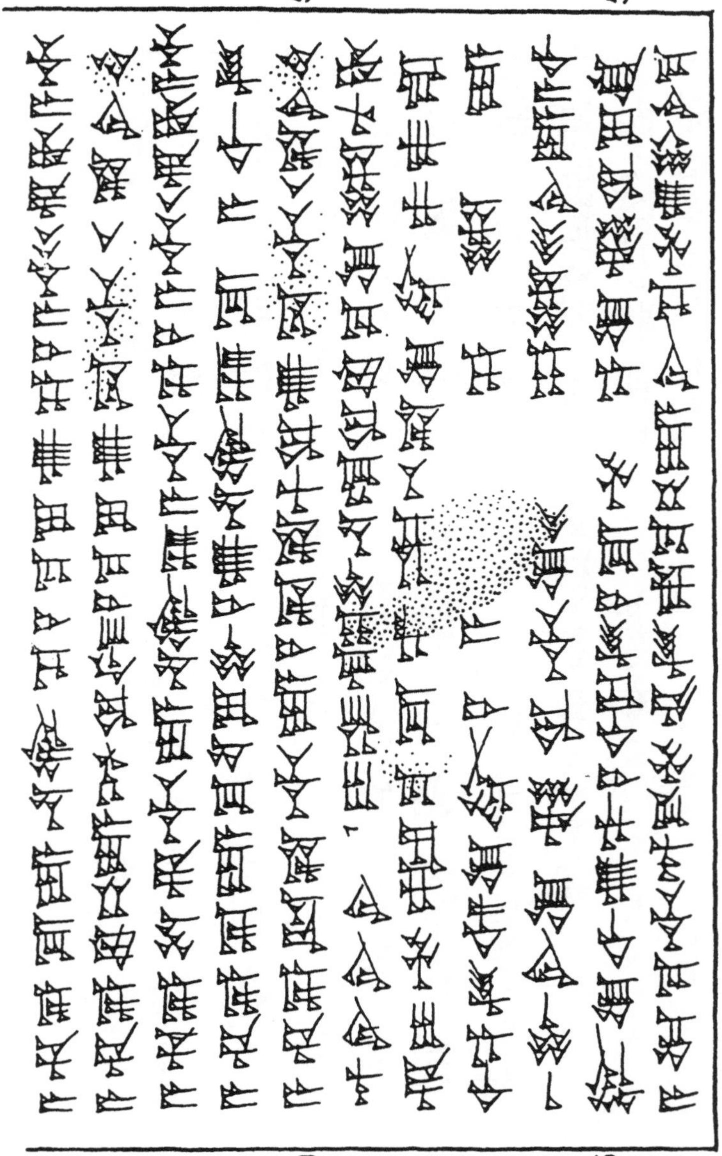

1. One sign erased by the scribe.

26187.

REVERSE.

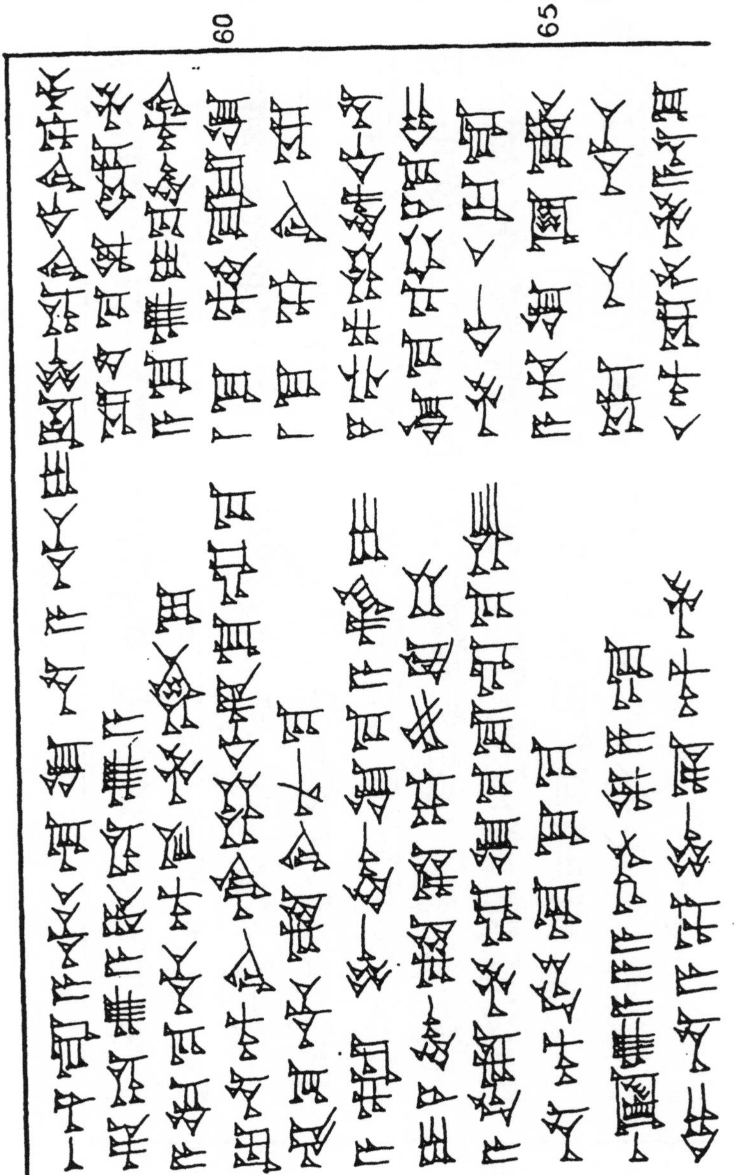

26187.

REVERSE (Cont.).

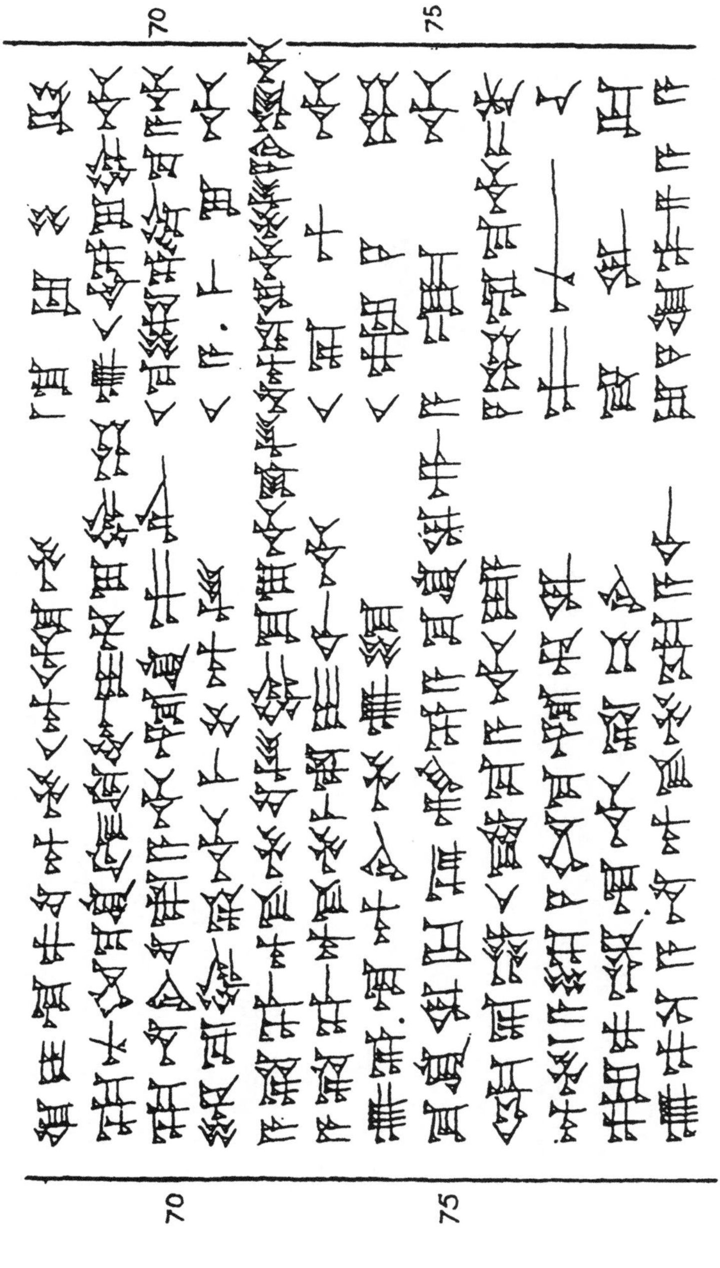

26187.

REVERSE (Cont.).

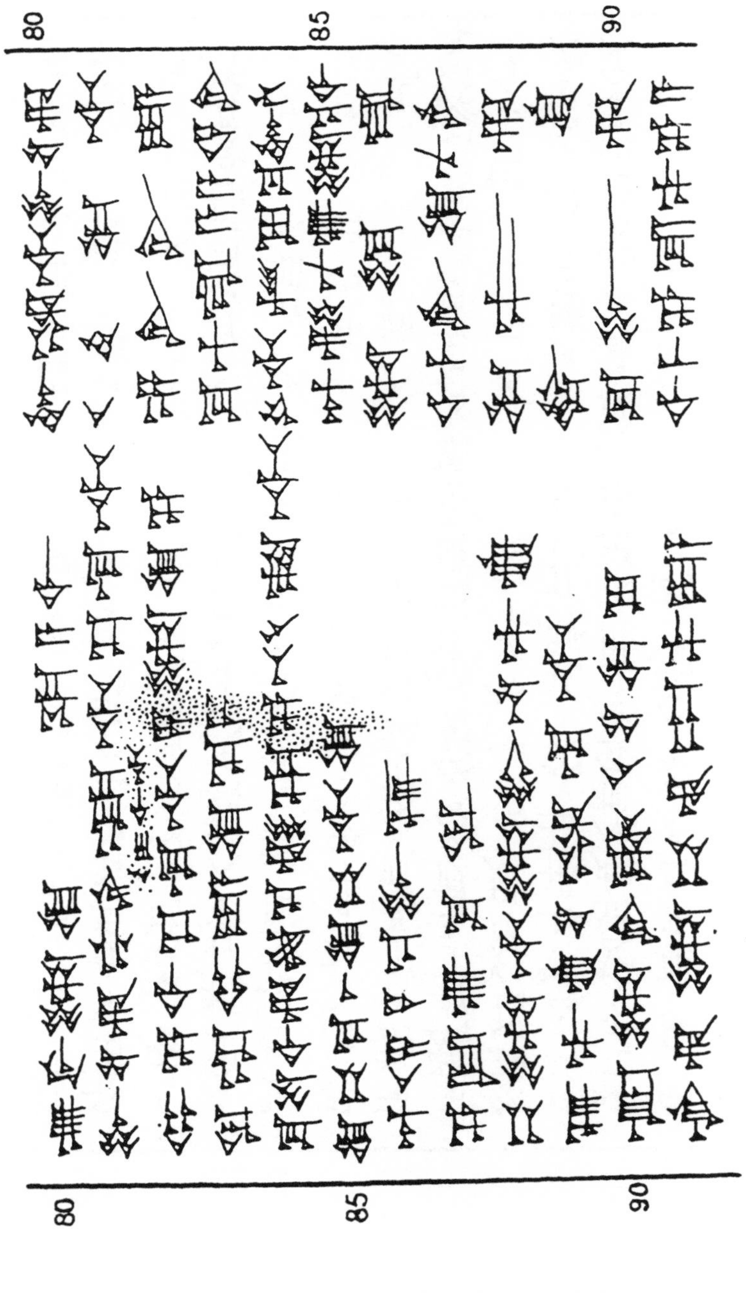

26187.

REVERSE (Cont.).

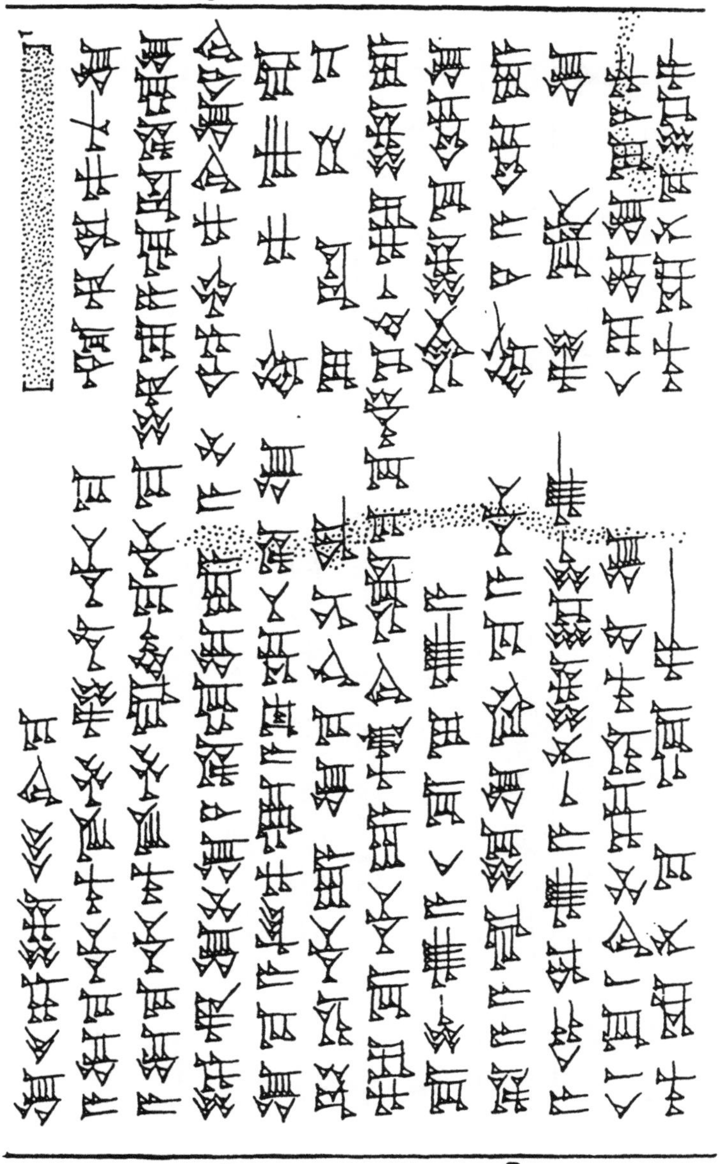

1. The second half of the line has been deeply erased by the Scribe.

26187.

REVERSE (Cont.).

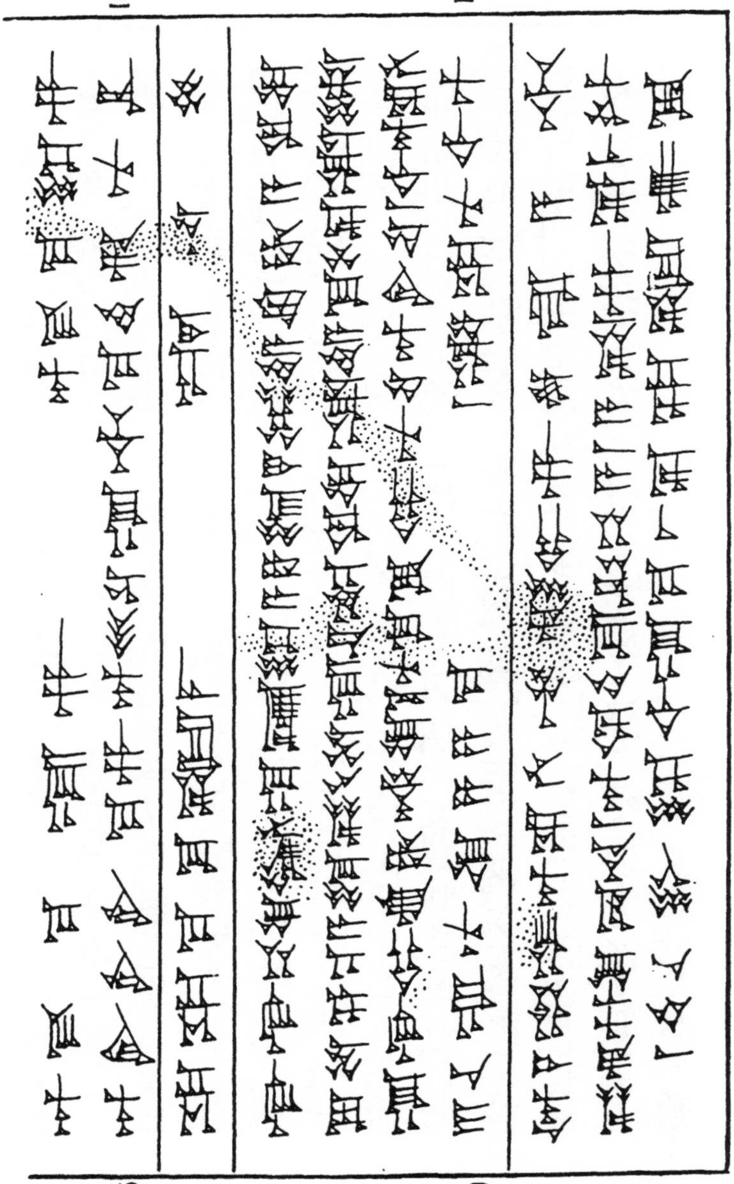

Index to Plates.

Index to Plates—*continued.*

Lightning Source UK Ltd.
Milton Keynes UK
UKHW040026200219
337611UK00001B/134/P

9 781616 405106